TERRORISM

TERRORISM
Threat, Reality, Response

ROBERT H. KUPPERMAN ▪ DARRELL M. TRENT

Foreword by Walter Laqueur

HOOVER INSTITUTION PRESS
Stanford University, Stanford, California

The Hoover Institution on War, Revolution and Peace, founded at Stanford University in 1919 by the late President Herbert Hoover, is an interdisciplinary research center for advanced study on domestic and international affairs in the twentieth century. The views expressed in its publications are entirely those of the authors and do not necessarily reflect the views of the staff, officers, or Board of Overseers of the Hoover Institution.

Hoover Institution Publication 204

The best lack all conviction, while the worst
Are full of passionate intensity.

William Butler Yeats
"The Second Coming"

Contents

Selected Readings

Foreword

I

The study of contemporary terrorism is only at its beginning and Dr. Kupperman and Mr. Trent's survey of terrorist technology and organization and of ways and means to counter them is one of the most important contributions in this field made in recent years. Further investigation of the general political context of terrorism is of course also needed, but while terrorist motives can be discussed endlessly (and usually inconclusively) as the result of the terrorist phenomenon, society is faced with difficult dilemmas here and now of both a general and a specific, "technical" character. Some of these dilemmas have been admirably clarified in this new study and for this we owe the authors a debt of gratitude.

All predictions about the occurrence of terrorism are risky simply because terrorism is not a mass movement, but carried out by very small groups of people. There is no accounting for the acts of fifty, or even five hundred, people in a society of fifty million: terrorism is possible at any time, in all free or semifree societies. It is perhaps more likely in some conditions than in others, and these conditions certainly deserve to be investigated, but accident undoubtedly plays a great role.

It has been argued that terrorism in our time occurs above all in the countries that were on the losing side in the Second World War, and far-reaching conclusions have been drawn from this fact (which is at best half-true). It could be argued with equal justice that there is a connection between terrorism and soccer, for the four countries which finished on top in the world championships of 1978 were all affected by terrorism (Argentina, Brazil, Holland,

Italy). To regard the "objective conditions" the key for the understanding of the occurrence of terrorism in our time is to chase a chimera. Native terrorism has not occurred, and is not likely to occur, in certain countries, such as Scandinavia. This may be connected with the fact that there is no tradition of political violence in these societies, but then it is also a fact that terrorism (except that of the nationalist-separatist kind) has seldom occurred in small countries or in small towns for the obvious reason that it is far more difficult to hide in such places than in the anonymity of the big city.

Recent manifestations of terrorism have shown some interesting innovations. Until recently, terrorist movements took pride in elaborate ideological justification, but this is no longer so. One looks in vain for a terrorist doctrine in political terms among German or Italian or Japanese terrorists similar to that of the Narodnaya Volya or the anarchists. Perhaps contemporary terrorists believe that no such ideology is now needed, or perhaps they are unable to formulate their strategy in a coherent manner. Events in recent years have also made it clear that terrorism is increasingly guided by remote control. This is not, of course, to say that all terrorist groups receive foreign help, or are guided by outside powers, nor is the phenomenon altogether novel: fascist Italy supported the Croatian Ustasha and other such groups in the 1930s. But of late, warfare by proxy has become more widespread, even if great care is obviously taken by the governments concerned not to leave any traces. Terrorists are men and women on the run. Without outside help they could not have possibly displayed such coordination and logistical sophistication, not to mention the problem of finances and the supply of arms, as they did, for example, in the kidnappings and murders of Schleyer and Moro. Such remote control may be difficult to prove in a court of law, and the countries affected may be reluctant in any case to make such charges against governments that are important oil producers or whose military power commands respect.

Lastly, there is the question of sympathizers, which has been a bone of contention, above all, in West Germany. It is ridiculous to cast aspersions on elderly poetesses and well-known novelists. In the same way it is reprehensible to brand as a sympathizer everyone who stands for political and social change. But there *are* sympathizers. When Rosa Luxemburg and Karl Liebknecht were killed in 1919, and again when Walther Rathenau was assassinated by terrorists of the extreme right a few years later, the German left quite properly pointed out that the murderers had not come from nowhere, that their actions should be viewed against the climate of violence that had been instigated by their intellectual mentors. The same is true today. Those who have been advocating "progressive violence" against "repressive toleration" did not envisage the indiscriminate killing of innocent people, and they can always argue that they should not be held responsible for the actions of the *terrible simplificateurs* who misunderstood their teachings. And yet . . .

II

There has been an upsurge of terrorism during the last year in Italy, Spain, Turkey, and a few other countries. The resurgence of Italian terrorism has been widely reported all over the world following the spectacular abduction and subsequent murder of Aldo Moro, the leading Italian politician. Italy's main terrorist groups, the Brigate Rosse (Red Brigades) and the NAP are believed to count no more than a few hundred members, and the "hitmen" among them may be no more than twenty. But they have shown a great deal of efficiency, the number of their supporters may be numbered in the thousands, and the fact that several police reports were found in a Rome flat abandoned by Brigate Rosse members shows that they have infiltrated the police and probably also the judiciary. The Italian terrorist scene is of interest furthermore because of the international connections between the terrorists and their sympathizers abroad, and the difficulty in documenting these ties in detail. As far as the background of the terrorist groups is concerned and the reason for their success, Italy presents few riddles; many if not most terrorist cadres belonged originally to Communist youth organizations and left the party because it was not activist enough. The success of terrorism in Italy, on the other hand, is quite obviously connected with the general crisis of Italian politics and society and the resulting weakness of the state.

Nor are the origins of Spanish terrorism shrouded in mystery. It is now almost entirely restricted to the Basque region and while its practitioners use extreme Marxist verbiage, their inspiration is quite obviously nationalist. The particular violence of ETA can perhaps be explained against the background of specific Basque fears of losing their national identity; Basques probably now constitute a minority in their historical provinces. On the other hand, as the recent elections have shown, the terrorists are a small minority in the nationalist camp. The feeling of isolation and of a race against time may have contributed to the intensification of the terrorist struggle.

Terrorism in Turkey, where some two hundred and fifty persons were killed during the first half of 1978, again presents unique features—it is conducted mainly between activists of the extreme left and the far right. The former specialize largely in abductions and armed robberies, the latter in individual assassination. The terrorists of the far left are predominantly of middle-class origin, those of the extreme right are to a large extent of proletarian origin; the extreme left dismisses them as "Lumpen-proletariat militants" but this is of not much help in understanding their social background. The situation is further complicated because the "right-wing" propaganda stresses the need to combat social injustice and, generally speaking, propagates a national socialist (but not fascist) line, and these happen to be also propaganda slogans of the extreme left. More than in Italy, and far more than in Spain, the universities have become the main battle scene of the terrorist struggle.

Terrorism in Argentina has been largely stamped out during the last two years in a wave of bloody repression in which not only many terrorists lost their lives, but also many people who had nothing whatsoever to do with terrorism. Less attention has been paid to the fact that terrorism in Argentina (as in Brazil, but not in Uruguay) has been distinguished from the very beginning by exceptional cruelty. Thus, the terrorists have seldom hesitated to kill innocent bystanders who happened to witness the preparation of one of their attacks, owners of cars that were seized for their operations, or even their own wounded comrades—for fear that they would talk when arrested. Today the once-Trotskyite

ERP has virtually ceased to exist, and the remnants of the left-wing Peronist Montoneros have transferred their activities to Rome, and, to a lesser extent, to Paris.

Palestinian terrorism, despite some spectacular exploits, has been on the wane during the last few years. In fact, there has been more internecine killing among Arabs than attempts to hit at Israel (the killing of the editor of *Al Ahram* in Nicosia, the murder of a cabinet minister at Abu Dhabi airport, the assassination of the North Yemen president and the PLO representative in London, and other such incidents). It remains to be seen whether this has been largely the result of the Lebanese civil war and the growing tensions within the Arab world, or whether the terrorists have been discouraged by the fact that attacks against Israeli targets have shown diminishing political returns. But this does not preclude, of course, a temporary revival of Palestinian terrorism.

Nationalist-separatist terrorism seems to be on the decline in Ulster, at least as far as the number of victims is concerned, but there has been an upsurge in France, mainly on the part of Corsican and Breton militant groups.

III

This short and incomplete survey of terrorist activities shows the great differences in the character of the terrorist struggle and the fortunes of the terrorist groups. In the United States there has been relatively little terrorist activity but a great deal of discussion—though not remotely as much as in Germany. But these debates have not been very productive, partly because there has been a great deal of confusion on the very topic of discussion. Books have been published in which Robespierre, Hitler, and Lenin appear side by side with Yasir Arafat and Carlos, in which every possible kind of political violence from above and from below is described and analyzed without much discrimination. Reviewing one such study, Conor Cruise O'Brien has noted that the author affixed the terrorist label to all those he disliked, a practice for which one may feel sympathy, but which hardly produces a better understanding of modern terrorism. On the xiv / FOREWORD

other hand, some overzealous political scientists have claimed that unless there is agreement on a foolproof, "scientific" definition of terrorism there can be no meaningful discussion of the subject; but is it likely that there ever will be such a comprehensive definition? The lack of discrimination in analyzing terrorist activities has unfortunate consequences inasmuch as statistics are concerned. To give but one example, what is the value of figures when an aircraft hijacking carried out by "bona fide terrorists" is lumped together with hijackings by armed men or women who are not members of terrorist organizations but were merely trying to escape from a police state—or even the actions of lunatics? A CIA report published in July 1976 flatly states that "more incidents were recorded [last year] than ever before." But the fact that more were recorded does not mean that more such incidents have actually occurred.

If the criteria used are, as admitted, quite arbitrary, the results will be equally arbitrary and comparisons, both on the historical level and between various regions, become quite meaningless. The study of terrorism in America will have to find its way between the Scylla of vagueness and confusion and the Charybdis of a sterile, purist fixation on definitions to make any progress at all. The West German experience has shown that computers may be of great value in apprehending terrorists, but they are of no help in understanding the mainsprings and the motivation of terrorism unless there is, in the first place, a minimum of conceptual clarity. And this, by and large, is not yet the case.

IV

We have to turn to Germany for the most extensive and in some ways most interesting discussions about the character of modern terrorism. There have been few terrorist operations in the *Bundesrepublik*: two citizens were killed in 1974, three in 1975, one in 1976, twelve in 1977, none so far in 1978. Many terrorist activists have been apprehended. But the terrorist phenomenon has occupied not only German politicians, but also historians, sociologists, political scientists, and educators, not to mention theologians and philosophers.[1]

Some results are trivial, such as the insight that there are no monocausal explanations; some simply translate well-known questions into professional jargon without enhancing our knowledge; some are manifestly wrong; some sound doubtful—this refers, for instance, to studies which claim that political violence appears predominantly in countries where fantasies of cleanliness are frequent.[2]

There is widespread belief that above all we need a general theory of terrorism—and that such a theory is possible. But even though at the end of the day we shall not be nearer to such a theory, certain suggestions have emerged that certainly warrant further examination. The neo-Marxist critique of terrorism is well known. As Herbert Marcuse recently put it: "The terrorists compromise the struggle for socialism which, after all, is also their own. Their methods are not those of liberation."[3] But if, according to Marcuse, the struggle against "repressive toleration" is a categorical imperative, it is not that obvious that one should reject terrorist operations, except perhaps for tactical reasons. If terrorism is rejected, and not just for tactical reasons, why assume that only the "methods" of the terrorists are not those of liberation? There is a strong totalitarian component in terrorism, as Bracher has shown, and in the "terrorist personality." Only if socialism is equated with the nationalization of the means of production, only if all the democratic, humanitarian, and libertarian aspirations of socialism are ignored, can the German terrorist's attachment to "socialism" be taken at face value. Bassam Tibi, a left-wing Arab political scientist teaching at a German university, has suggested that while terrorism in a democratic state is "criminal," this is not so in societies in which fundamental human rights do not exist.[4] This proposition seems at first sight irrefutable but Tibi's vision seems somewhat impaired as he singles out Iran, Chile, and South Africa as the main (or only) bastions of such repression. One can easily think of far bigger and more powerful countries in which elementary human rights do not exist. Is terrorism permissible there? Marcuse, for one, has been aware of the problem ("a very delicate one") but has so far found no satisfactory answer apart from claiming that terrorism in Franco Spain (the assassination of Carrero Blanco) was justified, whereas in East Germany it is not.[5]

Problematical in a different way are attempts from the other end of the political spectrum to interpret the origins of terrorism. Wilhelm Kasch, a professor of theology, has explained terrorism as the urge to destroy—the self and others—born out of radical despair, a new form of a "disease unto death" (shades of Kierkegaard and Heidegger), which manifests itself by way of the inability to make common cause with others (*Gemeinschaftsunfähigkeit*), the loss of the capacity to understand reality, aimlessness, and even the deterioration in the quality of the language used. This seems a fair enough description but Kasch then proceeds to postulate terrorism as an imminent part of a society without God, the consequence of "methodological atheism."[6] Of course, the basic concept is not new, but, on one hand, the decline of religion has gone on for centuries without leading towards terrorism, and, on the other, it would be only too easy to point to the incidence of terrorism in many lands during the Middle Ages precisely among religious sectarians and fanatics. Fanaticism, in other words, is not a monopoly of atheists.

According to Gerhard Schmidtchen and Hermann Luebbe, the roots of terrorism have to be traced to the general disorganization (of the society and the individual alike), to the decline of morality, and to the loss of democratic legitimacy and of the authority of democratic institutions.[7] There is little to quarrel with in such broad propositions but they apply to most modern societies, including many in which there has been no terrorism. On the extreme left a critique of this kind will be viewed as putting things on their head, for general disorganization and the decline in morality, the "legitimacy crisis" (and also terrorism) are in its view only secondary manifestations of the general crisis of capitalism.

In the case of Germany the specific German fate, the lack of German identity, and the *unbewältigte Vergangenheit* (the past that has not yet been mastered) are frequently invoked in this context—and not only on the left. This also refers to the fact that the purge of Nazism has been incomplete and the rejection of the fascist legacy not consistent, and to the difficulty of the younger generation to respect parents who were Nazis—or who failed to resist. If so, Austria should be a hotbed of terrorism. Austrian identity is even more dubious; pro-Nazi enthusiasm was, if anything, greater in Hitler's native country, and former Nazis, with perhaps a handful of exceptions, suffered no lasting harm in Austria after 1945.* Yet there is no terrorism in Austria—and thus the theory collapses.

Social and individual psychologists have enumerated a number of features characteristic for many terrorists: at the beginning there is always political and social engagement or, in popular language, "idealism." But the future terrorist fails to accept the inevitable frustration involved in growing up; the discrepancy between the ideals and the ugly realities that he faces in late puberty is too great—something in him gives way. This is accompanied by a disturbed relationship with authority on one hand and by a conflict in his own emotions on the other (fear of love) and thus he drifts towards terrorism—the only apparent alternative to drinking or taking drugs. Those suffering from individual problems transfer them on society and see the cure for their hangups in violent action and the overthrow of institutions.

The problems of adolescence are, of course, well known, but how much does such analysis contribute to an understanding of terrorism? How to explain that 99.9 percent of adolescents—even young radicals—react differently? The only plausible answer is that potential terrorists always exist, but that a variety of circumstances such as the cohesion of society, the strength of the state, and the general political situation determine whether they will actually proceed to terrorist action. Psychological interpretation could perhaps be of some help in explaining the high proportion of women among German terrorists; the explanation, one suspects, may not be that complicated, but it remains to be studied in detail.

Most of the interpretations that have been mentioned so far contain a kernel of truth, even though it is sometimes a minute one. But what they have to offer about the motivation of terrorism in Germany has no bearing on terrorism in other countries—least of all on nationalist-separatist terrorism, which is the most frequent form in our age. In many ways they try to explain too

---

*The case of Bernhard Vesper is frequently mentioned in this context. The former husband of Gudrun Ensslin committed suicide in a psychiatric clinic in 1971. He wrote an autobiographical novel (*Die Reise*, published posthumously in 1977) in which his relationship with his father, a literary luminary of the Third Reich, is described in detail. There has been no Vesper case in Austria.

much. World historical processes such as the cultural crisis, the crisis of legitimacy, or the crisis of "late capitalism" are invoked to explain the behavior of a few dozen people.

The contribution of criminology to the study of terrorism has been neglected so far but it is precisely in this direction that some advance seems most likely. There has been a notable reluctance to look at the criminological evidence, partly no doubt because the motives of the terrorists differ from those of the common criminal. But criminologists have been preoccupied for a long time with issues such as aggression and the problem of causality in crime; they know that people are more likely to kill in a group than individually, that the psychological obstacles to killing are reduced as the distance between the killer and the victim is increased. All this and other observations are of considerable relevance to terrorism. Above all, criminologists have known for a long time what students of terrorism are now learning from trial and error—that human beings are not arithmetical units that can be added up and divided in order to find a median, the "average terrorist."[8] As Thomas Aquinas wrote, *Individuum est incommunicabile.*

A great deal of work remains to be done on, for instance, the importance of ideology in terrorism and about the interaction between individual psychological motives and objective, i.e., political and social conditions. The serious study of terrorism is only beginning, but there should be no illusions about what it will be able to achieve. The issues involved are, in part, straightforward, obvious, and easily explicable. But there are also other aspects of terrorism that may forever remain beyond our comprehension. To accept this is not, however, to admit defeat; on the contrary, the present study shows convincingly in which directions our knowledge of the subject can and should be expanded.

WALTER LAQUEUR
Chairman, Research Council
The Center for Strategic and
International Studies
Georgetown University

Preface

During the 1970s, transnational terrorism became a stark reality to people throughout the world as the mass media transmitted, sometimes instantly, one horrifying spectacle after another. And as terrorist acts proliferated, controversy over terrorism heightened. Terrorism has become a rich topic for debate, a subject of intense disagreement on the floor of the United Nations. It has demanded attention as a serious policy issue. Studied by academicians, weighed and reported by journalists, and feared especially by the largest corporations—terrorism has come of age.

We have written this book because there is hardly any literature on the technological and management aspects of antiterrorism. No useful purpose could be served by another general treatise on terrorism. Walter Laqueur has provided the historical and political background. Brian Jenkins, among others, has analyzed the implications of terrorist actions and even ventured somewhat into the future.

We have personally dealt at senior levels of government with a wide variety of national security and domestic crisis management problems, having "faced the gun" more than once. For this reason, though our experience has not been confined to antiterrorism, the specter of an escalated terrorist threat is not an ethereal, academic matter to us. The physical consequences of major acts of terrorism are no different from natural disasters or large industrial accidents—but they have, of course, far greater political consequence. The essence of management is intelligent triage, allocating essential resources in order to minimize immediate and subsequent trauma.

In writing a work that connects the historical, political, physical, and management considerations of antiterrorism, we were faced with the difficult problem of "packaging" it. But we found that we could simplify our task if the material on the goal of developing a consistent national policy to combat terrorism was coupled with a discussion of federal emergency-preparedness.

The book's development is best understood by dividing it into five "phases," each phase consisting of one or two chapters. Phase I, which is composed of the foreword and the introduction, provides an overview of the policy and technical issues. As a self-contained unit, it will help the reader become somewhat knowledgeable about the field.

Phase II provides a brief historical analysis of terrorism (Chapter 1)—its heroes, its folklore, its effects on democratic governments, and its ultimate futility. It also deals with basic questions concerning contemporary terrorism: Who are today's terrorists? What have they done? Are they succeeding? What is the risk of a substantial escalation to acts of "national disruption"?

Phase III first treats the physical potential of acts portending national disruption (Chapter 2), including mass destruction terrorism. It then discusses counterterrorism technology (Chapter 3), focusing on the physical options available to a government for lessening the chances of successful terrorism.

Phase IV deals with incident management (Chapter 4), the problems a government faces in preparing to mitigate the effects of any substantial disaster resulting from terrorist acts. It discusses the requirements, as well as the choices available, for managing such a crisis.

Phase V describes our progress in establishing the means to combat terrorism. The first half (Chapter 5) is a discussion of the status of international cooperation, with recommendations for further refinement. The second half (Chapter 6) is a survey of the history of emergency preparedness and management in the United States, together with analyses of the incident-management apparatus, the new organization designated to deal with the consequences of terrorist acts, and the changes that are necessary to meet the evolving threat.

Eight essays, written by outstanding theorists and practitioners, make up the appendixes to the main text. Five of these pieces were prepared especially for this book, and three have previously been published. They bring into sharper focus some topics we were able only to touch upon: historical perspective and current trends, vulnerability of U.S. petroleum and natural gas industries, quantitative gauging methods, interaction between government and the media in time of crisis, and emergency medical care for victims of terrorism.

Some may fear that a book of this sort will give the terrorist new ideas and arm him with the means of executing devastating blows. We assure the reader that there are no terrorist tactics in this volume that are not already well known to the dedicated terrorist. The attacks on computers, electrical power systems, and pipelines, the poisoning of Israeli oranges, and the threats to use nerve agents and atomic bombs that have occurred attest to this.

We have been careful not to provide weapons design information. That certain biologicals can cause incalculable harm is common knowledge, but we have not instructed the terrorist in the art of growing anthrax. Any microbiologist could.

This book, then, places into perspective important technological and management issues that must be addressed by every government as well as industry if terrorism is to be kept within tolerable bounds. Terrorism cannot be controlled from a national position of ignorance. To behave as the three dumb monkeys—see nothing, hear nothing, and say nothing—offers little more than the prospect of living in the psychotic's world of denial.

Because our assumptions are necessarily simplified, our work must be considered preliminary. Over the last three years, departments and agencies of the federal government have participated in a series of comprehensive analyses of the developing terrorist threat. Reporting to the President through the Secretary of State and the Cabinet Committee to Combat Terrorism, they have recommended a broad range of procedures as well as substantive commitments of federal resources to improve government preparedness in this critical area. Their conclusions are particularly important because much of the apparatus for the management and coordination of a major crisis was dismantled by President Nixon in his Reorganization Plan Number One of 1973. Nixon divided the Executive Office functions of the Office of Emergency Preparedness among several federal agencies, thereby completely eliminating the critical bloc of analytical staff that had been charged with generating policy and coordinating authority for crisis management.

We participated in the work of the Cabinet Committee to Combat Terrorism, providing guidance for an analytical evaluation of its subject areas. But the views we express in this book do not necessarily reflect current government policy. We hope to provide a balanced evaluation of the terrorist threat as well as insight into shaping government policy and operations that would improve our preparedness. Terrorism promises to test our ingenuity severely in the years ahead. The importance of this study, we believe, rests in its proposal of ways to integrate a variety of federal resources to face that challenge.

Much of the material on incident management is based on the work Dr. Kupperman performed for the Law Enforcement Assistance Administration. We owe a great debt of gratitude to Mr. Perry Rivkind, LEAA's Assistant Administrator for Operations Support, for his courage and foresight. His support for the research projects of the Cabinet Committee to Combat Terrorism enabled completion of three primary reports that have set the direction for current federal initiatives. He has truly performed yeoman service in the cause of counterterrorism research. The LEAA has given us permission to cite freely from *Facing Tomorrow's Terrorist Incident Today*, a report by Dr. Kupperman that was publicly released in October 1977 by the LEAA. That work was the final report to LEAA for Grants Nos. LEAA-J-IAA-021-6 and LEAA-J-IAA-034-6.

Walter Laqueur is one of the world's leading authorities on terrorism. In his foreword to this book he helps set the stage for our examination of the technological and crisis management elements of terrorist incidents. We are especially appreciative of Dr. Laqueur's guidance and support in this project.

This study owes much to the helpful comments of many people. We are particularly appreciative of the assistance from Martin Anderson, Dennis Bark, Richard Burress, W. Glenn Campbell, Anna Clarke, John B. Condliffe, K.C.M.G., Richard Davis, Milorad Drachkovitch, Manfred Eimer, Franco Ferracuti, Peter Franken, Lewis H. Gann, Elizabeth Gehman, James Gregg, Paul Hanna, Conrad Hassel, Hans Josef Horchem, Kenneth Joseph, Jakov Katwan, Richard Keiser, Donald Kerr, John Kirsch,

Howard Liebengood, Robert McBrien, Lieutenant General E. C. Meyer, Tom Moore, Frank Ochberg, Anthony Quainton, Arthur Rovine, Richard Staar, Edward Teller, Jared Tinkleberg, H. D. Walton, Iram Weinstein, and George Weisz.

Any study of contemporary terrorism is constrained by the limited source materials available, particularly in regard to counterterrorism technology and crisis management. The supporting essays that appear as appendixes in this book are extremely important because they provide analytical commentary on a broad range of critical considerations. We would like to extend our deep appreciation to the authors of these papers: Yonah Alexander, James P. Bennett, Francis A. Bolz, Jr., Brian M. Jenkins, Bowman H. Miller, Charles A. Russell, Thomas Saaty, Maynard M. Stephens, Martin E. Silverstein, Harvey A. Smith, D. A. Waterman, and Richard H. Wilcox.

Our research assistant, Brian Berger, participated immeasurably in all the final stages of preparing the manuscript for publication. His long hours and dedicated analysis of structure and format, his efforts in researching, abstracting, integrating, reorganizing, and checking data—all were invaluable.

Liselotte Hofmann was of great assistance in editing the final manuscript. We are particularly grateful for her patience and understanding as well as her professional ability. Mickey Hamilton contributed to the completion of this project not only as general manager of the Hoover Institution Press but as a consultant and adviser on the technical aspects of the book's preparation. The long hours and hard work of Marcella Smith, Helen Sperry, Cheri Johnson, and Nancy Grey were invaluable in preparing numerous drafts of the manuscript.

We are also deeply indebted to our colleagues at the United States Arms Control and Disarmament Agency* and at the Hoover Institution for their comments, support, and encouragement.

*The views expressed in this book are the authors' and do not necessarily reflect the views of the United States Government or any of its agencies or departments.

TERRORISM

Introduction

Throughout the Middle East and Western Europe, German, Basque, Moluccan, Italian, and Palestinian terrorists have kept up a staccato of assaults. Their successes—and failures—are now legion, for they have managed to preoccupy large governments for weeks on end and have forced them to employ oppressive tactics. In desperation, Western European nations, using the Council of Europe, have banded together to protect themselves against terrorism. Yet kidnappings, bombings, assassinations, and industrial sabotage have become commonplace. Repetition has reduced their shock value—possibly to the point that they are somewhat tolerated.

The public has become acutely aware of terrorism, not only through news sources but through movies, novels, and television specials. Illustrating America's concern, a recent Harris Survey[1] revealed that "terrorism is viewed as a very serious world problem by 90% of the American people, and a very serious domestic problem by 60%." The survey went on to show that the public favors extreme measures in dealing with terrorists: 90 percent of Americans favor the development of commando teams such as those used by the Israelis at Entebbe and the West Germans at Mogadishu. Eighty percent favor airline service being cut off to and from countries that harbor terrorists; and more than half of the public would support the organization of a "special world police force which would operate in any country of the world and which would investigate terrorist groups, arrest them, and put their leaders and members to death."

Possibly just a momentary overreaction or conceivably the seeds of hysteria, the elements of a new vigilante justice are inescapable. America's reaction to domestic and international terrorism is especially interesting in that this country has been relatively free from terrorist assault. Transnational terrorists who have never set foot on United States soil have in part succeeded in intimidating the American public.

Terrorism Is Theater

Because *terrorism* is difficult—and possibly pointless—to define formally, its statistics are not fully catalogued. Nevertheless, apart from the civil war in Northern Ireland and repeated terrorist attacks in Israel, there are interesting statistics to note. During 1977–1978, Italy experienced over two thousand terrorist incidents and Germany about twenty. Over the past ten years there have been over three hundred kidnappings of business and political leaders in Latin America and Europe for whom several hundred million dollars in ransom may have been paid. Most have occurred during the past three years. With the exception of the Hanafi siege and the 1975 LaGuardia bombing, America has had little experience with major acts of terrorism. But there have been repeated bombings by the Weather Underground, the New World Liberation Front, and the Armed Forces of National Liberation (FALN) of Puerto Rico.

When compared with the national homicide rate, the death toll from terrorism is indeed small. In the past ten years terrorism has claimed the lives of about a thousand people. Yet it has become a major international issue. Why? Because terrorism is theater.

Anxieties have become high, but, unfortunately, the threshold for the spectacular assault has heightened as well. America and Western Europe have insatiable appetites for the novel, the bizarre. If we take this into account and accept the thesis that the terrorist's goal is disruption and that he must maintain his sense of "Broadway presence," we can readily speculate about the near future: terrorist organizations and their targets will *adapt* in order to stay ahead of governments' counterterrorist preparations and to maintain their façade of strength.

Who Are the Terrorists?

Terrorists are not part of marauding armies. In all, there are about three thousand of them grouped into some fifty organizations.* There may be an equal number of supporters. Four or five groups amounting to about two hundred terrorists—Germans, Italians, Palestinians, and Japanese—constitute the primary transnational threat. But they are at the tip of the iceberg, the action corps.

The "two hundred" have trained together in Cuba, Lebanon, Libya, and North Korea. Their weapons are supplied by Communist bloc countries, especially Czechoslovakia. Most frightening of all, they may have lost their political identity, having become increasingly nihilistic. One need only scratch the surface of their espoused Marxism to find their true purpose: destruction of the establishment, whatever government is in power. Although it might be overstating matters to posit central control (that is, the KGB), it is obvious that the Soviets have contributed substantially to their support. Weapons are not freely obtained from Communist countries; and the IRA, Weather Underground, and Black Panthers, as well as the "two hundred," are not trained in bloc countries without Soviet permission and promises of payment in kind.

What are their weapons? Not just pistols, submachine guns, and bombs, for there have been attempts to use heat-seeking, surface-to-air rockets (SA-7s) and Soviet-made antitank weapons (RPG-7s). German terrorists have threatened to disperse mustard gas and nerve agents, and in 1975 German entrepreneurs were arrested in Vienna for conspiring to sell nerve agents in the Middle East. There has been at least one incident in which a radioisotope of iodine was sprinkled on a train. Moreover, mass transit facilities have been attacked in Germany, broadcasting studios in Spain and Argentina, and nuclear power plants in France, Argentina, and Spain.

The terrorists may have their act together. It is not clear that the target governments do.

---

*If all terrorist "groups" were counted, some consisting of one or two individuals and often operating under more than one name, possibly several hundred could be listed. Examining the threat realistically suggests about fifty terrorist organizations of any consequence.

The Evolving Organism

Brian Jenkins has put it well:

> The use of terrorist tactics will persist. The actual amount of violence or threatened violence may increase, for terrorism has a built-in requirement for escalation if not in bloodshed, at least in audacity, drama, or magnitude of the threat. Potentially, terrorism could also decrease, for it has tended historically to be cyclical, with earlier waves of terrorism subsiding in the late nineteenth and early twentieth century. Future potential terrorists could decide that terrorist tactics are unproductive, perhaps even counterproductive, spectacles. The repertoire of the terrorists may change as new tactics are invented, old ones discarded, for there is a constant requirement for novelty. When terrorism becomes mundane, it may lose its effect. The sources of terrorist violence may move about the world as groups disappear or discard terrorist tactics as a means of achieving their objectives while new groups adopt them. But considering all things, the use of terrorist tactics is not likely to end, for the basic idea behind terrorism that a small but determined group, lacking other means of getting attention and of coercion, can achieve disproportionate effects through dramatic acts of violence has been repeatedly demonstrated to work, at least in the short run. And that is probably enough to preclude total abandonment.[2]

As their theatrical presence diminishes, there is little point for terrorists to increase the level of violence. Economic and other institutional forms of disruption are likely to be sufficiently effective. Obvious targets are the electrical power grid, water systems, commercial aircraft, pipelines, and communications systems. Acts of extraordinary violence—nuclear and other forms of mass destruction—would be counterproductive. In the unlikely case that they did occur, nations would unite to rout out the terrorists, anticipating, as one does in a war, losses along the way. Further, there is considerable room for maneuver between today's violence and the hobgoblins conjured to commit acts of nuclear, chemical, and biological terrorism. Far less than nuclear terrorism is needed to infect government with a case of the shakes. In the absence of national planning, the objectives of terrorism are all too easily achieved.

Terrorism has become a spectator sport, a theatrical event of nightmarish proportions. But we become bored easily. The next airline hijacking—or the next hostage episode—will no longer be spellbinding news. As we suggested earlier, the terror-organism may adapt, changing its target and awaiting its press reviews. One of government's most important jobs, therefore, is to "out-invent" terrorists, assessing as yet unexploited possibilities and devising countermeasures.

THE FUNDAMENTALS OF DEFENSE

Terrorism is hardly a new phenomenon; in one form or another it pervades recorded history. Yet, each time it reappears, still poorly defined, it looms as a new menace. Governments, especially the more liberal ones, find the phenomenon difficult to cope with.

The strongest band of terrorists is far weaker than the tiniest military force. Terrorists gain their leverage from the physical and institutional vulnerabilities of the societies they attack, and they magnify their exploits through massive media coverage. On a tactical level, terrorism has proven generally successful. On the strategic front, however, the scoreboard of struggle between nation-states and terrorists is not so clear. Walter Laqueur has placed the amorphous subject of terrorism in perspective.[3] He provides a panorama of terrorists and their times: the Zealots, India's Thugs, and the nineteenth-century anarchists. He compares these groups with their modern brethren—the Weathermen of the 1960s, the Palestine Liberation Organization (PLO) and its splinters, and the nihilistic Baader-Meinhof Gang.

Laqueur distinguishes between contemporary terrorism and its more ideologically based predecessors. The anarchists of the nineteenth century envisioned a just society and saw violence as a way of achieving their political ends. Contemporary terrorism, on the other hand, is indiscriminate and its practitioners seem to offer no grand visions of a "better world" and few, if any, realizable goals. Today's terrorist seeks to weaken governments, attacking the often tenuous bonds between government and the governed.

The nineteenth-century anarchists operated in a historical

vacuum, in the sense that no fundamental social revolution of the type they envisioned had yet occurred. If they were haunted by the possibilities lost in the collapse of the French First Republic, they also had a certain starry-eyed innocence, an implacable optimism that a healthy, free society would emerge out of the ashes of the existing social order, once it were put to the torch. Given the frankly authoritarian character of the various "People's Republics" established in this century, with their purges and Gulags, to hold such optimism today one would have to be truly blind. In fact, most contemporary terrorists display the cynicism of disturbed individuals playing out a desperate last chance.

Maintaining our fundamental freedoms and not caving in to terrorist demands are challenging tasks when we are under assault. Terrorism can succeed only if our willingness to face it realistically is replaced by governmental quaking and public alarm. Overreaction, such as government-imposed news blackouts or invasions of privacy, are unmistakable invitations to disaster.

The prescription is toughness. Governments must not appear to cower in the face of a few "killer bees." They must resolutely match wits with their antagonists, recognizing the range of targets, even economic ones, that are well within the reach of the more imaginative.

At root is the need to eliminate the causes of terrorism; but this could be achieved only through an uncertain, painful process. Certainly, the Arab-Israeli conflict will not be resolved easily. Governments, finding terrorism an intolerable form of dissent, are forced to combat it by means of *deterrence* and *damage limitation*. However measured, the profits of terrorism must be made to diminish. Thus, for example, terrorist acts should be treated as ordinary crimes rather than as lesser political offenses. Deterrence and damage limitation go hand in hand, for as terrorists become less successful, having often been embarrassed by the forces of government, their morale and available resources should wane. We must remind ourselves, however, that government's tactics should be tempered. The risk of an insidious state-repression, in the name of counterterrorism, is all too real. The "game" between terrorist groups and society is not straightforward—it is certainly not zero-sum.

There are practical defenses to be taken. The first is *intelligence*. Although it is easy to raise red flags about intelligence collection, having advance information about an impending terrorist assault is preferable to being caught unprepared.*

The second defense is *target hardening*, building "high-pass filters" that block the admission of amateurish terrorists and increase the costs to the more talented as well. Limiting access through physical means and controlling the accessibility of dangerous devices and materials are fundamental. Based upon threat assessments, *cost-benefit analyses* of the vulnerability of critical nodes of our society should be performed. For example, if a portion of the electrical power grid were to fail for an extended period, it would not be just the problem of the power industry; it would be a national catastrophe.

Were intelligence sources inadequate to thwart an incident and physical barriers too weak, we would be forced to manage government's responses to the assault. Thus, we come to the third defense. We need to develop an effective *crisis management system*, one that would take responsibility for a broad spectrum of nationally disruptive crises: rail strikes, natural disasters, fuel shortages, terrorism, and so on.

If terrorism continues at its present level of sophistication, the needed defenses are now being created. Tougher policies,

---

*The assessment of the threat of terrorism relies on intelligence techniques—observing known or suspected terrorists and, when feasible, penetrating their organizations. Unfortunately, the task of keeping up with terrorists in this fashion is overwhelming, for it is virtually impossible to tell when a formerly obscure or inactive group will suddenly spring into prominence. (The incident of March 1977 in which Hanafi Muslims terrorized Washington with three separate sieges illustrates this point.) On the other hand, terrorism that is widely advertised in advance may never take place, at least in part because of the intense counterefforts prompted by the advertisement.

Terrorist acts force the generation of their own countermeasures, as airplane hijackings led to screening of air passengers. Though politically explosive incidents still occur, the problem becomes a *quantitative* one, and countermeasures will be improved and developed until the probability of success for the particular form of terrorism appears tolerably small.

The first occurrence of a new mode of terrorism, however, usually appears as a *qualitative* problem, and it can be a grave one if it has not been anticipated. We must therefore attempt to "out-invent" terrorists, assessing as yet unexploited technical possibilities and devising countermeasures.

In estimating the frequencies of familiar types of attacks, qualitative errors in threat assessment are potentially more destabilizing influences on national policies toward terrorism than are quantitative mistakes. While avoiding actions that could cause widespread alarm, we must also avoid the contrary extreme of believing that because a certain type of incident has never yet occurred, it is therefore unlikely to occur in the future.

including trade sanctions and the termination of commercial air service to countries that harbor terrorists, as well as the development of rescue teams, will emerge as honed tools. But what if terrorists were to black out a major metropolitan area such as New York City? What if airline pilots were to go on strike because a surface-to-air rocket were used to shoot down a jumbo jet lifting off from Dulles or Kennedy? Obviously, we would face problems of greater magnitude. The socioeconomic effects of the terrorist attack could well outweigh the primary physical damage.

It would be no longer clear that law enforcement could take the lead, nor that we could find the appropriate target abroad to attack in retaliation. Broad-gauged but well-tuned crisis management machinery must be developed. Above all, we should not rely upon *ad hoc* solutions. Contingency planning and serious efforts at "gaming" the improbable event should be pursued vigorously, but they should be absorbed inconspicuously within the machinery of law enforcement, national security, and civil emergency preparedness—machinery intended to deal with the broader array of domestic and international crises we will undoubtedly face.

The Protection of Civil Liberties

The theatrical effect of terrorism is a means to an end, the end being the disruption, if not destruction, of a free society. We all walk a tightrope: the media are obliged to report the news, yet they can incite terror; government, by overreacting to the threat of terrorism, can appear ridiculous or repressive; and a government that has done little or nothing to prepare for the serious terrorist incident may cause irreparable injury to its people.

"You're damned if you do, and you're damned if you don't." That's the paradox of terrorism. But there is a middle ground. The news must be reported, but a code of ethics should arise from within the media. Government-imposed rules of conduct are bound to fail; besides, the terrorists would have won if they caused government to abridge the freedom of the press. Government must react but must continually balance its actions against the commitment to preserve civil liberties within its society.

As with other problems that threaten the social fabric, we tend to extrapolate to doom when the true effects would be far less serious. It is all too easy to point an accusatory finger at the media, the government, or any other convenient scapegoat. If we treat terrorism and its remedies simplistically, we will fall prey to ourselves.

CHAPTER 1

The Past Is Prologue

Terrorism has been correctly described as a strategy of the weak. The relationships of power between a terrorist organization and a sovereign state present a contrast in extremes. Like a muscle-bound giant, a great nation with full military resources can be reduced to impotence. By exploiting legal and cultural traditions that emphasize restraint, fairness, and the sanctity of life, terrorists seek to determine their adversary's response. They play on the inherent tension between freedom and order in all democratic societies.

The strategy of terrorism can be compared with the strategy used in various martial arts: the aim is to turn an opponent's strength against him. Terrorists seek reversals in the system of authority that is the framework of a civilized people—by demanding release for those who have been imprisoned according to due process, by attempting to dictate policy without regard to the structure of democracy, by aspiring to reorder society or determine its direction without consideration of, or in spite of, a majority consensus. A relative handful reject the basis of ordered existence, certain that they are working for something better. In this assumption of superior knowledge, transnational terrorists betray their essentially authoritarian character. Despite a rhetoric saturated with democratic and egalitarian imagery, these terrorists are no more committed to human freedom than are the various people's republics that they invoke as models of social organization. As was demonstrated by the Tupamaros in Uruguay, terrorists are much better at demolishing relatively humane, democratic structures than they are at providing new and better modes of governing.

Terrorists have always tried to deliberately provoke tyranny, in the mad hope that this will bring about the necessary preconditions for revolution. But, as in Uruguay, the conditions of tyranny they induce are more likely to stifle than to promote possibilities for change. The West German response to terrorism, while by no means tyrannical, already has been characterized by a diminution of civil liberties. However paradoxical, one of the responses terrorists desire is state tyranny. Clearly, when either through action or through a threat of action, the terrorist initiates this strange dialogue between himself and the target state, he is luring his adversary to join him on most slippery ground.

Perhaps the most perplexing characteristic of terrorism is the glaring disjunction between terrorist action and terrorist (stated) goals. What possible connection can there be between the cause of the Palestinians and the slaughter of Puerto Rican Christians at an airport in Israel or of New York-bound passengers at an airport in Athens? Why did a West German pilot have to die on his knees in Somalia? There are, of course, no satisfactory answers. Terrorist violence is by its nature random. Its immediate victims are of no real consequence to its perpetrators' goals. David Fromkin has stated the problem well:

> Terrorism is violence used in order to create fear; but it is aimed at creating fear in order that the fear, in turn, will lead somebody else—not the terrorist—to embark on some quite different program of action that will accomplish whatever it is that the terrorist really desires. Unlike the soldier, the guerrilla fighter, or the revolutionist, the terrorist therefore is always in the paradoxical position of undertaking actions the immediate physical consequences of which are not particularly desired by him. An ordinary murderer will kill somebody because he wants the person to be dead, but a terrorist will shoot somebody even though it is a matter of complete indifference to him whether that person lives or dies. He would do so, for example, in order to provoke a brutal police repression that he believes will lead to political conditions propitious to revolutionary agitation and organization aimed at overthrowing the government. The act of murder is the same in both cases, but its purpose is different, and each act plays a different role in the strategies of violence.[1]

By its very nature, terrorism is engaged in the disruption of norms, the violation of generally accepted standards of decency, including the rules of war as they apply to the innocent and the helpless. As we have discussed, terrorism is staged to call attention to an often unrelated situation through shock—creating situations of horror, doing the unthinkable without apology or remorse. It is consequently difficult to appraise in value-free language. To be effective, terrorism must evoke a severe emotional response.

While contemporary terrorism has an obvious relationship to state terror in its use of fear as a political weapon, it differs in its separation of actions from goals and in its usual indifference to immediate victims. Beginning with Robespierre, state terror has employed fear as a direct means of establishing authority and assuring obedience. It has proven particularly useful during the period in which a new state seeks to consolidate and legitimize its authority. The Soviet Union in its early days and Cambodia today provide examples of what we may expect if terrorists ever do achieve state power, but they tell us little about the contemporary terrorist problem. The real antecedents to contemporary terrorism are the various anarchist movements of the nineteenth century, in which the figure of Bakunin stands central.

Mikhail Bakunin devoted his life to bringing about a revolution in the semifeudal Russia of his day. An anarchist with decidedly vague ideas about the organization of society following revolution, he was primarily concerned with bringing about the destruction of the prevailing social order. In his *Principles of Revolution*, he wrote that "we recognize no other action save destruction though we admit that the forms in which such action will show itself will be exceedingly varied—poison, the knife, the rope, etc."[2] Though he thought of himself as a socialist, he was scorned by Marx and Engels, not only because he believed that a socialist revolution could first occur in Russia (which Marx dismissed as unlikely), but because he was viewed as a dangerous fanatic, thirsty for action but lacking a systematic philosophy. As such, he was clearly a forerunner of today's terrorist.

Bakunin was not, however, an advocate of the individual terrorism typical of nineteenth-century anarchists outside Russia.

He believed that an army of peasants and thieves would create the revolution, which would take the form of merciless, violent destruction of the status quo. His interest in a revolutionary alliance with the criminal underworld is particularly noteworthy in its anticipation of contemporary terrorist methodology. The idea had come from Wilhelm Weitling, the first German Communist and a major influence on Bakunin. In 1848, Weitling had proposed mobilizing murderers and thieves, "founding the kingdom of heaven by unleashing the furies of hell."[3] After Bakunin died, his followers retreated from such a coalition, opting instead for the "Propaganda of the Deed." This concept stressed the importance of individual acts of violence as revolutionary statements by members of an intellectual vanguard, and Bakunin's name became associated with this more European, propagandistic anarchism.

The context of nineteenth-century anarchism needs to be stressed. Like Marxism, it was largely a response to the failure of the revolutions that had swept Europe in 1848. These had been the efforts of Jacobin-style liberals, who were thought by many Europeans radicals, in retrospect, to have failed because they lacked the ruthlessness and the willingness to systematically pursue their stated goals. The anarchist or social revolutionary of the latter half of the century would consequently be noted for a single-mindedness of purpose that could accurately be described as fanaticism. Bombings and assassinations became increasingly common in the late nineteenth century; victims included at least one U.S. president, James Garfield (whether William McKinley's assassination in 1901 was the work of an anarchist or a madman remains an open question), and a Russian tsar, Alexander II. In Russia these developments occurred against a particularly oppressive backdrop augmented by a perceived failure of liberalism.

In their love of violence for its own sake, their desire to horrify and disrupt the society at large, as well as in the absence of any kind of systematic plan for social organization beyond the revolution, the nineteenth-century anarchists prefigure our contemporary terrorists. There are major differences, of course, and some of them are alarming: the present sophisticated organization of terrorists throughout the world, what one commentator has called "the New International"; the related phenomenon of today's terrorists claiming for themselves a global battleground, which makes a mockery of an international legal framework based on national sovereignty; and finally, the magnitude of damage of which contemporary terrorists are capable—the potential for nationally disruptive acts, including mass destruction, and the heightened degree of fear that they may consequently impose. Despite historical continuities, these characteristics make our terrorist problem an unprecedented challenge.

* * *

History teaches us that man learns nothing from history.
—Hegel

Does terrorism work? We can find, well before Yasir Arafat's reception at the United Nations in 1974, historical illustrations of terrorism's efficacy. Earlier in this century, some nationalist groups employed terrorist methodology successfully in their struggle against colonialism. But these efforts differed significantly from contemporary terrorism in that much of the violence was directed against a foreign presence, almost always European. The political goal of the violence was independence—departure of the foreign administration and establishment of a new nation. India, Israel, and Algeria, for example, employed varying degrees of terrorist violence in their drive for independence. In the case of Israel and Algeria, a strategic understanding was reached as to how the adversary's position of strength could be exploited.[4]

In India, terrorism in the years prior to World War II was conducted principally by disenchanted followers of Gandhi. One of the best-known groups, the Hindustan Socialist Republican Association, summarized its credo in *The Philosophy of the Bomb*.[5] This work expressed a pastiche of Russian-style anarchist violence and Marxian class warfare. Many of these terrorists were notably incompetent, likely to kill innocent bystanders while missing their targets. Somewhat more effective was the Hindu Mahasabha, a Brahmin group that inveighed against the English and the Muslims equally. Although none of the Indian terrorists were able to overshadow the tremendously popular, nonviolent Gandhism, Mahatma Gandhi was assassinated in 1948 by a member of the Mahasabha's terrorist wing, the RSSS. The unfortunate religious wars that have plagued India's brief history as a nation reflect the continued importance of the Mahasabha.

In Palestine, the Irgun (led by, among others, Menachem Begin), responded to the British betrayal of the Balfour Declaration by conducting a terrorist war against Great Britain. This small organization, with approximately a thousand members, had as its goal the opening of Palestine to the many Jewish refugees left homeless after the holocaust. Its strategy was to alarm the British into adopting a garrison-like presence in the country, with vast numbers of troops, which the Irgun correctly understood postwar Britain to be incapable of maintaining over an extended period. The Irgun's intention was to attack only property. However, nearly a hundred people died in the bombing of British Headquarters, the King David Hotel in Jerusalem, when Irgun warnings were ignored. While terrorists' actions did contribute significantly to the British decision to abandon Palestine in 1948, their violent methods put them outside the mainstream of Israeli politics, a situation exploited by David Ben-Gurion, who was able to prevent their leaders from participating in the coalition that ruled the new nation of Israel.

In Algeria, the tiny Front of National Liberation (FLN) was able to exploit to great advantage France's racist attitude toward the natives of its southern colony. Unlike other French colonies in Africa, Algeria was not a legally discrete entity; rather it was viewed as the southernmost part of France. The French had used this situation to maintain control and to discourage independence efforts: the Algerians were to think of themselves as Frenchmen. But once the FLN began its terrorist activities, which included the bombing of populous areas, the French responded by treating the entire non-European, Muslim population with suspicion. Native troops were replaced with European, and mass arrests were common. The French consequently forced all Muslims into an identification with the FLN, and the terrorist campaign conducted by a tiny group was able to shift into a popularly based guerrilla conflict.

The situations discussed above indicate the role of terrorism in various insurgent movements directed against specific colonial or mandated powers. They occurred in the context of the rise of the modern nation-state and were decidedly localized or regional in scope. Although the Algerian War was waged by dedicated Marxists, the conflict could be understood in purely nationalistic terms. The Cuban revolution, similarly, involved the toppling of an unpopular regime perceived as representing non-Cuban interests. Interestingly, the efforts to extend the Cuban experience as Marxist revolution elsewhere in Latin America faltered because the Cubans were unable to locate in an anticolonist setting ripe for the emergence of a new nation-state, as illustrated by Che Guevara's fiasco in Bolivia. The Palestinian terrorists, on the other hand, may well achieve their goal precisely because of the desperate need for a homeland of some sort. While transnational terrorists (German, Japanese, and others) may have helped the Palestinians pursue this goal, their role in their respective nations remains decidedly shadowy and their violence nihilistic.

CONTEMPORARY TERRORISM

The collapse of the great colonial empires in the wake of World War II engendered a vast and rapid reordering of global relations, carried out under the pressures of burgeoning nationalism in former colonies and protectorates. The postwar world order was of necessity somewhat hastily conceived and to no small degree jerrybuilt to fill the vacuum created by the demise of the Great Powers' empires. Although it has tended to serve well so far, this reordering has been under challenge since its inception. For many, and particularly for the peoples of the Third World, the prevailing mood of the postwar era has been one of transition, of a new world order emerging.[6]

Many of the terrorist groups committed to separatism or nationalism (the PLO being the best-known example) have operated in the knowledge that the use of limited force may be needed to carve out a niche for one's people. It is a classic application of Clausewitz's famous dictum that warfare is a continuation of diplomacy by other means, invested with a modern understanding of selective violence. Within much of the world community the pervasive anticolonialist sentiment of the postwar period has translated into a sympathetic attitude toward terrorism along these lines. At the same time, the writings of Mao, Guevara, Frantz Fanon, and Carlos Marighella illustrate strategy, foster a quasi-religious faith that history is on the side of the oppressed, and provide a theoretical link to ultraleftist terrorist groups in the advanced industrial societies of Western Europe and Japan.

A concurrent political development involves the growing awareness of the interdependence of all peoples, the sense that the great challenges facing mankind are of global scale. The postwar period has witnessed a proliferation of international organizations and efforts (the United Nations, International Monetary Fund, World Bank, the so-called North-South dialogue), all of which are predicated on a commitment to recognize and act upon this interdependence. An epiphenomenon resulting from this trend is the implicit notion that the advanced industrial nations bear direct responsibility for the state of development of the poorer nations. Whether or not this is accurate, it does contribute to an international climate in which self-appointed avengers may seek retribution through threats or acts of violence. This is typically the case in the kidnapping of foreign businessmen by Latin American terrorists, where exorbitant ransoms are extracted as "reparations" and murder is justified as execution.

A third concurrent development is the advent of satellite communications, particularly the capability, first realized in 1968, for transmitting television signals around the globe. The social implications of this technological innovation are far-reaching and as yet not fully understood. There can be no question that our growing perception of interdependence is inextricably linked to our advanced communications capabilities. Communication theorists of the McLuhan school would assert that the very concept of interdependence in its modern form is a child of satellite communications. Instantaneous worldwide television coverage of wars, insurrections, assassinations, and catastrophes contributes to and reinforces the sense of apparent disorder and instability that for many is the chief characteristic of our age, suggesting an environment in which the violent actions of desperate men and women are somehow appropriate. At the same time, television satellites provide a global audience for terrorist histrionics. We may yet see the global village held as hostage by terrorists with, say, a nuclear capability or access to advanced biological weaponry.

We must also consider what may be referred to as the cost-effectiveness of terrorism. A study prepared by the Rand Corporation examined sixty-three major kidnapping and barricade events staged by terrorists between early 1968 and late 1974. The conclusions (assignments of chance to risk and success) were striking. As summarized in a recent CIA research study, they showed:

- 87 percent probability of actually seizing hostages;

- 79 percent chance that all members of the terrorist team would escape punishment or death, whether or not they successfully seized hostages;

- 40 percent chance that all or some demands would be met in operations where something more than just safe passage or exit permission was demanded;

- 29 percent chance of full compliance with such demands;

- 83 percent chance of success where safe passage or exit, for the terrorists themselves or for others, was the sole demand;

- 67 percent chance that, if concessions to the principal demands were rejected, all or virtually all members of the terrorist team could still escape alive by going underground, accepting safe passage in lieu of their original demands, or surrendering to a sympathetic government; and

- virtually a 100 percent probability of gaining major publicity whenever that was one of the terrorists' goals.[7]

Although these statistics are disconcerting, one of the most dramatic examples of the efficacy of terrorism has been the emergence of the PLO's Yasir Arafat as the recognized spokesman for the Palestinian people, a position cemented by his unparalleled address to the UN General Assembly in 1974.

Even though it should not be too surprising, the heavy increase in the number of terrorist incidents as well as in the number of terrorist groups over the last decade is disturbing. So, too, are certain qualitative aspects of the expansion of terrorist activity.

Cooperation

There is evidence of increasing cooperation among national and international terrorist organizations in the form of common financial and technical support. As a result of this cooperation and of the extensive media coverage that terrorist activities have received, procedure techniques and even attitudes of particular groups are apparently being adopted by other groups.[8]

For example, Palestinian terrorist camps in Lebanon, Syria, Libya (and until 1970, Jordan) have trained revolutionaries from Western Europe, Africa, Latin America, Asia, and North America in terrorist techniques. Such groups have included representatives from America's Weathermen and Black Panthers, the Irish Republican Army, the Turkish People's Liberation Army, the Eritrean Liberation Front, Japan's United Red Army (URA), and West Germany's Baader-Meinhof Gruppe.[9] But the Palestinians have not restricted their training to leftists. They have also recruited German neo-Nazis, presumably on the basis of shared anti-Semitism. The following advertisement appeared in the ultrarightist *Deutsche National-Zeitung* in 1970–1971:

> Courageous and audacious young Germans are wanted to study the liberation war of displaced Palestinians. . . . Financial considerations should stop no one from participating. . . . If you are attracted by the proposed venture, contact us immediately.[10]

This Palestinian connection appears to be the main thread linking a diverse number of terrorist groups and events in what has come to be known as transnational terrorism. To the extent that there is an alliance, it appears to be quite loose, grounded more in common sympathies than in shared experience. This is clearly the case among those terrorist groups that grew out of the New Left movement in Western and Japanese universities. Although most of the students who participated in the New Left movement of the late 1960s have tended either to move into the mainstream of political activity or, more likely, to forego political interests entirely, a small number of those holding fairly extreme positions have intensified their efforts. And this, despite cultural differences that are often pronounced, is the common denominator among groups such as America's Weathermen, Japan's United Red Army, Italy's Red Brigades (Brigate Rosse), and West Germany's Red Army Faction (Rote Armee Fraktion), the group founded by the Baader-Meinhof Gang.

The Weathermen evolved as the ultraradical faction of the Students for a Democratic Society, the most important New Left organization in the United States. The United Red Army developed out of the Zengakuren, the extremist organization of Japanese university students. The URA combined contemporary revolutionary ideology with the highly warlike and suicidal tradition of Bushido (the code of the warrior), even using samurai language and swords in some of their hijackings. The Baader-Meinhof Gang represented only the periphery of extreme left-wing sentiment among students and intellectuals in West Germany. The group's ideology was heavily influenced by the "Frankfurt school" of political philosophy, which taught the validity of taking revolutionary action against property though not people. Their first act of terrorism was, appropriately, to set fire to a department store in Frankfurt. Their targets soon included people as well, and the gang would eventually be remembered for kidnappings and murders. The Hanns-Martin Schleyer kidnapping was undertaken by the "Movement of Second of June" in coordination with the hijacking of a Lufthansa flight by Palestinian terrorists, and underscores the type of transnational cooperation characteristic of contemporary terrorists. When a special German unit recovered the airliner in Mogadishu and thereby foiled the hijacking attempt, three gang members jailed in Stuttgart (co-founder Andreas Baader, his mistress Gudrun Ensslin, and Jan-Carl Raspe) committed suicide in their cells. A year earlier, founding member Ulrike Meinhof had hanged herself in the same Stammheim prison.

Italy's Red Brigades most recently occupied center stage with their bold kidnapping of former Premier and Christian Democrat leader Aldo Moro, killing the five men in his police escort and abducting him in broad daylight. The idea of kidnapping a major politician may have been inspired by the Baader-Meinhof Gang's

1975 abduction of Berlin mayoral candidate Peter Lorenz, whom they later freed in exchange for the release of five imprisoned terrorists. In kidnapping Moro, the Red Brigades hoped to bargain for the release of their founder, Renato Curcio, and eleven other jailed members then on trial in Turin. Curcio, once considered a brilliant sociology student at the University of Trento, had emerged from the turbulent period of the late 1960s a committed Marxist revolutionary. He founded the Red Brigades in Milan a decade ago with a group of other Marxist students from the universities of northern Italy. All shared similar middle-class backgrounds; none cared for the pro-Soviet Italian Communist Party. Originally committed to nonviolent revolution—the so-called *via pacifica* of orthodox Communist dogma—Curcio rather abruptly converted to a belief in violence as a necessary means of overthrowing capitalism. The conversion occurred while he was in the poverty-stricken countryside of southern Italy. There he reportedly witnessed a clash between day laborers and police in which two protesting workers were shot to death. In his outrage, he became convinced of the need for armed struggle.

Prior to the Moro kidnapping, the Red Brigades were already notorious for their maiming attacks on key figures in Italian public life, such as the crippling in June 1977 of Indrio Montanelli, editor of the Milan daily *Il Giornale Nuovo* and a leading anti-Communist. Montanelli was left with four bullets in his legs. Since murdering Moro, the terrorists have stepped up their maiming attacks.

The Red Brigades provide a frightening illustration of the power which a small band of dedicated fanatics can wield in a liberal democracy (particularly one like that of the Italians, never famous for its stability). They virtually paralyzed the already shaky political life of Italy by seizing Moro, who had recently been named head of the ruling Christian Democrats and was considered by many to be the most important politician in Italy. The Brigades' short-term goal was to subvert the "historic compromise" by which the Italian Communist Party would participate in a government led by the conservative Christian Democrats. Aldo Moro was largely believed to be the one man with the patience, tact, and skill necessary to hold this tottery coalition together.

A long-term goal of the group is to bring about "Europe's ultimate war: for communism." This is the basis of the Red Brigades' "Resolution on Strategic Direction," a sixty-page manual of revolution issued during the Moro affair. It portrays West Germany and Italy as "the strongest and weakest links in the western democratic system," therefore the battle ground for the first wave of the conflict. The Moro and Schleyer kidnappings were designed to trigger similar actions throughout Europe. The next stage foreseen in the manual is the formation of a single "Organization of Communist Combat" composed of all European leftist terrorist bands, which would then attack the West's "vital centers of multinational imperialism."[11]

The Red Brigades are known to have received extensive training in Czechoslovakia. Alberto Franceschini and at least three other Brigades leaders have trained in Czechoslovakia for periods ranging from several months to a year. Keys found in a Brigades hideout during the search for Moro were labeled "Prague" and proved to be for "safe-houses" in that city.[12]

The groups discussed above are responsible for a large measure of the terrorist activities of this decade. They are distinct from organizations like the IRA or the Eritrean or Basque terrorists in a way that is extremely illuminating for an understanding of transnational terrorism. What sets them apart is that they do not claim to be representatives of an oppressed class in their homeland. They are by and large the children of affluent societies, of modern industrial civilization itself. What they have rejected is their bourgeois origins, but not in favor of a downtrodden working class. Instead they have made a powerful identification with the struggles of the Third World, mythicized throughout the 1960s in the personae of such "heroes" as Che and Fidel. The very concept of the urban guerrilla that they embraced as a model was developed in Latin American revolutionary politics.* Horst Mahler, a recently jailed Baader-Meinhof member, put it this way: "We didn't feel German any more, but a kind of fifth

---

*Carlos Marighella's *Minimanual of the Urban Guerrilla* (Havana: Tricontinental, 1970), in which the Brazilian Communist applied Maoist theory to contemporary situations, was required reading for self-styled revolutionaries on American and Western European campuses. This work provides strategy for kidnapping, bank holdups, bombings, and other forms of "political violence."

column of the Third World." Suzanne Albrecht, one of the murderers of Dresden Bank chairman Jurgen Ponto (Suzanne's godfather and a close friend to her wealthy father), explained her radicalism by saying that she was "sick of eating caviar." The Baader-Meinhof Gang also spoke of its commitment to "destroy the islands of wealth in Europe."

This rejection of class origin and creation of a new antibourgeois identity on the model of an archetypal Third World revolutionary implies a shared set of values and a shared mode of action among such terrorists, the basis for extensive cooperation in the struggle against the common enemy (Western industrial democracy) on behalf of oppressed peoples of the Third World. (It obviously also suggests a high degree of personal alienation.) Finally, this is a shared perception of the world, defined in terms of struggle, in which alliance with more localized terrorist movements is not only logical but necessary.* Indeed, such movements continue to provide both inspiration and a conceptual framework for the Western terrorists. In 1970, for example, the Arab leader Dr. George Habash told the four hundred delegates at an international revolutionary congress held in Pyongyang, North Korea, "At this time of people's revolution against the worldwide imperialistic system, there can be neither geographic and political borders nor any moral prohibitions against the terrorist enterprises of the people's camp."

Although much of the terrorist violence carried out by the children of advanced industrial societies appears to be pure nihilism, from the perspective of radical Marxism (as opposed to the orthodox Soviet dogma) it does have a rather twisted logic that could be appealing to the true believer. Even from a traditional Marxist view, the commitment of the Western industrial nations to democracy is essentially an ideological mask, obfuscating the real conditions of production in a class society. The terrorist strategy (branded as adventurism of the worst sort by the

---

*A number of commentators have noted that the frequently austere religious backgrounds of the Western European terrorists and their families may suggest a Manichean world view in which the Christian battle of good against evil is replaced by a communist-capitalist struggle. The fact of central importance is that this struggle is felt to be both absolute and apocalyptic.

Soviet orthodoxy) is to force the liberal government to reveal its true, authoritarian nature and its primary commitment to a ruling elite and to property over human values, through restrictions on civil liberties as would be imposed in a crisis or state of siege. For the contemporary revolutionary raised in the advanced West, the most frustrating aspect of liberal civilization is its ability to integrate previously disaffected or disenfranchised elements of its society into the mainstream. The classic illustration here is the postwar success of the European social democratic movement in response to working-class interests. This integrative quality would seem to be one of the great virtues of our liberal civilization, but it has robbed the left of its proletarian vanguard. A large measure of Western and Japanese terrorism is consequently directed toward pushing the liberal government toward real or apparent tyranny as a necessary precondition for revolution. If the Baader-Meinhof group had succeeded, say, in forcing Bonn to suspend German civil liberties in the search for Schleyer, it would doubtless have felt that it had accomplished no small feat in heightening the level of alienation among the German people. Western terrorists employ such apparently self-defeatist if not infantile strategies in a clear effort to undermine the legitimacy of the liberal bourgeois state by throwing into doubt its commitment to liberty.

The record of transnational terrorism in this decade bears ample witness to what some experts are describing as a "New International." The route of the three Japanese United Red Army gunmen who committed the mass murders at Tel Aviv's Lod airport in May 1972 is a classic illustration of this ongoing cooperation among terrorists. The three first flew to the United States and Canada, then on to Paris, at the time a base of operations for their comrades in the Popular Front for the Liberation of Palestine (PFLP). From France they traveled to Lebanon, where they received commando training at a Fedayeen camp. They then returned to their friends in Paris, where they remained until false passports could be obtained from Frankfurt. Then it was on to Rome, where Italian terrorists supplied them with grenades and automatic weapons made in Czechoslovakia. A German sympathizer allowed them to store these weapons in his Rome apartment until they flew to Tel Aviv to complete their mission. Their route effectively circumscribes the international terrorist network of the early 1970s.

The eight Palestinian guerrillas of the Black September group who seized the Saudi Arabian embassy in Khartoum in March 1973 held three Western and two Arab diplomats as hostages. They demanded the release of jailed Baader-Meinhof terrorists from West Germany, convicted killer Sirhan Sirhan from the United States, all imprisoned Arab guerrillas from Israel, and seventeen terrorists from Jordan. When the target governments refused, the terrorists killed the three Western diplomats.

Such international rosters reflect the transnational character of contemporary terrorism; they are also typical of the cycle of violence into which terrorists and their targets are drawn. Events occur and are followed by arrests that are then followed by more events designed to free jailed cohorts. The famous June 1976 hijacking of an Air France jet to Entebbe, Uganda, was executed by a group of Palestinians and West Germans. After landing in Entebbe, they were reinforced by an Ecuadorian and more Palestinians. Negotiations were conducted by Waddih Haddad, operations chief of one of the groups most active in forging transnational links, the Popular Front for the Liberation of Palestine, then based in Somalia. Haddad demanded release of fifty-three terrorists held by the governments of five countries. Israeli commandos brilliantly foiled this effort. But this pattern of reprisals following arrests has had a serious dampening effect on the willingness of various governments to jail well-known terrorists.

Waddih Haddad, who reportedly died of leukemia in March 1978, was a true enigma in the already shadowy world of transnational terrorism. He was a Palestinian physician who fled Israel following the Six-Day War. Like many other Palestinians of the professional class at that time, he found refuge in Beirut, Lebanon. At American University there, he met Dr. George Habash. Habash and Haddad worked extensively in the refugee camps of Jordan, establishing a medical clinic and later founding the Popular Front for the Liberation of Palestine, a Marxist-Leninist organization committed not only to the annihilation of Israel and the establishment of a Palestinian state in its place, but to world revolution as well. They consequently viewed the oil-rich Arab capitalists as part of the same problem that the Israelis represented. Their struggle was against imperialism and oppression; as such, it attracted diverse leftist support, particularly among terrorists in Western Europe and Japan. Habash became widely known as the leader of the PFLP; Haddad went underground as chief of PFLP "special operations." He became a central figure, if not the most important individual, in the international terrorist network, running the secret camps where young and aspiring revolutionaries recruited from all over the world were trained to be terrorists. From various places in the Arab World, Haddad planned and coordinated a number of the major terrorist events in the 1970s, beginning with the hijacking of three jets, which were diverted to Dawsons's Field in Jordan where, before a world television audience, the PFLP blew up the aircraft. He was the mastermind of the Lod airport massacre of twenty-six people, many of whom were Puerto Rican Christian pilgrims. In this raid, his operatives were, significantly, not Arabs but three members of Japan's United Red Army.

Waddih Haddad was the immediate superior of the now-legendary Venezuelan terrorist Illich Ramirez Sanchez, known as Carlos Martinez, or simply Carlos, and popularized in the European press as Carlos the Jackal (after the terrorist who nearly assassinated De Gaulle). Carlos is known to have extensive contacts with the Baader-Meinhof Gang, the Basque separatists, the Turkish insurgents, the Arab Fedayeen, and the Japanese URA. After the Baader-Meinhof raid on a U.S. Army arsenal in West Germany, Carlos received some of the booty—M-26 grenades that he then distributed to Turkish, Palestinian, and Japanese terrorists. One of these American grenades was used by Carlos in the 1974 bombing of the Parisian nightclub Le Drugstore. Until 1975, Carlos ran the International Terrorists Collective out of an apartment in Paris. His group called itself the "Mohammed Boudia Commando." On June 27, 1975, when three French security agents appeared at Carlos's door with Michel Moukarbel, a Lebanese terrorist turned informer, he shot and killed Moukarbel and two of the agents, wounded the other, and then disappeared. The possibility that Carlos might have had Cuban backing seemed likely when, shortly after his escape, several Cuban diplomats were dismissed from their posts in the Paris embassy at the request of the French government.

Carlos's association with Cuba dates back to well before the Paris incident. In the mid-1960s, he was one of the young Latin Americans brought to Cuba for training in guerrilla operations under both Cuban and Russian personnel. He received instruction at Camp Mantanzas, which was run by General Viktor Simenov of the KGB. Carlos was one of the handful of trainees in Cuba sent on to Moscow for study at Patrice Lumumba University. He was dismissed from Lumumba in early 1970, reportedly for his "dissolute" lifestyle. A year passed before Carlos resurfaced in London, where his mother was then living. Almost nothing is known about Carlos's movements during this time, but in the early 1970s, he emerged as a major figure in the international terrorist network.

Working for Haddad, Carlos established an international network of terrorists under the aegis of the PFLP. Carlos has claimed to have forty professional terrorists in his control. It was this Carlos-Haddad network, now professing to be the "Arm of the Arab Revolution," that kidnapped the OPEC oil ministers in Vienna in December 1975. In 1976, members of this network hijacked the Air France jet to Entebbe. When they had landed in Uganda, with the cooperation of President Idi Amin, a second group of terrorists joined them. The leader of this "relief mission" was Antonio Bouvier, an Ecuadorian who had years before been Carlos's teacher in Cuba. In August 1976, in retaliation for the Israeli rescue at Entebbe, Carlos's operatives blew up a transit lounge in the Istanbul airport, killing four people.

Besides running secret training camps for terrorists of diverse nationalities in Southern Yemen, Iraq, and other rejectionist states, the PFLP is also known to possess a type of Soviet-built light antitank rocket launcher, the RPG-7, and a heat-seeking ground-to-air missile, the SA-7 or Strela. In September 1973, PFLP members were arrested during their attempted use of Strelas near the Rome airport. In January 1975, at Orly airport in Paris, two terrorists fired a Russian-made RPG-7 rocket launcher at a Boeing 707 of El Al as it taxied toward the runway. The Israeli pilot took evasive action and the rocket crashed into another plane but did not explode; a second shot hit an administration building, causing some damage. The terrorists escaped, leaving the launcher behind. In January 1976, members of the PFLP were arrested at the perimeter of the Nairobi airport while preparing to fire Strelas at an El Al jet coming in to land. The weapons are thought to have come from the Libyan and Ugandan governments. An SA-7 may have been used by black nationalist guerrillas in Rhodesia to shoot down a passenger plane in early September 1978, a crash in which thirty-eight people died. Of the eighteen survivors, ten were massacred before rescue parties reached the site.

The PFLP is believed to run a workshop that is the central supply system for false passports and other documents used by terrorists around the world. Examination of numerous captured documents confirms that they originate from a single source. Palestinians, West Germans, Japanese, and Carlos himself have all traveled on these false papers.

The exchange of personnel in domestic and foreign terrorist operations has also been well documented. During a 1970 Palestinian attempt to capture an Israeli airliner in London, Israeli security agents killed a Nicaraguan terrorist carrying three passports, including an American one. A captured member of the Turkish People's Liberation Army informed the Israelis that the killing, in May 1971, of the Israeli Consul General in Istanbul was in payment for a debt owed by the group to the PLO. The May 1972 Lod airport massacre was a joint suicide mission of the URA and the PFLP. After that, the Japanese URA established a headquarters in Beirut. When Lebanese Christians captured the Palestinian Tel Zatar camp in July 1976 one of those who surrendered was a member of the URA. There is also evidence available of other alliances: the close association between the IRA and the Breton and Basque separatists; the exchange of training and arms support among the Eritreans, Al Fatah, the PFLP, Syria's Sai'qa, and the Arab countries; and similar exchanges among groups in Argentina, Uruguay, Peru, Venezuela, and Nicaragua.[13]

In 1974, revolutionary groups in Argentina, Bolivia, Chile, and Uruguay established a central organization called the Revolutionary Coordinating Junta (JCR). The following year they were joined by Dominican, Colombian, Paraguayan, and Venezuelan revolutionaries at a meeting in Lisbon, where the pact was formalized. Together they have raised a sizable amount of cash, mainly from ransoms paid for kidnapped businessmen. The Argentinians alone are believed to have collected over two hundred million dollars within a recent three-year period.

In mid-October of 1977, *The Times* of London reported that the junta had set up a headquarters in Paris that "has become a kind of clearinghouse for international terrorism," specializing in the publication of revolutionary pamphlets and field manuals.[14] According to *The Times*, the head of the junta is Fernando Luis Alvarez, known as "Pelado." Alvarez is married to Anna Maria Guevara, the sister of Che. The report said that there were relationships between the junta and an unnamed left-wing group in Britain, the IRA, and Carlos. It was unknown whether their activities were linked to recent terrorist events or whether their function was mainly to put out propaganda. Some experts on world terrorism, including Dr. Richard Clutterbuck of the University of Exeter, suggest that the drive for more central coordination in transnational terrorism is being directed by the junta.[15]

It is widely believed that the administrator of Argentina's Montoneros introduced Red Brigades leader Renato Curcio to Ulrike Meinhof at a secret Paris meeting in 1970. Much of the subsequent cooperation in European terrorist operations can be traced to this Latin American connection, as can most of the "seed money" with which European terrorist organizations began their operations at the end of the last decade. A good deal of speculation points to the Cuban DGI (its secret service) as the organizers of the JCR.[16]

Summit meetings of the transnational terrorist leadership have occurred at least twice: in Lebanon in 1972 and in Larnaca, Cyprus, in July 1977. These meetings were attended by Germans, Japanese, Iranians, Turks, and the IRA and paid for by the Palestinians.[17]

Government Cooperation and Support

Terrorist groups are known to receive substantial financial and military support from cooperative governments. This is one of the most disturbing aspects of the terrorist problem, and it has a long history. Before World War I, the tsarist government of Russia covertly supported the Serbian Black Hand, a secret organization whose activities in the Balkans were a major factor in the outbreak of war in Europe in 1914. In the 1930s, the Italian government supported the separatist Croatian Ustasha, even providing asylum for several known assassins, while denying any involvement. "We do not give our hands to murderers. Those who want to implicate Italy are cowards and liars," roared Mussolini in a mockery of righteous indignation. This sort of claim would be repeatedly echoed by such governments as those of Libya and Algeria in the 1960s and well into the 1970s—with about as much veracity.

There are, of course, many ways a government may support terrorist activities, ranging from the apparently passive provision of safe harbor or use of air space to actively promoting and supporting terrorists with money, arms, or training. The list of nations that are now or have recently been involved in supporting terrorism includes Libya, Cuba, the Soviet Union, China, North Korea, Algeria, the People's Democratic Republic of Yemen (Southern Yemen), Tanzania, Congo, Zaire, Egypt, Syria, Iraq, and Lebanon.[18]

Among the most active has been Libya, which supported and continues to support a wide range of nationalist groups of various ideologies. Much of this backing has been covert, but in the summer of 1972, Colonel Muammur Qaddafi, Libya's dictator, began openly to boast about his contributions to world terrorism. Qaddafi told an interviewer that, besides establishing training camps for volunteers and providing refuge for Arab hijackers, he was supplying arms to the IRA in Ulster and to Muslims in the Philippines. He added that he would be happy to supply weapons to blacks, "unfurling in the United States the banner of the struggle against American racism." In September 1972, Qaddafi gave Yasir Arafat five million dollars as an "expression of gratitude" for the Fatah-Black September murder of eleven Israeli athletes at the Munich Olympics.[19] At a secret meeting in November 1976, Libya and Algeria assumed responsibility for "arming, financing, and training the Basques of Spain and the Bretons and Corsicans of France."[20]

With somewhat more secrecy, the training of terrorists was

occurring in Communist countries. In the late 1960s, Mexican guerrillas received training in North Korea and North Vietnam. In the early 1970s, African insurgents fighting the Portuguese were trained in the use of sophisticated weaponry, including ground-to-air missiles, by Soviet officers at bases within the Soviet Union.

Throughout the 1960s, the Soviets underwrote Cuban training programs in which Third World youths were given instruction in guerrilla methods. Similarly, in the 1970s, most of the Soviet support for terrorist groups has been channelled through client states and other intermediaries. Since 1969, Moscow has been providing funds, weapons, and other assistance to Fedayeen groups through a complex system of intermediaries. Much the same approach is used for the support of Western terrorists. There is no question that the Soviets view terrorism as dangerous primarily because of its uncontrollable nature, and their support for it outside the Middle East is highly selective, dictated by strategic considerations. Since the end of World War II, for instance, the Soviet Union has been the principal backer of the exile Croatian separatist movement, primarily to create problems for the Yugoslavian government under Marshal Tito.

There are indications that the international community is far less tolerant of terrorist violence than was once the case. Radical Third World states are increasingly less willing to face the threat of sanctions for aiding terrorist operations. A fairly encouraging development in this respect occurred recently. Both the kidnapping of Hanns-Martin Schleyer by Baader-Meinhof members on September 5, 1977, and the hijacking of the Lufthansa jet to Somalia by Palestinians on October 13, 1977, were efforts to force the West German government into freeing three Baader-Meinhof leaders (Andreas Baader, Gudrun Ensslin, and Jan-Carl Raspe) and eight jailed colleagues. When the hijacking occurred, Lebanon, Syria, Jordan, Kuwait, Oman, and Southern Yemen closed their airports to prevent the hijacked plane from landing. All these countries have been traditionally sympathetic to Palestinian terrorists in the past. Equally significant, the nations in which the imprisoned Germans had sought asylum (Algeria, Libya, Iraq, Southern Yemen, and Vietnam) all refused to admit the terrorists. According to German authorities, this was a major factor in the suicides of Baader, Ensslin, and Raspe.

Domestic Terrorism

The United States has been relatively untouched by the storm of terrorist activities of the past decade. Any number of hypotheses have been brought forth to explain this, ranging from our people's basic confidence in this country's ability to respond to injustice to just plain luck. Although we would not attempt to offer a definitive explanation, certain factors do come to mind. Unlike the nations of Western Europe, America has never had a popular, broad-based left—nor a broad-based right, for that matter. Our tradition of mainstream, consensus politics has tended to preclude extremism, and consequently offers little if any history of efficacious extremist activity. Critical exceptions abound, certainly, dating back to the Boston Tea Party, a proto-typical terrorist event, but the continuity of our democratic republic is characterized by the peaceful transfer of authority and by peaceful change.

To some degree, certainly, America has always represented a myth of infinite futures, the promise of new beginnings inherent in our conception of the frontier. So it has avoided the claustro-phobic atmosphere that is characteristic of older societies in which history is a nightmare, a burden on the living, tormenting both the intelligentsia and the disenfranchised. More specifically, we have no immediate experience of fascism to haunt our young and to be repressed. All of this is not to say that we have had no terrorist problem, nor can we necessarily dismiss the threat of terrorism in the future. As the following discussion makes clear, a tiny number of isolated individuals are capable of doing no small amount of damage. But, clearly, terrorism in America has not been the apparently endemic problem faced by the people of Italy, West Germany, and Japan.

Terrorist violence in America has for years been associated with right-wing extremists like the Ku Klux Klan and the American Nazi Party. Most leftist terrorism has occurred in recent years, and is largely an outgrowth of the radicalization of American youth that erupted in the 1960s over the Vietnam War and the perceived failure of the nonviolent civil rights movement to achieve social and economic justice for American minorities.

The Weather Underground Organization, or Weathermen, was

the radical Marxist wing of the Students for a Democratic Society (SDS). Since the breakup of the SDS in 1969, the Weather Underground has claimed credit for more than thirty bombings, the targets including a number of federal buildings. Leaders of the group have received aid (including safe exile and transportation) from Cuba. Two of the founders, Ted Gold and Diane Oughton, were killed in 1970 in an accidental explosion in their New York City bomb factory, while two others, Mark Rudd and Jane Alpert, have since turned themselves in to the police. Co-founder Bernardine Dohrn remains at large, but the group has been inactive in the last few years, and its present viability remains in doubt.

Far more active currently is the New World Liberation Front (NWLF), primarily based in the Pacific Northwest. The NWLF has claimed credit for well over fifty bombings. Frequent targets have included public utilities (Pacific Gas and Electric) and large corporations (ITT, General Motors, Adolph Coors Company). The group's anticorporate stance has extended to terrorism on behalf of environmental issues. A so-called Environmental Assault Team has exploded bombs at several PG&E substations and at the visitor center of the Trojan Nuclear Plant in Rainier, Oregon. The NWLF has claimed links with the short-lived Symbionese Liberation Army, both groups having been to some degree outgrowths of the Venceremos Organization, a now-defunct militant radical movement active in Central and Northern California during the Vietnam War.

The Armed Forces for National Liberation (FALN) of Puerto Rico perhaps exemplifies the degree of horror that a tiny group can achieve with no popular support. Despite overwhelming indications by all public opinion research that the people of Puerto Rico wish to remain part of the United States, and in fact favor statehood, this Marxist-Leninist organization, with approximately a dozen members, has claimed responsibility for over sixty bombings in the New York City area in the name of Puerto Rican national independence. These included the bombing of the annex to the Fraunces Tavern in 1975, which left four people dead and more than forty others wounded.

The Black Panther Party, founded in 1966 by Huey Newton and Bobby Seale in Oakland, California, attempted to capitalize on frustrations arising from the slow progress in the civil rights movement. Adopting a rhetoric of counterracism, it became a paramilitary organization demanding revolutionary change. In its first five years, numerous party members and police were killed in what appeared to be a running battle between the Black Panthers and law-enforcement authorities. Those who remain in the group no longer espouse violence as a means of change and are heavily involved in local politics in Oakland.

Transnationals in the United States

For many observers, the real terrorist threat to America will not be from indigenous sources at all. No American terrorist groups have succeeded in achieving the broad support of sympathizers that European groups enjoy. But there is the strong possibility that as European nations step up their fight against terrorism, often at the cost of civil liberties (as has already occurred in West Germany and Italy), America's open society will attract foreign terrorists, both as a land of exile and as a potential stage for new terrorist activities. Transnationals will of course strike anywhere they think their actions will be effective and America, with its vast global interconnections and relatively high degree of personal freedom (including freedom of movement without identity cards and such), may appear as a vulnerable target. On July 20, 1978, a suspected member of the Baader-Meinhof Gang was arrested after illegally trying to enter the United States. Kristina Ketherina Bersta, wanted in West Germany for belonging to a criminal organization and for criminal conspiracy in using explosives and counterfeit documents, was apprehended in Vermont after attempting to cross over from Canada by foot. She had in her possession a false Iranian passport. According to news reports, three other suspected Baader-Meinhof members with whom Miss Berster was known to have stayed at a Canadian hotel tried to cross the border at the same point but returned to Canada after being questioned by border patrolmen. One or more of them may have successfully entered the United States.[21]

It is of course impossible to estimate how many other foreign terrorists have found safe exile in America, or what their intentions may be. A score of nations have unwillingly played host to transnational terrorist events, at the risk of their citizens' safety, the security of their property, and even the legitimacy of their governments. As crackdowns in Europe proceed, we must recognize that our own country could conceivably become the stage for a new wave of transnational activities, even as we hope that foreign terrorists do not come to see America as their last frontier.

POTENTIAL DEVELOPMENTS IN TERRORISM

In *International Terrorism: Trends and Potentialities*, Brian Jenkins offers insights that demand consideration. Jenkins identifies two key sources of modern terrorism: (1) the failure of rural Cuban-style guerrilla warfare in Latin America, typified by the Guevara's Bolivian fiasco, and (2) the major defeat of Arab forces against Israel in 1967, which led the Palestinians to abandon their reliance on the conventional military power of the Arab states in favor of various forms of terrorism, ranging from rural, guerrilla-style border raids to sophisticated disruptions of advanced technological society, such as multiple jetliner hijackings.[22] Both of these historical sources illuminate the essentially desperate character of those who turn to terrorism as well as the fact that terrorism is a weapon of the weak, a poor man's warfare that does not require the popular base of support necessary to engage in a more conventional struggle.

Jenkins forsees a number of potential developments in terrorism, all of which portend serious ramifications for incident management and for overall government policy. There is, first of all, the potential for the escalation of violence. At least two factors are of major importance here. The first involves the phenomenon of a society grown numb to what may once have been perceived as shocking levels of violence. The earliest airline hijackings, for example, were genuinely frightening media events that led to a public demand for tighter security and a public acceptance of the various delays and other inconveniences inherent in routine X-ray and physical search. Today, hijackings are standard TV fare and must involve some bizarre twist if they are to garner serious media attention. (An example is the October 1977 Lufthansa hijacking to Mogadishu, Somalia, which was linked to the kidnapping in Germany of industrialist Hanns-Martin Schleyer.) The question is: Will terrorists feel that it is necessary to escalate the threat in order to maintain "Broadway presence" and their ability to horrify a jaded populace?

The second factor involved here, as we suggest in our discussion of the terrorist arsenal (see Chapter 2), is the potential for nationally disruptive acts, if not mass destruction. What sort of constraints, if any, can we assume on the part of desperate or psychotic individuals, given the availability of mass-destruction technology, particularly if they view their political goals as beyond attainment? This is a little like the hypothetical question of whether Hitler, had he possessed the means to trigger a nuclear holocaust during those last days in Berlin, might not have extended his final gesture of destruction to civilization at large. An individual (or group), concluding there is nothing to lose, undermines the presumption of rationality inherent in all nuclear deterrence theory.

Another potential development is that terrorist groups will become more like traditional criminal organizations. There are clear parallels, for instance, between Mafia-controlled kidnappings of executives for ransom in Italy, long a common form of crime in that country, and the "politically" inspired kidnappings of foreign executives in Latin America. The latter have proved so profitable an industry that they could easily continue without the indictments of "crimes against the people" made by the various revolutionary tribunals, or they could simply maintain their revolutionary trappings as a mask for activities of an essentially criminal nature. This suggests the emergence of a "quasi-political crime syndicate engaged in criminal activities" such as kidnapping, protection rackets, and other forms of extortion, while maintaining a political profile to exploit mass resentments or revolutionary sympathies within the populace.[23]

This potential development represents one of the ways in which a terrorist subculture could become a permanent fixture in our world. Another involves terrorism supplanting Marxist, Maoist, or other revolutionary ideologies to become an ideology in and of itself, attracting nihilistic elements of society as well as embittered marginal groups and individuals more inclined toward exacting some form of revenge than toward righting social wrongs. Certainly anarchistic terrorists are more concerned with living in a present defined by action than they are with achieving a systematic, long-term revolution along Marxian lines. Indeed, many of the European transnational terrorists seem to be propelled by a profound self-hatred, a nausea concerning their own historical-material identities that leads them to seek the negation of the very culture which nurtured them. Consequently, such personalities appear less interested in contributing to the establishment of a just society than in triggering the apocalypse.

Jenkins sees in much of terrorism a reaction to the general trend toward increasing centralization of authority in modern nation-states, with its concomitant loss in regional autonomy. He asserts that "the intense nationalism of the late nineteenth and first half of the twentieth century is being replaced by intense regionalism and ethnicity."[24] This is clearly at the heart of the various separatist movements. At the same time, if and when such groups succeed in bringing about the formation of smaller national units (a Palestinian state may set the precedent), the temptation may be great for these relatively weak states to employ terrorism, or threaten to do so, as a surrogate for conventional warfare. Sadly, the wisdom of yielding to this temptation would be borne out by a "cost-benefit" analysis based on the efficacy of past terrorism.

Another, similar potential development involves the increasing importance of nonstate actors in the international community, with groups like the PLO attaining global recognition as ethnic representatives without a national base. Again, we would confront a situation where a relatively weak organization could dictate terms to powerful nations on the basis of the threat of irrational or disruptive behavior. There are some eight hundred separate ethnic groups in this world, and although it would be difficult to assess how many (perhaps it would be more accurate to say how few) have the potential to make their presence felt on the world scene, those with global aspirations do have a model of "how to succeed" in the history of the PLO.

Further terrorist activity may originate from extreme right-wing groups lacking confidence in the ability of legitimate authorities to deal with leftist terrorism or concerned with what they perceive as a more general threat from the left. Whether this takes the form of vigilantism, as it already has in Argentina, or of covert operations structurally similar to those of the terrorist left, as has been the case in Italy and Spain, such activity constitutes a further erosion of the rule of law, contributes to the cycle of violence, and is symptomatic of a society that has lost its bearings. It is, in short, no less a threat than terrorism of the extreme left.

Publicity

As discussed earlier, modern terrorism is inextricably linked to advanced telecommunications. Terrorists seek media coverage. Their actions are designed to dramatize and advertise their existence and cause. Through their violent acts they often seek to convince the uncommitted to withdraw their support from an institution or regime and therefore make wider revolutionary activity possible. In order to be effective, terrorists must inform and involve the general public. In many cases of South American, Canadian, and European terrorist actions, groups have included among their demands the publication of so-called manifestos in exchange for release of hostages.

Whenever possible, terrorists will employ strategies aimed at throwing the ruling government into crisis, which in the parliamentary model of Europe and Canada could lead to the forced resignation of the prime minister. There was some discussion of this in West Germany during the Schleyer-Lufthansa affair, and it might have occurred had the raid on Mogadishu failed along the lines of Sadat's Cyprus fiasco of 1978 (fifteen hostages held by Arab terrorists were freed, but in a gun battle with Cypriot National Guard forces fifteen Egyptian commandos were killed, another fifteen wounded, and the remaining taken into custody). The kind of pressures brought to bear on the ruling coalition in Italy during the Moro affair illustrate the influence a small band of extremists can exert in a free society. The treatment a government receives from its national press is of course critical in determining the popular impression of its competence in crisis management.

There is evidence that successful terrorist techniques will be borrowed by other organizations around the world and repeated.

The mass media play a key role in this phenomenon and in general terrorist communications as well.[25] Recently the Symbionese Liberation Army skillfully utilized California news media during the Hearst case. Their choice of victim assured them extensive coverage by the national and particularly the West Coast media. According to the testimony of one behavioral expert, "If one could cut out publicity, I would say you could cut out 75% of the national and international terrorism."[26]

If the terrorist group is linked directly with a political party, terrorist activity may soon be a political liability. A constant danger among political movements engaged in terrorism is that they may become caught up with the acts of terrorism and lose sight of long-term political goals. At such a time as it becomes important to quell terrorist attacks and seek greater legitimacy and an active role in the government, cracks may develop within the group's organizational structure. Sometimes more radical elements will form dangerous splinter groups. For example, in seeking to be recognized as the legitimate representative of the Palestinians, the PLO tried to disassociate itself from its more radical elements. During this attempt the organization was forced to execute some of its more radical members. Dissent among Middle Eastern terrorist groups over recent peace moves has led to the reemergence of the radical "Rejection Front," dedicated to upset any political settlement unpalatable to its members.

Structure and Strategy

How does the drama of a terrorist event translate into a realigned social or political structure? A terrorist act involves three primary actors, and their actions are likely to be influenced by three important audiences. The first actor is a group that threatens or carries out a violent act in order to discredit responsible authorities or gain some other political end. The second actor is the group against which the violent act is threatened or conducted; it is incidental to the political outcome sought and is selected only because it has intrinsic or symbolic value to the third actor. And the third actor is the government or other authority that the terrorist wishes to discredit or influence by virtue of its responsibility and concern for the safety of the object of the threatened or actual violent act. Audiences before whom the drama is enacted, and whose attitudes may affect the manner of its conduct and outcome, include the people for whom the target government is responsible, other governments with similar interests and responsibilities, and other terrorist groups with both a tactical and a political interest in the contest.

It is interesting to think of terrorism as theater, but possibly more useful to think of it as a form of warfare, for terrorism is consistent with the essence of classical military strategy: the efficacious use of force to achieve a desired policy end. Terrorism is a particularly pernicious form of conflict because by its nature it poses the quintessential dilemma for the target government: that is, how to defend citizens, institutions, and interests against the threat of terrorism while preserving their essential character, popular support, and willing compliance. In a free society, the terrorist exercises the initiative and, within limits, can determine the intensity, scope, and issues that characterize the campaigns in the struggle. The only long-term security against terrorism, therefore, is elimination of deeply felt grievances. That is obviously a very long way off. In the interim, in order to limit the range within which the terrorist can seek to operate, governmental action must be taken to improve international cooperation, security, and countermeasures and to enhance preparations for crisis management.

Well-trained, highly organized, and well-financed terrorist groups are usually formed in structured units, independent and unknown to one another, with a central controlling group. In the early phases of their organization these units are often small "cells" with three or four bases. The initial task of these units is to solidify the organization. The next major task is to achieve media recognition. Initially, this is accomplished by attacking defenseless targets without immediate political or military value, such as prominent individuals, office buildings, and banks, the main objective being to spread fear. Palestinian terrorists have been known to pass up targets such as clearly marked and vulnerable military vehicles and to attack instead school buses full of children. Such attacks are often designed to draw new members who are attracted by the group's notoriety and its ability to embarrass authorities. In 1970, for example, the PFLP burst upon the scene with a spectacular multiple hijacking, followed by the televised destruction of three captured jets at a Jordanian airfield.

As a general rule, a terrorist group escalates the violence of its attacks in order to sustain the fear of the population and government, but these actions take place within bounds that make them appear to be a natural response to the provocation of officials. In later stages of its campaigns, when the group has grown in size, support, and popularity, targets increase both in complexity and in variety, while taking on more pragmatic military and political values. The strategy at this stage is to avoid general battles but to persistently attack the government and frighten its defenders. Often at this stage, governments compound their problems by taking repressive measures, striking out irrationally, and further alienating the citizenry. It is difficult to conceive of a worse overall response.

Generally, terrorists are highly selective in choosing their targets. Since all terrorist events are theatrical, the terrorists tend to assess the symbolic, publicity, political, and military values of a proposed attack. For example, during the Cuban revolution Castro quickly abandoned widespread bombing attacks in Havana in order to avoid alienating potential supporters. The danger of this kind of widespread alienation has definitely been a check on some groups who are capable of mass-destruction terrorism.

Nevertheless, radical factions of the PLO and the URA have shown a greater willingness to cause increasing numbers of fatalities in their assaults. The URA suicide attack at Lod airport in 1972, in which twenty-six were massacred and over seventy wounded, included the use of automatic weapons and hand grenades against defenseless civilians. Right-wing Cuban terrorists in 1976 planted a bomb in a Cuban airliner, causing it to plunge into the Caribbean, taking the lives of all seventy-three aboard.[27]

As the CIA has noted, the self-imposed constraints of terrorists regarding mass violence are largely determined by national traditions as well as by the credo or ethos of the particular group.[28] It is consequently difficult to generalize, but clearly it is unwarranted to assume that whatever constraints have limited the magnitude of terrorist violence up to now will continue to operate indefinitely. Given the potential for nationally disruptive terrorism, it would be wise to prepare rather than be taken by surprise.

Terrorists have repeatedly demonstrated their interest in national disruption. The assassinations of Hanns-Martin Schleyer and Aldo Moro as well as the kidnapping of bankers in Barcelona are examples of attacks against the institutional structure, symbolized by these powerful individuals. Although these attacks lacked technical sophistication, terrorists have demonstrated interest in the more technically difficult act. For example, within a week of the Aldo Moro assassination, terrorists attempted to black out Rome. They hit the electrical power system but they were not as yet sufficiently sophisticated to know which components to attack. Nevertheless, they did manage to cut off the power for some of the suburbs of Rome.[29] In 1977, Palestinian terrorists injected Israeli oranges with liquid mercury, thereby disrupting some 40 percent of their European market for the fruit. Interestingly enough, liquid mercury is not very toxic.[30] No one was hurt, yet the terrorists managed to perform a sophisticated act that was nonviolent and caused significant disruption.

Nationally Disruptive Terrorism

Terrorism conducted at a level that would disrupt national political, economic, and social processes is a threat that cannot be taken lightly by either government or the private sector. Individual acts or a series of acts of this magnitude would challenge the preparedness and flexibility of local, state, and federal authorities. The full attention of government would be absolutely essential. A government would have to use all its resources to react to the severity of the terrorist challenge and at the same time measure the awareness of the private sector and the threat to the safety and well-being of the citizenry. Nationally disruptive terrorism involves acts of mass destruction that are overwhelmingly significant as well as lesser acts that accomplish the purpose of disrupting national life. Terrorism at either level could cause a degree of disruption that would have serious national and international consequences, particularly if carried out in a country like the United States. It is the purpose of this investigation not only to determine and analyze the limits of a particular event as it relates to national disruption but also to evaluate the impact of an event or a series of events on the operation and functioning of government.

Biological and chemical agents, though readily attainable, have remained largely unused and therefore do not appear to be likely terrorist weapons. Yet, documentation of many other incidents of the use of biological and chemical agents since World War I exists. As late as 1967 the Egyptians were reported to have used toxic agents against the Yemenites. There are also reports that the Baader-Meinhof group recently threatened to use mustard gas against West German cities. In many respects, chemical and biological agents represent the terrorist's easiest avenue into the mass-destruction arena. In contrast to the concern over nuclear materials, the control and safeguard of chemical and biological agents have not been given adequate consideration. Indeed, it is far easier to culture anthrax than it is to steal or fabricate a nuclear device; and an anthrax attack is potentially more lethal than a nuclear explosion. A small nuclear device could kill a hundred thousand people if detonated in a dense population center. By contrast, an aerosol anthrax attack could rival the effects of a thermonuclear device.

Relatively few terrorist attacks have demonstrated technical sophistication. Nevertheless, there have been isolated incidents of terrorist assaults involving the use of highly toxic agents and there have been at least fifty threats to employ nuclear weapons in the United States. Iodine 131, a radioisotope, has been sprinkled over a train in Europe. The alphabet bomber in Los Angeles had developed a number of sophisticated explosives and, when arrested, was apparently attempting to synthesize a nerve agent. In January 1972, two college youths were charged with conspiracy to commit murder in a plot to poison Chicago's water supply with "typhoid and other deadly bacteria." West German authorities, a year later, received similar threats to introduce anthrax into the country's water supply. These threats did not involve complex technology but they did underscore the obvious fact that there are crazies willing to threaten society and, possibly, willing to kill thousands of people. These should not be confused with rational terrorist groups who have shown no predisposition to engage in acts of high violence. However, as Walter Laqueur stated recently in *U.S. News & World Report*, terrorists do not necessarily calculate rationally.[31] Technology is here and we must attempt to minimize terrorist ability to use it. Although mass destruction is quite unlikely, other far less violent acts of national disruption are not. Advanced societies are extremely vulnerable. The electric power grid, water supply systems, computer systems, computer networks, natural gas and crude oil pipelines, and airline transportation systems are examples of highly sensitive targets. The loss of critical components of any one of these systems could prove catastrophic. Few, if any, seriously conceived countermeasures have been taken to minimize these vulnerabilities. Unfortunately, the terrorist's task of disrupting our vital networks has been made easier with the advent of readily portable antitank and antiaircraft weaponry. Terrorists have obtained small, highly portable, and sophisticated antitank and surface-to-air rockets, virtually all of them Soviet-made.

The proliferation of simple, effective, precision-guided munitions, such as the LAW and RPG antitank weapons and the Redeye and SA-7 antiaircraft weapons, represents an equally serious consideration because their potential use threatens destruction with major national implications. These and other weapons used by clever, desperate people against sensitive targets could cause one or a series of major crisis situations.

Will we be forced to confront acts of nationally disruptive terrorism in the future? Here our "crystal ball" breaks down. Some terrorists may already have the capacity for mass destruction. It is clear that we cannot afford to be unprepared. Any terrorist event, by its nature, demands a response. It forces the adversary to make the next move. The question we pose is whether our government will have to make a major policy choice in a decisional vacuum? It seems to us far preferable to develop preparedness for a wide array of contingencies, even as we hope that such planning will never need to be utilized.

CHAPTER 2

The Terrorist Arsenal: The Physical Potential for Nationally Disruptive Terrorism

Compared with the tools of modern warfare, the arsenal of terrorist assaults is usually primitive. Thus far terrorists have rarely used more than pistols, submachine guns, and crude bombs. Yet terrorists have achieved considerable tactical success. What are possible arsenals available in the future, should terrorism advance in sophistication and audacity?

An increased degree of sophistication of the terrorist arsenal could be marked either by the use of more advanced weaponry or by the use of the present crude weapons to attack more technologically sophisticated targets. Man-portable antitank and surface-to-air rocketry, chemical and biological agents, and nuclear weapons would fall into the first category. Use of explosives to knock out a main transformer of the electric power grid, sabotage against crude oil or natural gas pipelines, and destruction of critical computer installations fall into the latter category. (Obviously, a sophisticated antitank weapon could be used to destroy a key installation as well. Thus, the categories are not mutually exclusive.)

Although we expect that terrorism will take on new and more harmful forms—and the possibility of irrational acts of mass destruction cannot be excluded—we do not anticipate mass-destruction terrorism. We view the very existence of alternative weapons and the consequent opportunities for implicit or explicit extortion as posing an important issue. This chapter is therefore largely devoted to a discussion of some of the more awesome possibilities.

Our purpose is to acquaint the reader with the damage that a small band of terrorists can wreak; we do not wish to inspire terrorists to new heights, nor to write a "how-to-do-it" book. We assume—as is clearly the case for the Germans, Palestinians, Basques, and some Latin Americans—that terrorists have access to machine shops and university-level laboratory facilities, and that they might employ a handful of Ph.D.-level scientists and engineers.*

The Plausibility of Mass-Destruction Terrorism

Speculations about terrorist use of mass-destruction weaponry have been characterized as wild and sensational. It is argued that terrorist use of such weaponry is unlikely for several compelling reasons. First, safeguards against terrorist access to suitable nuclear materials should prevent such incidents. Second, biological and chemical agents have long been available but have gone unused.† Third, and perhaps most important, the use of mass-destruction weaponry would be counterproductive to terrorists— alienating followers and potential supporters and provoking effective countermeasures.

Today, as ever, violence is a common vehicle of political change. Worldwide resource shortages and distributional inequities are subjects of increasing Third World attention and protest. Multinational corporations and international organizations such as OPEC have emerged as powerful influences in international affairs, often diverging from the interests of nation-states and alienating populations.

---

*Illustrating the reasonableness of this last assumption is the fact that several tens of thousands of Arab students have received graduate-level technical training in the United States and Western Europe. We need only assume that ten of them actively support the more extreme Palestinian groups.

†Strictly speaking, this is not true. There have been isolated instances in the United States and abroad in which chemical and biological agents have been employed. Fortunately, their use to date is best described as inept.

A projected proliferation of fissile materials has underscored the erosion of superpower dominance and has been accompanied by increasing Third World militancy. Agreements precluding the use of nuclear, chemical, or biological weapons may be beyond the ability of impoverished nations to enforce, and are not binding upon terrorist groups.

As the ability to create nuclear weapons spreads, greater numbers of countries may seek deterrents. Finding the nuclear alternative impractical, some may seek more rapidly accessible but equally potent forms of destructive capability, such as biological weapons. Although the penalties for using these mass-destruction agents may be too high for industrialized and developing nations, extremely poor national and certain subnational groups may be less cautious. The possession of mass-destruction weapons might be viewed as a quick route to political recognition by groups or countries with heretofore marginal political power. It is also possible that a mass-destruction capability will come to be perceived as a lever in the struggle for global redistribution of wealth and power. The extortion potential will always be high where the capacity for massive violence is present. As we have tried to suggest, hostage situations of the future may yet involve entire populations.

Thus the arguments against the plausibility of national or terrorist use of mass-destruction agents may not be as compelling, for the longer term, as they now appear. First, even the best-protected nuclear installations are subject to attack. The United States possesses no monopoly of nuclear technology and may not be able to assure the use of safeguards and physical security throughout the world. National accountability for fuels of nuclear plants in Third World countries may not be any better than their accountability in other matters. Moreover, corruption could create flourishing black markets in such materials if governments or subnational groups are determined to acquire them for weapons production.

Security in nuclear energy plants outside the United States may not always be of a high degree, and there is a possibility of terrorists holding a plant in a hostage-barricade situation, threatening leakage or other sabotage unless demands are met. For many, this scenario is more plausible than that of terrorists obtaining fissile material and constructing a nuclear bomb. (There have reportedly been several instances of college students attempting to design a fission bomb—but most of these designs are of dubious validity.)[1]

Second, nations have demonstrated their willingness to use biological or chemical agents. For example, in the 1960s the Egyptians reportedly used toxic agents against the Yemenites, and the Japanese during World War II experimented with biological agents against the Chinese. Numerous other examples of the use of chemical and biological agents since World War I exist.[2] Such agents may grow increasingly attractive as a sort of "poor man's deterrent," as they are inexpensive, readily attainable, and effective.

The third argument against terrorist use of mass-destruction weaponry, based upon the alienating effects on supporters and worldwide opinion, may be the most cogent. But recent terrorist trends may make even this argument less convincing.

Terrorist groups have not been deterred from widespread killing; the Rome and Lod airport massacres establish this. Mass-destruction weaponry may prove highly appealing to nihilistic groups bent on causing shockingly destructive incidents. In 1975 and 1976 the Baader-Meinhof Gang in West Germany threatened to use chemical agents against German cities.[3] Apolitical, criminal groups might also be attracted to lucrative opportunities for mass-destruction extortion.

Radical factions of many terrorist movements such as the Palestinian "Rejection Front" may not fear the alienation of world opinion and may be attracted to mass destruction in the pursuit of their disruptive goals. Repressive countermeasures that may discredit a democratic government are certainly one terrorist goal.

Successful extortion and the undermining of national decision-making processes do not require actual use of such weapons by terrorists. The mere possession of mass-destruction agents by a terrorist group would focus widespread publicity on their cause and could provide significant political leverage.

Violent acts against the government and society are possible today and may not be totally improbable in coming years. The LaGuardia bombing and the specter of "Philadelphia Fever"* convey the message; the clock is running, the irrational may occur.

No amount of theorizing can decide whether incidents of mass destruction will or will not occur. We tend to extrapolate easily to near safety or doom from scant data even though the social and physical processes governing longer-run terrorist tactics are highly complex and unpredictable. One tenet is obvious: Even if mass-destruction terrorism were as highly improbable as many believe, its potential consequences could not be ignored. We must try to understand the physical as well as the more complex socioeconomic effects of heightened acts of terrorism. The easier task is the assessment of physical effects, which we touch upon in the balance of the chapter.

EXPLOSIVES, AUTOMATIC AND LIGHT ANTITANK WEAPONS, AND SURFACE-TO-AIR MISSILES

It is difficult to assess and predict the plans of various terrorist groups. It is similarly difficult to know which weapons they might use. But because of availability and previous use, there are certain weapons that we must expect to find in terrorist hands.

The most readily available weapon to a terrorist organization is the crude, homemade explosive that can be fabricated from seemingly innocuous materials found on the open market. Next in availability is the automatic weapon. Typical examples are submachine guns and machine pistols made in the Soviet Union, Czechoslovakia, and Poland. Such weapons have been used extensively in terrorist operations. By contrast, heavy machine guns, such as the U.S. 50 caliber, are difficult to conceal and to move covertly. Light antitank rocket launchers, principally the Soviet-made RPG-7 and the U.S. LAW, are known to be in the hands of terrorist groups. For example, the RPG-7 was used in

---

*The sinister "Philadelphia Fever" or Legionnaires' Disease of the summer of 1976 was apparently not a terrorist incident; yet to some it had the earmarks of homicide. Its impact on America was considerable.

the January 1975 attack on El Al Airlines at the Orly airport, Paris. The U.S. LAW and other antitank weapons, such as the French Strim F-1, have been issued in quantity to the military forces of various nations. They are portable and easy to conceal. Surface-to-air missiles, while the least readily available of the weapons discussed, are known to be in the possession of Palestinian groups.

Explosives

Terrorists, as a rule, employ two types of bombs: explosive and incendiary. Explosive bombs are of either fragmentation or blast type. The most commonly encountered fragmentation bomb used by terrorists is the pipe bomb, utilizing gunpowder as the explosive agent. Blast-type bombs usually contain commercial- or military-type dynamite with a blasting cap for detonation.

The effectiveness of explosive charges can be significantly increased by the employment of the shaped-charge (or cavity charge) principle to "focus" the force of an explosive in a desired direction. The charge can be either conical for penetration or linear for a cutting effect. An air space is required between the explosive and the target for this principle to work effectively; the charge is usually placed a short distance from the target.

Fire bombs are quickly and cheaply constructed, easy to use, and capable of inflicting extensive damage. The typical fire bomb consists of a glass bottle filled with an inflammable mixture (usually gasoline containing thickening additives, such as motor oil, to cause it to adhere to the target). A fuse is attached to the bottle, being designed to ignite the flammable mixture when the bottle is shattered against the target. No matter how crude, explosives and fire bombs are the most common terrorist weapons. Used by terrorists here and abroad, they vary in sophistication from time-delay fused and barometric bombs to the primitive truckload of fertilizer mixed with fuel oil that destroyed the Army Mathematics Research Center at the University of Wisconsin. Other than the risks inherent in dealing with explosives, bombings are relatively safe hit-and-run operations. They are difficult crimes to solve; witness some seventy bombing attacks against Pacific Gas and Electric, the Fraunces Tavern tragedy, and the

LaGuardia Airport bombing of 1975. It appears that as terrorist groups mature, having gained experience and polish, they turn from bombings to more difficult acts such as hostage-taking. This is especially true of European and Palestinian terrorists. Other than the Symbionese Liberation Army's kidnapping of Patricia Hearst, America's terrorists rely almost exclusively upon the bomb.

Automatic Weapons

The automatic weapon is basically an antipersonnel weapon, but it can also be used to penetrate the skin of a commercial aircraft or automobile. It is a favorite of terrorist groups because of its availability, concealability, high rate of fire, and psychological impact on lightly armed security forces or unarmed civilians. There are two basic types of automatic weapons: the assault rifle and the submachine gun. Assault rifles can be acquired in their many military versions or in semiautomatic commercial versions. The automatic versions are readily available in Europe and the Far East; the commercial version can be purchased from arms dealers. Similarly, the submachine gun and its miniaturized cousin, the machine pistol, are especially suitable terrorist weapons, which can be easily obtained.

The most likely heavy machine guns that terrorists might acquire are the US 50 caliber and the Soviet 12.7 mm. Both machine guns are effective sniper weapons and can destroy aircraft and lightly armored vehicles. These weapons are cumbersome and cannot be easily transported by a single individual.

Precision-Guided Munitions and Light Antitank Weapons

Possibly the most dramatic recent development in individual weaponry is precision-guided munitions (PGMs). PGMs are devices that can launch missiles whose trajectories can be corrected in flight. On cloudless days their accuracy is very high. Many PGMs are man-portable; that is, they are lightweight and can be carried and operated by one or two men. Generally speaking, their purpose is to destroy aircraft and tanks. Obviously, the man-portable PGM can meet terrorist requirements as well. In fact, terrorists have attempted to use them, especially the Soviet-made SA-7 (Strela).*

There are a number of man-portable, surface-to-air rocket systems, the most important of which are the American-made Redeye and its successor, the Stinger; the Soviet-made SA-7; and the British Blowpipe. Sweden has developed the RBS-70, which is a tripod-mounted antiaircraft system, but its bulkiness makes it less attractive to terrorists than the SA-7 or Redeye.

The SA-7 and Redeye employ infrared devices, heat-seeking sensors that guide the missile to a heat source, such as an aircraft engine. They weigh under thirty-five pounds and their effective range is several kilometers.

America's Dragon and the TOW missiles are precision-guided antitank weapons that are in the operational inventory. (The TOW system was used successfully in Vietnam.) Similarly, the Soviets employ the Sagger. These missiles are wire-guided in order to make in-flight correction. They use lasers for target acquisition, are relatively lightweight, and have ranges of several kilometers. The projectiles, employing shaped charges, can pierce several feet of homogeneous armor plate.[4]

Precision-guided weapons are found in many countries. In the estimate of Brian Jenkins,

> First-generation PGMs such as Strela and Redeye will be available to 30 to 40 countries in the Third World. It is not realistic to expect that all of these countries will maintain strict security measures; some may find it in their interest to make these weapons available to nongovernment groups. If we postulate a conservative loss rate worldwide, by theft or diversion, of one-tenth of one percent over the next five years, then man-portable PGMs will be "loose" in the hundreds by the beginning of the 1980s.[5]

Although PGMs represent an exceptionally great future menace for the future, terrorists have already used related, but less

---

*In 1973 at Rome a Palestinian terrorist plot employing two SA-7s to shoot down an El Al airliner was foiled. Similarly, in 1975 at Kenya, an analogous plot was also thwarted. In 1978 a Rhodesian airliner may have been shot down with an SA-7.

sophisticated light antitank rocket launchers against armored vehicles and commercial aircraft. Though not precision-guided, the Soviet RPG-7 and U.S. LAW can achieve deadly results at ranges of over a hundred meters.

The LAW is a free-flight missile fired by a percussion mechanism from a disposable tube. The LAW weighs about five pounds and has an antiarmor warhead whose effective range is about 300 meters against a stationary target but less than half that distance against a moving target. The successor to the LAW is called Viper. Although slightly heavier than the LAW, it has a far greater range and a more effective warhead. The Viper is presently in the engineering development phase.[6]

Rocket launcher systems are lightweight, compact, and self-contained, and require no support equipment. They can be dismantled and easily transported in a suitcase or disguised as something other than a launcher tube. (X-rays of baggage may disclose a silhouette of the weapon system and its components.)

They are particularly useful against targets such as limousines, aircraft, transformer banks, trucks carrying casks of radioactive waste, and pipelines. Unfortunately, these weapons are made available to terrorist organizations by some of the less responsible countries and the black market. (Recent conflicts in the Middle East and Southeast Asia have given rise to the potential for large numbers of them being placed on the market.)

NUCLEAR EXPLOSIVES AND CHEMICAL, BIOLOGICAL, AND RADIOLOGICAL WEAPONS

The development of radiological weapons (excluding construction of a nuclear explosive), the synthesis of nerve agents, and the culturing of small amounts of suitable biologicals are straightforward matters that are discussed today in the open literature,[7] especially in a now-famous study popularly known as the "Superviolence Study."[8] Moreover, dangerous agents such as cobalt-60, the insecticide TEPP, and specimens of anthrax are commercially available. Although growing virulent biologicals is a hazardous activity for the amateur, and making large quantities takes considerable skill and judgment, many thousands of people are sufficiently trained to perform such tasks.

There are various ways to compare nuclear, chemical, and biological weapons. One basis is the weight required to produce heavy casualties within a square-mile area under idealized conditions. In the table below in which this measure is used, various agents are ranked in terms of effectiveness.*

TABLE 1

COMPARISON OF AGENTS

Agent	Grams
Fuel air explosions	320,000,000
Fragmentation cluster bombs	32,000,000
Hydrocyanic acid	32,000,000
Mustard gas	3,200,000
Nerve gas (GB)	800,000
Crude nuclear weapon (fissionable material only)	5,000
Botulinal toxin (Type A)	80
Anthrax spores	8

This table makes a remarkable point. Compared in such a manner, chemical weapons, especially nerve agents, can be more than an order of magnitude more effective than fragmentation weapons; some biological agents cannot only rival thermonuclear devices in effectiveness but are a hundred thousand times more devastating than nerve agents.†

It is easy to illustrate theoretical aspects of nuclear explosives as well as those of virulent toxins and live pathogens, but there is a wide gulf between the theoretical and the practical. Though theoretical construction of nuclear explosives has become an

---

*Mean lethal "doses" of the agents are distributed uniformly in a one-square-mile area. In the case of a nuclear explosive, a standard "cookie cutter" interpretation is appropriate. Further toxins are uniformly dispersed as a line source, a 120 m/min wind is present, and the target is unprotected. The results are best viewed as order-of-magnitude estimates. (This comparison was derived by Conrad V. Chester of the Oak Ridge National Laboratory, transmitted in a June 20, 1975, letter entitled, "Perspectives on the CB Terrorist Threat."

†Lest we need reminding, the Black Death (bubonic, pneumonic, and septicemic plague) caused an estimated seventy-five million deaths in the period 1347–1351, and influenza claimed more than twenty-one million lives in 1918.

armchair pastime, first popularized by Mason Willrich and Theodore Taylor over four years ago,[9] the fabrication of a reliable nuclear explosive is a difficult and dangerous task that would not be undertaken lightly by a terrorist organization wishing to preserve its meager technical assets, especially its scientific personnel. Similarly, though theoretical estimates of casualties from chemical, biological, and radiological attacks are easily made, the dispersal of these agents is not a trivial matter. In large water supplies such attacks are virtually impossible; and for the agents to be dispersed efficiently as an aerosol, the help of a competent aerosol engineer and a meteorologist might be essential. Compared with nuclear explosives, and despite the many difficulties associated with efficient dispersal, effective chemical, biological, and radiological attacks are readily accomplished. Mass destruction, however reasonably measured, is technically feasible. But it is a myth that one can accomplish it by tossing a small quantity of a "supertoxin" into the water supply.

Nuclear Explosives

Recently a great deal has been written about the clandestine fabrication of a nuclear weapon. It has been fertile ground for movies, novels, and TV shows. Enterprising MIT, Harvard, and Princeton students have "designed" nuclear weapons, and a student-led course in nuclear weapons design was proposed to be given at the University of Connecticut. Possibly there is enough open information available to make a nuclear bomb. In fact, to the physicist the most important fact of all was learned when the first nuclear explosion was announced: supercritical masses explode.

The terrorist who intends to explode a nuclear device need only ensure that it goes "bang" and that the time-honored mushroom cloud is obvious to all. High reliability and predictable yield are requirements for the military, not the terrorist. Toppling one of the towers of the World Trade Center would suffice—lower Manhattan need not be demolished. It would be foolhardy to believe that a small, dedicated group could not build an inefficient atomic bomb, yielding between a few hundred tons and a kiloton in TNT-equivalents—hardly a trivial challenge.

The ingredients of a nuclear weapon include a high explosive and a special nuclear material (SNM). Clearly, the first obstacle would be obtaining the special nuclear material: uranium 233, uranium 235, or plutonium 239. Other than stealing the material or an actual nuclear weapon from a government installation, the terrorist would have to depend on the nuclear fuel cycle as the primary source of SNM.

There are many nuclear reactors in operation, the most common being light-water reactors that employ *low-enriched uranium* as a fuel.* The low-enriched uranium cannot be used in a nuclear explosive. On the other hand, once the fuel has been processed by the reactor, it does contain plutonium 239, which can be used to fabricate a nuclear weapon. Fortunately, the spent fuel from the reactor is highly radioactive. The plutonium cannot be retrieved without sophisticated handling and chemical separation processes. These may be out of the reach of many small nations, let alone terrorists.

There are, of course, other types of reactors, including the Canadian heavy-water reactor known as CANDU, which uses natural uranium as a fuel and also produces plutonium. In addition, there are breeder reactors that produce plutonium and uranium-233.

Plutonium 239 is the most widely available SNM. It is produced by neutron bombardment of uranium 238.† Were a clandestine nuclear explosive made, by all odds plutonium 239 would be the fissile component of the bomb.

Two basic nuclear weapons designs exist. First, there is the

---

*Naturally occurring uranium consists of the nonfissionable isotope uranium 238 and the fissionable one, uranium 235. Uranium 235 is only 0.7 percent of the mixture. Enriched uranium has a higher percentage of uranium 235. For uranium to be of practical use in the "core" of a nuclear explosive, it should be highly enriched.

†Upon neutron bombardment, uranium 238 captures a neutron, becoming uranium 239. Uranium 239, which has a short half-life, decays to neptunium 239, which in turn decays to plutonium 239. The half-life of neptunium 239 is only a few days; but plutonium 239 is quite stable, having a half-life of some 24,000 years. From the point of view of military weapons fabrication, it is important to obtain *weapons-grade* plutonium 239. Plutonium that is recovered from a light-water power reactor will contain a substantial amount of the isotope plutonium 240, in that plutonium 239 also captures neutrons. The two isotopes are virtually inseparable because they are chemically identical. The presence of plutonium 240 makes *reactor-grade* plutonium undesirable for use in weapons. Plutonium 240 fissions spontaneously and unpredictably, thus affecting the rate of fission of a critical mass of plutonium 239. As a result, a nuclear explosive employing reactor-grade plutonium could be of unpredictable and of lesser yield than one fabricated from weapons-grade material.

implosion weapon, utilizing a high explosive to implode symmetrically upon a mass of plutonium 239 that would be the core of the device. The more symmetrical the implosion, the greater the efficiency of the weapon. A sufficiently asymmetrical design may produce little or no nuclear yield. Next is the simplest, the *gun-type* weapon, which usually employs uranium 235. Because of a preinitiation problem, plutonium is not used in a device of gun-barrel design.

How easy is it to construct a crude nuclear weapon? The question is best answered by asking analogous questions: How easy is it to teach a bright, thoroughly inexperienced individual enough surgical procedure to perform an appendectomy? Would a patient be satisfied with his would-be surgeon, the "surgeon" having just read a surgery text for the first time? Well, the same problem may beset the would-be nuclear weapons designer. At one extreme Theodore Taylor,[10] who is an experienced weapons designer, feels that an enterprising amateur could fabricate such a weapon. Few would argue that another Manhattan Project would be required, but most would conservatively estimate that it might take a half-dozen technically trained and mechanically adept people to accomplish the feat in safety. In addition to the SNM and high explosive, the project would require time, space, and money as well as technological abilities. Individuals with training in nuclear chemistry, physics, metallurgy, and electronics, as well as those with some experience in handling high explosives, would be especially desirable. Once the SNM is obtained, an exceedingly difficult matter in itself, the remaining tasks concern weapon design, engineering, reliability, and safety. Playing with near-critical masses of fissile materials is a dangerous business, indeed. Moreover, high explosives are known to have detonated at the most unwanted moments.

The Effects of a Nuclear Detonation   Suppose a nuclear bomb having an effective yield of five kilotons of TNT is detonated at ground-level in midtown Manhattan. Skyscrapers and multistory buildings in the immediate area of the explosion are demolished. At the center of this area is a crater 120 feet wide and 50 feet deep. Although structural damage to the multistoried steel- and concrete-reinforced buildings decreases as one moves several blocks from the point of explosion, the absorption of thermal radiation by flammable substance, along with the large number of short-circuited wires and ruptured gas lines, starts intense fires throughout a large area.

Despite the use of fire-resistant materials, the closeness of the buildings and the intense drafts through shattered windows facilitate the spread of fire. Ruptured water mains near the explosion can lead to a collapse in water pressure throughout Manhattan. Firemen are confined to fighting localized fires caused by flaming debris. Attempts to bring rescue vehicles into the destroyed area are blocked by heavy debris on the streets.

About twenty minutes after the explosion a fire storm may begin. Because of the strong inward draft the fires would not spread much beyond the range in which they started soon after the explosion. However, virtually everything combustible within this range would be destroyed.

Because of the characteristics of the bomb and its method of employment, the local fallout is severe. Over 60 percent of this radioactive material descends in early fallout. The accompanying rain caused by condensation from the fire precipitates additional large amounts of radioactive materials into the area.

Assessing the number of fatalities from such a bomb is difficult and subject to wide variations. But a conservative estimate can be made that as many as fifty thousand to one hundred thousand people would be killed in the immediate area of explosion. The number of fatalities in the surrounding area would add significantly to this figure.

Although the preceding scenario is fanciful and a five-kiloton weapon is quite unlikely to be within reach of even a sophisticated terrorist group, it does provide obvious measures of destruction.[11] Nuclear weapons effects can be divided into two categories: immediate and delayed. Immediate effects are blast, thermal radiation, and nuclear radiation. Delayed effects, other than those that result from injuries and burns and not including food shortages, sanitation, and service problems, are limited to radioactive fallout.

Except for promoting blast overpressure, nuclear explosives are quite unlike conventional explosives. A crude device producing a kiloton yield, a weapon that might be within reach of terrorists, would produce an overpressure of ten pounds per square inch (psi) at about 1,200 feet from ground zero. A peak overpressure of ten psi would produce considerable structural damage and, according to Glasstone,[12] result in an expected mortality rate of about 10 percent of the exposed population, were the effects of translation and flying debris ignored.* Thermal radiation from the fireball would presumably result in a similar mortality rate. On the other hand, there is another and probably more pronounced danger from a low-yield nuclear weapon. Prompt nuclear radiation would be expected to cause a 50 percent mortality rate among the exposed human population at a radius of about 2,400 feet from ground zero.

All those exposed to lethal doses of prompt radiation would not die immediately. There would be a sizable population of "walking dead." Except for very high doses, nuclear radiation is not immediately lethal. At lower doses the human body's responses are more variable. It might take several weeks after the explosion to determine the full effects.

Delayed radiation effects due to fallout would depend upon meteorological conditions, height of burst, and the terrain and soil characteristics of the region. Distribution of fallout is a complex matter and is not fully predictable. Some facts, however, are basic. Fallout will not be distributed in a radially symmetric way about the point of detonation; there will be, in fact, *hot spots*. The more active, shorter half-life particle emission will diminish in intensity after a short while, leaving long-lasting but low-level sources of radiation. Immediate health hazards resulting from the fallout of a low-yield nuclear explosion should end after some eight hours from the time of detonation. But the longer-run risks of induced cancers, while not great, obviously cannot be estimated accurately.

Chemical and Biological Weapons

Chemical and biological weapons stir deep public fear because of misperceptions and popular acceptance of half-truths about the

---

*In an urban environment the mean lethal radius diminishes to the four-psi level. This adjustment from the free-field estimate is necessary because of flying debris. Even with minimal warning, people would lie down, thereby raising the threshold to seven psi.

potency of nerve gas and the ease with which plagues of medieval scope could be engendered and propagated. The threat by terrorists to use such weapons could well breed panic. There are many chemical and biological agents of extreme potency; but their effective delivery as weapons of mass violence, whether by means of water supplies, food distribution, or aerosol, would be formidable obstacles to the amateur. Weaponry in the hands of the technically resourceful, however, can be partially ranked:

> In terms of fatalities, conventional weapons such as machine guns and small bombs constitute the least threat. They can produce tens or hundreds of casualties in a single incident. Chemical weapons such as nerve agents constitute a substantially greater threat, being capable of producing hundreds to thousands of fatalities. A small nuclear bomb could produce a hundred thousand casualties, but biological agents—both toxins and living organisms—can rival thermonuclear weapons, providing the possibility of producing hundreds of thousands to several millions of casualties in a single incident.[13]

Chemical Weapons　　There are tens of thousands of highly poisonous chemicals. Some are commonplace but generally unknown to the public, and others are exotic. We limit our discussion to two classes of poisons and two biologically produced toxins. The first two are the *fluoroacetates* and the *organophosphorous compounds*, popularly known as *nerve agents*. The biologically derived toxins are *botulinal toxin*, which causes botulism and is produced by a microorganism (*Clostridium botulinum*), and *ricin*, which is a violently poisonous protein derived from the castor bean.

Fluoroacetic acid was first synthesized at the turn of the century, but the toxicities of fluoroacetic acid and its derivatives were not realized initially. Fluoroacetates attack the normal cell functions, leading to cell death and ultimately to death of the human being. The basic cellular chemistry is affected by inhibition of various enzymes. The fluoroacetates block biochemical reactions that metabolize hydrates of carbon to carbon dioxide and water, a process that releases the energy required for normal cellular functioning. Fluoroacetate compounds are available commercially, as, for instance, the rodenticides known as compound 1080.

The synthesis of fluoroacetates is relatively straightforward, and the procedures are well documented.[14] Relatively small changes in chemical structure can produce an order-of-magnitude change in toxicity.[15] Although certain of the fluoroacetates are extremely toxic, and a moderately competent chemist could easily produce tens of kilograms of them, these agents cannot be equated with a practical mass assault by terrorists. Dissemination would be the next and most difficult step.

Among the most toxic chemical compounds, other than those produced by living organisms, are the organophosphorous compounds, the so-called nerve agents. There are tens of thousands of them.[16] The first one to be synthesized was tetraethylpyrophosphate, produced in the mid-1800s. Commercially known as TEPP, it is among the most toxic organophosphates. Many organophosphates are available commercially as insecticides. TEPP is one of them. Another is parathion, an insecticide that has proved to be quite hazardous.

The Nazis pursued the study of organophosphorous compounds for insecticidal and chemical warfare purposes, and the German chemical industry developed two highly toxic substances: tabun (ethyl NN-dimethylphosphoramidocyanidate) and sarin (isopropyl methylphosphonofluoridate). There is a vast open literature on organophosphorous compounds. Partly because of military interest, but largely because of academic and commercial relevance, this family of compounds has achieved considerable economic importance as insecticides. The chemistry of these compounds has also been of value for basic research on the electrochemical transmission of nerve signals. Organophosphorous compounds interfere with the action of acetylcholinesterase, which is essential to the transmission of electrochemical signals from one nerve ending to another.[17]

When taken orally, sarin is ten times as toxic as TEPP to humans. Because of its high volatility, it has relatively low dermal toxicity; but a small quantity of sarin splashed on the skin can produce a vapor concentration high enough to exceed the mean lethal inhalatory dose with a single breath.[18] In aerosol form, sarin has a mean lethal dose of 70 mg min/m^3. At a normal rate of respiration this equates with a lethal dose of about 0.015 mg per kg of body weight.

Although sarin is considerably more toxic than TEPP, there is yet another group of nerve agents, known as the V-agents. These are far more toxic than sarin. VX is the best known of this family, and its method of preparation was first published by the British Patent Office.[19] SIPRI has reported that VX, when inhaled, is 10 times as toxic as sarin, but dermally it is 300 times as toxic.[20] A moderately competent organic chemist, with limited laboratory facilities, can synthesize sarin and VX. The operation would not be without considerable personal risk.

Botulinal toxin and ricin are produced from living organisms;[21] they are not synthesized in a laboratory. (It is a tossup whether to call them biological or chemical agents.) The toxin that causes botulism is produced by the organism *Clostridium botulinum*, which is found virtually everywhere. Improperly prepared sausage and canned tuna are classic sources of botulism. The virulence of the toxin is incredible. When compared with the most toxic nerve agents, botulinal toxin is a thousand times more effective. Although the mean lethal dose is not known precisely, it is measured as low as a few tenths of a microgram.

As a terrorist weapon it could be devastating; yet there are limits to its usefulness. Dissemination is the hardest step. As with other agents, it would be virtually impossible to poison a large water supply: hydrolysis, chlorination, and the required quantity of the toxin are the inhibiting factors. Distribution via the food supply and aerosol dispersal are potential alternatives. As should be expected, the food processing industry is intensely concerned about botulinal contamination. Although technically feasible, and very frightening, a terrorist attempt to contaminate canned products would be of limited effect. Aerosol dispersal would be a difficult and risky matter as well. Were terrorists to attempt a toxic aerosol attack, they would probably use other agents.

Botulinal toxin is easily produced and there is a considerable literature on its anaerobic growth and care. Serologic typing for virulence is a standard task for the microbiologist; techniques of continuous culturing are well understood; and the separation and purification of the toxin are also widely known.

As we mentioned earlier, ricin is a plant protein that is

obtained, among other methods, by solvent extraction from castor beans, the seeds of *Ricinis communis*. Crystalline ricin is an order of magnitude more toxic than sarin, comparing in toxicity with Indian cobra neurotoxin and with tetrodotoxin, which is found in globefish and certain salamanders. Ricin has no warning smell and its effects are often delayed. When milled and dispersed in solid form, its toxicity degrades owing to heat and mechanical stress. Although its toxicity is great, it is three orders of magnitude less than botulinal toxin and would make a poor weapon of mass destruction.

Biological Agents   Unlike weapons derived from plants or bacteria such as *Botulinum clostridium*, live pathogens could be successfully employed by terrorists and potentially inflict great harm. Some microorganisms, including certain bacteria and viruses, are of nearly incalculable virulence. Depending on the (average) particle size of an aerosol, meteorological conditions, vertical dilution, sedimentation, and so on, a mass-destruction attempt using live biologicals against a densely populated target might produce anywhere from a few hundred to hundreds of thousands of casualties. Even the "uneventful" attack producing a few hundred casualties could cause government disruption and public panic. (The disorder effected by the "Philadelphia Fever" of 1976—which was not, as far as we know, terrorist-inspired—is illustrative.) Table 2 indicates various pathogens that could be employed by terrorists bent upon mass destruction.[22]

Unlike chemical agents, a small seed culture, when in the hands of a knowledgeable microbiologist having university-level laboratory facilities at his disposal, can be multiplied to a large quantity. Moreover, once an individual is infected, the microorganisms can multiply prodigously, subject to body defenses (white cells and antibodies).

The balance of our discussion of biological agents is devoted to what is perhaps the most available, yet devastating agent within reach of the terrorist—pulmonary anthrax. The pneumonia-like illness caused by *Bacillus anthracis* is nearly 100 percent fatal when untreated. The only treatment, massive doses of penicillin, is not usually effective, because by the time the symptoms of pulmonary anthrax appear, antibiotic therapy is useless. There being

TABLE 2

EFFECTS OF VARIOUS BIOLOGICAL AGENTS

Agent	Mean lethal dosage	Means of transmission	Incubation period (days)	Lethality category	
				Treated	Untreated
Anthrax *Bacillus anthracis*	10,000–20,000 spores	aerosol	2–3	very high	100%
Pneumonic plague *Pasturella pestis*	3,000 cells	aerosol, food, water, vector	3–4	low	100%
Tularemia *(Francisella tularensis)*	50–100 cells (inhalation)	aerosol, food, water, vector	2–7	low	40%
Cryptococcosis *(Cryptococcus neoformans)*	high infectivity	aerosol, food, water	unknown	very high	very high
Smallpox *(Variola virus)*	high infectivity	aerosol, contact	3–22	(supportive therapy only)	moderate

SOURCE: This table is derived from Advanced Concepts Research, *Superviolence*, and SIPRI, *Problem of Chemical and Biological Warfare*.

few volunteers to test its deadliness on themselves, its mean lethal dose is not known precisely. Various authors, including Rothschild,[23] estimate it to be ten times more toxic than botulinal toxin.

Nearly all microorganisms die quickly when exposed to sunlight. They are adversely affected by high temperatures and succumb easily to desiccation. Simply put, they are fragile. This is not the case for anthrax. It is a hardy organism. In spore form it can live for decades, withstanding wide variations in environment.

How easy is it to prepare? Unfortunately, after having obtained a virulent strain, even a modestly trained microbiologist could continuously culture the organisms. The techniques for its preparation and care are well known.[24] Although *Bacillus anthracis* is extremely infective, its dissemination as an aerosol is not a trivial matter.

Illustrating the effectiveness of anthrax, the *Superviolence* study has described an aerosol attack designed to subject five million residents of Manhattan, the Bronx, and New Jersey to infectious doses of anthrax spores. Having assumed good meteorological conditions, a large quantity of the agent, and, in our view, considerable technical sophistication of the terrorists, the authors of the study concluded that more than 600,000 deaths would result. Although experts might take exception to the casualty estimate, few, if any, would disagree with the principle.[25]

Radiological Weapons   Aside from nuclear explosives, fissionable material used as a radiological weapon differs radically from other types of mass-destruction weapons. A nuclear explosion disperses radiological materials of sufficient activity to cause large numbers of casualties; but when plutonium material is used as a dispersion weapon, the effects are not prompt. In fact, evidence of radiological damage—leukemia, genetic defects in offspring, fibrosis of the thyroid or lungs—might not appear for years.

The half-life of many dangerous fissionable materials is such that the length of time during which the affected area is contaminated rivals, and even exceeds, the duration of contamination for areas sprayed with anthrax. The radiological effects on humans resulting from long-time exposure can be minimized by evacuating the contaminated area. Rehabilitation would depend on whether the area could be cleared of most of the fissionable material and, if not, whether the value of the contaminated area is so vital that its rehabilitation outweighs the statistical risk of possible long-term physical effects.

Examples of such dangerous radioactive agents are plutonium 239, polonium 210 and cobalt 60. Plutonium 239 does not occur naturally in any abundance but is a plentiful by-product of nuclear reactors. Because it is a basic ingredient of a nuclear weapon, it is subject to strict material accountability and physical security measures. Polonium 210, which is also very dangerous to humans, is controlled by Nuclear Regulatory Commission licensing and is available only in small samples for laboratory experiments. Cobalt 60, a nasty gamma emitter, is available in larger amounts in hospitals and medical centers where it is used for cancer research and therapy.

Although we do not try to minimize the dangers of plutonium 239 and other radioisotopes,[26] it is a myth to think that terrorists can easily disperse them, for instance through an air-conditioning system. Perhaps the greatest danger associated with the threatened dispersion of plutonium 239 is the popular exaggeration of the threat. Not only because of its intrinsic harmfulness, but because of the fears surrounding radioactive substances, plutonium 239 and other isotopes are necessarily objects of great concern for government. Dispersion weapons utilizing radioactive isotopes (especially isotopes of plutonium) could become a powerful terrorist threat.

SOCIETY'S CRITICAL NODES

Highly industrialized nations—especially those that place a premium on competition and market efficiency—are fragile in the sense of being vulnerable to catastrophe. Commercial aircraft, natural gas pipelines, the electric power grid, offshore oil rigs, and computers storing government and corporate records are examples of sabotage-prone targets the destruction of which would have derivative effects far greater than their primary losses would suggest. Consider the recent New York blackout. Disproportionately high damage occurred—nearly uncontrolled looting and arson, resource shortages, and a further loss of already low public confidence. Suppose, instead of its two-day span, the blackout had lasted just three days more. The city would have been paralyzed. It is not difficult to invent stark—possibly realistic—scenarios: looters would run wild, fires would be started at random, and jittery National Guardsmen might shoot into crowds of panicked people; food and water would become scarce and food spoilage would be nearly total; as the sanitation system collapsed, the specter of disease would become an overriding concern; the rats, outnumbering the people, would be close to achieving a permanent victory.

The point is that "nature," with the aid of human inefficiency, produced the two-day siege. A trained, but quite small, paramilitary force could virtually put New York City—or any large metropolitan area—out of commission for an extended period of time.

Thus far our experience with terrorism has been limited to diminutive acts. Even so, the world was riveted to the TV screen when the Munich killings occurred in 1972; and it was blind luck that the Hanafi Muslims did not choose a more interesting target. Because we are implicitly willing to accept the human and political losses, we are prepared to handle the "Hanafi" assaults; but a slight upward deviation from the projected pattern of familiar incidents could bring about terrible hardships. Thirty years ago terrorists could not have obtained extraordinary leverage. Today, however, the foci of communications, production, and distribution are relatively small in number and highly vulnerable—and the media balance themselves on tightropes, doing their jobs of reporting the news, yet being perilously close to inciting further terror.

Terrorists need not use atomic bombs or biological agents to bring about devastation. A clever terrorist who understands the vulnerable pressure points of government can inflict grievous harm. Unless governments take basic precautions, we will continue to stand at the edge of an awful abyss.

This section is devoted to a discussion of the fragility of

society's interconnections—our "choke points." Most are obvious and the rest should not be made public. Thus, we limit ourselves to a general discussion in order not to provide "cookbook" information for would-be terrorists. Fabricating a nuclear weapon, or concocting chemical or biological agents, is technically demanding, but an individual bent upon inflicting considerable harm upon America needs only the most primitive weaponry, once he is armed with the detailed knowledge of our important choke points.

The balance of this section touches upon some of the more obviously fragile but important networks. In particular, we comment upon the vulnerability of energy delivery and computer systems. (A far deeper treatment of the vulnerability of the natural gas and petroleum systems is presented in an essay by Maynard Stephens on pages 200–223.)

The Electric Power Grid

The vulnerability of the electric power grid to blackout, even to those of regional extent, has become all too obvious. Few blackouts have resulted from sabotage. In the days of the Office of Strategic Services and the resistance movements of World War II, raids were made behind enemy lines on electric power plants. Today terrorists generally live within the boundaries of a targeted power plant, there being no formally declared sides. Even so, terrorists have found the electrical power system an attractive target. Somewhat after the Moro event, Italian terrorists, having downed high-power transmission lines, succeeded in temporarily blacking out a portion of Rome;[27] and Puerto Rican terrorists have accomplished similar feats. Thus far the attacks upon the power grid have not been notably effective. Generally speaking, the grid has many "loops," enabling it to sustain a considerable amount of damage without general or even regional collapse. Nevertheless, the Northeast blackout of 1965 demonstrated the potential of cascading, domino-like failure of the grid.

Beyond power plants the likely targets are transmission lines and transformers. There are about 250,000 miles of power transmission lines in the United States; some 55,000 miles of these are the so-called extra-high-voltage (EHV) lines used for cross-country transmissions of large quantities of electricity. In addition to large switching centers, the key elements of the cross-country system are the EHV transformers, which are used to step up voltage in order to achieve the economies-to-scale of high-voltage transmission and subsequently to step down power at the consuming level in order to achieve local distribution. These large transformers are ready targets for demolition, short-circuiting, and rupturing that would cause the loss of coolants. Some are protected; others are not.

From the viewpoint of both the government and the terrorist, the crux of the problem is to identify those relatively few choke points in the transmission system whose destruction would cause the most hardship. Based upon the perception of threat as well as the consequences of failure, investments in greater redundancy and better physical security deserve serious cost-benefit analysis.

The Vulnerability of the Petroleum and Natural Gas Industries

Maynard Stephens is quoted in *Newsweek* as saying, "The system is vulnerable all along the line. I could take a handful of Boy Scouts and, in an hour, deal a damaging blow."[28] From pipelines and refineries to offshore oil and gas fields, the system is insecure. For example, offshore oil platforms are vulnerable to aircraft, surface boats, swimmers, and saboteurs. In the same *Newsweek* article Captain Robert Denton, who heads Naval Intelligence in Panama City, Florida, warned that the threats are real: "Offshore emergency assets are essentially unprotected, and we are vulnerable to overt, clandestine or covert attack."[29]

The pipeline system is an easy target. Pipelines are easy to identify, since they must be marked each time they cross a waterway or road. It would be all too easy to take out the larger pipelines, especially the few that carry several million barrels of crude oil a day. The result would be serious disruption of the Northeast's petroleum supplies.

Texas and Louisiana are the nation's two top-ranking producers of natural gas. In 1974 Texas and Louisiana marketed about eight million cubic feet each. Further, Louisiana plays a dominant role in the interstate movement of natural gas, since it contributes about one-half of all the gas used in the United States. Further, a high percentage of gas flowing from Texas to the Eastern U.S. market passes through Louisiana's larger pipelines.

Unlike electrical power transmission, if natural gas transmission were interrupted there would be no ready way to exchange gas from one company's pipeline to another. Any substantial disruption of a major trunkline could severely disrupt natural gas delivery. The importance of this problem is underscored when it is understood that some 35 percent of the nation's energy is supplied by natural gas. It has been estimated by Stephens and others that a small band of terrorists could shut off three-quarters of the flow of natural gas to Eastern markets in one night's work without having left the state of Louisiana. The problem is similar with crude oil and petroleum pipelines. It would not be difficult to put a big "dent" in the system. Pumping stations and river crossings are key targets. A well-planned paramilitary effort against our natural gas and petroleum transmission systems could immobilize America.[30]

The Vulnerability of Computer Systems

Today's Luddite might object most to the computer. Over the past two decades we have witnessed an unparalleled transition from assorted machines and labor-intensive jobs to a computer-intensive economy. New jobs, new jargon, new machines, new invasion-of-privacy problems—amidst inundating piles of well-managed data, we have succumbed to the era of the microprocessor and the ubiquitous Social Security number. Our sense of personal identity has never been lower. Yet the computer and information revolutions have barely begun.[31] Can the sorcerer counter his apprentice's spell? Even if he cannot, terrorists may try.

The pursuit of commercial efficiency has brought brilliant, fixed points of control into being, critical nodes whose destruction would be comparable with brain death. Billing systems, Social Security and Internal Revenue Service accounts, load-sharing in the electric power grid, airline scheduling, manned space flight, and nuclear-tipped missiles are within the computer's span of influence. Yet, with the exception of computers under military aegis, nearly all large computer systems are insecure—naked targets for enterprising terrorists. Whether by crude demolition or by deft use of electromagnetic pulses, computers can be brought down, their memory banks and outputs discredited.

Some governments and large corporations have begun to store their most vital records in oversized bomb shelters that serve as their emergency corporate seats (for example, at Iron Mountain in New York State), preparing to survive the worst. Few can afford this level of protection, but nearly everyone can afford the electromagnetic shielding needed to save the major department store from possible bankruptcy.

CHAPTER 3

▬▬▬▬

Security and Countermeasure Technology: An Assessment

Technology is but one means of countering terrorism. It is not offered here as a panacea for an advanced society lacking the commitment to remain vigilant in its own defense. Counterterrorism must necessarily use intelligence, police, and military operations as well as psychological, medical, and behavioral science techniques before, during, and after threatened or actual incidents. Technology's role is to support these efforts.

The most practical way to judge the relative usefulness and breadth of application of various technologies is to divide counterterrorism into functional tasks. The discussion and evaluation of technology can then be furthered by comparing these tasks with various scenarios. We suggest that the job of counterterrorism be divided into the following four, not mutually exclusive, functions.

Prevention   The avoidance of terrorist incidents by denying access to suitable instruments where possible, by successful protection of critical targets should an incident be attempted, or by deterring incidents through a combination of denial and protection.

Control   The timely establishment of mechanisms for command and control of governmental resources to assure an efficient response to an incident, with adequate informational and decision-making provisions, designed to seize the initiative from the terrorists.

Containment   Emergency measures taken to delimit the terrorist act in a physical sense and to "decouple" it in a psychological sense from the intended political consequences. Actions to limit damage and provide emergency health care are included.

Restoration   Deliberate actions to conclude the incident and restore the situation, lasting until the situation is returned to normal and routine services are again available.

CONCEPTUAL FRAMEWORK FOR RESOURCE ALLOCATION

To parallel the four functional tasks, we can divide the management of terrorism problems into four phases—prevention, control, containment, and restoration. Although the ways of managing these phases and their concomitant technologies are interrelated, the requirements that systems and devices must meet are quite different in the various phases. A further useful distinction is that between broad general-purpose measures and specialized devices tailored to a particular type of incident or threat.

Raising Barriers

The first and last phases—prevention and restoration—primarily involve general-purpose measures. Screening of passengers and baggage at airports, fences, guards, and alarms handicap terrorists. Although there can be no guarantee against circumvention by a skilled and determined effort, screening limits potential terrorism to the most talented groups (a high-pass filter) and so tends to inhibit terrorism. Such measures, to be effective, must be generally applied lest they merely divert terrorists from one opportunity to another where the protective measures are lacking. (For instance, international air pirates, such as those involved in the Entebbe incident, arrange to board at points where security is known to be lax.) When the opportunities are numerous, the protective systems and devices used must be economically feasible. Multipurpose systems are preferable to a proliferation of dedicated, single-purpose systems. Installing a sophisticated, single-purpose cobra venom detector at each U.S.

airport, for instance, would be ludicrous. On the other hand, a device that could, with moderate reliability, detect a wide variety of poisons, explosives, and drugs might be useful if its cost were not too high.

Many of the emergency measures that would help restore well-being and tranquility in the wake of terrorist events would not be substantially different from those normally associated with natural disasters.

Measures intended to prevent terrorism will typically be costly since they must be generally applied if they are to be effective. Most of the restorative measures have a joint utility in alleviating other sorts of calamities. Restorative measures related directly to disasters would not cost as much as preventive measures because they would be applied after the fact to deal only with a particular incident. Thus, such restorative measures might be feasible at a relatively high unit cost (per installation) in contrast to preventive measures.*

Attempting to allocate counterterrorism resources on a marginal analysis basis poses extremely complex problems because of the vast number of potential targets and variety of possible countermeasures, leading to a multitude of investment alternatives. These alternatives can, of course, be grouped but they then must be weighed on the basis of lives and property saved and sovereignty preserved. Ultimately, one must fall back on sensitivity analysis and professional judgments.

Specialization

The control and containment phases of terrorist problems contrast sharply with the prevention and restoration phases. In prevention and restoration, generality of purpose is a desired feature. In controlling or containing a terrorist incident, precise

---

*The technologies and uses of prevention and restoration gadgetry may be likened to antiballistic missile defense and the game-theoretic allocation of resources of attacker and defender. If we view terrorists as highly resourceful opponents, we could also view means for prevention as examples of "terminal" defense and the means for restoration as examples of "preferential" or "area" defense. Borrowing liberally from the analytical literature of the ABM field, one might conclude—as we do in the case of ABM analyses—that for moderate defense budgets and small attacks, the entire defense budget should be spent on restoration. As our perception of the threat increases, means of prevention become more desirable.

tailoring of the response to the nature of the threat is needed. If it becomes apparent that a terrorist is credibly threatening to use cobra venom, the availability of an antidote becomes crucial. Moreover, it does not need to be ubiquitous. Subject to obvious logistic constraints, a limited antidote supply, matched to the terrorists' resources and their capability of using them, would suffice. It might therefore be worthwhile to invest in developing highly specialized technology on a very limited basis (in terms of numbers of devices produced) to deal with particular cases that may occur.

All contingencies cannot be covered, so the possibility of rapid access to a wide variety of experts and equipment is the principal strategy to adopt. Nevertheless, we can aspire to a higher technology than would be feasible in the prevention mode, with its high initial investment for the masses of ubiquitous equipment; we can develop more specialized devices for dealing with the threats we judge most likely.

Joint Usage

From our abstract viewpoint, the technology of containing the consequences of a terrorist incident differs from that of controlling the incident primarily in its being more adaptable to dual purposes. Just as restoration from the effects of terrorism has much in common with restoration from the effects of other disasters, so with containment. Whether a chemical or biological disaster is terrorist-inspired or accidental, its consequences are hardly distinguishable. The havoc wrought by terrorist bombing of an aircraft does not differ much in its immediate physical effects from that caused by aircraft accidents and industrial explosions. Both the control and containment phases of antiterrorism technology can be highly specialized and fairly costly, but the containment can often depend on systems that are present anyway, such as ambulances and fire engines at airports and the resources of disease-control centers.

The control phase of antiterrorism appears to be the one most amenable to the application of highly specialized technology. It is interlinked with the prevention phase, at least in the case of extortion attempts, through the credibility of the terrorist's threat. A few years ago the Croatian hijackers of a TWA 727, for instance, were deterred by airport security precautions from taking bombs aboard. Confidence in the system by the crisis managers, however, was not sufficient to allow them to call the terrorists' bluff. In general, the assessment of the threat credibility will depend on the preventive measures that are in effect and on their perceived reliability. Moreover, the willingness to act on a judgment that a threat is probably a bluff will depend on the means available for mitigating the consequences if the judgment proves faulty—that is, on the resources devoted to the containment and restoration phases.

A quantified analytical approach to dividing resources among various phases of antiterrorist activity or among the various potential terrorist threats does not appear possible. One must rely, ultimately, on estimates of comparative worth and probability of occurrence. We have tried in the above paragraphs to offer some qualitative bases for making the judgments.

HARDENING THE TARGET

A clearly useful way to meet the threat of terrorism is to create conditions under which it would be impossible for terrorists to successfully attack critical targets. The goal is idealistic; for political, economic, and social reasons it would be difficult to meet. Nevertheless, there is a great deal that can be done to prevent some forms of terrorism. Employing technology to "harden the target" is an obvious area for exploration. At risk is the openness of our society were we to employ repressive security means—for then the terrorists would have won. Although a somewhat subjective matter, the application of technology is especially desirable when it denies the potential terrorist the leverage he seeks, without fostering policies that deny civil liberties.

Hardening the target has prophylactic value. It entails denying terrorists access not only to arms and explosives but also to their intended targets. The objective is to make the potential terrorist act so difficult that the amateur is defeated and the professional finds the cost too high. Thus hardening the target is synonymous with establishing barriers, some managerial and others physical. The physical methods of hardening aim to reduce the terrorist's ability to damage a specific installation and, for networks, such as the electric power and communications systems, to increase the number of critical nodes. Here we consider two types of barriers: (a) denial of means and (b) security devices and procedures.

Significant improvements continue to be made in methods for detecting devices and materials terrorists might use and in methods for preventing access to potential terrorist targets. But none of the present or anticipated devices has a long-range detection capability; none of the present and anticipated types of barriers is impenetrable. Sensors are most useful in preventing terrorism by making it difficult for potential terrorists to obtain and transport arms, explosives, or chemical, biological, and radiological agents.

In the balance of our discussion of target hardening we distinguish between measures to deny access to weapons and the means by which targets can be protected if weapons have been obtained.

Explosives, Automatic and Light Antitank Weapons and Surface-to-Air Missiles

Explosives   Terrorists employ high explosives, which are usually homemade devices and which produce casualties by blast effect rather than by fragmentation. Explosives offer many advantages to a terrorist: they are available everywhere and crude bombs can be fabricated locally; they are concealable and can be readily disguised so that X-ray and magnetometer inspection are ineffective defenses. The most obvious means of making it more difficult for terrorists to obtain explosives would be to restrict their purchase and impose better security and inventory control procedures on business. Obviously, even if these suggestions were implemented, there would be no way of preventing terrorists from making a crude bomb out of fertilizer and oil. Moreover, industry would balk, and justifiably so. Denial of access to explosives seems impractical at best.

The matter of target protection is similarly thorny. Any crowded area, such as an airline terminal, an auditorium, or a sports arena, is an obvious target for bombing. As a practical matter, protection of a diverse set of targets requires the technical ability to detect explosives quickly and unobtrusively at entrances. Just as important is limiting access to clandestine or forced entry.

An explosive detection device must provide for rapid processing, have a low false alarm rate, and be capable of detecting small amounts of explosives in sealed containers. (Some of the more experimental devices activate in the presence of nitrobenzene, an ingredient of black shoe polish.) The task could be somewhat simplified were all commercial detonators impregnated with easily detected taggants. The U.S. Bureau of Alcohol, Tobacco and Firearms has been at the forefront in coordinating research on taggants. While there are electronic means of explosive detection under development, the most reliable detector is a well-trained dog.

Technological progress is needed, for there is clear enough evidence of repeated tragedy. However, the problem is far more than technological. It is political, it is economic, it is regulatory, and it is legislative.

Small Arms   Terrorists have used pistols, rifles, machine guns, and sawed-off shotguns. In the United States alone, there are nearly 200 million guns in the public's possession. Although the possession and sale of automatic weapons are strictly controlled, terrorists—including the Symbionese Liberation Army—have had little difficulty in obtaining them. Whether they are stolen from military supply depots or smuggled in from abroad, the automatic weapon is all too plentiful. And in the Middle East, or for that matter, virtually anywhere in Europe, the machine gun is a common sight.

Denying terrorists access to small arms is a hopeless goal. Interdiction through technological and intelligence methods are the fundamental defenses, the requisite tools being customs inspections and X-ray and magnetometer examinations. But we must not ignore the physical security of military depots and the need for good inventory control systems. Of course, alarm systems, as well as passive and active barriers, are essential.

Small arms are used for assassinations or for the taking of

hostages. Airline passengers, industrial and governmental VIPs, or just about any small group of people who could be isolated in a defensible barricade are potential targets. Obviously, the number of possible targets is overwhelming. There would be no way of protecting even a minuscule fraction. Nevertheless, the more critical and likely targets can be provided some protection by devices designed to detect the presence of small arms.

Office buildings are virtually unprotected. Even federal office buildings are easily penetrated. Uniformed guards and identification cards are trivial challenges to the trained terrorist. Magnetometers, like those used to screen airline passengers, could be used to screen all entrances at moderate cost but doing so would slow admittance to buildings substantially. Though such inspection procedures would be acceptable to frightened VIPs—wealthy European industrialists being obvious examples—the widespread use of magnetometers is unlikely.

Clearly, bulletproof clothing such as kevlar jackets and other body armor, armored cars, bodyguards, and executive training programs intended to minimize the dangers of terrorist attack are all available. While not exotic by contrast with the more sophisticated weapons described earlier, a crude handgun can be as lethal a weapon as the bubonic plague. Ironically, the difference between these weapons is the degree of personalization, the bullet being more selective than the germ.

Man-Portable Rockets   Lightweight antitank and antiaircraft rockets can transform the poorly trained and inexperienced individual into a capable mass killer. In such a person's hands, the first-round hit probability on an armored vehicle several hundred meters away, or a jumbo jet shortly after takeoff, is extremely high. As we discussed in the last chapter, the primary weapons are the Soviet RPG-7 and the United States LAW. The antiaircraft rockets concerned are the Soviet SA-7 and our own Redeye. Relatively small and lightweight, they can be easily hidden; some can even be transported in a small suitcase and fired clandestinely.

These missiles have been used in Southeast Asia and in the Middle East, and they have been sold or transferred to scores of nations. As a practical matter, therefore, they are out of Soviet or American control. Through private purchase, through a gift from a friendly foreign government, or by theft, terrorists can continue to obtain and use these weapons. Unfortunately, crossing national boundaries has rarely been a problem for terrorists. As before, the basic defense is interdiction—customs inspections that employ magnetometers, explosive detectors, and X-ray devices.

The United States has taken substantial security measures to prevent the theft of antitank and antiaircraft weapons. However, the poor physical security and inventory control of these weapons, when in the hands of Third World nations, pose substantial risks to every nation. It is worth noting that there has not been a recent Soviet-influenced conflict in which the recipients of Russia's support were not carrying RPG-7s.

In addition to physical security, tagging devices to facilitate accountability and tracing are important. Active and passive transponders, as well as a variety of electronic, magnetic, infrared, odorous, and visual devices could also be employed.

Denying access to these weapons may be the only practical defense. Thus interdiction of such weapons at national boundaries, physical security, and good inventory control are among the most important objectives. The problems of protecting a wide variety of targets (commercial aircraft, armored limousines, or power centers) are substantial. Traditional close-in security measures can be overcome by a standoff attack. If terrorists were to adopt the tactic of shooting down commercial airliners, the security radius from the airport would have to be several miles, and noise abatement rules would have to be abandoned were aircraft to stay out of the SA-7's intercept-envelope. Similarly, limousines cannot be hardened sufficiently to defeat the RPG-7, but development of "soft" armor may be worth pursuing. Once the terrorists have gotten their hands on man-portable rockets, protection at acceptable levels of economic and social cost may be impossible to achieve.

Nuclear Explosives and Chemical, Biological, and Radiological Weapons

Nuclear Explosives   As we discussed in the preceding chapter, terrorist use of nuclear or other weapons of mass destruction is highly unlikely. Yet, were terrorists to use any of these, the consequences could be devastating. For some weapons, especially nuclear explosives, denial of access is feasible but in the long run not guaranteeable. On the other hand, protection against a terrorist nuclear attack is virtually impossible. American civil defense, unlike that in the Soviet Union, is sparse. Other than for short-term fallout effects, shelters would be of little or no use were a nuclear weapon detonated without warning.

Were a nuclear explosion to occur in an urban environment, 50 percent of the exposed population would die at the 4 psi radius from ground zero. Obviously, with sufficient warning the area could be evacuated. Property destruction would be high but few lives would be lost. Even with short warning time, the 4 psi mean lethal overpressure could be increased to 7 psi (for instance, people might lie down). Fissile materials are well protected. Moreover, the U.S. Department of Energy has formed Nuclear Emergency Search Teams, which employ spectral gamma and neutron particle detectors in order to locate hidden atomic bombs. Were the threat of nuclear extortion to become aggravated, fairly standard nuclear detection equipment could be placed at national borders, thereby becoming an unobtrusive part of the normal customs inspection procedure. Though the equipment could be standardized, and need not be sophisticated, to be effective it would be required at a vast number of buildings, airports, harbors, and other facilities. Thus, even with low unit cost, the total cost could be high.

Chemical, Biological, and Radiological Agents   Highly toxic chemical agents are commercially available. For small, not widely destructive terrorist acts, household cleaning agents could prove lethal. Certainly, the more toxic insecticides, such as parathion or TEPP, although requiring an exterminator's license, are essentially unregulated items. Whereas a mixture of bleach and ammonia could kill a few people and irritate the mucous membranes of a small crowd, TEPP sprayed onto a crowd by a crop duster would annihilate hundreds to thousands. The sad fact is that there appears to be no practical way of controlling toxic chemical agents except for militarily significant stocks of sarin or VX.

Interdiction is also a difficult matter. First, there are vast numbers of highly poisonous chemicals, most of which are commercially available in nearly all countries. Next, the means of detection are highly selective. Using a technique such as Raman spectroscopy, we must generally know what to look for in order to detect the agents. Protection against a chemical attack is primarily dependent upon warning. Were the threat of chemical attack made, and demands imposed on government, it might be possible to thwart the assault. As a practical matter, however, the target would have to be isolated. Certainly, a convention hall, office building, or sports arena is quite vulnerable. Complicating matters further, were a chemical attack intended to discredit government and cause socioeconomic disruption, randomness of target and frequency of attack would be basic terrorist tactics. Generally speaking, chemical detectors could be used to interdict selected chemicals were close-in inspections feasible. Obviously, if chemical detectors were distributed widely, they could give warning during the first minutes of such an attack.

There are many similarities between a terrorist's threat involving bacteriological agents and one involving chemical agents. In a positive vein, there is limited commercial availability of deadly pathogens. Moreover, the growth, care, and dispersion of biological agents require more technological sophistication than does the dispensing of chemicals. If prior intelligence is lacking, denial of access is the apparent defense against a biological attack. Cultures of anthrax and bubonic plague can be obtained through unlawful means; they can also be grown clandestinely. The means of denial must include rigid physical security and clever methods of inventory control, for unlike chemicals which do not "grow," pathogens do. Basic research into the remote sensing and identification of hazardous bacteriological agents would be useful. Aside from the terrorist's threat, such research and development could have other valuable military and medical applications.

Without sufficient warning, the odds are that a bacteriological attack would be successful. Unfortunately, by the time the symptoms appear for some diseases, such as pulmonary anthrax, it is too late. With warning, target vulnerability can be reduced through the use of filtering masks, application of heat, immune serums, vaccines, and antibiotics. To repeat, the key is early sensing and diagnosis.

Radiological agents are controlled; yet radioisotopes such as cobalt 60, iodine 131 and polonium 210 are weakly safeguarded. By comparison, plutonium is extremely well protected. Fortunately, near-field detection of radiological substances is far easier than detection of toxins. Although the term "radioactivity" evokes an often irrational fear, the physical threat is largely limited. If terrorists obtained these materials and we were unable to interdict them, it would be virtually impossible to thwart their attack. The only resort would be mopping up—employing decontamination techniques.

Applications of Technology to Prevention of Terrorism

Sensors   Although, as we noted earlier, there has been considerable development of tools for remote detection of terrorist devices, materials and activities, none of the present or anticipated detection devices has long range. Sensors will be especially useful at focal points of transportation and at barriers such as airport boarding gates and custom inspections.

The category of intrusion sensors spans a wide variety of uses. Among the less sophisticated devices are the widely used door switches, conductive tapes, and photoelectric detectors used for home, store, and factory alarm systems. At the high end of the spectrum are sensors developed for the war in Southeast Asia, sensing vibration, sound, and heat. Experience with these devices has shown that they are very useful for sounding an alarm but must be accompanied by quick investigation and a backup guard force. Furthermore, the alarm system itself is often inadequately protected. Although intrusion sensors can increase the effectiveness of a guard force, they require continual testing for malfunctions and other weaknesses.

Closed-circuit television (CCTV) has become fairly widely used to expand the surveillance area of a guard force. The lowered cost and improved reliability of CCTV systems will probably lead to even wider adoption. But the number of cameras that can be monitored effectively by a single guard is limited.[1] Moreover, cameras can be blinded in various ways, although warning signs will usually be present. One technique, developed for the protection of nuclear reactors against diversion of fissionable material, causes a CCTV to sound an alarm if any motion occurs in selected areas of the picture. Although such a capability increases the cost and complexity of a surveillance system, it can extend the number of cameras a single guard can monitor if the absence of motion in the field of view is the normal condition. The U.S. Customs antiterrorism program includes CCTV as a part of its plan, and some customs facilities already have the system.

There are a great many examples of installations using advanced sensor systems, but the Sinai effort is possibly the best-known application. The United States established and operates in the Sinai an early warning system that is intended to monitor the approaches to the Mitla and Giddi Passes. The system uses advanced types of intrusion sensors (acoustic, seismic, etc.) emplaced in arrays to detect all intrusions. There are also devices designed to monitor the sensor fields; these include day-and-night imaging systems to determine the nature of the intrusion.

The detection devices are generally effective against a number of possible terrorist instruments and, of course, against many types of attack. And sensors, as we noted earlier, are most useful in this task of prevention by making it difficult for potential terrorists to obtain and transport arms, missiles, explosives, and chemical, biological, and radiological agents. This is not exclusively the case with techniques that permit tracing the terrorist instruments after the event. Use of these in the restoration task can improve our diagnosis of the event and help prevent future attacks, particularly if a counterterrorist intelligence system receives the information.

Metal Detectors   Metal detectors, such as those used to screen passengers before boarding airliners, have become fairly familiar. It is not necessary to describe the units and their strengths and weaknesses, except to note that their public acceptance has been encouraging. This may indicate that more comprehensive screening of people and baggage will be accepted if it is shown to be needed. Metal detectors, however, seem to have limited utility for screening checked baggage and cargo because of the large amount of metal present in innocent cargo.

Metal detectors are most useful in locating small arms as

terrorists pass through transportation nodes such as airport loading gates. It is possible that increased use at customs barriers would further interdict international transport of small arms.

X-Ray Machines   X-ray machines are presently used for inspection of airline carry-on baggage. Their increasing use for inspection of checked baggage and cargo is expected, but the interpretation of the X-ray shadowgraphs of large volumes of luggage will be tedious and possibly imperfect. Development and acquisition of contrast enhancement and of attachments for automatic pattern recognition would be potentially worthwhile.

Explosive Tagging and Detection   A number of techniques for automatic detection of the characteristic vapors given off by many explosives are under active development. There is considerable variation among explosive compounds in the amount and detectability of vapors emitted, but some of the most common ones (TNT, dynamite, ANFO, and RDX) emit detectable vapors. The two most useful and promising detection methods are specially trained dogs (which are expensive to train and manage) and electron capture vapor detectors, but neither is yet completely satisfactory. The broad utility of such detectors in preventing a wide range of terrorist threats indicates that their development and procurement should receive priority, as is discussed later.

Another technique for combating the use of explosives is tagging them with distinctive chemicals at the time of manufacture so that the presence of an explosive can be determined easily, either before or after detonation. This should make identification of terrorists easier, but some development is needed, and economic or legal impediments to mandatory tagging need to be overcome.

In view of the frequency with which explosives are used by terrorists, research and development on better detectors, with longer detection range and improved effectiveness against a spectrum of explosives, is imperative.

Tagging Advanced Weapons   The great potential destructiveness of modern, portable, homing antitank and antiaircraft missiles makes them attractive weapons for terrorists. They are readily available as a result of their use in Mideast and Southeast Asian wars. Counterterrorism measures have been directed toward both protecting military stocks and screening baggage and cargo that are to cross national boundaries. The tagging of military stocks to provide stricter control deserves serious analysis. Although there are a number of promising principles, each has some drawbacks. Further research is needed to determine if an acceptable method is possible and, if so, what costs and operational problems might be encountered.

Detection of Chemical Agents   Although many hazardous chemicals are nominally controlled in the United States, it is relatively easy for knowledgeable terrorists to acquire the materials to make highly toxic agents. Since almost any public gathering is a potential target, terrorists cannot always be denied access to their target. Technology may be able to reduce this threat through detectors for trace amounts of hazardous substances. Since it is nearly impossible to remove all traces of some agents from the outside of a sealed container after filling, trace detectors could be useful. A considerable amount of development is still needed because there are many potential chemical agents.

Detection of Biological Agents   For terrorism through biological attack, the situation is very similar to that involving chemical agents, except that detection of the agents either before or after attack seems to be more difficult. In theory, however, there are promising techniques of detection and identification. Considerable research would be needed to bring the state of the art to a practical reality. If this were accomplished for reasons of antiterrorism, medicine would benefit substantially as well.

Detection of Nuclear Agents   The techniques for control and detection of nuclear materials, either bomb materials or radioactive agents, are much better than those for chemical or biological agents. The public anxiety and the potential number of injuries from a nuclear attack make the threat of such an attack appealing to terrorists. Added protective barriers and tightened security at nuclear installations are the major areas for improvement. But improvement may be difficult and expensive because much of the easier work has already been done.

Preventing Access to Potential Targets

The erection of fences and barriers against intruders is a fairly standard practice at installations that are likely targets for terrorist attack. Unfortunately, many of these were designed to be effective against petty thieves or the curious. Defenses against a determined, well-equipped terrorist group must be stronger and much more sophisticated, but any barrier serves a useful purpose by excluding the less determined potential intruders. The use of advanced sensor systems, including closed-circuit television, has already been discussed. The following, more traditional techniques are also effective.

Fences   The chain-link galvanized steel fence, sometimes topped with a few strands of barbed wire, is probably the most common perimeter barrier. When backed up by a guard force it is quite effective against casual and even determined intruders unless they are well equipped. There is always the danger, however, that maintenance will be neglected; holes caused by ground erosion or faulty gates will make access easy. Furthermore, determined intruders using wire cutters, ladders, or even heavy vehicles can penetrate such barriers. Nevertheless, a well-maintained, well-lighted, and well-patrolled chain-link perimeter fence is probably the first priority in defense against saboteurs. When such a perimeter is frequently patrolled or monitored by closed-circuit TV or intrusion sensors, it can be effective against surreptitious attack. A good perimeter fence also prevents intruders from entering a facility to reconnoiter and plan a later attack, and it is an effective screen against contact-fused missiles that can be fired from outside the barrier.

Vision Barriers   Detailed analysis of the vulnerability of important installations indicates that erection of vision barriers can be vital in preventing saboteurs from planning or executing an attack. Obviously, vision barriers are of reduced value if the target installation routinely permits visitors to tour and note vulnerable parts of the facility. For particularly sensitive installations, such policies may need to be reexamined, or limitations may be necessary for tour routes.

Heavy Barriers   A truck loaded with explosives could damage some important heavy structures. Intervening heavy walls, or even piles of sandbags, could delay or perhaps defeat such an attack. As with any protective measures, the choice of methods to use at a particular installation must be made on an individual basis. (The high cost of heavy barriers probably will be an important factor.)

Armored Cars   Since dignitaries are a frequent target for terrorists, mobile protection, such as the use of armored cars, is necessary. While recent progress in armor has made the closed armored car a less vulnerable target for terrorists armed with handguns, the availablity of hand-launched antitank weapons has increased the threat. The development of new types of armor for such cars may help reduce this threat.

Increasing Guard Force Effectiveness   This study of physical impediments to terrorist access to important installations has made it clear, if it was not before, that an alert guard force is needed to back up barriers and intrusion sensors. Determined intruders, in time, can defeat the strongest barrier if they are uninterrupted. Training and constant analysis of potential weakness are needed.

Normally, terrorist attacks occur so rarely and at such widely dispersed locations that guard procedures and training often do not take into account the possibility of intentional destruction by a group of well-equiped, well-prepared terrorists. Since each installation is likely to have its own peculiar weaknesses, the most serious threats can be countered only by examination of each location.

A number of the discussed antiterrorist techniques should improve a guard force's capability to detect and respond to attempts at intrusion. Such responses must be quick and forceful. Each potential target facility requires "plans of action" in case of attack.

When a possible intrusion is detected, the guard force must know:

Who goes to investigate.
Who takes over the investigator's duties.

Who calls where for reinforcements.
What communications are used.
What the backup communications are.
What to do if two intrusions occur at the same time.

Completely satisfactory answers to such problems may be very difficult and expensive for some installations, but the process of thinking them through should facilitate emergency planning and make management aware of weaknesses in security that need correcting.

CONTROL, CONTAINMENT, AND RESTORATION

Preventing the terrorist act is our first priority. Yet despite our efforts at prophylaxis, the terrorists may still attack. In response, therefore, government must *control* its diverse assets; it must limit damage and provide emergency health care to *contain* the incident; and it must *restore* the target.*

The Hostage-Barricade and
Small-Arms Attacks

Imagine the Hanafi siege or the Entebbe and Mogadishu skyjackings, where as many as several hundred people were held captive by terrorists armed with automatic weapons and in some cases explosives. At risk were many lives, nationalistic images, and the political futures of national leaders. Although only a microcosm of violence, these events blew up into disproportionate media spectacles. The first, and possibly the foremost job of government, is to appear to be in *control*. Because terrorism is highly theatrical, the appearance of a self-assured, organized governmental response would be equally as important as "countertheatrics" as it would be for saving lives.

The taking of the Air France airbus gave rise to a theatrical production that met the perceived needs of Palestinian and Ger-

---

*Restoration to normalcy in the case of a nuclear explosion or an anthrax attack may not be realistic. Thus, "restoration," as we use the term, includes abandoning the target area, redistributing population, and having the option to rebuild elsewhere.

man terrorists and gave a platform to the comic villain, Idi Amin. America—indeed, the entire Western world—was both intensely involved and absorbingly entertained. Large governments were helpless; capitulation seemed inevitable. Were the terrorists to have won fully by obtaining the release of prisoners from Israel, France, and Germany, the matter would have ended on an ominous but boring note. A superhero was needed; a romantic rescue force led by an Israeli "John Wayne" was the answer. Israel took a big risk, having had to improvise the countertheatrics hastily; but it had little choice. The terrorists were vanquished, the hostages were saved, and several movies were made. (A similar feat was performed in 1977 by the German border police at Mogadishu.) Now quite a number of countries have developed their own rescue teams. (Even the Egyptians shot it out with Cypriots at Nicosia's airport in 1978.)

Suppose that a Hanafi-like incident were to occur in Los Angeles. Who would be in charge? On the surface, it would be the problem of the local authorities. But, if it were learned that Palestinian terrorists were involved, and if some of the hostages were senior foreign officials, all hell would break loose. Within minutes of learning of the incident, the President of the United States might attempt to take charge. Depending upon his relationships with the governor of California and the mayor of Los Angeles, federal intervention would or would not be smooth. Possibly the chief of police of Los Angeles might be under orders to force the FBI into a secondary role; but equally likely, state and local governments might tell the President that they would cordon off the area, wanting no part of the central problem, and suggesting that the federal goverment "take the heat."

The stage is set for the terrorists holding their hostages, a tense relationship between federal, state, and local officials, and an emerging media event of compelling importance. There are many players, but there is no script. Yet improvisation need not be totally blind.

Control   What are the ingredients of government being in "control"? Having matters in hand, or at least appearing to have them so, implies that a considerable amount of homework has been done. Certainly, "luck" enters into the equation, but so do

well-conceived organizational arrangements, ironed-out jurisdictional questions between local, state, and federal authorities,
and planned uses of technology. At an operational level, the
problem of gaining control is analogous to creating "impedance
matches" between the policy level of government, its field
operations, and the terrorists. The keys to dealing with the
hostage-barricade situation, as well as less-focused small arms
and rocket attacks, include securing radio and telephone communications, isolating the physical foci of terrorist activities,
developing tactical intelligence, and creating an initial plan.

First, consider the hostage-barricade case. Having secure communication denies information about government's tactical operations (the compromise of which could jeopardize its responses
to the incident) to the terrorists as well as to the press and the
public.* Commercial telephones are initially suitable, but direct
lines between the scene of the incident and the appropriate
operations centers need to be established. Obviously, traffic concerning the incident should not be carried on normal police
radio bands. Secure-voice, police, and military radio nets would
be vital.

The area could be isolated in a number of ways, the extent of
isolation being determined at the time of the incident. As a matter
of standard practice, adjacent buildings and streets are usually
evacuated and a police perimeter is established in order to restrict
the terrorists to their present barricade. These precautions having
been taken, command and communications needs become
dominant.

The initial terrorist demands may have been telephoned to the
police or they may have been transmitted by some other means
(for example, a radio station). At the onset, the negotiators would
identify themselves to the terrorists, attempt to determine who
they are and what they represent, try to learn the identity and
condition of each of the hostages, and attempt to get the terrorists
to state their demands fully. The purpose of such an exchange is
to obtain preliminary intelligence, allowing authorities to re-

---

*At the time of the Hanafi incident, reporters were in contact with the terrorists,
interrupting communications with the police and divulging valuable information about
government's tactics to them.

search intelligence files on known terrorists and to devise an initial strategy, employing behavioral science techniques used successfully in hostage negotiations by the FBI and various police organizations.*[2]

An initial physical, behavioral, and intelligence estimate can now be assembled. Yet, basic issues requiring early resolutions remain. These include the question of whether to rescue now or wait and the means of stalling, of gaining further intelligence, and of establishing a barter system with the terrorists (for instance, a hostage or some other concession for some food). The first three or four hours are crucial. If none of the hostages is killed early on, the chances of the incident being resolved without loss of any hostages become quite good.

The second and more general problem is that of "attack by fire." Governments have been confronted with threats and actual incidents of assassinations, explosions, sabotage, and the use of surface-to-air rockets to down commercial aircraft. Gaining control, and thus dealing with such incidents as these, is more difficult than coping with a hostage-barricade episode. The reason is simply that the hostage-barricade situation is highly focused: we know where the terrorists and their hostages are. But when an "attack by fire" is threatened, the location of the terrorist is not known, nor is it clear that we could identify the target either.

At minimum, an operations center must be established. Secure communications and a means for intelligence collection and analysis are also basic. The relevant technologies are the same as those discussed in the hostage-barricade situation, but the allocation of police and military forces may be quite different. This last point follows from the concern that there may be a very large number of likely targets. Were a threat received involving automatic weapons, public and private security services could be alerted; but the number of magnetometers, X-ray units, and explosive detectors needed for effective protection could be overwhelming. If the use of SA-7 rockets were suspected, the

---

*The pioneering, practical research in this field was performed by Dr. Harvey Schlossberg and Capt. Frank Bolz, Jr., both of the New York City Police Department. See pages 393–404 for Captain Bolz's description of hostage-negotiation techniques.

military—at least the National Guard—would have to be called upon. Here, the current state of technology does not appear to be a boon for antiterrorist operations.

Containment   By definition, containment involves taking time-urgent measures to decouple the terrorist act from the derivative, potentially costly, socioeconomic effects from the immediate physical consequences of the act. Obviously, the objective is to limit damage physically and politically.

Small-arms attacks cannot be stopped. At best, we can limit the terrorist's choice of targets by taking increased security measures. These measures, which are preventive, afford leverage to the terrorist. Moreover, he can wait until the cost and inconvenience of security unduly burden government. The high payoff tactics, then, are in seeking to defeat the terrorist psychologically and in getting him involved in a series of communications leading either to his surrender or to a mistake that will aid the authorities in capturing him. The FBI has taken the intellectual and operational leads in developing these methods. If the public were to learn of the terrorist's threat, government would have to make every effort to convince the people that it is in control; but just as one accepts the risks of accident and disease, there are dangers of terrorism to be borne as well.

As is true for the matter of control, the hostage-barricade problem is sufficiently well defined to be amenable to the more apparent containment measures. Following the initial moves to gain control—and assuming it is judged that the chances of a successful rescue operation can be improved with time and deliberate preparation—a number of actions might be taken. These would be designed to improve the government's position versus that of the terrorists, further isolating them and lessening their apparent leverage.

Gaining time has value in itself. For example, fatigue is induced and opportunities are created for gathering relevant intelligence and developing rescue plans. Successful stalling depends on convincing the terrorists that the government is moving with all deliberate speed to consider their demands, but that political and technical problems impede progress. The essential components of stalling are credibility and management of the information flow to the terrorists.

Intelligence can be further developed by getting the terrorists to release one or more of the hostages who, by reason of age or physical condition, may require medical attention. Such persons can be valuable intelligence sources. Other good sources are electronic means, as well as infrared or ambient light night-vision devices. Information concerning a barricaded building's floor plan and utilities can be gained from people familiar with the site, from architectural plans, and by inspecting similar buildings nearby. Vital information concerning the background, motivation, and habits of the terrorists might be gathered from intelligence files and factored into the development of a rescue plan.

If the terrorists start shooting hostages, a hasty assault may be ordered with whatever police resources are available. But in the more likely case that time is available, specially selected, highly trained police assault teams can be marshaled, briefed, and prepared for a forceful rescue operation.

There are ways to control the extent of isolation. In addition to a security cordon, the site can be additionally interdicted by turning off telephone, electricity, gas, and water service. Local jammers can be used to blank out portable radios, thus providing the government with a monopoly on the information flow to the terrorists.

A successful conclusion of the incident may require deception of the terrorists and initial withholding of evidence from the press, both of which carry risk for the government.

Containment efforts may continue to tighten the noose, the vigil taking from several hours to several days or even weeks (for example, the two Dutch incidents in May 1977 involving the take-over of a train and a school were very lengthy). The desired outcome is the terrorists' surrender, resulting from their isola-tion, loss of initiative, and consequent feelings of helplessness. If they do not surrender, and appear unlikely to, at some point the decision must be made to rescue the hostages and terminate the incident.

Restoration   As we have used the term, restoration implies taking actions to conclude a terrorist incident, reinstate routine services, and return to the normal, preattack state. This may not be feasible; yet its attempt would be vital.

If a jumbo jet were downed by SA-7 rockets, the immediate problem would be the same as with any other air crash. The delivery of emergency health care, including triage, would be essential. Obviously, trained professionals ranging from trauma surgeons and orthopedists to a well-trained cadre of paramedics would also be indispensable. Unless terrorist attacks were to become commonplace, no nation would develop an efficient system for health care delivery for terrorism alone. Still, the consequences of terrorist acts include mass casualties. Mechanically induced injuries, such as sucking-chest wounds caused by flying missiles and burns, are common to terrorist-caused explosions, industrial accidents, and natural disasters. If the consequences of terrorism were included in the larger and more reliably occurring list of disasters, an efficient emergency health care delivery system would be clearly justifiable. A common resuscitation model, portable ventilation equipment and surgeries, helicopters, exercised logistical arrangements, and specialized management information with which to match up patients and hospitals are the needed ingredients. (Dr. Martin Silverstein, a leading authority on emergency health care delivery, discusses treating mass casualties on pages 349–392.)

As we can readily see, technology cannot be divorced from the people who would use it or from the unifying concepts embracing its uses. Were the terrorist attack to cause a regional blackout, or to damage telephone switching systems, or to interrupt a fraction of our natural gas supplies, backup systems would be needed. A thorough understanding of the possibilities for rerouting, substitution, and sources of alternate supply would be as important. Obviously, clever uses of technology, other than management information systems and mathematical models of damaged networks, are but small parts of the management problem confronting government.

As we discussed earlier, the job of restoration is far better defined for the physically focused terrorist incident. The hostage-barricade incident is a classic example of a situation in which the use of highly specialized technology could have predictable payoff.

Let's assume that the use of behavioral techniques have not

been successful in a hostage-barricade incident, and that a command decision has been made to conclude the episode by force. Once this decision has been made, a number of options exist. Unfortunately, all of them entail considerable risk. We assume that the terrorists are armed with automatic weapons and possibly with "dead man"-fused explosives. Further complicating matters is the possibility that our intelligence may be faulty. We may not accurately know who the terrorists are (for example, terrorists have been known to force hostages to carry unloaded weapons in order to confuse the authorities). When the non-Jewish hostages were released at Entebbe, they were intensively interrogated about all the physical and behavioral aspects of the siege. (One of the principal concerns of the Israelis before they embarked on the raid was whether or not the terrorists had explosives.)

Storming a barricade involves several tasks. These include surprise, entry, and incapacitation of terrorists. Surprise can be achieved by acting quickly, executing the assault in a very short time. It may be facilitated by terrorist fatigue, environmental conditions within the barricaded area, and the use of technical means to cause disorientation. Entry can be gained in various ways, including conventional explosives, especially if the hostages are shielded. The usual agents available for riot control, such as the tear gases, would not incapacitate quickly enough to prevent retaliation. Unfortunately, the nonlethal, instantly incapacitating gas may not exist. (In any case, we are constrained by a biological factor of about ten seconds, the time needed for one full circulation of the blood.) The above methods have been used in a number of instances, possibly the most dramatic having been the Dutch Government's storming of a hijacked train and schoolhouse in 1977.

A major advantage that can accrue from coaxing the terrorists out of the barricade is the opportunity to employ snipers and thus immensely simplify surprise and penetration. A trained, coordinated, radio-directed sniper team should be able to fire simultaneously from up to two hundred meters and kill an equal or less number of terrorists. Given adequate communications and teamwork, this could be done with less risk to the hostages than any form of barricade assault.

The hostages having been released, and the terrorists dead or captured, the business of cleaning up is apparent and routine. But the perception of the incident and response to it by the press, the public, and by other potential terrorists may be as important, if not more so, than the fact of a successful conclusion. Unfortunately, the most successful techniques and technical applications must receive the least visibility to ensure their usefulness when next called for. Thus, we have limited our discussion to generalities.

Weapons of Mass Destruction

In Chapter 2 we discussed the ease of fabrication and effectiveness of various weapons of mass destruction. Although the definition of "mass destruction" is necessarily vague, an order-of-magnitude increase in violence over the sorts of incidents we have seen to date would be envisioned. The agents are nuclear, chemical, and biological. Stated candidly, if terrorists were able to obtain the weapons, and if we did not have prior intelligence about an intended attack, there would be little or nothing that could be done to prevent it. It cannot be overemphasized that good intelligence is the key.

Control The first thing to realize is that if a threat of mass destruction is taken seriously, or worse yet, if a mass-destruction attack were to occur, America would be in a state of siege. We would face a civil emergency of unprecedented proportions. Concern about martial law, evacuation, logistical arrangements, housing, food, and health care would be dominant. Even people living in unaffected areas would be consumed with fear. The derivative political and social effects could overwhelm America.

With a chemical attack, if the target is not known in advance, the government must be prepared to clean up afterwards. The army would be called upon to decontaminate the terrorist's target and remove thousands of bodies. Obviously, teams equipped with chemical detectors as well as technical means for decontamination would be required. Army technical teams would be brought in to identify the agent, determine the extent of damage, and set forth safe procedures for entering the affected area.

With no warning of an attack whatsoever, there may be severe technical problems in rapidly diagnosing the cause of death. As hideous as it is to contemplate, were a vast number of bodies discovered, it would be of utmost importance to determine the cause of death quickly.

For the biological and radiological agent there are similar problems. Here, however, the near-term effects might not be nearly so dramatic. In the case of biologicals, two or more days may pass before symptoms are noticed; and in the case of the dispersal of radiological agents, months could pass without anyone realizing that a great many people were exposed to dangerous levels of radiation. If the terrorists were to warn us of the attack, or tell us that the attack had occurred, we might be slightly better off. With a nuclear explosion the effects would be obvious; about as much, if not more, of the technical and managerial tools of our civil defense program would be strained beyond credibility.

The contributions of technology to the task of control are limited to the use of specialized detectors, decontamination equipment, and managerial tools as information systems to allocate emergency resources and mathematical models to estimate the extent of damage and the duration of danger. It would also be quite useful to develop technical means to perform rapid diagnosis and to identify specific pathogens.

Containment   Were a weapon of mass destruction used, there are a few technological means for containment that would prove useful. Here, the problem may be divided into two functions: first, to prevent further attacks, and, second, to contain, or limit, the physical effects of the initial attack. If there were no communications between the authorities and the terrorists, the first goal could be achieved only through intelligence and police means. On the other hand, if the terrorists and the authorities were in regular contact, behavioral techniques could prove valuable as well.

To meet the second goal, the public must be informed about decontamination and antiseptic procedures, as well as suitable sheltering. Further, if the attack unleashed a highly contagious disease, such as pneumonic plague, containment would crucially depend on early detection and diagnosis as well as quarantine procedures.

Restoration   As difficult as it was to define the technology needed to deal with the limited hostage-barricade incident, the technology needed for the mass-destruction event is even more elusive. The technologies required for control, containment, and restoration are often the same. Dividing the mass-destruction problem into threat and execution stages, we see that the problem of restoration rests with the latter stage. It entails a massive cleanup, an unprecedented decontamination effort, and the feeding, sheltering, and logistical support of thousands of people. If the event were localized, such as for a chemical attack, the problem might not be overwhelming.

In the case of biologicals, the need for antibiotics, serums, and vaccines would be great, if only for their placebo value. Since sunlight and high temperatures destroy virtually all microorganisms, restoration should be simplified. In the case of anthrax, however, the problem would be far greater. Spores of anthrax can survive for twenty or more years. Prodigious quantities of bleaches would be needed.

Were a radiological agent employed, especially in an urban environment, the decontamination process would be horrendous. Washing it away would do little good, for it would spread it into the sewer systems and the isotopes could ultimately end up in the drinking water. With the long half-life of a substance such as plutonium 239, decontamination of a large office building might be impossible, especially if stringent environment and occupational safety and health standards were maintained. The net result would be the abandonment of major commercial and industrial facilities, or even whole neighborhoods.

Other than the contagious spread of some pathogens, the nuclear explosion poses all of the restoration problems of chemical, biological, and radiological agents. There is no point in elaborating upon the complexities of the task. They would be immense. We refer the reader to the classic Herman Kahn books, *Thinking about the Unthinkable* and *On Thermonuclear War*.[3]

VULNERABILITY ISSUES

However security measures are viewed, the bottom line is the protection of critical industries. It is all too easy to invent the hobgoblin who attacks New York City with an atom bomb, and there is hardly a biological attack that can be thwarted. Yet, for the focused target, such a nuclear power plant or an airliner, government is held especially accountable for its failure at contingency planning.

Vulnerability of an installation is both physical and symbolic. Thus, if a block of EHV transformers were blown up, the symbolism would be great, but the lights would go out as well. By contrast, if a nuclear power plant were attacked by a small band of terrorists bearing nothing more than small arms and explosives, very little physical damage would occur, but the symbolic effects—the hysterical fear of a core meltdown with its insidious cloud of radioactive materials—would cause the severest political ramifications and might force the industry to shut down partially. Thus, it may not be enough to limit the potential for substantial physical damage; we may need to win so overwhelmingly that the perceived damage would be insignificant.

No target can be hardened absolutely. Therefore an analysis of an installation's vulnerability to attack must include a projection of probable threat (its likelihood, mode, and size); the effectiveness of various physical defenses, depicted by the four criteria (prevention, control, containment, and restoration); and the monetary as well as social costs of providing the various defenses. Though hardly a simple matter, sophisticated analyses of vulnerability can be performed.

The downside costs of failure, such as would arise from the disruption of the electrical power system or the shooting down of a jumbo jet, could exceed the costs attributable to the primary losses. One aspect of a usable negotiation theory (or the wisdom of taking governmental actions in response of judgments about threat credibility) is the risk of failure and consequent losses. Analyses of vulnerability should include the expected cost of failure—in other words, the downside costs attributable to governmental initiatives. To borrow examples from other subjects, the economics of building a dam should account for its possible collapse and resulting liabilities. Similarly, Howard, Matheson, and North wrote about probabilistic considerations when deciding to seed a hurricane.[4]

Such risk analyses require the construction of decision trees, setting out alternative actions, governmental responsibilities, possible damage, various probabilistic estimates, and so on. Structuring the event space and the decision tree are useful exercises even when undertaken by themselves, but estimating the conditional probabilities is at best an "iffy" matter. Delphi techniques may be important exploratory tools, providing high and low estimates of the probabilities and thus offering the possibility for limited sensitivity testing.[5] (See pages 244−284.)

If our problems with terrorism increase, the legal and political aspects of governmental responsibilities will become all too evident. In our contingency planning efforts, we therefore should begin to account for the full downside costs of our potential actions. All too often this subject is treated as a painful afterthought.

Attacks on Nuclear Power Reactor Sites

The safety of nuclear power reactors has been discussed and debated widely; so much so, that terrorists might consider a sabotage attempt to be disproportionately attractive to the actual damage that could be inflicted. Part of the potential attractiveness of these sites is the prospect for releasing even small quantities of radioactive materials, thus causing considerable notoriety and possibly unwarranted alarm.

The task of *preventing* attacks on nuclear power reactors requires closing many avenues now open to potential terrorists. General-purpose restrictions on acquisition of explosives and firearms (particularly automatic weapons and antitank missiles) are clearly useful in making attacks on nuclear installations, as well as on other potential targets, more difficult. The detection of explosives is a matter both of availability of funds and of technological capabilities. As with much of the currently feasible support technology, a review of our priorities, given the potential threat, is in order.

Governmental *control* of a threatened attack on nuclear power plants entails enhancement of security at threatened installations and intensified search for the terrorists and their instruments (firearms, explosives, incendiaries). Good counterterrorism intelligence and a good crisis-management system would be most helpful against such threats as well as against threats to a wide variety of other potential targets.

Containment of terrorist action against a nuclear installation has a structural similarity to containment of many other types of attacks. If terrorists were to occupy a nuclear reactor site and threaten its destruction unless their demands (ransom or political concessions, for example) were met, then the situation would be similar to the hostage-barricade situation that occurs frequently. Law enforcement authorities now use some psychological techniques, communications equipment, night-vision devices, body armor, and long-range, accurate weapons for containment of such threats. Considerable technological improvement in these methods is possible and necessary. Because such situations occur so frequently (although not at nuclear sites), development and acquisition of countermeasure technology would be extremely useful.

In the case of attack against a nuclear reactor site, specialized radiation-detecting equipment would also be needed. Such equipment is available for purchase and could be acquired and stocked at regional centers for deployment where needed. Predictive capabilities that would permit law enforcement authorities to estimate where radioactive contamination would go if released are now technologically possible. Such capabilities would also aid in the control phase by limiting necessary measures to the area of hazard.

If the postulated terrorist attack took the form of a "hit-and-run" attempt at destruction, containment of the incident would take a different form. It would become essential to determine the type and extent of damage (based on confirmation of predictions, if available) and then to prevent further damage. In the nuclear case, the potential release of radioactivity is the most unusual feature and the one that may cause the most widespread actual or psychological damage. Technology can help by determining in a convincing way the location and intensity of any radioactivity that might have spread. Instruments for this are available at nuclear power sites and could be obtained from the damaged installation if the terrorists did not destroy or take them.

Restoration of the situation after an attack on a nuclear reactor could entail decontamination measures. In cases where the damaged nuclear power reactor is a major power source for an isolated region, with little capability of receiving of power from other, unaffected sources, alternate, emergency power sources might be deployed to the area.

Attacks on the U.S. Electric Power Grid

Extremely high-voltage transformer substations and certain switching centers, which are critical elements in the power transmission system, are vulnerable to attack because not only are they poorly protected, but they can be damaged by a variety of weapons, and repair or replacement of their tailor-made transformers is a relatively long-term operation. Even the destruction of a small number of key transformer substations or switching centers could cause prolonged power outages over wide areas, significantly affecting individual consumers, essential services, and industry. Although various of protective measures are available and generally would serve to deter vandalism or the less dedicated type of terrorist effort, they would have little or no value against a determined terrorist attack using sophisticated standoff-type weapons. Effective action currently depends on the initiative of private industry. Efforts are now being made to identify areas best suited for remedial action, though primarily for the short term.

Analysis of the four functional tasks in countering such attacks shows that the key substations of the power grid are typical of a number of kinds of terrorist targets: the substations are important, but protected only by exclusion and division barriers with small or nonexistent guard forces.

Prevention of such attacks can be aided by better barriers, intrusion sensors, and guard forces, but the cost of such added protection would be high to cover the large number of installations. Intelligence of terrorist plans and tactics would permit concentration of counterterrorism resources and firearms; missiles and explosive detectors at transportation nodes would be useful against these and similar threats.

Control and *containment* of terrorist threats against the power grid must rely on the same measures and techniques as those for a nuclear reactor attack except, of course, radiological detection equipment is not pertinent.

Restoration after an attack on the power grid would require finding alternate electric power transmission paths until repairs could be made. The amount of power interrupted could be far too large for deployable power sources (gas turbine generators, for example) to give much relief. Such an attack would probably make it necessary to increase protection at other substations, move toward standardization of EHV transformers and switch gear (to speed replacement), and increase the redundancy in the power grid to lessen the reliance on any one substation. Thus, the task of restoration should provide the needed insights and impetus to prevent the next attack on the grid. Alas, this appears to be the fate of all open societies.

Attacks on the Airline Industry

The threat to the airline industry posed by surface-to-air missiles (SAMs) or antitank weapons in the hands of terrorists indicates that airplanes are most vulnerable to such weapons during takeoff. Thus, the area in which a SAM launcher could be located extends far beyond airport boundaries. Complete surveillance and control of such areas is not possible without vast expense. The first line of defense against SAM attack, therefore, seems to be exclusion of such weapons from the United States. Should a credible threat emerge, some airport approach and departure paths could be partially guarded and searched by local police and perhaps other security forces. This defense would, however, be very expensive and intrusive.

A mitigating factor in this bleak picture is that even the high hit probability of a modern heat-seeking SAM (such as the Russian SA-7 that has been used by terrorists) does not guarantee that the aircraft will crash. The pod-mounted engines on many airliners are far enough from structural members so that destruction of an engine need not down the aircraft. A hit on the engine mounted in the vertical stabilizer of some airliners could be quite serious, however, and hits on Boeing 707-type aircraft engines could cause structural wing damage.

The ease, publicity effect, and high chance of producing damage make a SAM attack attractive to terrorists. Careful screening at customs for entry of SAMs and effective security of such weapons in the hands of military forces seem to be our most useful countermeasures.

The threat to aircraft on the ground and to air control installations posed by antitank missiles in the hands of terrorists is also a serious matter. Current airport security measures tend to reduce though not eliminate the threat here, but air control centers and electronic installations are usually remote and not heavily protected. An attack on one of them could easily be successful. Although it would result in considerable damage, hazard to personnel, and publicity, such destruction would not cripple the airline industry, because there would be overlapping control center coverage. Successful attacks on several installations would be more serious and would cause substantial curtailment of operations.

Since antitank missiles are now available in this country, they pose a likely threat. Although careful study of each air control installation is necessary, the provision of perimeter fences at a considerable distance from these installations and the erection of barriers to screen and detonate contact-fused missiles seem to be first-priority countermeasures.

Attacks on the airline industry differ from the previous scenarios mostly because the potential hazard to lives is much greater. Although the number of people near substations in the power grid is likely to be small, many people are typically vulnerable at air control centers, in airplanes, and at airport terminals. This human element most certainly explains the high appeal of such targets for the terrorist. Attacks on the airline industry simply have a greater potential for hostage-barricade situations where people are the hostages. If the threats are carried out, *containment* and *restoration* measures may have to deal with assault and treatment of casualities. The *prevention* and *control* phases involve techniques similar to those recommended in the earlier scenarios discussed except that the frequency with which airplanes have become targets may warrant installation of special antiterrorist measures. An example would be the installation of microphones inside a plane's cabin and jacks on the outside of fuselages to permit law enforcement authorities to hear conversations inside the craft should a terrorist incident occur.

The containment phase of a hostage-barricade incident involving people could be aided by a large variety of listening, seeing, and assault devices. During the course of our research in technology assessment we found a number of possibilities and the programs discussed earlier in this chapter contain recommendations for development of such devices.

Attacks on Public Officials and Foreign Dignitaries

Terrorist groups are willing to go to elaborate measures to execute a successful attack. The military-style kidnapping of Aldo Moro is a case in point. Fortunately, this extensive preparation can make such an operation vulnerable to police, FBI, and Secret Service intelligence efforts.

To penetrate the mystery that presently surrounds terrorist groups requires even greater reliance on techniques such as monitoring what may appear as insignificant but related events: signs of growing radical activity; acts of subversion; accumulations of arms and explosives; and clandestine meetings to discuss militant acts. Such information then requires accurate evaluation and quick dissemination of intelligence received in order to lead to successful deterrence.

The statistics on past assassination attempts indicate that attacks on motorcades are quite frequent and modern automatic weapons seem to be preferred. The growing availability of hand-held antitank weapons is ominous. Restricting the entry and exchange of such weapons is an important near-term measure. Other helpful measures would be the armoring of security vehicles so that security personnel cannot be so easily immobilized or injured in an attack, and more frequent use of military or charter aircraft rather than commercial carriers to effect a better separation between possible terrorists and the targeted individual. In kidnap prevention, a wide range of methods have been put forward in the wake of the Moro affair. The use of unobtrusive armored cars, the varying of routes from home to office, and the general development of a low profile for public officials and foreign dignitaries are being put forth as ways to make the would-be kidnappers' task more difficult. The increasingly common purchase of kidnap insurance by corporations for their executives has given new impetus to the security-management industry and may lead to the further development of counterterrorist measures in the private sector.

Examination of past attacks on public officials indicates that preventive measures such as controlling and detecting firearms at transportation nodes can be useful, but that it is not possible to completely exclude potential attackers from approaching their targets. This is done as much as possible, but having good antiterrorist intelligence has been a most valuable asset in some cases.

Generalizations

The vulnerability matters just discussed show a great deal of similarity in the measures needed to prevent, control, contain, and restore a situation. This similarity occurs because terrorists attempting such attacks usually employ small arms, explosives, incendiaries, or missiles. Interdiction of the supply or transport of such instruments is one of the few means we have to inhibit or prevent these attacks. (Interposition of barriers and having good intelligence of terrorist plans are others.)

An equally important similarity involves the fact that the scenarios discussed above (with the exception of assassination) may well involve hostage-barricade situations. As mentioned earlier, it would be extremely useful to develop as much as possible our ability to handle this type of development, because containment of these situations is likely to involve similar techniques. In addition to developing specialized technology (various types of visual and aural monitoring devices, special long-range weapons, body armor), it might be a particularly good investment to expand our understanding of the psychological and behavioral aspects of these tense confrontations as they affect *all* participants. This is also an important area for game development, in which players would gain insight into the various strategic possibilities on both sides of the barricade.

Counterterrorism technology potentially plays an important role in combating the more technically advanced instruments of terror: chemical, biological, and radiological/nuclear attack. These are more commonly thought of as instruments of mass terrorism because their potential for mass destruction is so great. The specific kinds of counterterrorism technology that are applicable depend strongly on the specific terrorist instruments.

CHAPTER **4**

▬▬▬▬

Fundamental Policy Choices
and Incident Management

Although denial is temporarily a more comfortable state, the first lines of defense may fail: we may not get advance information of an impending terrorist act or the target may not have been sufficiently hardened. If the attack were another skyjacking, it would not be pleasant for government; but the world has become accustomed to such events. On the other hand, were a DC-10 shot down by a surface-to-air rocket, or were terrorists to create their own "Philadelphia fever," government would be under the greatest stress. It appears axiomatic that the tools of incident management should be created ahead of time; government should be organized to deal efficiently with such crises; and the operating and policy levels of government should simulate terrorist incidents in order to obtain some experience at handling them.

At a time of crisis we must expect to face management problems but we must also anticipate that our sovereignty will be assaulted. Fundamental policy choices would present themselves: To what degree and in what ways would we consider meeting the terrorists' demands?

FUNDAMENTAL POLICY CHOICES

On the face of it, governmental policy should prohibit concessions to terrorists. This posture may indeed be appropriate when the lives of a handful of individuals are threatened. However, the policy of "no substantive bargaining with terrorists" would be reevaluated in the event that society was threatened with mass destruction of lives and property. Indeed, should the destruction of a major city be considered a real possibility, the government would have little choice but to consider major concessions, concessions that could potentially undermine its ability to govern.

Preconditions for Bargaining

In the case of "intermediate" terrorism (downing commercial aircraft, sabotage of power or communications facilities, and other nationally disruptive acts), we are not dealing with the kind of threat that could permanently cripple the nation or irreparably rupture the foundation of modern society, but neither are we dealing with the kind of threat that can be dismissed out of hand as unworthy of substantive negotiation. We must therefore attempt to strike the difficult balance between a willingness to make meaningful concessions and an unwillingness to bargain at all.

Although often of nihilistic basis, we must assume that terrorist violence is the product of people with rational (to them) political or financial goals. We are thus led to a fundamental policy question that must be resolved: although we may or may not understand the specific aims of a particular terrorist group, what kind of concessions would we be willing to make in the event of an "intermediate" terrorist threat?

Before attempting to outline a defense, it is essential that we identify the ramifications we fear most. The immediate physical damage is a lesser danger than the impact the incident might have upon our socioeconomic structure. The greatest dangers arise from the persistent secondary effects. For example, should a terrorist group be successful in destroying a jumbo jet at takeoff, the institutional and psychological effects could be far more significant than the actual destruction. In some cases, such as attacks upon electric power or communications networks, the secondary effects upon society could approach those of "mass destruction."

In light of this potential, our preeminent goal is to "decouple" the secondary effects from the primary incident. If both potential terrorists and government become convinced that "intermediate" acts of violence need not have far-reaching societal repercussions, we would be in a far better position to exclude strategic concessions from consideration.* But if government becomes panicky and overreacts to a terrorist incident, what can government expect of the media and the public?

It cannot be too strongly emphasized that strategic capitulation must be excluded from the bargaining table. If it appears that extortionists can command political and financial power by threatening us with serious assault, the impetus for others to attempt similar ventures could become irresistible. Success begets success!

Bargaining with Terrorists†

The least difficult variety of extortion to accede to is that involving a financial demand without any political or institutional implications. This is more or less common in the private sphere. Although we could expect it to reach greater proportions when directed against a government, it would probably not deal a crippling blow to national sovereignty. In such a case, the government might attempt to protract negotiations in an attempt

---

*The distinction between "strategic" and "tactical" is qualitative: a mere tactic to one person may be a matter of strategic importance to another. Here, strategic concessions are those that, if revealed, would undermine either the political or financial stability of the government. By contrast, tactical concessions are intended to limit short-run damage and are not of a magnitude that would enhance the terrorists' leverage. The use of "bait money" to buy time and gain needed intelligence, techniques to wear down the captors during a drawn-out hostage-barricade ordeal, and false promises of safe passage are examples of tactical concessions. Such tactics can be risky and are often inherently deceitful. If they were published after the fact, we might have fewer courses of action to deal with during a subsequent incident. Thus, in an operational context a proposed concession must endure the rigors of heated debate and policy-level decisions to assess whether it is "tactical" or "strategic."

†Our discussion of the tactics of bargaining and substantive concession is not intended to be an endorsement of either; rather, at a time of crisis their consideration would be a matter of political reality. Above all, deterrence should be the objective of all nations because the first publicly known concession may have a pronounced contagious effect. Yet, governments cannot afford to stand as rigid tin soldiers by refusing to concede to unimportant demands. The "game" between terrorists and government is not zero-sum—it is cooperative and rich with mixed strategies. When faced with the credible prospects of mass destruction, every concessionary move is tactical—and potentially strategic. In order of preference, enough time will have been borrowed to locate and disarm the terrorists, we will have succumbed to the extent of endowing the terrorists and becoming each other's hostage, or we will have conceded fully.

to locate the extortionists. If it were unable to do so because of a strict time limit imposed by the extortionists, it might be preferable to pay at least a portion of the demand rather than to test their willingness to carry out the threat. The success of politically motivated terrorists may also attract criminal groups to the lucrative opportunities for extortion.

Threats requiring a change in government policy are a different matter. They are decidedly unconventional because they cannot be levied against an individual or group but only against an official decision-making body of a legitimate government. Accession to such a threat could undermine that government's domestic and international credibility. However, even within the context of political extortion, there is a broad range of possible demands and an equally broad range of possible responses.

For example, a terrorist group may present the target government with a list of required incremental policy shifts, shifts that could plausibly occur over a period within the context of administration policy. In such a case it might be possible to negotiate without overtly undermining national sovereignty. In the long run it might be possible to thwart the extortionists' designs as the government learned about their operations; but in the short run the government might attempt to bargain and be forced to accede—partially or in full.

The target government would face a much more serious problem if the terrorists announced their threat to the public or if the media somehow became aware of it. (The problem of maintaining secrecy about the threat could be exacerbated by a terrorist group demanding a dramatic and immediate shift in policy that could not possibly occur within the context of the Administration's programs.) Once it becomes apparent that a small group can force a legitimate government to alter its domestic or foreign policy, there is evidence that a "bandwagon" effect could be significant. Other fanatic groups might quickly realize that they too could enter the arena of political power by resorting to threats of major consequence. Should the threat become public or should there even be rumors of the threat in the press, widespread panic could result. Because we have never faced this problem, and thus have no experience in coping with it, one can only speculate about the impact that a distraught public might have upon government officials responsible for making crisis decisions. It is quite possible, however, that the pressure to accede (or not to accede) to any or all terrorist demands would be enormous, thus further constraining the target government's options.

Although maintaining secrecy while bargaining would certainly be preferred, some terrorist groups might consider it advantageous to publicize their threat. Publicity would make them more visible and might also cause a panic-stricken population to exert pressure upon the authorities to comply with terrorist demands. This problem could be further complicated if the terrorists imposed a strict time limit upon negotiation. In such a situation, if the authorities were unable to persuade the terrorists to lessen their demands or to convince them that great violence would not further their cause, the target government would have to make the ultimate decision: accede to their demands, either partially or in full, or test their willingness to carry out their threat.

When the target government is dealing with a terrorist group that seeks a permanent stake in the international system—such as the PLO—the chances for cooption (endowing the terrorists with resources they will be forced to protect in bargaining) and confidentiality are reasonably high. Because the group wants to be a part of the system, it would gain little by making it impossible for nations already in the system to accede to their demands. Such groups want to be coopted.

By contrast, nihilists may believe that terror is in their interest. Because nihilists despise the established order and have no desire to become a part of it, the target government may not be able to persuade them to maintain confidentiality. Their tactics alone may preclude the possibility for maintaining secrecy. Consider a scenario in which the terrorists overrun a nuclear weapons storage site and are subsequently surrounded by military forces. Such a case could not be kept confidential; the authorities would have to cope with the threat in public. The major political damage would already have been done once the terrorists were successful in taking over the storage site.

Although the publicity factor might complicate matters in one sense, this scenario presents fewer bargaining and logistical problems than do many others. The threatened area could be evacuated, intelligence operations could be limited because the culprits are surrounded, and the area of potential physical damage is identified in advance. In this classic barricade setting, the authorities might refuse to negotiate at all, finding it preferable to mount a full-scale attack against the terrorists. The biggest concession to these terrorists that could be considered is their initial safe passage out of the area.

In the above cases, bargaining possibilities might be greatly increased if the extortionist demands remained secret and if the group itself had a desire to be coopted. Many times this is clearly impossible. Nevertheless, because secrecy and cooption may represent the target government's best chance to limit damage, they should be considered as bargaining objectives when the use of force cannot succeed.

Let us examine the philosophical premises and tactical procedures for implementing the strategy of cooption.

- The target government must be able to convince the terrorists that, should they insist upon public humiliation, negotiation may be impossible.
- In order to make this strategy operational, the target government must be willing to consider some concessions. Without them it might be impossible to prevent the terrorists from publicizing their threat in order to bring public pressure to bear upon the government.
- By conceding in part, the government must demonstrate that the terrorist gains could be lost in escalating violence. If they obtain assets that a target government can retaliate against, the target government then acquires a hostage. Once the terrorists have a stake in the system, their desire to destroy it may fade away.
- Cooption of terrorists is designed to promote a situation of deterrence, not friendship. (Indeed, if at any time during or after the negotiations it becomes possible for the government to disarm the terrorists, such a course of action would be "fair play.")
- There remains the possibility that terrorists may refuse to negotiate or that they may negotiate only to gain publicity

and intensify the drama. In such an event one must attempt to preempt.

We do not suggest that the cooption of terrorism is a panacea for dealing with a potentially devastating extortion. There is none.

INCIDENT MANAGEMENT AND DAMAGE LIMITATION

The first two lines of defense can fail. Enough advance information may not be obtained to thwart a terrorist attack. Also, if it is worth the cost, any physical security system can be defeated. Thus we come to the last line of defense, the efficient management of the incident, including the "clean-up" phase. All that lies between a full loss of public confidence in government, possible chaos, and government's saving of face is the public's perception that government did all it could. The truth may be irrelevant.

Just how would we respond to an extortion or assault? Our actions to date are mixed. For the small hostage incident we have developed behavioral techniques that seem to work well. A bigger event, such as the LaGuardia bombing, can escalate to open Presidential involvement within hours. In the case of the Croatian skyjacking, our no-concessions policy eroded. At the hijackers' insistence, their propaganda message was published and leaflets were airdropped over London. And in the Hanafi matter, it was hard to tell who were the heroes—the police, the psychiatrists, or the Muslim ambassadors. Somehow, whether by muddling through or by using honed behavioral tools, a massacre was avoided. Over the past five years there have been various nuclear weapons extortions, all of which were handled competently by the FBI and the Department of Energy. Fortunately, the threats were amateurish. The "Philadelphia fever" does not appear to have been a terrorist act; yet it was mysterious, frightening the public and forcing the Bellevue Stratford Hotel, where the disease erupted, out of business.

There are many terrorist objectives and an even greater variety of potential terrorist acts. We shall confine ourselves to a discussion of those situations where timely crisis-management action is possible and productive. Crisis management techniques can be effective when a terrorist's preliminary actions have not obviated the need for further governmental action to limit damage. These techniques can be usefully applied to the hostage-barricade situation; to politically motivated hijackings of aircraft, trains, or ships; to economic or institutional hostages (for instance, seizure of nuclear power stations, sabotage of electric power grids or of elements of the Federal Reserve System); and to threats of mass destruction, including nuclear, chemical, or biological extortions. In these instances the terrorists have not fully engaged their ultimate destructive potential, so government has several options, including bargaining with the terrorists and limiting damage in the event that bargaining attempts are unsuccessful.

The mere existence of a capability to counter a terrorist action or to limit and repair the damage done is worth little if that capability cannot be exercised in a controlled way. Most large nations possess enormous inherent capability. The problem is mobilizing it in face of terrorist attack and, moreover, doing so in a manner consistent with the legal, ethical, and political constraints of the particular society.

Whether the case is a threat, a convincing demonstration followed by a threat, or an outright assault, the upshot will be fear and confusion. What should one do first? How should government respond? Who is in charge? Who are the terrorists? What are the hostages—a few people or a planeload, a major city, or the electric power grid? What sort of weapons do the terrorists have—pistols, submachine guns, explosives, or weapons of mass destruction? Can government meet their demands? Are they thinkable (for example, the payment of money or the release of specified prisoners)? Or are the demands so outrageous that they cannot be met by government (for example, the imposition of a capital levy that would reduce the wealthiest to a level of, say, $100,000)?

The willingness to execute a threat, the assessment of the terrorists' technical competence and resources, and the discerned costs and benefits attributable to both government and terrorists are inextricably interwoven. Government's flexibility is limited by the demands themselves, the toughmindedness of an established policy to deal with terrorists, the personal strength of a chief executive, and the forethought that has gone into organizational and other contingency planning to meet such crises.

The balance of this chapter is devoted to a discussion of assessing threat credibility, organizing government to deal with a terrorist-caused crisis, contingency planning, developing management information systems, applying gaming techniques, and limiting damage should terrorists attack. These topics are components of the management machinery needed to implement the "last line of defense."

Judging the Credibility of a Threat

If threatened with massive violence or national disruption, what actions should we take to minimize the short-term dangers to the "organism"? No study can adequately treat this question, for no amount of forethought can relieve the President of having to make "seat of the pants" judgments if the risk of catastrophe is perceived. Even though predictive models cannot be built, the problem can be bounded. At a minimum the credibility of the threat must be assessed and the penalties for failure understood.

Credibility assessment is a complex matter requiring intelligence as well as behavioral and technical information. If the PLO threatened to use nerve agents unless their demands were met, the credibility question might center on their resolve to execute the threat rather than on an attempt to verify the existence of the nerve agent. By contrast, if less well-catalogued terrorists made comparably difficult demands, interest in analyzing their motivation would not be lost, but concern would center on determining their technical ability to carry out the threat.

Credibility is not a static phenomenon; intelligence and behavioral factors play influential roles as each act of the drama is improvised. In contrast to the conditioning experience of moviegoing, the tragic fact is that the "good guys" do not always win, even in the end. We may have to settle for probabilistic outcomes, uncertain shades of gray.

By itself a credibility assessment may not be useful; rather, the assessment must be linked to a class of possible actions government might take in response to the threat. Moreover, cost is measurable in different ways: there are monetary and political costs, risks to human life because of panic created by a federal action, losses of civil liberties, jurisdictional disputes with state and local governments, and, at the extreme, the destruction of the organism itself, whether through miscalculation of the opponent or by government's own hand.

It is not difficult to imagine the simplest act causing panic—for example, using specialized equipment to search for a hidden nuclear bomb. If the equipment were too obvious, the attempt to locate the "weapon" could cause widespread panic, especially if the search were centered in a major city.

A Crude Taxonomy   The credibility of a threat might be judged by a ranking scheme. At the base of the scale would be obvious hoaxes and crank calls. Ascending the scale would be events involving multiple messages, ongoing communications with the terrorists, and definite evidence of the terrorists' ability to inflict great harm. At the high end of the scale there might be demonstration attacks and finally the execution of the full threat, such as the detonation of a nuclear weapon. Corresponding to each of these events would be a set of actions and their costs. Thus, for example, at the low end of the credibility spectrum there should be little source for jurisdictional disputes with state governments; and at the top of the scale state governments might be only too happy to turn the problem over to the federal government. In this case we may find that government's largest costs occur in the mid-range of the credibility scale. The same may be true of the public affairs issue. By contrast, however, the cost of disaster relief peaks at the high end of the scale. Although the measurements would be highly subjective, it would be useful to set up a taxonomy based on credibility and cost indicators. From this we could derive some crude policy guidelines. (A way of measuring costs and benefits is presented by James P. Bennett and Thomas L. Saaty on pages 244–284.)

Intelligence Collection and Assessment   In order to deal successfully with terrorist extortion, the government must obtain good intelligence, which includes gathering information on trends of terrorism and the more difficult matter of monitoring the day-to-day dynamics. Special attention must be given to assessing the terrorists' technical sophistication.

In the event of a mass-destruction threat the intelligence community would be called upon to perform monumental tasks of supplying background information on the terrorists, locating their weapons, and assessing their capabilities and intentions. Research and development of equipment for detecting nuclear, chemical, and biological agents must be an integral part of our intelligence collection capabilities. Obviously, new and innovative approaches to these problems are essential.

The assembly and dissemination of accurate and timely knowledge of terrorist activities and plans is probably the most useful countermeasure against terrorism. Intelligence may enable us to prevent some attacks. The wide range of vulnerable targets in our open society makes it prohibitively expensive to give adequate protection to all potential targets. Good intelligence permits concentration of expensive defenses on likely targets.

An important aim of good intelligence must be the development of a sophisticated morphology (see Table 1), both for comparison of various terrorist movements and for development of in-depth understanding of individual groups, their historical backgrounds, and particularized aims. Quite simply, it is the kind of knowledge one would want to possess regarding a potential adversary—an assessment of significant variables that locate each group in a range of historical and political contexts. We include this analytical tool here as an indication of the massive task our intelligence agencies must undertake.

Technical Assessment   The technical estimation of threat credibility may be quite difficult. Designs and some details of nuclear devices that, in principle, can be made to work exist in the open literature. Unless there is some obvious flaw in the design that can be readily identified by nuclear weapons experts, it may take considerable time and effort to determine whether a specific design is practical and, if so, whether it would have a yield of a few tons or a few kilotons. Given the fascination of popular writers and the media with this subject, in the years ahead more information about nuclear weapons design will be publicly available. The evaluations of such threats may rely in part on the accountability of nuclear materials to determine whether plutonium or highly enriched uranium has been diverted.

TABLE 1

INTERNATIONAL AND TRANSNATIONAL TERRORISM:
SIGNIFICANT VARIABLES

GROUP CHARACTERISTICS

Name of the organization or, if none, of the political, military, or bureaucratic entity controlling the actors

Country of origin

Relationship to the government of that country

Size and organization

Leadership

Composition (the occupational and educational qualifications of the members and their age range)

Credo/ethos

Elementary Typology*

Particularistic (ethnic, religious, linguistic, or regional)

Nationalistic (irredentist or anticolonial)

Ideological

　　Anarchism

　　Radical left (revolutionary socialists, Trotskyites, Maoists, Guevarists, Castroites, and other ultraleft fringe groups)

　　Orthodox Communism

　　Extreme right

　　Other

Pathological

Domestic base (extent of popular sympathy and support links with legitimate social or political organizations, and links with other domestic dissident groups)

Foreign links (ties with other terrorist organizations, with international or legitimate transnational organizations, and with foreign governments)

Life cycle (date of formation, period or periods of transnational or international activity, and, if applicable, date of demise)

TABLE 1 (Cont.)

EVENT CHARACTERISTICS

Location of incident

Nature of act

Elementary Typology

Kidnapping

Barricade and hostage

Bombing (any type of explosive charge or device, including letter and parcel bombs)

Armed assault or ambush (with or without sophisticated weapons)

Hijacking (aircraft, ship, or other means of transportation)

Incendiary attack or arson

Assassination or murder

Chemical, bacteriological, or radiological pollution

Other

Number, status, and nationalities of human victims

Nature and national association of physical target

Number, nationality, and organizational affiliation of the perpetrators

Nature of demands (publicity, prisoner release, ransom, political action or change, arms, or safe passage)

Targets of demands (governments, corporations, or international organizations)

Outcome (duration of incident, identity and posture of governmental and transnational actors participating in its resolution, extent to which terrorists' demand were satisfied, fate of human victims, fate of terrorists, extent of property damage, and, if applicable, identity of nations granting or facilitating safe haven)

LOCAL ENVIRONMENTAL CHARACTERISTICS

Type, repressiveness, and effectiveness of government (representative democracy, authoritarian, or totalitarian)

Societal traditions and attitudes with respect to authority and violence

Homogeneity of the population

Current levels of popular malaise and internal strife

Current level of socioeconomic development (including per capita GNP; levels of industrialization, urbanization, and literacy; and the proportion of the population with higher education)

TABLE 1 (Cont.)

Recent and current socioeconomic growth rates (as above)

Societal inequities (markedly unequal distribution of income, discriminatory practices, and systematic limits on social and political mobility)

GLOBAL ENVIRONMENTAL CHARACTERISTICS

Technological advance

Sophisticated man-portable weaponry (development, deployment, and international trade in such weapons)

Proliferation of nuclear facilities

Communications advances (developments affecting both media coverage and tactical communications)

Mobility-related developments

Interdependence

New vulnerabilities (those links binding our increasingly interdependent world—e.g., commercial and communications centers, transportation hubs, international power grids and pipelines, supertankers, and jumbo aircraft—that presently, or that may in the future, offer potentially highly disruptive targets for terrorist attack)

Reactive upsurge of nationlism and ethnicity

Modernizing social and economic change

Destabilizing local effects

Large emigre-worker concentrations

Political environment

"Revolutionary" atmosphere highlighted by the challenge to the existing world order raised by the "have not" nations

Controversy over illegal versus justifiable political violence

Shifts in priorities and values and the emergence of a strong sense of "social conscience"

Dispersion and erosion of political authority

Proliferation of nonstate actors and the parallel increase in the number of international and transnational organizations providing moral or material support to national liberation or leftist revolutionary formations

International agreements, treaties, and conventions relating to terrorist acts

TABLE 1 (Cont.)

<hr>

Behavior of states providing direct and indirect support to terrorist groups
Transnational contact and cooperation among terrorist groups
Significant international economic trends and developments
Extracyclical events
Cyclical fluctuations

<hr>

*Major categories are not mutually exclusive.
Source: Milbank, "International and Transnational Terrorism," pp. 35–37.

Unlike special nuclear materials that are maintained under comparatively rigorous inventory control, there are biological and chemical agents that can be manufactured with relatively limited resources. Almost no control mechanisms exist for the commercial purchase and transportation of these agents. If biological or chemical threats were made, the extortionist group could submit a sample of the agent. Threat credibility would then hinge on the evaluation of the terrorists' ability to employ the poison or pathogen, assuming they gave some indication of how it might be dispersed.

If a terrorist makes outlandish claims about the potency of his agents of destruction, it will be necessary to identify with some certainty the destruction potential of such agents. Clearly the actions, risks, and approach to any negotiation will depend on having as clear an understanding as possible of the potential damage that might be inflicted.

Behavioral Assessment After a threat is verified to be authentic, crisis managers will be concerned with formulating steps to meet the emergency. At some point in this process a critical behavioral analysis of the threatening group's motivation, intention, and capability must be made, either intuitively by decision-makers on the spot or with the assistance of specialists.

Although each terrorist and each incident are unique, behavioral techniques may be the only means of prediction. Ideally, predictions become more accurate as more background data become available. From such intelligence, behavioral scientists make initial judgments about the motivations, capabilities, and intentions of terrorists as well as their probable responses to various negotiating tactics.

Although there is no distinct "terrorist personality," researchers have produced profiles of those who commit acts of terror. These include, with overlap, the psychotic, the psychopath, and the political ideologue.

Because behavioral scientists have dealt with these personalities in other contexts, there is a substantial data base that may be applicable to terrorist activities. For instance, federal behavioral experts were able to assemble a large amount of intelligence on the Symbionese Liberation Army. From press reports, and from the taped statements, criminal records, and activities of the SLA, these specialists were able to construct a group profile which, had it been available at the time of their attempted apprehension of these terrorists, might have served to facilitate successful negotiations with them.

As a member of a terrorist-threat management team the behavioral scientist should serve as a consultant to the crisis manager. Any background material on the perpetrators and all relevant information concerning the incident should be made available to the behavioral consultants. From information on the modus operandi of a terrorist group—the type of attack, weapons used, types of demands, amount of planning indicated, and the size, ideology, resources, communications, and training of the group— behavioral scientists may be able to provide guidance concerning the likelihood of success of particular counteractions. Given information about past interactions of a terrorist group with local governments, such as its willingness to negotiate, compromise, allow deadlines to pass, or take violent actions, behavioral consultants could analyze the probability of the success of specific negotiating tactics. For example, behavioral specialists might be able to suggest certain characteristics that should be considered in the selection of persons to serve as negotiators in particular circumstances.

Other areas of interest to behavioral scientists in their effort to formulate successful responses will include the number of terrorists and hostages involved, the capability of the terrorist to engage in prolonged negotiations, the age, sex, nationality or ethnic origins of the terrorists and hostages, and, of course, any information on the past history of the individual perpetrators.

The nature of the perpetrators' demands can also provide behavioral experts information as to their identity, motivation, capabilities, and real intentions. Generally, political terrorists and criminals have limited themselves to immediately satisfiable demands—the release of prisoners or payment of cash, as opposed to policy changes that are more subtle and time-consuming. Most organized groups will be aware of the impossibility of many types of demands, such as the resignation of elected officials, and will realistically limit themselves.

Another mark of serious political terrorists will be whether or not they offer their targets a means of communicating the negotiations. Terrorists with a sincere desire to have their demands met, as opposed to a deranged individual or a publicity-seeking group, may also be motivated to keep the threat unpublicized.

The threat itself may also be a guide to characteristics of the perpetrators. The amount of financial investment, technical skill, special materials, and personnel necessary to successfully mount a given threat may disqualify the credibility of many groups. The threat may be accompanied by various forms of proof such as plausible credit for past incidents, diagrams, or materials that can further characterize the perpetrators. Other clues might be available from explanations of the choice of victims, targets of demands, or the presentation of manifestos to be published.

Although the state of the art may preclude absolute answers to many management problems, local police departments and federal agencies, notably the FBI, have found the behavioral approach very useful. No longer should decision-makers be forced to depend solely on their intuition for important psycho-political assessments of the threatening party.

In conclusion, there is a substantial need for additional research in the behavioral assessment of terrorist threats. The insights obtained from this research could make a significant contribution to an effective crisis-management system, and excellent pioneering research has been done.[1] The inclusion of a properly prepared behavioral adviser to the crisis management team might also bolster the effectiveness of the government response to the terrorist threat of mass destruction.

Organization of Government and Contingency Planning

Typically, authority for dealing with various aspects of a terrorist incident is dispersed over a number of government departments and jurisdictions in a manner that is well suited to handling day-to-day concerns but that may impede efforts to deal with a crisis.* To maintain public confidence that the government is reacting capably, it is important not to resort to unnecessarily alarming emergency measures and to handle things through channels—up to a point. At a certain level of public concern, on the other hand, handling things "through channels" may appear callous or stupid and the public will be more reassured that everything possible is being done if the Chief Executive is visibly involved. This is a very fine line to walk, and fraught with hazards for the Chief Executive who is suddenly thrust into the midst of a developing situation.

To overcome this problem, we suggest that the primary organizational arrangements for dealing with terrorist incidents remain fixed along traditional law enforcement and diplomatic lines, but that a small group at the highest level of government, and having the confidence of the Chief Executive, be given both the responsibility of monitoring emergent crises and the authority to coordinate and expedite government actions when necessary (see Chapter 6). With such an arrangement the Chief Executive should be able to participate in management of a major threat in an informed way, to the degree he desires, and with the amount of public visibility that seems appropriate.

---

*The details of present organizational arrangements are more elaborate than illuminating. They are steeped in statutory and bureaucratic precedent rather than tuned to meet the external threat. In fairness, however, as the terrorism problem becomes increasingly felt, "incremental" improvements are made. Progress is evident in the nuclear extortion and airline hijacking areas. Further, the Federal Preparedness Agency has developed the Federal Response Plan for Peacetime Nuclear Emergencies (FRPPNE). We point out, however, that Canada's crisis coordination center, led by Robin Bourne of their Solicitor General's ministry, is among the world's best-conceived incident-management mechanisms.

Because public alarm is often the terrorist's objective, the perception of the government's reaction by the press and the public can be of utmost importance. Maintaining "business as usual" where possible, and facilitating a smooth transition to high-level coordination and management when necessary, seem the surest means of reassuring the public as well as deserving its confidence.

A straightforward terrorist attack may pose impressive problems for the government's disaster-relief agencies and for those concerned with tracking down and prosecuting the criminals. A major attack might even warrant the sort of high-level coordination described above. A threat of national disruption, however, presents a much more complicated set of problems. As we have discussed earlier, the first of these is the credibility of the threat. This is an extremely delicate matter, especially in the case of chemical, biological, and nuclear threats. Being too easily alarmed can lead the government into hasty, foolish actions that can serve the terrorist's ends with no further need for action on his part. Being too phlegmatic can lead to tragedy if a valid threat is ignored. As we have emphasized, rapid access to the requisite expert advice from appropriate scientists is crucial to making informed judgments of the credibility of exotic threats, but advice from behavioral scientists may also help determine the credibility of particular threats. The high-level monitoring group we suggest could serve to buffer the government from overreaction to negligible or unevaluated threats as well as to expedite response to a threat deemed valid.

The same organizational idea is the model for the national security community; the National Security Council staff serves as the buffer between the President and the major actors. Preparations to manage the effects of a nationally disruptive terrorist act are part of civil emergency preparedness, a program that may exist in name only.

Contingency Planning   The initial steps in organizing to combat terrorism are those of planning and of delineating responsibility. Within the executive-level group we have suggested as desirable, clear lines of responsibility must be drawn and plans developed. But to assure smooth functioning in time of crisis, the organization must be exercised so that it can develop routines. The senior advisers we envision can scarcely be expected to engage frequently in such exercises, but aides familiar with their interests could do so. Moreover, a small staff drawn from the agencies most likely to be involved in terrorist incidents, and serving as liaison with those governmental agencies, should be established. The staff would conduct exercises aimed at developing smoothly working routines. These should involve collaboration with the other levels of government, local officials, and other interested parties to resolve the difficulties posed by sample terrorism scenarios. The emphasis should be placed on finding ways to draw on needed resources and to arrive at decisions in a crisis atmosphere. The objective would not be to prepare for specific crises but to develop modes of operation and an awareness of the available resources, to establish how to get access to those resources, and to understand the logistics involved in using them. By conducting such exercises, it would be possible to experiment with the use of a variety of information networks, computer-assisted searches, and automatic checklists of factors relevant to decisions, and to ascertain the relative utility of various forms of data bases concerning terrorist groups. As the process proceeded, the effective modes of operation should become understood and the requirements necessary for coping successfully with a variety of terrorist groups and incidents should become clearer. The design of such exercises must be worked out in advance with great care in "blackboard exercises" by the staff. They should serve as a useful model of reality without becoming so complicated that they confuse more than instruct.

Although computer-assisted decision aids can be of considerable value, they do not replace the artful crisis-management team. But if we are dealing with giant logistical problems, such as the delivery of emergency services, including health care, or if we are plagued with major resource interruptions, such as communications or electrical power failures, sophisticated computer aids and large management-inventory systems are indispensable. Such systems should be intelligently designed—and thus meet the needs of the crisis manager—or they will grow cancerously.

Gaming is an extension of the "case-method" of research. For the small-scale hostage event we already have a sizable amount of data. Techniques to handle these events are emerging. In fact, there are several successful training programs dealing with the behavioral and tactical aspects of hostage-barricade situations. (The FBI National Academy and the New York City Police Department are prime innovators in this area. See pages 393–404 for a description, by Captain Francis A. Bolz, Jr., of "the New York plan.") But when there are no data, the "cases" must be simulated. Obviously, simulations do not replace live experiences, but it would be difficult to find a sane person who wants to experience the management problems of mass-destruction terrorism. Gaming should prove to be indispensable for training and planning and may turn out to be as valuable during an actual incident.

Simple heuristic models, on-line displays that ask the right questions and set forth a protocol of "dos" and "don'ts" are essential. (An example of the application of heuristic modeling techniques to international terrorism is offered by D. A. Waterman and Brian M. Jenkins on pages 285–330). An on-line listing of pertinent experts must be immediately available. These and other informational aids, such as EMISARI, are crucial tools for the President and the crisis team.*

A considerable amount of effort is required to construct the models, data bases, and management information systems needed for effective crisis management. The path is largely uncharted.

Media Relations   The media are star actors in a terrorism play. The media can emerge as forces for good, limiting the derivative societal repercussions of an attack, or they can incite terror. Media coverage cannot be eliminated, nor would that be desirable in free societies. If the media were not to cover terrorist events, terrorists might commit even more acts—or escalate the level of violence—in order to attract public attention.

---

*There are a number of practical illustrations of using on-line management systems during crisis management situations. Some of the early developments occurred during the ninety-day wage-rent-freeze of 1971. An on-line management information system called EMISARI (Emergency Management Information System and Reference Index) became the matrix for the national and regional managers of the freeze. An extension of the system, called RIMS (Resource Interruption Management System), was used in conjunction with railway strikes and fuel shortages.

When exercises are conducted, it would be worthwhile to ask representatives of the media to participate in them. Otherwise the "games" would suffer from an obvious lack of reality and not serve as teaching or learning devices for government or the press. Any attempt by a democratic government to unilaterally dictate a code of ethics for the media would be a serious mistake. Such a code must emerge from within. Openness and understanding of one another's roles in dealing with incidents of terrorism are essential if the terrorist is not to succeed in turning a relatively small attack into a circus. (For an excellent overview of the problems encountered in media relations, see Yonah Alexander's essay on pages 331–348.)

Constructing the "Game"   Although no one method of gaming is fully defensible, there are certain ground-rules for constructing "games."* Among the more obvious tasks, we must establish a skeletal crisis-management organization, "Red" and "Blue" Teams, as well as a system for refereeing. Further, to make the exercises concrete, representative scenarios must be chosen. Above all, they must appear to be tractable. Thus, a mass-destruction terrorist attack killing hundreds of thousands of people, followed by political demands and a threat to kill millions, is an impossible case. Such scenarios are far enough removed from reality to make the "game" unattractive to potential players.

The objectives of gaming include training, but an inclusive concept of clearly defining the tasks confronting government is the encompassing goal. Ideally, the "game" should be played at the highest levels of government; but this is probably an unrealistic aim. The initial versions of the "game" are likely to be primitive: scenarios will be chosen, messages simulated, and the crisis team will attempt to communicate with the operating elements of government.

Initially, referees should not attempt to give numerical scores. They should instead point out the lessons to be learned, defining the managers' tasks more clearly, noting their failures and, when

---

*Although we do not cite specific references on gaming here, there is a sizable literature on the subject. We include various references to gaming and simulation in the bibliography.

possible, suggesting practical means to solve some problems quickly. For example, if we were to decide to concede partially, and if a great deal of money were required, how could the money be gotten quickly? How should we deal with a recalcitrant state government holding "political" prisoners? When should the leadership of the Congress be consulted? Are government's operations centers adequately "netted," one not operating independently of another but all being under central control? What sorts of experts will we need quickly—technical, behavioral, medical, political, public relations? Etc., etc.

It seems that a requisite for belonging to the crisis management team (here, the "Blue Team") is knowledge of the bureaucracy—and, hence, access to the right people. Moreover, there are some obvious areas of expertise that should be embodied in the crisis management operation: politics, international relations, technology, law, military, public relations, and law enforcement. The crisis management team, which is likely to be headed by the President at a time of crisis, should be regularly led by a ranking official, for it must appear to have clout, it being the liaison between policy and operations.

The "Red Team"—the pseudo-terrorists—need not be as elaborately equipped. In fact, the composition of the "Red Team" should be scenario-dependent. By contrast, the refereeing system should complement the "Blue Team," employing people of diverse backgrounds, including representatives of state and local government, members of Congress, lawyers, scientists, police, foreign policy experts, journalists, and the like. The referees will have the toughest job of all. Unlike judging a sporting event, refereeing here can rely on no simple numerical scoring system to escape from the difficulties of performing penetrating analyses.

The "game" should be run many times in order to discover our weaknesses and strengths—and thus build our national incident-management system. After three or four "games" have been played, sophisticated numerical weighting schemes, such as the one proposed by Bennett and Saaty, might be employed. Fault-tree analyses and other mathematical tools might be used to calculate downside costs, and so on. Once we reach this point, we will have arrived at a sophisticated stage.

There is a "chicken and egg" problem. Is the "game" to be played first and the crisis management team to be developed afterwards? Or is the crisis management team to be formed and the team subsequently tasked to construct and play "games"? Although the organizational ideal of a crisis management team that does gaming may be appealing, the two concepts are interwoven. So we must resort to an iterative procedure, guessing initially at the composition of the crisis management team and the rules of the game. After three or four iterations, the crisis management team and the "games" it plays should be clearly distinguishable.

What is the bottom line for gaming? The crisis management team is in the business of coordinating government operations, buffering the President and the senior-most officials from moment-to-moment operational problems. Should a major terrorist incident occur, confusion must not reign. Thus, as far as possible, government's emergency response should occur in a preplanned context. The end products of gaming are sets of options to meet the more obvious sorts of scenarios, the crisis managers' full knowledge of government's emergency capabilities, and the ability to rapidly transform agencies (performing their normal functions) into emergency configuration. Once obtained, skills must be exercised and information put to use; otherwise the investment in gaming would grow stale.

Structuring the Event at a Time of Crisis   The problems of uncertainty are exacerbated by the dynamic nature of many crises. Thus, with limited information and resources the manager may find it difficult just to keep up with rapid developments, let alone improve the overall picture of the situation.

During a crisis, not only does a manager suffer from poor information, but he has the problem of identifying his objectives and then allotting them priority in accord with his limited resources. He has relatively little time to analyze available alternatives (his own or those of an adversary) or to develop new capabilities. (If domestic and international tensions are to be mitigated with greater success, the important role of the "crisis avoider" must be recognized.)

The main objective of crisis management is to convince an opponent that the immediate and long-run costs of opting for, continuing, or increasing hostilities exceed the immediate costs of accepting an offer to resolve conflict that minimally promises face-saving opportunities to the leaderships. Negotiations with an adversary rest, at bottom, on conveying to him the costs of opposition as dictated by his own value system. (In many cases these may be opportunity costs, that is, costs attributable to lost or deferred opportunities.) Moreover, for our position to be credible to an opponent he must perceive that the costs we propose to meet in gaining our objectives are acceptable to us within our value system.

A number of difficulties are common to the management of crises: uncertainty, poor data-handling methods, too few data, too many data, inadequate communications, differing value systems, changing management objectives, political harassment, little planning, and insufficient time in which to learn. Added to these conceptual difficulties are the psychological and physical problems of confusion and fatigue. Clearly, the successful crisis manager must be a versatile person—a resource allocator, a communicator, and an artful negotiator with a tough hide.

Although contemporary methods of systems analysis have been used in attempts to organize data and clarify options, they have generally been of little use in presenting an accurate picture of an opponent's values and perceptions. Even though he may benefit from available data and analytical models for allocating constrained resources, the crisis manager has few given measures of utility. He is forced to make highly subjective judgments. He must compare "apples and bananas." But there are no firmly established "pricing" rules; nor is there a free marketplace from which to infer the "prices." So we need to develop hybrid weighting schemes, such as delphi methods, which are useful for gaming and incident management. The inputs to a weighting scheme are subjective and its structural form is artificially linear. Nevertheless, the essence of "price" formulation is fiat or feedback. This can be accomplished in the context of an automated delphi technique, such as the EMISARI system mentioned earlier. Bennett and Saaty (see pages 244–284) have developed a plausible weighting scheme that has the ability to depict negotiating options at a time of crisis.

Damage Limitation

In the event that the government's bargaining strategy is not completely successful, measures must be taken to limit the potential physical, institutional, and psychological damage that the terrorists can inflict.

The havoc wrought by terrorists closely resembles the effects of natural calamities and accidents. We have seen industrial accidents spread deadly chemicals in a fashion any terrorist might well envy. (In 1976 such an accident, releasing a highly toxic industrial agent known as TCDD, devastated the Italian town of Séveso.) Earthquakes can outdo any bombing terrorists might threaten—even with thermonuclear weapons. But what terrorists can do is to increase the frequency with which we must endure such catastrophes, thereby making preparation against them more urgent. Moreover, terrorists hold out the threat of repeatedly induced catastrophes that accident and nature do not.

Resources developed to limit the effects of terrorist-inspired disasters and to restore the damage can be used to deal with industrial accidents, floods, earthquakes, and storms. If logistical and emergency health care delivery were developed to meet the large-scale terrorist attack, much more could be done to alleviate human suffering in the event of industrial accidents or natural disasters. Therefore, preparations needed to cope with terrorist damage need not stand out like a "sore thumb." They can be included in the emergency preparedness efforts of all governments.

During a terrorist crisis, one of a government's foremost responsibilities is to maintain public confidence in its ability to cope with all contingencies. As long as a government can convince its citizens that it has the ability to govern despite whatever concessions are made or physical damage is inflicted, the terrorists will be denied a major objective and government's leadership will remain unshaken.

In order to limit damage, government should mobilize its resources to accomplish the functional tasks of control, containment, and restoration. Unfortunately, damage-limiting actions cannot always be easily put into effect. But because maintaining public confidence in the government is of supreme importance, appearance may often be more important than reality.

Controlling an Ongoing Terrorist Act and Containing the Damage   For purposes of this discussion we distinguish two types of terrorist actions, the *hostage-type* action and the *surprise attack*. The essential difference is that the hostage-type action allows time for the government to "bargain" and devise tactics for controlling the outcome, whereas in the surprise attack, little can be done to control the situation, and damage limitation and restoration become the primary concerns.

The hostage-barricade situation is an extremely fruitful area for the application of technology. The problems include getting information from behind the barrier, penetrating the barrier physically, and incapacitating the terrorists while limiting damage to the hostage. All of these are fairly well-posed technical problems subject to solution by physical and behavioral science techniques.

As an incident develops and the nature of the threat becomes manifest, highly specific and sophisticated technology may be applicable to control the outcome or contain the damage done. It may prove well worthwhile to develop highly specialized technical resources to deal with certain types of likely terrorist incidents. In an emergency rapid access to a wide variety of experts and equipment rather than ubiquity is the crucial factor determining usefulness of such resources. The technical means of organizing such availability by various prearrangements and by the use of management information systems is an important technological aspect of combating terrorism. If, for example, a terrorist *does* threaten to use an exotic toxin, it then becomes important to be able to deal with it if the threat is carried out.

As previously noted, damage done by terrorists has everything in common with industrial accidents and natural disasters except frequency and intent, so only a strengthening of the systems required for such calamities and a shortening of the time required for the systems to operate appear to be indicated.

Medical Rescue as an Antiterrorist Measure* The public does not yet hold governments fully responsible for rescue after natural disasters, but demand is growing. Governmental responsibilities are being assessed and rescue operations dissected, although the resulting mortality is still regarded as inevitable and as an "act of God." No such leniency, however, is guaranteed the "decision-maker" during and after a terrorist attack if efforts to save lives are inadequate or bungled. It is insufficient merely to remove the injured to overloaded municipal hospitals. The public may expect special efforts on behalf of the health of victims of enemy action.

The myths of overwhelming weaponry and hopelessness of large disasters can be disproved by the research data of modern medicine. A superior system of medical rescue can be devised to produce a higher salvage rate than is presently obtained.

Although it would be conceivable to justify a national emergency system purely as a counterterrorism measure, no such justification is necessary. The citizens of each nation have a right to protection of life and limbs, whether the etiological agent be a terrorist, an industrial accident, or a natural disaster. Technology has grown too complicated, populations too congested, and the incidents of regional medical emergencies too frequent to place sole reliance on the local community or the neighborly volunteer approach. Disaster planning for large events has been largely unsuccessful because it has been partitioned from the successful emergency medical systems that operate daily. The personnel disappear and become untrained, and rehearsals tend to be unrealistic. Perhaps the necessity of counterterrorism will bolster the need for national emergency medical systems.

The topic of emergency health care delivery is not strange to government. It is receiving considerable attention, but possibly not enough. It is a complicated matter involving logistical and other management problems, resource allocation, communications, training programs for paramedical personnel, stockpiling of equipment and drugs, and clinical research and evaluation objectives. Considerable technological development is needed to make a national system truly efficient.

---

*As indicated earlier, Dr. Martin Silverstein discusses this subject on pages 349–392.

The Military Option   No discussion of the management of transnational terrorist incidents would be complete without exploring a military solution. It is clear that if negotiations fail, nations must be prepared to use military force. Yet few countries have an adequately trained or equipped paramilitary force that could deal with a fast-breaking crisis.

We think that a time will come when a well-conceived, highly trained, and versatile international paramilitary force is available to all. The risks of tactical failure should be spread equitably among many nations. If acts of international terrorism are to be faced squarely, they must be viewed as international peacekeeping problems, not merely domestic law-enforcement challenges. Individual nations should not be expected to bear the military and political burdens alone.

The military option, whether internationally implemented or not, must be an "on-the-shelf" ability. Lack of effective international cooperation means that the major powers will have to have some operational military force capable of mounting the sort of rapid and effective response exhibited by Israel at Entebbe and by West Germany at Mogadishu. Improvisation with hastily assembled military units will only aggravate and confuse matters. We comment further on this topic in the next chapter.

CHAPTER 5

International Considerations

Contemporary terrorism claims for itself a global battleground. The transnational character of so many terrorist events reflects a fundamental element of the problem: that is, the terrorists' exploitation of legal traditions that emphasize the sovereignty of the nation-state. Terrorists do not define their field of action in terms of national boundaries; yet up to now, those same boundaries have provided terrorists with an effective means of escape or with safe havens.

Terrorists have even succeeded in bringing nations to the point of hostilities short of war by creating situations in which the sovereignty of two states is in conflict. In the incident at Entebbe, the host nation, Uganda, decided to provide sanctuary and to support and defend the terrorist hijackers of the Air France plane. Israel felt compelled to take action and did so successfully, though in violation of Uganda's sovereignty and by means that could have been construed as an act of war. In the Mogadishu incident the host countries, Somalia and Southern Yemen, did not know how to deal with a terrorist event that they in no way wished to support. Fearing involvement, Southern Yemen decided to return to the terrorists the German pilot who had managed to escape. He was executed and Southern Yemen found itself implicated in his death. Only the West German rescue operation prevented further loss of life. Again this would have been a violation of national sovereignty had Somalian resistance been encountered. The Israeli invasion of Lebanon in 1978 may well have represented a counteroffensive directed against Palestinian terrorists—but at the same time it destabilized the Lebanese government and added new tension to the precarious balance in the Middle East. The tragic farce in Cyprus, where Cypriot forces clashed with Egyptian commandos over who would deal with the Palestinian murderers of a prominent Egyptian, throws into comic relief the potential for disaster ensuing from this sort of jurisdictional debacle.

Despite the bravado performances of the Israelis at Entebbe and West Germans at Mogadishu, such operations are not guaranteed to work. Additionally, they run the risk of violating basic understandings regarding the fundamental right and responsibility of a state to deal with criminal activities within its borders. Transnational terrorists operate in full knowledge that the international community lacks a comprehensive framework for dealing with them. The worst they may encounter are haphazard efforts undertaken in a context of international confusion and conflict. Furthermore, they know that one of the cherished principles of national sovereignty is the right of a state to grant asylum to those whose crimes in another state are deemed "political" in nature.

We are consequently faced with the dilemma that any long-term planning to counter transnational terrorism must necessarily take one beyond the nation-state to the formulation of a transnational response, while at the same time, the crisis management operations that we have witnessed so far reinforce the primacy of the nation-state. The failure of the international community to manage terrorism has to be seen in the larger context of the community's limited ability with respect to what Stanley Hoffman has described as "the global and regional management of force in a world of multiple arms races, in which violence across borders is the last resort not only of states but of frustrated groups and individuals, in which weapons of mass destruction may become cheaper to produce and easier to deliver, in which the resort to force can still often appear as a rational means toward political ends, in which the build-up of force may, even more often, be an end in itself."[1] In fact, the efforts in this century to formulate an international framework for the prevention and punishment of transnational terrorism do indeed parallel international efforts to control larger-scale conflicts and have been hindered by many of the same problems.

Background

The first international efforts to deal with the problem occurred in the League of Nations, primarily as a response to the assassination of Yugoslavian King Alexander I. Alexander was murdered in Marseilles in 1934 by two Yugoslavian nationals who were then harbored by Hungary. The League of Nations approach was two-pronged: in November 1937 two conventions were presented to the League for consideration, one for the Prevention and Punishment of Terrorism, the other for the Creation of an International Criminal Court. The Prevention and Punishment proposal was aimed at international incidents involving heads of state and other internationally protected persons. According to the convention, such crimes could not be deemed political. On the basis of the second convention, member states that captured those accused of such offenses would have the option of committing the accused to the International Criminal Court for trial. The first convention was signed by twenty-four nations but ratified by only one (India); the second convention received not a single ratification. Nevertheless, the League of Nations effort has served as a model for subsequent comprehensive plans.

In 1954 the International Law Commission of the United Nations submitted to the General Assembly a draft Code of Offenses Against the Peace and Security of Mankind, while another UN agency drafted a plan for an International Criminal Court. The draft code included a paragraph on terrorism, describing as an offense against mankind "the undertaking or encouragement by the authorities of a state of terrorist activities in another state, or the toleration by the authorities of a state of organized activities calculated to carry out terrorist acts in another state."[2] The draft code has never been voted on, however, owing to the failure of the UN to formulate a legal definition of aggression—a problem as slippery as defining terrorism. Two postponements of consideration of the draft code, in 1957 and again in 1968, suggest that it may never be acted upon.

Existing and Proposed Agreements

In the years since the draft code was conceived, terrorism has of course become an increasingly serious problem. The international response, in the UN and elsewhere, has been erratic, characterized by disparate efforts, many of them unsuccessful either in adoption or in practice.

Existing agreements include three conventions on hijacking. The Tokyo Convention of 1963, formally entitled the Convention on Offenses and Certain Other Acts Committed on Board Aircraft (entered into force December 4, 1969), gives jurisdiction over in-flight crimes to the commander of the aircraft, who may take necessary action to restrain hijackers, and establishes a system whereby the commander may land in any contracting state and turn the hijacker over to that state. The convention gives the state receiving the hijacker the option of returning him to his state of origin or to the state of registration of the aircraft.

The Hague Convention of 1970, formally the 1970 Convention for the Suppression of Unlawful Seizure on Aircraft (entered into force October 14, 1971), has as its principal purpose a system for ensuring the prosecution or extradition of aircraft hijackers. It applies to any unlawful seizure.

The Montreal Convention, formally the 1971 Convention for the Suppression of Unlawful Acts Against the Safety of Civil Aviation (entered into force January 26, 1973), concerns aircraft sabotage. It requires the extradition or submission to prosecution of persons who commit acts of sabotage or otherwise destroy aircraft or who endanger the safe flight of an aircraft by damaging it or by destroying or damaging air navigational facilities. It also covers acts of violence against persons on board aircraft, as well as bomb hoaxes that endanger the safe flight of aircraft.

A proposed convention submitted to the International Civil Aviation Organization (ICAO) by the United States and several other nations failed to be adopted by the Rome ICAO conference in 1973. The sanctions envisaged by the proposed convention included suspension of aviation rights under the Chicago Convention (1944 Convention on International Civil Aviation), the International Air Services Transit Agreement, bilateral air services agreement, or any other relevant agreements. The possible sanctions also included suspension of all international air navigation to and from the violating state. The Soviet Union and France insisted that international sanctions could not be imposed except by the UN Security Council acting under Article VII of the

UN Charter. However, there have been numerous instances of state collective actions, including sanctions, outside the framework of the United Nations.

The Organization of American States (OAS) Convention, formally the 1971 Convention to Prevent and Punish the Acts of Terrorism Taking the Form of Crimes Against Persons and Related Extortion That Are of International Significance (entered into force October 16, 1973; the United States became a party to the treaty on October 26, 1976) commits the contracting states to prevent and punish acts of terrorism, especially kidnapping, murder, and other assaults against the life or physical integrity of those persons to whom the state owes a special duty of protection under international law. The convention is the OAS precursor of the United Nations effort to develop effective legal deterrents to crimes against diplomats and other foreign officials. Once again, extradition or submission for prosecution is the basic obligation of each contracting state.

On December 14, 1973, the United Nations General Assembly approved the United Nations Convention on the Prevention and Punishment of Crimes Against Internationally Protected Persons, including Diplomatic Agents.* The convention obligates each party state to establish as a crime under its internal law the international commission of any of the following:

> Murder, kidnapping, or other attacks upon the person or liberty of an international protected person.
>
> A violent attack upon the official premises, the private accommodations or the means of transport of an internationally protected person likely to endanger his person or liberty.
>
> A threat to commit any such attack.
>
> An attempt to commit any such attack.
>
> An act constituting participation as an accomplice in any such attack.
>
> Extradition or submission of the case for prosecution is the enforcement technique.

---

*The United States is a party to this convention. Implementation of domestic legislation was also enacted. PL 94-467, an "Act for the Prevention and Punishment of Crimes Against Internationally Protected Persons," was signed into law on October 8, 1976.

In September 1972 the United States proposed to the UN General Assembly the adoption of a convention on "exported" general terrorism. Developed after the massacre of eleven Israeli athletes in Munich, the United States draft Convention for the Prevention and Punishment of Certain Acts of International Terrorism was intended to extend the principle of the Hague and Montreal Conventions to a broader range of crimes. It represented a skillful effort to proscribe international terrorist activities while avoiding the stickier issue of violence in the context of a colonial or civil war—that is, an internal context involving the right of peoples to self-determination. As one legal scholar has described it, the draft convention's main achievement was its success in "localizing internal conflict situations by providing international measures for the punishment of those zealous revolutionaries who seek to dramatize their cause by acts of terrorism in foreign countries."[3] This is achieved in Article 1:

1. Any person who unlawfully kills, causes serious bodily harm or kidnaps another person, attempts to commit any such act or participates as an accomplice of a person who commits or attempts to commit any such act, commits an offence of international significance if the act
   (a) Is committed or takes effect outside the territory of a State of which the alleged offender is a national; and
   (b) Is committed or takes effect
      (i) Outside the territory of the State against which the act is directed, or
      (ii) Within the territory of the State against which the act is directed and the alleged offender knows or has reason to know that a person against whom the act is directed is not a national of that State; and
   (c) Is committed neither by nor against a member of the armed forces of a State in the course of military hostilities; and
   (d) Is intended to damage the interests of or obtain concessions from a State or an international organization.

The American draft convention was formulated as an international legal response to the terrorists' claim to a global battlefield. The UN reaction illuminates the current difficulty in achieving such a response effectively. Rather than voting on the American proposal (which by all estimations would have been defeated), the General Assembly created a thirty-five-member Ad Hoc Committee on Terrorism. Almost immediately, fourteen non-aligned states within the committee (Algeria, Congo, Guinea, India, Mauritania, Nigeria, People's Democratic Republic of Yemen, Syria, Tanzania, Tunisia, Yemen Arab Republic, Yugoslavia, Zaire, and Zambia) drafted a counterproposal that defined terrorism as "acts of violence and other repressive acts by colonial, racist, and alien regimes against peoples struggling for their liberation." The counterproposal further asserted that "when people engage in violent action against colonialist, racist, and alien regimes . . . the international community, when it has recognized the validity of these objectives, cannot take repressive measures against any action which it ought, on the contrary, to encourage, support, and defend."[4] Not surprisingly, the Ad Hoc Committee eventually reported that it had been unable to arrive at a consensus on any proposals.

The General Assembly majority was opposed to the U.S. draft convention, primarily on grounds of interference with rights of self-determination. The U.S. initiative was thus effectively stifled at the United Nations and is now unlikely to be revived there or in any other international forum.

The 1972 Convention on Prohibition of the Development, Production, and Stockpiling of Bacteriological (Biological) and Toxic Weapons and on Their Destruction (entered into force March 26, 1975) is not directed at the problem of terrorism as such, but it is relevant to the issues analyzed in this book. The convention obligates the parties not to develop, produce, stockpile, or acquire biological agents or toxins "of types and in quantities that have no justification for prophylactic, protective, or other peaceful uses," nor weapons and means of delivery. All such material was to be destroyed within nine months of the convention's entry into force.

One of the relatively encouraging international developments occurred on February 15, 1973, when Cuba and the United States signed a Memorandum of Understanding for the return of boats and aircraft and the prompt extradition of certain categories of terrorist (including hijackers). The agreement developed out of a situation in which American aircraft hijackers regularly sought asylum in Cuba, while anti-Castro Cubans were similarly commandeering air and water craft to the U.S. coast. The agreement demonstrated that a radical socialist state with a commitment to international revolution could view certain types of terrorism as detrimental to its own best interests. (Cuba was well aware that most of the hijackers were not "revolutionaries"—just plain criminals or loonies.) The 1973 memorandum is no longer formally in force, but its provisions may continue to be observed. Although the agreement was definitely a step forward, if only because it slowed the influx of sanctuary seekers to a trickle, it does raise the question of whether we must experience a major escalation of terrorist activity directed against a large number of target states of various ideologies before effective international legal steps can be taken. In other words, how far must international terrorism go before the majority of nations recognize that it is in their own interest to oppose it?

The member nations of the Council of Europe have entered into a treaty that would deny political asylum to terrorists. Signers would agree not to consider as political acts crimes in which a bomb, grenade, rocket, automatic weapon, or letter bomb was used. For the purpose of extradition, airplane hijackings, kidnappings, assassination attempts, and bombings would not be regarded as political crimes. Furthermore, the Federal Republic of Germany intends to seek UN General Assembly approval of an international convention to prosecute takers of hostages, in most cases airplane hijackers.

On July 17, 1978, in Bonn, the leaders of the United States, West Germany, France, Britain, Japan, Canada, and Italy signed a joint statement pledging to act together to escalate the fight against international terrorism by suspending air traffic to and from countries that fail to extradite hijackers and return hijacked aircraft promptly. The text of this most recent antiterrorist agreement is as follows:

> The heads of state and government, concerned over terrorism and hostage-taking, declare that their governments will intensify their common undertaking to fight international terrorism.
>
> In cases where a country refuses extradition or prosecution of those who have hijacked an aircraft and/or do not return such aircraft,

the heads of state and government are jointly resolved that their governments should take immediate action to cease all flights to that country.

At the same time, their governments will initiate action to halt all incoming flights from that country or from any country by the air-lines of the country concerned.

The agreement was an unexpected result of a summit convened to address economic problems. Terrorism had not been on the agenda, nor had it been covered in any of the preparatory meetings prior to the summit. The decision to issue the statement came following a spontaneous suggestion by Japanese Prime Minister Takeo Fukuda, which was then developed by Canadian Prime Minister Pierre Trudeau. The apparent haste with which the statement was drawn up may explain its vagueness concerning the length of time that would be allowed for extradition and/or aircraft return prior to the enactment of sanctions, and the process by which sanctions would be enacted. The statement also fails to define standards to be used for determining what would constitute acceptable prosecution in lieu of extradition.

These formal arrangements are an important reflection of the seriousness with which some countries see the terrorist threat. It is urgent that more countries share this perception, and accede to and ratify the multilateral conventions outlined above. Important as they are, however, they are at best a beginning. More is needed in several areas.

The Failure to Create An International Framework: An Analysis

At the sixty-seventh annual meeting of the American Society of International Law, Professor John Dugard discussed what he felt an ideal United Nations treaty to combat terrorism should do. According to Dugard, such a treaty would:

1. reaffirm that all States have the duty in all circumstances to refrain from encouraging guerrilla activities in another State;
2. prohibit acts of terrorism which disturb the international order and clearly identify the international element which brings the act within the jurisdiction of international law;

3. oblige States to extradite or punish offenders under the Convention;
4. reaffirm the international community's abhorrence of State-controlled terrorism as expressed in the Nuremberg principles, the Genocide Convention, and the human rights provisions of the U.N. Charter.[5]

As Dugard noted, the principles of this "ideal" treaty, with the exception of Section 4, were actually embodied in the U.S. draft Convention on the Prevention and Punishment of Certain Acts of International Terrorism. This is particularly disturbing, of course, given the utter failure of the draft convention to gain acceptance in the UN General Assembly. A number of legal scholars have speculated on the implications of the draft convention's failure with respect to the development of an international framework for controlling terrorism, notably Professor Dugard, John Norton Moore (former counselor on international law in the Office of the Legal Adviser of the U.S. State Department), and Professor Jordan J. Paust.[6] All three agree that the draft convention represented the best plan yet devised for controlling terrorism without proscribing those types of armed struggles legitimized by the UN Charter-guaranteed right to self-determination. Professor Dugard has suggested that there are two main obstacles to achieving a consensus in the United Nations on a convention of this type: first, the ambiguous status of wars of national liberation, with which the nonaligned majority in the General Assembly tend to identify, which they will generally tolerate, and which many terrorist movements aspire to create; and second, the fact that most states do not wish to lose their right to grant asylum to those who commit what they view as essentially political offenses. Traditionally, political criminals have not been viewed as threats to the life or property of citizens of other states and have thus generally been granted asylum. But Dugard asserts that when an individual takes action which "threatens the stability of other States or undermines the international order, he ceases to be a political offender and becomes a criminal under international law, like the pirate or hijacker."[7] Dugard cites the Meuniers case, in which an English court allowed the extradition of an anarchist on the ground that "he was not an opponent of one government but of all governments."[8]

John Norton Moore has suggested that the slow response of the international community to developing cooperative measures, despite the horrors of Munich and other massacres, can be traced to three myths pervasive not only in the nonaligned majority but in Western nations as well. The first is that "to oppose the actions of terrorists is to oppose the self-determination of peoples."[9] This, Moore argues, poses a "false congruence between self-determination and terrorism."[10] In fact, the UN Charter does not grant the right to unlimited actions to achieve the objective of self-determination, and the General Assembly has never condoned attacks against civilian populations nor against those uninvolved in a conflict. Additionally, the 1949 Geneva Convention forbids the taking of hostages when they are in no way actively involved in the hostilities.

The second myth is that antiterrorist measures are actually disguised forms of repression directed against a particular movement or cause, such as the Palestinians'. But as the activities of Croatian terrorists or anti-Castro Cuban refugee extremists make clear, terrorism may cut across ideological as well as national boundaries. Moore rightly notes that terrorism is a threat to all established governments.

The third myth, according to Moore, is that dealing with the causes of terrorism has primacy over measures taken to control terrorist activities. This myth underlies the report of the UN Ad Hoc Committee, which preferred to rant over the various "repressive and colonialist" forces in the world rather than to take positive action on the draft convention for control of terrorist crimes.

Jordan Paust has argued that the failure of the draft convention to gain UN acceptance was due at least in part to a confusion among the nonaligned concerning what it attempted to control as well as what it did not seek to control. Paust suggests that it is necessary to make clear that the draft convention's prohibitions on international terrorist strategies "do not proscribe activities compatible with the UN Charter, such as permissible revolution, self-determination, anti-colonial struggles, and quests for independence or other macro-political purposes."[11]

Paust makes the fascinating argument that when a state supports a terrorist or insurrection movement in another state, it actually violates the right to self-determination of that other state. A prohibition on the strategies of terrorism is in fact in congruence with the principles of self-determination and the fundamental freedoms of individuals because "terrorism as a strategy to coerce others through violence offends not only the free choice of the whole people, but also the freedom and dignity of the individual."[12]

The failure of the United Nations to take action on the development of an international legal framework reflects a basic lack of consensus on the arguments discussed above. The prospects of action being taken by the United Nations in the future are not encouraging, and perhaps point to the need for more regional agreements, along lines of those discussed earlier in this chapter. The United States should sponsor new multilateral treaties to limit terrorist activities and foster multilateral agreements for cooperative management of transnational incidents while continuing to press for UN action. The concept of an International Criminal Court should be seriously considered at the same time that extradition agreements are formulated and enforced. Paust has articulated two basic points on which a consensus is essential for international cooperation of any kind: first, the "need for legal restraints on violent coercion"; and, second, the "unacceptability of 'just' excuses per se."[13]

The rationalizations of terrorism, as in the myths described by Moore, overlook the fundamental threat to civilization embodied in terrorist crime. The tolerance of the rhetoric that seeks to justify coercive violence to some degree indicates a loss of confidence in the humanistic values of our civilization, which seek to preserve the lives and freedoms both of individuals and of peoples at large. The international community cannot afford to lose sight of its commitment to those values. As UN Secretary General Kurt Waldheim has stated:

At all times in history, mankind has recognized the unavoidable necessity of repressing some forms of violence which threaten the very existence of man himself. There are some means of using force, as in every form of human conflict, which must not be used, even when the use of force is legally and morally justified, and regardless of the status of the perpetrator.[14]

Potential Areas of International Cooperation

In a global legal system predicated on the primacy of the nation-state, one major obstacle to the creation of international agreements on counterterrorism is likely to involve the issue of sanctions, particularly as they relate to sovereignty. Third-party responsibilities for damage, arrangements governing search and seizure, and the general problem of indentification are all areas about which current international law has little to say.

Clearly, sanctions are best approached cautiously, issue by issue. Even with the more familiar forms of terrorism, such as the seizure of aircraft, sanctions are hard to articulate, let alone impose. Possibilities are limited. For instance, let's say armed terrorists descending from a national flag carrier were clearly not properly inspected before boarding. The question of responsibility then needs to be divided between airport authorities and the carrier. The obvious potential sanctions are nonuse of the airport facilities by other carriers and denial of landing rights for the responsible carrier at other airports. Either move, however, has high costs for all countries affected. There is yet insufficient international concern about terrorism to inspire acceptance of this sort of reduced commerce. Nevertheless, it is possible to discourage tourist travel to those countries with unsafe airports and to reduce the number of passengers on their flag carriers. This can be done by apprising travelers that particular airports or airlines are unsafe.

Another approach would involve international (that is, ICAO) ad hoc inspection. In many airports, notably at Rome and Athens, technically reliable systems are in place, and airport personnel have been trained in their use. Yet the will to use systems efficiently and to apply procedures rigorously seems lacking. International ad hoc inspection with the implicit sanction of adverse publicity could improve this situation.

For the time being, it seems reasonable to suggest that programs which avoid the more difficult issues arising from the fact of national sovereignty are most likely to be enacted. What seems required initially are limited approaches designed to bring at least the same degree of common understanding to the international side of the terrorist problem. We need to bring about an international climate of common threat perception. Only in such an atmosphere will a web of comprehensive, formal international undertakings to inhibit terrorist activity develop.

As one might expect, nations should build on existing channels of communication, the establishment of relations among embassies, foreign offices, interior ministries, and intelligence agencies. The pipelines are there and can be used effectively. As within the United States government, the problem abroad is to achieve interest in terrorism, inspire coordinated planning and research, and ultimately induce reallocation of human and budgetary resources.

There are a number of areas of potential international agreement regarding deterrence measures. Mutual efforts involving shared resources (personnel, information, technology) represent a logical development for an international community committed to combating the global problem of terrorism. We currently appear to be at the stage where difficult, fundamental truths about necessary policy measures are only just emerging.

Specialized Rescue Teams

The Entebbe raid was counterterrorism theater at its best. Perhaps the greatest significance of this event was its graphic public demonstration that direct sanctions are possible, and that sanctuaries are vulnerable. The Entebbe experience suggests opportunities for common contingency planning and coordination and cooperative exercises by states that fear terrorist attacks on their own soil or against their citizens and property abroad.

The United States currently maintains special military forces with counterterrorist capabilities. At the center of this counterterrorist program are uniquely trained units, with 252 men each, drawn from nine U.S. Army Special Forces battalions: five battalions at Fort Bragg, North Carolina, two at Fort Devens, Massachusetts, one in the Canal Zone, and one in West Germany. Trained for preemptive action, these units are capable of carrying out all hostage rescue operations along the lines of the raid on Entebbe. Additionally, selected armed forces units are prepared to participate in counterterrorist operations, though not as a primary responsibility. These units include two U.S. Army Ranger battalions, geared for support of special counterterrorism units, nineteen platoons (14 men each) of Navy Seals, one company (180 men) of Marine Reconnaissance Forces, an 1,800-man Marine amphibious unit, Marine battalion landing teams (1,200 men), and Air Force Special Operations Forces and military airlift command units.[15] All of these additional forces are geared for overseas operations, and would not conceivably be called into action except in the most serious international crises. None could be deployed in a domestic terrorist crisis without an explicit Presidential waiver of the Posse Comitatus Act (18 U.S.C. 1385), which prohibits use of the Army or Air Force for law enforcement within the United States except when expressly authorized by some other provision of the law (such as 18 U.S.C. 351, relating to attacks on federal officials).

One nonmilitary team that could be activated for a domestic crisis is the Nuclear Emergency Search Team (NEST) in the Department of Energy, operating independently of the military. NEST conducted the search for nuclear material following the Soviet missile crash in northern Canada in 1977.

The United States is not now engaged in training the forces of other nations in counterterrorist operations. This could easily be achieved through existing international military programs. Further work needs to be done on advanced contingency planning with selected countries. This might involve United States or international use of landing and other support facilities, as well as coordination of international crises. We may also want to consider the use of selective demonstration exercises in overseas support facilities by two or more countries as a potential deterrent.

At least twelve other nations maintain special commando units trained for counterterrorist operations. Undoubtedly, the two most famous of these units are the Israeli Saiyeret and the West German GSG-9. The Israeli Saiyeret executed the Entebbe raid in July 1976. Prior to this sensational event, the Saiyeret foiled the hijacking of a Belgian Sabena airliner at Israel's Ben-Gurion International Airport in May 1972 by posing as mechanics and bursting into the plane.

The GSG-9 is widely considered to be the best existing anti-terrorist team. Created by the West German government after the Munich Olympic slayings, the Grenzschutzgruppe-9 (Border

Protection Group 9) is composed entirely of a select group of volunteers, all with above-average IQ's and all trained to master a variety of skills, including karate, scuba diving, knife fighting, and use of a wide range of weapons. The German team utilizes the most recent equipment and is highly mobile. It is divided into five-man units and each is assigned two high-performance Porsche automobiles. The units operate in the field with three men in one car and two in the other. The two-man car is specially outfitted for communication equipment and support weapons that can be used to deal with a terrorist confrontation. These units are backed up with helicopter support and fixed-wing aircraft. The team is headed by Colonel Ulrich Wegener, who, in preparation for this command, trained for almost a month at the FBI Training Center at Quantico, Virginia, and for about another month at Israeli paratroop schools.[16] Wegener went on to lead the highly successful raid on the Lufthansa airliner in Mogadishu.

The ten other countries that have counterterrorist commando units are Britain, France, Switzerland, Belgium, Denmark, Italy, the Netherlands, Norway, Austria, and Indonesia. The British Crown Colony of Hong Kong also has such a unit.[17]

Nearly all the teams are of recent vintage. The British team is perhaps the oldest. It has served as a model for various countries, among which are undoubtedly Israel, Germany, and the United States. The British unit is drawn from the Special Air Services Regiment (SAS). The SAS was formed during World War II for offensive operations involving deep penetration, first in the western desert and subsequently in Europe.[18]

France has several commando units trained to deal with hijackings as well as prison riots and the protection of public officials. Best known are the French Foreign Ministry's antiterrorist brigade and the Gigene (from the French for National Gendarmerie Action Group) of the Defense Ministry. These teams have seen action more than sixty times both inside and outside France. One well-known instance involved a 1976 operation in Djibouti, then in French territory. The commandos rescued children of French military personnel held by four terrorists from neighboring Somalia.[19]

The Dutch have two antiterrorist units. One is drawn from the

Dutch marine corps and is trained for hand-to-hand combat with terrorists. The other consists of sharpshooters from the army, navy, and military police. They provide cover fire for the marine commando operations, as in the June 1977 storming of the hijacked train and schoolhouse where South Moluccan terrorists held some fifty hostages for twenty days.[20]

The Swiss are in the process of forming a commando unit to carry out operations as in Mogadishu and Entebbe. They also have approximately 2,700 "sky marshals," specially trained security officers who accompany the nation's commercial airline flights. The sky marshals also ride on Egyptian commercial flights.[21]

The Belgians have a special commando unit named Brigade Diane, after the Roman goddess of the hunt. The group is drawn from selected state police volunteers. Similarly, the Italians have a special fifty-man "Squadro Anti-Commando."

The existence of these various teams points to the tremendous potential for international cooperation in counterterrorist operations. The limited cooperation that has already occurred clearly needs to be extended to programs of joint training as well as to counterterrorist operational contingencies that are multinational.

Increasing International Cooperation

It is reasonable to suggest that the Moro and Schleyer kidnappings have moved the Europeans in this direction. Since Moro's abduction and slaying, a counterterrorist network of police and intelligence services has been developing. At a secret meeting in April 1978, the nine Common Market countries and Austria and Switzerland agreed to pool resources to combat terrorism on the Continent. The French have been involved since September 1978. According to Austrian Interior Minister Erwin Lanc, this network is designed to provide a "direct and fast exchange of information, coordinate strategy, install personal contact among our police forces, harmonize police equipment and radio wavelengths, set up a computerized Europe-wide data bank in many fields such as car markings, license plates, hot money, and movements across frontiers, share our acquired knowledge and experience."[22]

With respect to the terrorist arsenal, perhaps the greatest area of international concern involves the possibility that terrorists will someday acquire weapons-grade fissile material through piracy of the commercial traffic in fissile materials. Some international measures have already been undertaken. The United States and many other nations are signatories to the 1969 Non-Proliferation Treaty. A Suppliers Conference has been meeting in London for quite some time to set security standards. The International Atomic Energy Agency (IAEA) in Vienna is an organization of more than 130 nations established to regulate the flow of nuclear materials. The U.S. Nuclear Regulatory Commission (NRC) has established stringent requirements concerning the security and transport of fissile materials. The U.S. internal standards for control of these materials are very high. In other countries, however, despite international standards established by IAEA and the Suppliers Conference, we can be less certain of the security of plutonium 239 and uranium 235. Prospective suppliers of nuclear fuels, plants, and components clearly need to specifically recognize the terrorist threat in implementing their export licensing programs. Stringent international plant security and transport standards, paralleling NRC guidelines, could be required by supplier states.

Another major area for international cooperation involves conventional arms transfers. Arms sales conditions set by supplier states could include use of certification procedures to ensure that weapons are not subsequently sold to terrorists. Under such procedures potential violators would face the threat of a cutoff of future supplies if they diverted arms to third parties in violation of nontransfer agreements. Admittedly, enforcement of such agreements would not be easy, particularly given the big-business character of arms sales. A somewhat more promising area involves control of conventional explosives through a comprehensive tagging program.

During the last few years, the Bureau of Alcohol, Tobacco and Firearms in the U.S. Treasury Department has taken the lead in the development of explosive taggants.[23] Put simply, taggants provide a means whereby concealed explosives would activate a detector. A successful program of detection would prevent the introduction of explosives into a given area for illegal use. Work is also being done on development of taggants for identification, that is, after the explosion has occurred. While important for event analysis and tracing of ownership, tagging for identification would not substantially deter the criminal use of explosives. Tagging for detection is a simpler process (if only because the taggant need not remain intact following detonation), and we are currently very close to realizing a program of this kind.

Tagging requires the addition of some chemical material to the explosives that would activate a detection system, signaling the presence of the tagged explosive. Most of the work so far has concentrated on developing vapor taggants, which are simple and can be detected by inexpensive instruments. Detection systems would be built into doorways, into the circulating systems of buildings or aircraft, or in portable units for the search of an area.

Explosives would be tagged at manufacture. Blasting cap-sensitive explosives (dynamites, water gels, and slurries), explosive powders, semigelatinous materials (plastic explosives), and military explosives could all be effectively tagged. Blasting agents, which account for 80 percent of the three billion pounds of explosive materials detonated each year, are not susceptible to tagging because they result from the mixture of components, generally an oxidizer and a fuel oil, which are not in themselves explosive and therefore not government-regulated.

Current emphasis is on development of vapor taggants for cap-sensitive explosives—which account for 20 percent of all crime-related explosions and for a disproportionately high percentage of resulting damage (69 percent of all deaths, 68 percent of all injuries, and 79 percent of all property damage)—and for plastic explosives, which are commonly employed by terrorists in letter bombs. The Bureau of Alcohol, Tobacco and Firearms expects to have a trial program in operation within the next few years in conjunction with the National Pilots Association.

But the critical factor in a truly successful taggant program (which conceivably could drastically reduce the incidence of crime-related explosions) is that it must be international in scope. If it is not, a detection program could be easily circumvented by terrorists using nontagged explosives of foreign origin. Additionally, an international tagging program can be effective only if detection systems are employed consistently on a worldwide basis. Although explosives industry and law enforcement experts look forward to a day when advanced technology makes detection of all explosive materials possible without the use of taggants, chemical vapor tagging is currently feasible at a reasonable cost. It is clearly an area where comprehensive multilateral agreements could yield a tremendous payoff to signatories. Because it is essentially nonpolitical and seeks to control a form of criminal activity universally perceived as heinous, it may be an ideal area for United Nations action.

Another concern involves the development of conventions protecting oil rigs and other structures in international waters. The issues of the vulnerability of offshore oil rigs is quite substantial. Over the next decade in the Gulf of Mexico there will be thousands of oil rigs, all of them quite prone to assault by terrorist groups. The same is true of oil rigs in the North Sea.

Conventions relating to the protection of oil rigs and other facilities in international waters need to be considered in light of the third Law of the Sea Conference (1975), which adopted verbatim Article 15 of the 1958 Geneva Convention on High Seas. This article condemns illegal violent acts on or under the seas but fails to specify exactly what constitutes an illegal action. Additionally, Article 15 states that any act of violence undertaken in the cause of independence or liberation cannot be considered piracy. As noted above in relation to the UN Charter, this type of qualifier can well be exploited by any terrorist organization. The third Law of the Sea Conference thus created a mile-wide loophole for terrorist activity in international waters.[24]

The areas of potential international agreement discussed above by no means exhaust the possibilities. They do suggest approaches that are currently feasible and, particularly in the case of nuclear fuels, urgently needed. We have tried in this chapter to indicate the tremendous constraints that operate in the field of international law and that have heretofore prevented the development of comprehensive international programs to combat terrorism. At the same time, we hope we have indicated those areas where agreement and cooperative action are possible.

Perhaps the greatest stumbling block to all such efforts is the absence of what we have described as an international climate of common threat perception. Until the international community recognizes the serious nature of the threat posed by terrorism, there is a severe limit on what kind of cooperative action can be achieved. Because contemporary terrorists do not define their field of action in terms of national boundaries, the problem is global and cannot be fully met if those same boundaries provide terrorists with an effective means of escape or with safe harbor.

CHAPTER 6

Restructuring Federal Emergency Preparedness

We have considered numerous aspects of the terrorism problem: its historical roots, the activity of the past decade that we have termed "contemporary terrorism," the implications for nationally disruptive acts, the technological aspects of threat and counter-measure, the principles of deterrence, the requisites for incident management and damage limitation, and the progress of nations in banding together to combat this very significant threat.

In this chapter we focus on U.S. emergency preparedness, emphasizing two related aspects: one, management of an emergency incident; and two, management of the consequences of such an incident. The federal premise is that incident manage-mand and consequences management, as they relate to terror-ism, are divisible, that they can be conducted separately but con-currently, with consequences management receiving relatively less emphasis and being assigned to an agency below the level of the Executive Office of the President. Were terrorism to remain qualitatively the same, there is little question that this distinction would be reasonable. We have become proficient at dealing with today's events, their consequences lying below the perceived threshold for national pain. On the other hand, if nationally dis-ruptive acts of terrorism—even mass-destruction terrorism—were to beset America, we believe that this dispersion of author-ity would prove cumbersome. In this chapter we explain why, in regard to acts of national disruption, the artificial distinction between incident and consequences management could create serious problems.

We consider, first, America's vulnerability to terrorism. We then comment on President Carter's decision to form the new Federal Emergency Management Agency, which, among other responsibilities, would be concerned with the coordination of federal efforts to mitigate the consequences of terrorist acts. We then capsulize the history of U.S. organizations created to deal with emergency preparedness generally (that is, incidents and consequences) and point out why, in comparison with some earlier developments, the present structure, which is yet to be tested, may not be adequate to deal with higher-order acts of terrorism. Finally, we examine the management challenges that lie ahead. Our comments, while at times critical, are offered in a constructive spirit. During the past few years a good deal of progress has been made. But we may not have come far enough.

America Is Not Immune

Transnational terrorism is a phenomenon of the 1970s that has come to be widely perceived as a serious threat to democratic societies. The strong interaction between once loosely connected terrorist organizations further highlights the vulnerabilities of advanced industrialized nations. Sponsorship and support of terrorist activities by Libya, Algeria, Iraq, and the East European bloc of nations are well documented. What is not clear is these nations' degree of involvement in encouraging terrorist activities.

The Middle East situation is a case in point. The paramount objective of Palestinian terrorists has been expressed in many public statements: namely, the establishment of a Palestinian homeland. Fortunately, the United States has not been used as a shooting gallery for publicizing this struggle, perhaps because our government has been perceived as less than totally committed either in opposing or in supporting the establishment of a Palestinian state. But America has not escaped entirely; it has paid a human and economic price for the Middle East conflict. Although OPEC's cutoff of oil exports in 1973 was the most vivid act, it should be remembered that Sirhan Sirhan wrote in his notebook that it was "necessary" to murder Robert Kennedy by June 5, 1968, the first anniversary of the 1967 Six-Day War in which the Israelis captured Sirhan's birthplace, East Jerusalem. In the same notebook a newspaper clipping was found that characterized Kennedy as hawkishly pro Israel, further evidence that the New York senator was the victim of an assassin motivated by concern over his lost homeland.[1] This tragedy was only one incident in a ten-year wave of Palestinian terror.

As President Carter becomes more involved in mediating a Middle East settlement, one must certainly question whether the center stage for terrorist activities will continue to be the Mediterranean and whether the United States will continue to enjoy its relative immunity. Ambassador Heyward Isham, former director of the State Department's Office for Combatting Terrorism, assessed the situation in July 1978:

> The US government is seen by radical Palestinian organizations as a pivotal political actor in the Mideast. We are aligned, to be sure, with Israel, their primary enemy. We are, as well, supportive of the moderate Arab regimes, particularly Egypt and Jordan, whose peace initiatives threaten the solidarity and viability of the Rejectionist Front. We have been fortunately spared Palestinian terrorist operations within the US to date. As the likelihood of some accord in the Mideast becomes greater, and as the US is increasingly perceived as having vital interest in such initiatives, this country will become an irresistible target of forces bent on sabotaging any accord. It is, frankly, only a matter of time, given the current alignment of forces.[2]

A high degree of uncertainty is ever present. Anyone writing a book on current public policy issues runs the risk of being overtaken by events. Alas, there is no "crystal ball." But the determination of individual countries to combat terrorism and the extent of international cooperation can substantially influence the magnitude of the threat. So it is important to analyze American policy initiatives that are already in being and to try to evaluate their potential effectiveness. Does the United States have a program of incident management and emergency preparedness sufficient to meet tomorrow's terror? Can we be certain that the problem will not migrate here?

AMERICA'S INCIDENT MANAGEMENT MACHINERY

In 1977, an extensive review of U.S. policy and procedures for dealing with the terrorist threat took place under the sponsorship of the National Security Council (NSC) and resulted in policy guidelines.[3] It was determined that within the NSC its Special Coordinating Committee (SCC) would function as the primary liaison between the council and the government's planning and operating elements responsible for countering acts of terrorism.

Although it would be virtually impossible to keep the President from assuming the central position in a major terrorist situation—witness President Ford in the 1975 LaGuardia bombing issuing a public statement and directing his federal agencies to conduct an extensive review of airport security—the establishment of a well-conceived structure to manage a crisis is of primary importance. America's incident management system is based on delegation of authority. Responsibility for managing international incidents has been given to the State Department, while the Justice Department is to take the lead on internal matters.

Ambassador Anthony Quainton, director of the State Department's Office for Combatting Terrorism, in congressional testimony during September 1978 discussed the organizational aspects of managing a terrorist incident:

> With respect to the handling of the US Government's involvement in a terrorist incident in progress, the SCC, chaired by the President's National Security Advisor, has been charged with assisting the President in the management of such crises. Its membership includes the statutory members of the NSC and other senior officials, as appropriate. In practice, the SCC would probably directly exercise this responsibility only in the event of a major terrorist incident requiring highest level decisions. In general, the US Government's response to terrorist incidents is based on the lead agency concept: the State Department has operational responsibility for international incidents; the Department of Justice and FBI handle domestic incidents coming under Federal jurisdiction. They work closely with state and local law enforcement authorities where there is overlapping jurisdiction. Aircraft hijacking is a special case—the Congress has mandated by law that the Federal Aviation

Administration shall have primary responsibility in this field. Each of these agencies can and does draw upon the support of other Federal agencies with relevant expertise. Where interagency policy issues arise during the course of an incident, senior officials of concerned agencies can meet, under NSC Staff leadership, to resolve them.[4]

The federal government's contingency planning and incident management mechanisms are derived from the NSC's Special Coordination Committee. Contingency planning and coordination issues are handled by a working group on terrorism and its executive committee, which are chaired by the State Department, with a Justice Department official serving as the vice chairman for both. The Executive Committee has representation from the Departments of State, Defense, Justice, Treasury, and Transportation, and from the Joint Chiefs of Staff, the CIA, and the NSC staff. The Working Group, which is laden with interested but not directly involved agencies, serves as the focus for information sharing. The Working Group has been divided into various functional subgroups dealing with policy and planning issues (research and development, security policy contingency planning and crisis management, public relations, and international initiatives).

It is important to emphasize that the Working Group and its Executive Committee perform coordinative and planning functions only. As we noted earlier, the management of the terrorist incident is based on a lead agency concept: the international incident is the province of the Department of State, and the responsibility for managing a domestic incident rests with the Justice Department. The Special Coordinating Committee is the binding matrix linking the operating agencies with the President.

Were an international incident to occur that involved citizens, property, or interests of the United States, the State Department would assume responsibility for its management. Although the lead-agency concept that preordains the State Department's central role may be straightforward, a lot can go wrong. For relatively simple incidents—the sorts of events we have seen to date—the concept is viable, but a strict adherence to bureaucratic etiquette may not suffice if the terrorists prove to be unobliging.

It is impossible for a lead entity to deal effectively with serious acts of terror without having done its homework. To become prepared, it would be of great value to simulate a broad range of possible situations in order to focus legal and other research and to test contingency plans were an actual confrontation to occur. As the terrorist threat continues to evolve, the legal constraints within which the .government must operate need an ongoing review. In some instances, new legislation will be required. After new legal authorities are established, a method must be devised to test them through the simulated dynamics of a variety of realistic scenarios. In an actual terrorist situation, legal guidance beyond existing authority may often be required.

The members of an effective crisis management team must be carefully selected and authorized to deal completely with a myriad of complex problems. Since crises always seem to occur at the least convenient times, steps must be taken to guarantee that trained people are always available.

A carefully planned, adequately equipped, and fully operational command post is a central requirement. The State Department and the other major actors in the international security community have established command posts that are continuously operational. These command posts must answer the need for adequate communication and information, but this can be gleaned from live or simulated experiences. Communications needs extend from secure telephone networks to radio and microwave equipment and to satellite relays, thus ensuring necessary linkages between central control and the most remote areas of the world. But just as vital is the fullest "netting" among command posts. They must act in symphony. If one were to act out of step from the others, great tragedy might result. Unfortunately, we have had several bitter lessons.

Good information is the key to realistic assessment of an ongoing terrorist incident. Having considerable data about the area within which the event is unfolding would be important. As a related matter, it would be necessary to make an assessment of the terrorists' weapons and equipment and to obtain pschological profiles of the terrorists. The technologically sophisticated incident could present government with especially difficult problems. Good intelligence could thus play a determining role.

Under certain circumstances, there would be legal restrictions on the sharing of intelligence information.

Another requisite is flexibility. We must not inflict grievous self-injury by denying ourselves basic tools. All of the above-cited factors governing an ongoing incident must be integrated. We repeat an earlier message: it would be useful to simulate events so that people can work together under conditions that closely approximate those of an actual event. Gaming and other such exercises are needed to maintain a workable lead-agency concept.

During the past three years, federal authorities have considered these factors of incident management. Embassies throughout the world are aware of their potential involvement in a terrorist situation. The special task forces set up by the State Department in actual terrorist situations have involved other departments and agencies. Thus, policy formulation and contingency planning are being given serious attention.

A basic structure for incident management is in place. Simulations are being contemplated, military exercises have been conducted. The special U.S. military forces discussed in Chapter 5 (pp. 153—154) could function as an effective operational arm. (These units should be capable of dealing with a broad range of terrorist situations in which force or containment is required.) Although vexing questions about the adequacy of the decision-making structure remain unanswered, a degree of responsible progress is evident.

The Justice Department, supported by the Federal Bureau of Investigation, is responsible for the law enforcement aspects of domestic terrorist incidents. An office similar to the State Department's Office for Combatting Terrorism operates within the Justice Department. The Protection of Foreign Officials (PFO) statute, passed in 1968, expanded FBI responsibility for terrorist actions. The bureau's research and contingency planning efforts are centered in its Special Operations and Research Staff (SOARS),* which was conceived and developed by John M. Kirsch, a brilliant strategist with a vast operational background.

---

*SOARS was formerly known as TRAMS, an acronym for Terrorism Research and Management Staff.

SOARS, which is housed at the FBI's Training Division, has been able to explore a broad range of terrorist situations, to interact with the most capable law enforcement officers from around the world, to give relevant seminars, and to support local officials during actual incidents.

In some domestic terrorist situations, the federal government, including the FBI, may not have sufficient legal authority to become actively involved. However, the FBI interacts closely with law enforcement agencies throughout the country by training their officers in the use of the latest equipment as well as teaching them current paramilitary and hostage-negotiation techniques. Through these efforts local, state, and federal law enforcement agencies learn to support one another.

The interaction between the federal government and local jurisdictions is crucial, but it is nevertheless a murky, ill-defined matter that must be worked out before a serious terrorist assault occurs. The problems of communications and coordination are critical. Here again the FBI's training efforts have paid off.

THE CONSEQUENCES OF A TERRORIST ACT

President Carter announced Reorganization Plan Number 3 on June 19, 1978, establishing a new agency to deal with civil emergency preparedness. This Presidential initiative merges the federal government's emergency preparedness and disaster response programs. Five existing agencies and six additional disaster-related responsibilities are being combined to achieve a more manageable and responsive federal system. For emergencies ranging from natural and manmade disasters to nuclear attack, the reorganization is perceived as a consolidation of federal preparedness responsibilities. Two emergency functions not previously assigned to any specific federal agency are incorporated into the new plan: "(1) coordination of emergency warning and (2) federal response to consequences of terrorist incidents."[5]

By law (Section 906 of title 5, United States Code), sixty working days were provided for Congressional review of the proposed

Presidential reorganization plan. By not vetoing the reorganization plan, Congress endorsed its implementation. The new governmental agency has been given a significant terrorist response assignment. The Presidential action is an acknowledgment of the developing terrorist problem and provides a new apparatus for planning and emergency preparedness functions to deal with terrorism.

How will the new agency work? What is the extent of its responsibility? Little information is available to explain the intent of the President in this new assignment. But, if the new agency is to be effective, it must emphasize the readiness of the federal government to act decisively to mitigate the consequences of nationally disruptive acts of terrorism.

Much was unclear after the brief mention in the White House Fact Sheet of the assignment to the new agency of "federal response to consequences of terrorist incidents."[6] The testimony before Congress during the hearings on the reorganization plan did not provide much more insight into this highly significant mission. Neither the remarks by the President at the time he announced the emergency management reorganization nor his transmittal letter to the Congress provided details on the new authority to coordinate terrorist incidents. Yet this assignment could very well be one of the most important aspects of the new agency. If properly developed, this authority could become the basis for the kind of planning that would be so necessary were terrorist activities in the United States to intensify.

Just days before the reorganization plan became effective, Ambassador Quainton wrote an excellent commentary, "Dealing with Terrorism," which appeared in the *Christian Science Monitor*.[7] He stated that terrorism continues to be a serious problem and that the international implications are critical, but he did not discuss the relevant responsibilities of the recently reorganized emergency management agency. After pointing out the need for cooperation and consensus among nations, Ambassador Quainton discussed the domestic need in the United States for effective coordination. Because of the complexity of this country's political system, terrorist incidents may touch on responsibilities and require resources of the Departments of State, Defense, and

Transportation as well as agencies of the intelligence community, FBI, and local governments.

Before President Carter established policy guidelines for terrorist incident management, the bureaucratic tangle of authorities had been coordinated by the National Security Council and the Working Group of the Cabinet Committee to Combat Terrorism.[8] More than twenty-eight agencies have had some policy or operational interest in managing crises. The implications of assigning to the Federal Emergency Management Agency emergency preparedness and disaster responsibilities as they relate to terrorism have yet to be spelled out. The House Committee on Government Operations submitted a report on the new agency with only a brief reference to terrorism: "The President intends to give the new agency . . . coordination of planning to reduce the consequences of major terrorist incidents," and "the reorganization plan is part of a broader program to consolidate Federal emergency preparedness functions."[9]

In the report from the Senate Committee on Governmental Affairs relating to Reorganization Plan Number 3, one section deals with a range of possible consequences of terrorist incidents. Concern is expressed that should terrorism change from isolated events to coordinated offensives, the results could be devastating. Countries would be forced to contend with substantial loss of life, extensive property damage, and severe threats to their political stability. A major escalation in terrorist attacks "could cause more serious and more nationally significant social, economic and political consequences."[10] The Senate's report went on to say that terrorist incident management is being handled by the Special Coordinating Committee of NSC and will so continue. The Senate recognized the crux of the dilemma:

> When the requirement exists, the SCC coordinates the actions of the Federal law enforcement agencies involved in responding to the criminal act of terrorism. None of the responsibilities of the SCC or the law enforcement agencies will be changed by the reorganization.
>
> By contrast, the responsibilities for consequences management are not clear. As a result, Federal agencies are reluctant to plan or com-

mit resources. The President has no one source he can turn to for reports on the damage incurred, the resources available to respond, and the relief actions underway. To fill the void, the new agency will monitor terrorist incidents in progress and, as required, report the status of consequences management efforts to the President. Consequences management in terrorism will thus be a capability in the broad all-risk, all-emergency functions of the agency. The vulnerability assessment activities of the new agency will be directed toward identification of physical actions that might be taken to reduce damage against specific kinds of targets, and identification of areas and types of scenarios that will require consequences management.

Immediately after a terrorist attack in cases where the domestic situation would be so serious as to become a matter of national security concern, it is anticipated that the SCC and the White House Emergency Management Committee would meet together and develop joint recommendations on response for the President.[11]

What are the implications of the proposed interaction between the new agency and the NSC described in the Senate report? Providing a considerably more detailed commentary than the House report, the Senate sees the new agency being set up to have, in addition to management responsibilities for consequences of major terrorist incidents, an assigment to monitor, report, and advise the President on the status of the consequences management effort. Stating the Administration's position, James T. McIntyre, director of the Office of Management and Budget, affirmed that the President would assign the new agency responsibility for "coordination of preparedness and planning to reduce the consequences of major terrorist incidents. This will not alter present executive branch responsibilities for the prevention and control of terrorist incidents."[12]

The United States has been extremely fortunate not to have been more involved in the transnational terrorist incidents of the last decade. This country has the most sophisticated and complete media coverage of any nation on earth and terrorism is theater seeking as broad a viewing audience as possible. What stage could be better than the United States?

THE ANTECEDENTS OF THE FEDERAL EMERGENCY
MANAGEMENT AGENCY

Our present civil emergency machinery is the outgrowth of an earlier emergency management agency and is rooted in civil defense preparedness (which even now receives primary defense emphasis in the Soviet Union). But the efficiency of the U.S. apparatus could well be hampered by the position it has been allocated in the federal bureaucracy.

In order to be effective, the crisis management authority must be able to orchestrate the activities from departments and agencies across the federal spectrum. President Carter's new reorganization plan seems to include a basis for these essential elements of immediate response. If this is the President's intention, the plan's origins can be traced back to President Roosevelt, who in 1941 assigned responsibilities in case of war, flood, drought, or other conditions threatening public peace or safety to the Office of Emergency Management. Further development of this concept occurred in 1950 with President Truman's Federal Natural Disaster Program, which substantially involved the federal government in recovery efforts after a natural disaster. It was, in fact, a crisis management program. From its inception, the program was viewed as an extension of the Chief Executive's authority and was financed from the President's Disaster Relief Fund. After the Disaster Relief Law was enacted in 1950, Truman delegated responsibility for its application to the administrator of the Housing and Home Finance Agency.

The first test of the new law came with the great Midwestern floods of 1951, and the program, with responsibility for its administration relegated to one of the line agencies of the executive branch, did not work. In order to coordinate the federal response of all the agencies, Truman found it necessary to place responsibility for the emergency management operation in his Executive Office of the President. On July 19, 1951, he sent a letter to the director of his Office of Defense Mobilization requesting that he "direct and coordinate the activities of the Federal departments and agencies toward restoration of the general economy in the areas."[13] This order established the second phase of what is now being organized as the Federal Emergency Management Agency.

Every President in the modern era has been confronted by the bureaucracy of the executive branch, a bureaucracy that controls the steps and procedures that must be completed before a Presidential order or directive can be carried out. It is the mechanics of government. It is exemplified by the frustration of a President who has issued an urgent order to carry out a particular directive, waited for the bureaucracy to act, and finally realized nothing would happen. Jonathan Daniels, a key aide to Presidents Roosevelt and Truman, observed:

> Half of a President's suggestions, which theoretically carry the weight of orders, can be safely forgotten by a Cabinet member. And if the President asks about a suggestion a second time, a wise Cabinet officer will give him at least part of what he suggests. But only occasionally, except about the most important matters, do Presidents ever get around to asking three times.[14]

Truman was decision-oriented and insisted on preserving his prerogatives as the Chief Executive. His sense of unease with the federal bureaucracy was profound and, in his letter to the director of the Office of Defense Mobilization, he made clear his perception that a void existed in the executive branch that could not be allowed to persist. He also recognized the similarity of different emergency-management responsibilities, reinforcing the necessity for merging regular management operations such as those relating to natural disasters with civil emergency preparedness. Significantly, these responsibilities remained in the Executive Office until President Nixon's cutback reorganization of 1973, when authority was dispersed among different parts of the federal government. As Truman understood, the kinds of management necessary for defense preparedness and for disaster preparedness are, in fact, markedly similar in structure. Carter has added "response to consequences of terrorist incidents"[15] to these emergency considerations. This generalized thinking about emergency preparedness should quite rightly underlie federal efforts in the development of a single agency capable of managing a wide range of crisis situations.

Richard Nixon accepted and effectively used the emergency functions that had been initiated by Truman and expanded by Eisenhower, Kennedy, and Johnson. In fact, the emergency management agency's capacity for effective crisis management was never more amply demonstrated than in the years just prior to its dismemberment by President Nixon. During this period it responded to some of the greatest challenges of any time since its formulation in 1950. On August 15, 1971, when the President announced that he would impose a wage-price-rent freeze for ninety days to stem inflation, the agency offered the only critical mass of staff in government that could be immediately mobilized to administer this complex program. In September 1970, after the Shultz Cabinet Committee had submitted its report to the President recommending an energy policy, the President deferred action on the committee's findings, giving the Office of Emergency Preparedness (OEP) responsibility for coordinating energy policy.

During the Nixon years, an unprecedented number of natural disasters struck the United States, inflicting billions of dollars of damage. The emergency management functions were expanded and improved to respond to the increased demands from all sectors of the economy in states throughout the country. This crisis management operation provided information and coordinated federal programs to contend with a series of transportation stoppages, coal shortages, fuel problems, and a postal interruption. The operational aspects of these situations required development of a staff oriented toward and skilled in dealing with crises, disasters, and nonwar emergencies. Fortunately, the organization was never tested by a critical terrorist incident and the government has not yet been confronted with anything similar to the Munich slayings, the Entebbe incident, or the OPEC kidnapping.

President Nixon's Reorganization Plan Number 1 of 1973 abolished the Office of Emergency Preparedness in the Executive Office of the President. There was a pervasive feeling at the time that the move was largely political, given Nixon's commitment to reduce by 50 percent the size of his Executive Office. It was further suggested that the OEP's dire warnings of an impending energy crisis prior to the 1972 election had made it something of a political liability. Although the stated purpose of the reorganization was to improve the quality of federal preparedness, a general consensus has arisen during the Carter reorganization study that the dismantling of the OEP and the dispersal of its functions in a variety of departments and agencies in the federal structure severely handicapped the government's capacity to deal with emergency situations.

THE FEDERAL EMERGENCY MANAGEMENT AGENCY'S LACK OF CLOUT

A possible shortcoming of the new Federal Emergency Management Agency is that the new agency has the same status as all the other federal agencies. It is reminiscent of the original effort by Harry Truman in 1950 when he assigned emergency management functions to one of the line departments. After his first emergency experience in 1951, the responsibility was elevated to the Executive Office of the President, where it remained for twenty-two years. The significance of locating the emergency management function in the Executive Office of the President lies in the necessary involvement of many federal departments and agencies in any critical situation.

The Executive Office of the President is generally accepted to be the coordinating level of government speaking for the President. In any national security emergency the key actor would be the National Security Council, which is an Executive Office agency. Similarly, the Office of Management and Budget could not function effectively outside of the Executive Office. By contrast, the General Services Administration is an example of an agency that has broad coordinative authority, but is outside of the Executive Office and has limited influence within government.

Crisis management is an unusual challenge. For example, in an emergency management situation it is often necessary that individuals of low governmental rank deal directly with department or agency heads. This may seem to be a petty matter but it could prove to be binding at a time of great strain. The point is that individuals of relatively low rank can function as representatives of the President if they belong to the Executive Office. Under the present plan, the emergency management agency is at the same level as other agencies, a level that is somewhat below the relative status of Cabinet departments.

Fortunately, Mr. Carter is establishing an Emergency Management Committee, chaired by the new agency's director, which would report directly to him. Membership would include the Assistants to the President for National Security, for Domestic Affairs and Policy, and for Intergovernmental Relations, as well as the director of the Office of Management and Budget. The committee would establish broad policies for exercise of emergency authorities and advise the President on alternative courses of action in national civil emergencies and on the costs and benefits of alternative policies for improving performance and avoiding excessive costs. In the past there has been a tendency to build staff to support the functions of an active committee. It will be interesting to see how the staff requirements of the Emergency Management Committee are met and what relative position this committee will hold, in relation both to the new agency and to the Executive Office of the President. We will find out whether the chairmanship of this high-level committee will be able to compensate for the inferior location of the new agency.

The underlying reason for the reorganization, which consolidates the various emergency management functions, was that these functions were scattered throughout the government. The result was an ineffective civil emergency apparatus. The rationale for the consolidation of the natural disaster, civil emergency preparedness, and civil defense programs should apply to the separate responsibilities for counterterrorism preparedness and incident management as well. Will the separate but parallel authorities for these two different but interlocked assignments be impossible to administer without conflict and confusion? At this stage it would be difficult to say, but in the end much of the operation of any organization or system depends on the caliber of the individuals involved and their ability to interact with their counterparts in other agencies. Coordination between federal agencies has often been a difficult task.

How would the FBI react if ordered by a new agency to clear, subordinate, or coordinate all administrative decisions regarding a domestic terrorist incident before taking action in order to reduce the possible consequences of a terrorist situation? How would the Department of Defense react to directions from a second- or third-level agency to make transportation, communication equipment, and personnel available to deal with a crisis situation? How would the State Department respond to limitations or restrictions on its authority to coordinate and deal with international terrorist situations or to the monitoring and reporting role of an outside independent agency charged with responsibility for mitigating the consequences of a terrorist incident?

It is, of course, fundamental that complex governmental action at the federal level requires decentralization of responsibility and power. But it is equally fundamental that, as Graham Allison puts it in his classic *Essence of Decision*, "the necessity for decentralization runs headlong into the requirement for coordination."[16] The need for a truly effective preparedness program on the federal level has never been greater, and we submit that a critical mass of experts is preferable to the kind of ad hoc bureaucratic shuffle that has been experienced during the last five years. It is obvious that the crisis management structure previously dismantled and now reconstructed can operate most effectively with clear and comprehensive authority delegated from a strong Chief Executive. The relationship between dealing with the terrorist incident and mitigating its consequences needs to be carefully thought out.

CONCLUDING OBSERVATIONS

As of today, we are poorly prepared to deal with nationally disruptive acts of terrorism. Our capability to manage terrorist crises is limited. Our state of preparedness is not adequately developed. The international community is not integrated into preplanned modes of response. Research on terrorist behavior, target hardening, and the problem of restoration after attack is only in its infancy.

President Carter's recognition of the problem and his initial step of reorganization are a beginning. He has established a basis for development of a national incident-management system including a crisis management team and a civil emergency pre-paredness program with immediate access to the highest levels of government. The management role must be set by pre-established authority. The team must do contingency planning, refine and negotiate strategies, determine resource and management in-formation needs, and coordinate the operations of government at times of crises. The team's development and organization must be related to a support staff of "critical mass" size, oriented toward and trained in dealing with crises and disasters that have provided practical experience for its operations.

The necessary standby arrangements for aircraft, communica-tions, personnel, and other resources must be made before the crisis occurs. Further, a roster of experts and the means to summon them quickly are fundamental. Consistent with the law, remotely accessible data bases must be constructed for planning and operational purposes. Terrorist's tactics and operations, their weapons, and their organization and training all should be catalogued and studied as an intregal part of a national incident-management system.

The U.S. program must be based on international arrange-ments to combat terrorism across borders, making use of extradi-tion agreements and elimination of safe havens, multilateral controls on the transfers of antitank and antiaircraft weapons, and agreements for technical assistance and the exchange of intelligence. Whether developed on a national level or through cooperative international arrangements, large nations must have the specialized paramilitary ability to perform rescue operations such as those at Entebbe and Mogadishu. Countering terrorism can be accomplished only by funding a vigorous research and development program. There are rich opportunities for behav-ioral and technological research. Even limited efforts could make dramatic contributions.

Observing the behavior of modern terrorists, we are reminded of the world depicted in William Butler Yeats's poem "The Second Coming," a world in which "the best lack all conviction, while the worst / Are full of passionate intensity." To curb terrorism before it produces more serious sacrifices to the deities of apocalyptic destruction, architects of an effective counter-terrorism strategy must begin to have conviction—to care enough about the importance of their task to prevent the gratuitous waste of further killing. Equally important, our society must retain conviction in its own endurance and in the resilience of democratic institutions.

Countering and managing incidents of terrorism are not direct or fully prescribable tasks. One does not take a teaspoon of medicine every four hours to cure the scourge. At best, nations will be forced to live with the disease symptomatically, and pray that its spread is containable.

To pursue the metaphor, if the symptoms are treated too aggressively, both doctor and patient may die. If the disease frightens the doctor into submission, then the prognosis is congenital weakness. The malady infects us all and the statistics of morbity and mortality worsen each time the least painful course of action is taken.

There is no doubt that mass annihilation is feasible—and resourceful, technically oriented thugs are capable of achieving it. Their leverage over nation-states is disproportionately high. But the day of mass destruction will be thrust upon us by ourselves; terrorists are as strong or as weak as society's fear of hobgoblins admit. Some thought and courage are all that lie between the usual perils of civilization and the specter of self-inflicted carnage.

SELECTED READINGS

Introduction to Selected Readings

Contemporary terrorism and its implications have been discussed in selective detail so as to provide an overall perspective of considerations of threat, reality, and response that must be addressed by the United States and other free nations. In order to enhance the analysis and the policy initiatives set forth in the preceding pages, we have selected eight essays written by well-known theorists and practitioners. Five are original works prepared at our request to offer more detailed information on significant areas in the main text; three are reprints of important articles.

The first paper, by Bowman H. Miller and Charles A. Russell, examines the current trends of terrorist groups, chronicles the near past, and submits a glimpse of the future. In view of the terrorist's quest for high-leverage targets, Maynard M. Stephens, in the next essay, pinpoints the vulnerabilities of the U.S. petroleum and natural gas industries to terrorist attack.

The emphasis in our book has been on technology and crisis management. Other than developments in physical security, and techniques to analyze their effectiveness, there is no formal discipline of technologically based countermeasures to terrorism. Possibly our discussions of threat and countermeasure will stimulate further inquiry. Crisis management is the art of the possible, and in developing our study of it we drew heavily on our own experience. In the third essay, Robert H. Kupperman, Richard H. Wilcox, and Harvey A. Smith provide an overview of crisis management problems and suggest analytical techniques that could aid decision-making in time of strain. James P. Bennett and Thomas L. Saaty then present, in the fourth paper, a novel quantitative technique to aid decision-making. The fifth essay, by D. A. Waterman and Brian M. Jenkins, is a particularly interesting discussion of the progress that has been made in applying heuristic modeling techniques to the topic of international terrorism. Crisis managers need checklists of "dos and don'ts" when disaster strikes. In a terrorist situation, the time for theorizing is past and the effectiveness of the management effort may well rest on the application of "decision rules" that have been previously developed and can be applied to help guide government through a dangerous and uncharted labyrinth.

In the sixth essay, Yonah Alexander tackles an especially sensitive subject. During times of crisis, the relationship between the media and government can be fiendish. Whether the public perceives a government operation as successful or as an illustration of governmental impotence may largely depend on the news coverage. The issue of government control and freedom of the press is particularly important in crisis management situations.

Emergency medical care for victims of terrorism is an area of crisis management that deserves special attention. Martin E. Silverstein, in the seventh essay, links emergency medicine with systems theory as he presents a cogent thesis about salvaging lives in the event of mass casualties.

The final essay, by Francis A. Bolz, Jr., offers guidelines for developing workable methods to manage hostage-barricade sieges. In his practical approach, Bolz provides a brief but impressive insight into the complex operational and psychological considerations involved in humanely resolving a hostage situation.

The Evolution of Revolutionary Warfare: From Mao to Marighella and Meinhof*

BOWMAN H. MILLER and CHARLES A. RUSSELL

The Evolution of Revolutionary Warfare

Within most areas of the world, one of the more significant developments during recent years has been the steady movement of revolutionary forces from a rural to an urban environment. Whether nationalist, nihilist, or Marxist in political outlook, many of these revolutionary elements have abandoned serious efforts to create insurgent bases in the countryside. Rejecting the dictates of guerrilla theoreticians such as Mao Tse-tung, Ho Chi Minh, Giap, Guevara, and Debray—all of whom urged the creation of rural-based guerrilla cadres—most revolutionaries of the 1970s have opted for urban terrorism. Instead of a rural guerrilla force capable of expanding and, in the words of Mao, ultimately "surrounding the cities," present-day revolutionaries have reversed the sequence of events. Operations are now initiated and developed within a nation's cities, turning these and not the countryside into the real focus of revolutionary efforts. In view of this significant shift in the locus of revolutionary effort, this study examines some of the pragmatic, ideological, and tactical considerations involved as well as the long-term impact of these changes on the future development of revolutionary activity worldwide.

In general, the change to an urban focus for revolution appears attributable to a combination of factors. Primary among these are

---

*The views expressed in this paper are the authors' and do not necessarily reflect the views of the U.S. government or any of its agencies or departments.

(1) an increasingly sparse rural population resulting from continued and accelerating urbanization; (2) the presence in many metropolitan areas of a growing, articulate, and generally aroused cadre of students and young intellectuals willing to embrace terrorism as the most effective means to topple governments they consider corrupt or ineffective; and (3) the ready availability in urban versus rural areas of the basic necessities for successful revolutionary activity (targets, funds, intelligence, medical supplies, and even food).

Although urbanization has long characterized many nations of the world, within recent years this trend has accelerated generally. Rural dwellers, formerly willing to remain a part of an often semifeudal agrarian society, are now being drawn to urban areas in increasing numbers. Attracted by the prospects of employment and improved living conditions, many migrants from rural areas see the cities as a means to escape the grinding poverty of some countrysides. When these considerations are coupled with often inhospitable rural areas (as in portions of Latin America and the Middle East), the net result is frequently an underpopulated countryside and overpopulated urban areas. In these circumstances, a rural-based revolutionary effort has little chance of success simply because the countryside lacks the popular base to support it.

Within even traditionally urbanized areas such as Europe, portions of the Middle East, and sections of Latin America, population flow to major cities is a demographic fact of life. Traditionally the focus of education and intellectual life—as well as industry and employment opportunities—cities contain a majority of the the literate citizenry and student population. And it is from these latter two groups that present-day terrorist organizations draw most of their members. Often educated in the law and humanities, these students and young intellectuals have difficulty integrating into societies that demand increasing numbers of technicians, engineers, and skilled artisans. Frequently the product of a university system influenced by Marxist economic and political doctrines, these individuals form a highly volatile and articulate group. When their political activism and demands for social/political change are met with governmental lethargy and inactivity, they become ideal candidates for terrorist recruitment.

Familiar with the city and its customs, these individuals find an urban environment a natural combat area. Inspired by the writings of such terrorist theorists as Abraham Guillen, Carlos Marighella, and their Palestinian and German imitators, and encouraged by the success of city-centered revolutionary movements in Latin America, the Middle East, and Europe, these students and intellectuals have opted for urban terrorism versus rural guerrilla warfare.

In selecting a combat area, these groups also have considered more pragmatic matters such as target availability, access to funding, and sources of medical equipment and food as well as the availability of useful intelligence.

Terrorist targets   Within an urban area target selection is virtually unlimited, including foreign embassies, diplomatic personnel, foreign and domestic business firms and personnel, governmental officials, and so on. All can be attacked with relative ease. In contrast to the acts of rural guerrillas who may have little impact upon a central government for an extended period of time, the kidnapping of a diplomat or the destruction of a foreign business immediately focuses world attention on the terrorists and their demands. Of equal significance is the fact that such acts embarrass a government and undermine public confidence in its ability to provide protection for its citizens and prominent visitors.

Funds   Critical in all revolutionary efforts are funds to support the movement, protect its personnel, and procure needed weapons and other equipment. Readily available for attack in urban areas are banks and foreign business firms. Also lucrative is the kidnapping of foreign or domestic business personnel. In the almost nine years between January 1, 1970, and November 1, 1978, known paid ransoms alone for terrorist kidnap victims have exceeded $145,000,000.[1]

Food   Always a problem in rural areas where guerrillas have to live off the land, in urban centers food supplies are as close as the nearest market; their acquisition is not dependent on a degree of acceptance by the local population as it often is in the countryside.

Medical Assistance   Frequently a crucial area in rural guerrilla operations, for the urban terrorist pharmaceuticals are readily available through purchase or theft. In addition, medical students at local universities can provide skilled surgical assistance when needed (as in the case of the Uruguayan Tupamaros and the various Italian terrorist groups).

Weapons   In even such a basic area as arms procurement, the urban terrorist has a substantial advantage over his rural counterpart. Whereas the rural guerrilla normally obtains additional weapons from an enemy killed in battle, or via shipments smuggled into the country, the cities offer a variety of sources. When weapons cannot be purchased openly or through the black market, police stations, armories, gun clubs, and similar facilities offer lucrative targets. While retention of an arsenal seems uppermost in the mind of Marighella,[2] one wonders if weapons pose a problem to many urban terrorists when so many are abandoned during attacks.

Intelligence   In regard to intelligence, critical in any revolutionary effort, the urban terrorist organization has a substantial advantage over its rural counterpart. Composed primarily of individuals from middle- or upper-class families, urban terrorists generally have personal or family connections extending into many echelons of both national governments and their economies. Through these links and those of friends and associates, they are often able to obtain quite accurate information on governmental counterterrorist operations.[3]

In addition to those basic demographic and pragmatic considerations that have played an substantial role in moving the focus of revolutionary activity from the country to the city, significant tactical concepts also have been important.

Terrorist Tactics and Techniques:
The Practitioners' Response

The terrorist is an enigma for many reasons, not the least of which is his unique combination of idealism and pragmatism. His idealism usually springs from a "true belief" in revolutionary change and the ultimate promise embodied in this process of which he feels a part. Pragmatically, however, the terrorist also is fully aware of his weakness. It is this important "self-admission" regarding a lack of power and followers that literally propels him toward the tactics of terrorism.

During the twentieth century, we have seen an emphasis on several key notions in the development of the doctrines of revolutionary warfare. The Vietnamese Truong Chinh stresses the tactics of harassment, borrowing from Mao and even Clausewitz the standard military tenets of ambush, surprise, and maximum concentration of force for attack followed by immediate dispersal. Truong Chinh's treatise preaches patience, endurance, and the need to "prolong the war," to tire the enemy force and its supporting government.[4] Marighella only in his later writing sees the significance of demographic change in Latin America as a major factor speaking for guerrilla warfare against the large urban centers. But his basic thinking remains tied to rural insurgency, with urban attacks simply a precursor to major rural insurgent operations.

Not until we take up Abraham Guillen do we find a tactical thinker whose notions are reflected in the actions of those terrorists operating today.

> Today the epicenter of the revolutionary war must be in the great urban zones . . . it is . . . necessary to count on a vast urban guerrilla force to give to the revolutionary war a political dimension. . . . What is important is not to win space, but rather to destroy the enemy and to endure longer.[5]

> If 70 percent of a country's population is urban, the demography and the economy must dictate the specific rules of the strategy of revolutionary combat. The center of operations should never be in the mountains or in the villages, but in the largest cities where the population suffices to form the army of the revolution.[6]

Recognizing the urban center as the core of population, as the site of the major targets available for attack, and as the ideal environment in which to conduct individual operations from a clandestine base, Guillen depicts his strategy of progressive harassment in graphic terms:

> The "strategy of the artichoke" is the most prudent or safe one for urban or rural guerrillas: to eat the enemy bit by bit, and through

brief and surprise encounters of encirclement and annihilation to live off the enemy's arms, munitions and paramilitary effects.[7]

The image here is most apt. The strategy of the terrorist is to harass, to select individual victims whose fate is highlighted for a much broader audience. Terrorism is theater for effect. It presupposes that its primary product (fear) will be aroused among the many as they are forced to witness in detail the awful violence perpetrated upon a few select victims. The terrorists are militarily and politically weak. They need political supporters and operational recruits. They can ill afford the bad public relations resulting from failure or even perhaps too great a success. The German government's counterattack at Mogadishu in October 1977 cost the German terrorists dearly in morale, in their ability to attract potential recruits, and in cadre per se. By the same token, the LaGuardia locker bombing of 1975, which killed twelve, the proposed German terrorist operation against Pope Paul VI, and similar activities were counterproductive in the terrorist view and were either abandoned or left unclaimed.

Regardless of objectives, group orientation, favored tactics, or cadre experience, terrorist groups today have several characteristics in common. These shared traits result from the types of persons involved and the tactics available. They stem only secondarily from existing intergroup linkages and contacts. All terrorists are hit-and-run artists. Once a situation evolves into open warfare as in Rhodesia, Nicaragua, or Ethiopia, isolated acts of terrorism are replaced by civil war or large-scale insurgency. The incidents in a campaign of terrorism remain quantifiable. They have a beginning and an end and are carefully planned in advance.

Terrorists select targets that promise minimal risk while retaining satisfactory, if not optimum, political attractiveness. These variables of risk to the terrorists and target attractiveness are in a direct relationship. Only the terrorist group—and then only at a certain time—can and does determine how much risk is acceptable in any given operation. Although a head of state ideally may be the most attractive target, he or she presumably is well protected and thus less vulnerable to assault or seizure. Circumstances within the group, its recent activities, pool of available operatives, experience level, and self-confidence dictate the potential targets and tactics. Often the habits of potential targets prior to any operation confirm or eliminate them as "possibles" in terrorist deliberations. Routines, access, physical and personnel security, and other factors all weigh in this target selection process. External conditions, such as political events, previous operational successes or failures, or debts owed to other groups, all tend to play a role in target selection and the timing of an attack.

These factors and considerations are a matter of course for the terrorists whose prime concern is a positive outcome from each operation. These, they hope, will lead to respectability before some constituency, the embarrassment of a government, and an ill-conceived reaction by that government while under pressure to "do something." "The main point," George Habash once said, "is to select targets where success is 100% assured. To harass, to upset, to work on the nerves through unexpected small damages."[8] Habash's tactics coalesce with those of Truong Chinh. He advocates gnawing away in a prolonged fashion, as does Guillen with his artichoke strategy, and stresses success over target attractiveness. And well he might, for it was Habash's Popular Front for the Liberation of Palestine (PFLP) that introduced aircraft hijacking into the basic terrorist inventory. Certainly others have diverted planes but not in an orchestrated campaign to aggravate an enemy state that was otherwise nearly immune to guerrilla attack.

Terrorists in the last decade have changed the rules of combat. Again it was Habash who let it be known that there are "no innocent victims" in this world. The means are justified by the ends and those means emphasize leverage attained through fear, intimidation, and coercion. Human lives are the key ingredient for the terrorists' success—not their own lives but those of their victims. At times those victimized are chance selections—air passengers, visitors to terminals, hotels, and the like, or other opportunity targets such as restaurants, bars, or public transportation. Analysis reveals that the transnationally capable and active groups—largely the fedayeen terrorists and the Japanese Red Army—have specialized in hijackings and in attacks on facilities. On the other hand, groups that are nationally delimited in their tactics and range of operations have emphasized kidnapping and outright assassination. All groups use bombs and all perhaps began with the bomb in their embryonic phase.

Terrorists detest the notion that persons in those groups that they hate and attack continue to feel comfortable and untouched by terrorist acts. As a German terrorist quoted in an interview expressed it, "All members of the ruling class should be unsure of their status, they have slumbered peacefully long enough. They are to be forced to protect every conceivable facility with a force of pigs [police]."[9]

As the terrorists seek to prove that governments are failing to provide protection to the governed in an orderly society under a rule of law, they hope to force government officials to respond in a way that portrays an image of bungling against minute groups of "criminals and gangsters" and has a negative impact on the citizenry in general. If an overreaction can be induced that alienates the middle class, some groups feel a grass-roots revolution can be developed. In this respect, Castro's victory over Batista is a model held up for emulation. No doubt the Sandinistas in Nicaragua feel the Cuban success can be duplicated against the Somoza regime.

Terrorist tactics are simple but effective from the practitioner's point of view. By the same token, bombing, kidnapping, assassination, the seizure of facilities and conveyances, and maiming are not the monopoly of the terrorist. They are the trade of the criminal, the violently deranged, and even the wartime saboteur. The distinctions lie not in the acts themselves, since murder, assassination, and execution are all forms of homicide, but in the motivation for the deed and in the selection of the victims. Both Marighella and Guillen are quick to point out the distinctions between guerrillas and outlaws (from their perspective), and they caution, as does Regis Debray, against a group losing sight of its politics and becoming a Mafia.[10] The practice of terrorism is not to become an end in itself but to remain a revolutionary tool. One can ask whether groups such as the West German Revolutionary Cells and the Japanese Red Army adhere to this notion or are approaching nihilism.[11]

The choice of any particular tactic by a group is largely contingent on any combination of the following factors: the group's capabilities, weapons, general support apparatus, cadre experience, unique skills, operating environment, target pool, government countermeasures, level of sophistication, clandestine havens, and external support. From the perspective of operational sophistication, one can construct a hierarchy of these tactics that illustrates their relative positions on a scale of competence, as in the figure below.

Bombing is a readily available, easily learned technique that can be undertaken with minimal risk to the perpetrator. The bomber operates with time and distance on his side. His operation is a momentary one and allows him to commit a violent act without the necessity of witnessing its effects upon the victim(s). Though the bomb is a simple tool, the varieties of explosives available and the possible operations for their use are almost infinite.

A stand-off attack on a target using short-range conventional weapons (bazooka, mortars, grenade launchers, and the like) is more demanding than a bombing but primarily because of the nature of the weapon. It is man-operated rather than timed to operate. Once again the attack is of short duration. Barricade operations involving hostage seizures demand one essential prerequisite for success: a potential safe haven. From an analytical viewpoint the value of such stand-off operations, involving a mutual stalemate, appears limited and sophisticated groups now tend to avoid them. In these actions, the hostage-takers themselves become hostages.

Assassination can take many forms. Restricting our attention to gunfire assaults on one or more victims, the requirement for good operational planning to insure success and escape is greater than in the previously mentioned tactics. Few, if any, terrorists (of the crusader variety) are actually suicidal; that is, they do not shun the possibility of an escape from the scene of the attack. Escape presupposes planning, timing, precise coordination, excellent firing ability, rapid movement, and good clandestine tradecraft as well as secure operational arrangements. Assassination using weapons brings the killer face to face with the human victim. This, it would seem, demands more resolve and perhaps greater commitment than other tactics.

Hijacking has become a headline tactic. In actuality, however, it occurs relatively infrequently. It is a special tactic and, in the case of aircraft, demands a planeload of passengers as well as a safe haven for landing and escape. By definition, hijacking is virtually limited to transnational groups. Nationally limited terrorists avoid it. The tactic demands patience on the part of the operatives and an ability to handle a "duration operation." The world is attuned now to the possibility of hijackings, and countermeasures in this sector are the most developed, if also of varying degrees of effectiveness.

Although the foregoing tactics are significant, from the terrorist perspective it is kidnapping that is the most demanding and promising. The operation requires intricate planning, split-second timing, a large support apparatus to sustain the group holding the victim, and the ability to remain secure while still communicating demands or negotiating with third parties. In the Schleyer and Moro kidnap/murder cases, there also were protective details that raised the risks—but not high enough to affect the terrorists' willingness to operate. The killing of bodyguards was seen and accepted as an operational necessity. The fact that this was accomplished without harming the target persons illustrates the commitment and sophistication of the groups involved. Kidnapping cases can last, and have lasted, for a year or more. The ability to conceal locations, movements, and support in such situations is no mean achievement.

Urban Terrorism: The Track Record in the 1970s

Depending upon which commentator is read, the significance of today's terrorist actions ranges from a general continuation of politically motivated violence to an unparalleled scourge capable of destroying society. Few treatments, however, are able to quantify the phenomenon in any meaningful way. As a result, we are left with general observations and tentative conclusions.

Using a data base developed by one of the authors that contains detailed information on major terrorist incidents since January 1970, the writers can with reasonable accuracy quantify the terrorist phenomenon.[12] Setting aside the few instances of major ongoing civil strife or insurgency (including Northern Ireland, Israel, and several African states) where terrorist attacks are interspersed with larger military operations, this data set includes over 5,000 incidents (offensive terrorist operations, either actual or attempted). The casualties from these attacks have amounted to at least 2,735 killed and 3,472 wounded. In addition, 3,286 hostages were seized. The following ratios reflect the fatalities by type of operation (or tactic) involved: 49.3%—facilities attacks; 27.3%—bombings; 21.2%—outright assassinations; and only 1.3% and 0.9% kidnapping and hijacking incidents respectively.

The most popular and perhaps most versatile terrorist tactic involves the use of bombs.* Since 1970, terrorists have carried out thousands of bombings. Our data set includes 3,043 bombings through September 1978, selected on the basis of the significance of the target, the sophistication of the particular techniques used, or the damage/casualties inflicted. But such data must be seen in some perspective: Between January 1969 and November 1977 there were over 10,000 recorded bombings in Northern Ireland alone. These resulted in at least 476 deaths. Between 1973 and

---

*Marighella, in fact, at one point in his "Minimanual" defines terrorism as "an action, usually involving the placement of a bomb or fire explosion of great destructive power. . . . Terrorism requires that the urban guerrilla should have an adequate . . . knowledge of how to make explosives." (See note 2.)

1977, over 436 million dollars in damages were registered in this area.[13] Although our data set indicates approximately 62% of all terrorist attacks to have been bombings, it is subject to upward revision, so that perhaps the figure is closer to 80%.

The breakdown of the remaining operations by tactical typology shows 15.8% of all terrorist operations to have been facilities attacks; 11.8% assassinations; 6.9% kidnappings; and only 1.6% hijackings. The remaining, less than 2%, include disruption-oriented operations and some 65 maimings (maiming/leg-shooting data cover only the period since 1975).

If one focuses on the targets or victims of terrorist operations, regardless of the tactic used, the proportional breakdown is as follows:

> Business: 33%
> > Domestic: 17%
> > Foreign, non-U.S.: 6%
> > U.S.: 10%
> Police Military: 18%
> > Non-U.S.: 12%
> > U.S.: 6%
> Diplomatic: 12%
> > Foreign: 9%
> > U.S.: 3%
> Other governmental: 8.8%
> > Foreign: 8%
> > U.S.: 0.8%
> Transportation: 5.1%
> > Foreign: 5%
> > U.S.: 0.1%
> Utilities: 3%
> > Foreign: 2%
> > U.S.: 1%
> Political parties: 6% (all foreign)
> Media: 3.2%
> > Foreign: 3.0%
> > U.S.: 0.2%
> Others: 10.9%

By nationality, 1,168 or 22.2% of all targets in these cases were American. The major categories within this set of only U.S. victims were: business—46%; police/military—25%; diplomatic—12%; other U.S. government—4%; utilities—5%; and others—8%. Of all attacks against business enterprises, regardless of nationality, 30% have been directed at American firms.

Regionally, terrorist attacks have been most frequent in Europe (50%) and Latin America (21%). North America (14%), the Middle East and North Africa (11%), Asia (2%), and subsaharan Africa (2%) round out the count. In 1970 there were twice as many operations in Latin America as in Europe. By 1978 (through September) the ratio was reversed. In the first three quarters of 1978, Europe counted at least 506 incidents, led by Italy, compared with 256 in Latin America. Distinct variances exist between regions in the use of specific tactics. For instance, 62% of all kidnappings have occurred in Latin America while Europe has witnessed 54% of all bombings and 44% of all assassinations. The data base lists, for North America, some 667 incidents, of which 575 or 86% have been bombings.

Dollar costs attributable to terrorism would run into the billions if direct losses, additional security resources (private and public), insurance, and similar costs could be tallied. In those instances where the media have reported direct losses in terms of damages or ransoms paid, the figure amounts to more than 380 million dollars. Based on an estimate of the proportion of the data that report on such losses and on other available materials, a more accurate reflection of costs probably exceeds a billion dollars since 1970.

Outlook

Although few would dare forecast the future of terrorism, there are particular trends or indicators that seem to bear watching. In the political framework, the tendency of some groups to abandon notions of constituency or any political basis for operations can signal nihilists at work, groups for whom terrorism becomes a strategy rather than a tactic. For such groups, terrorism is literally a way of life and a means of self-gratification. Smaller ethnic groups bound up in larger states and others frustrated by the uselessness of conventional methods also undoubtedly will continue to apply terrorism for attention and leverage.

Among terrorist operatives, more and more women are appearing in leadership and operational roles. Younger persons also are moving into some terrorist groups in large numbers. Gradual increases are evident in group membership for technically schooled young persons and those who have not attended universities. Increased participation by technically inclined personnel makes operations directed at mass disruption of key technologically based systems and industrial sabotage more plausible.

Many groups will undoubtedly continue to follow established patterns and time-tested techniques. But it is the possible move by others toward mass disruption operations that is most alarming. With the increased technical skills now available in the terrorist inventory, it is in this area of mass disruption that the greatest future danger appears to lie.

NOTES

1. All statistical materials contained in this chapter, unless otherwise indicated (and particularly those appearing under the chapter sub-caption "Urban Terrorism: The Track Record of the 1970's") were derived from a terrorist incident data-base developed by Dr. Charles A. Russell, presently associated with Risks International, Inc., Alexandria, Virginia. The data and conclusions drawn from it are the property of Risks International and under copyright of that organization. This material is reproduced in this chapter with the express permission of Roy Tucker, President, Risks International.

The incident data-base in question contains detailed data on over 5,000 terrorist incidents since January 1970. Incidents are broken down by date, time, country and city, target, nationality of target (if an individual, the corporation and his position therein), group involved, number in group, weapons or explosives used, ransoms demanded or paid, hostages taken, disposition of hostages, other demands. Materials are filed by incident types. These are kidnapping, assassination, facility attack, maiming, hijacking, and bombing. Only selected bombings are included, those in which the damage/casualties are significant, the device unique, or the method of emplacement unusual.

2. Carlos Marighella, "Minimanual of the Urban Guerrilla," *Tricontinental* (Havana), January–February 1970, p. 26.

3. For additional data on this and other characteristics of terrorist operatives, see the authors' article "Profile of a Terrorist" in *Military Review*, August 1977, or in *Terrorism: An International Journal*, 1, no. I, November 1977.

4. Truong Chinh, *The Resistance Will Win* (facs.ed.), in Bernard B. Fall, *Primer for Revolt* (New York: Praeger, 1963), pp. 111–115, 178–84.

5. Abraham Guillen, *The Philosophy of the Urban Guerrilla: The Revolutionary Writings of Abraham Guillen*, trans. by Donald C. Hodges (New York: Morrow, 1973), p. 233.

6. Ibid. p. 237.

7. Ibid. p. 250.

8. George Habash, interviewed by Oriana Fallaci in *Life*, June 12, 1970, p. 34.

9. An unnamed member of West Germany's Revolutionary Cells, quoted in the *Westdeutscher Rundfunk* documentary "Terrorismus," aired on May 14, 1977.

10. Guillen, *Philosophy of the Urban Guerrilla*, pp. 260, 269; Marighella, "Mini-manual," p. 17; Regis Debray, "Prologue" to *Los Tupamaros en Acción* (Mexico City: Editorial Diógenes, 1972), p. 41.

11. For additional discussion of this topic, see Charles A. Russell, Leon J. Banker, and Bowman H. Miller, "Out-Inventing the Terrorist," in *Terrorism: Theory and Practice* (Boulder, Colo.: Westview, forthcoming).

12. See note 1.

13. *ABC* (Madrid), November 17, 1977, p. 30.

The Oil and Natural Gas Industries: A Potential Target of Terrorists

MAYNARD M. STEPHENS

The petroleum industry, including closely related natural gas operations, can be divided into a number of distinct segments, each functioning as a unit within itself, yet tied to, serving, and coordinated with, other units of the industry. Figure 1 shows a generalized model of the petroleum and natural gas industries.[1]

This discussion will not stress the exploratory phases of the industry for, though a saboteur can cause serious damage to company equipment, certainly no national impact will result from sporadic attacks on wells being drilled, especially those in remote locations.

Established petroleum and natural gas operations, their pipeline interties, and associated tankage and storage are the most attractive targets of dissidents. But there is no part of the industry that is immune to being seriously damaged by someone who has a little knowledge of it or makes an effort to learn its frailties. It is no wonder that security personnel and management become almost "paranoid" at the thought of having attention drawn in publications to the vulnerability of the industry. Installations are constructed to serve efficiently specific functions, giving little or no attention to security measures needed to protect the facility from potential attacks. But how does one know what dangers and threats to guard against? Although some sabotage has occurred, there is no history of organized and sidespread sabotage in the petroleum industry in the United States. Nevertheless, as we become more and more dependent on our limited domestic supplies of oil and gas, our national security becomes increasingly threatened and, in time of an oil embargo or created shortage of

Fig. 1. The national petroleum and natural gas system model

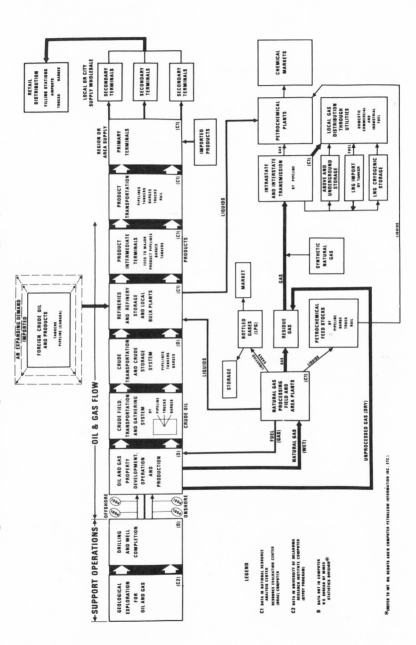

supply, damage done to even a fragment of the domestic industry takes on greater importance.

There are several levels of local, national, and international tensions, or situations, that might in themselves identify the potential for sabotage to the industry. Some are tabulated as follows:

1. A disgruntled employee or local dissident acting solely for one of a multiplicity of reasons;
2. A small group, or cult, seeking press attention to forward a "cause";
3. A group acting for monetary gain only, using threats, sabotage, and executive kidnapping to strengthen its demands;
4. A group having some "patriotic" cause, or strong national commitments, and seeking extensive press coverage;
5. Revolution, internal strife, and guerrilla activities within a country;
6. Limited warfare between nations;
7. Total warfare.

The level and intensity of tension will determine the type of oil and gas operations most likely to come under attack.

The flow of domestic petroleum, natural gas, and refined products advances to major national importance as the "conflicts," tabulated above, approach total war conditions. Much national attention has been directed toward the crucial role of energy. If the Gross National Product is plotted along with the use of energy, the two curves relate directly to each other (see Figure 2). A shortage of energy immediately reflects in the country's ability to generate goods, services, jobs, and transportation. Since 75 percent of the nation's energy is furnished by the oil and gas systems, it becomes an obvious corollary that anything that impairs the full function of these operations adversely affects the nation's economy and ability to function effectively.

Further, police and military services are mobile; all depend on petroleum products. No protective organization can function without a generous supply of the proper fuel, when and where needed. The present petroleum system is so efficient that planners

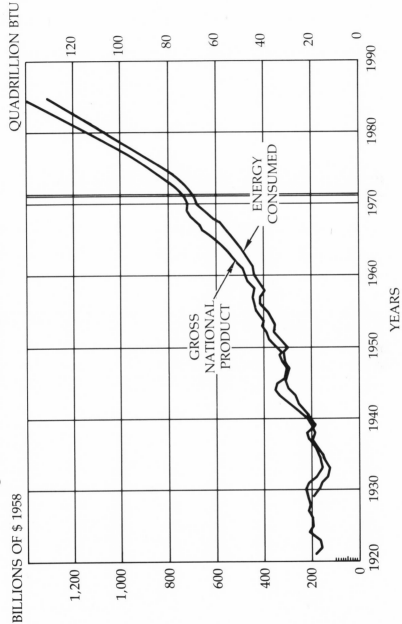

Fig. 2. Ratio of U.S. energy consumption to real GNP

tend to be lulled into a false sense of security, since almost unlimited volumes of fuel are presently available. Such probably will not be the case under conditions of even a minor, organized conflict in which deliverability of products is impaired.

Our present petroleum supply is not designed to withstand attack. It can be seriously damaged by a small band of knowledgeable, dedicated dissidents, even to the extent of impairing military functions. In addition, great localized chaos can be created where petroleum products suddenly become unavailable.

There has been planning for contingencies in the past, but such foresight seems to be in current disfavor. Most state plans, and, certainly, federal plans, are not fully updated to relate the constant changes in personnel and organization taking place within both industry and government. Most existing plans are obsolete or grossly inadequate to cope with the potential problems that the nation will surely face should a "cold war" or other types of attrition and stresses continue to plague it.

It is unfortunate that serious contingency planning, as it relates to oil and gas, has been grossly underfunded in the past ten years on a federal level and almost totally neglected on a state level. In view of planning done by some major nations, one must conclude that the United States has not kept pace and, if this trend continues, it could become a scenario for disaster.

VULNERABILITY OF OIL OPERATIONS

The *Oil and Gas Journal*[2] reports that, during the week ending October 6, 1978, the daily average of domestic oil production was 8,768,000 barrels (42 gallons per barrel). In spite of a record number of drilling rigs in operation during this same period (2,341), production was still 53,500 barrels of oil per day, less than during the same period in 1977. Oil discoveries are not keeping pace with escalating daily demands of the country. The Department of Energy[3] reports a product demand of 18,100,000 barrels per day, average, during May 1978. In this period, domestic production was up somewhat, but still a shortfall of about 40 percent of the total national demand occurred. The OPEC countries supplied about 82 percent of the crude oil imported to the United States in this period, or in excess of 4.6 million barrels per day. Refined products added to this supply. This oil is moved by tanker. Domestic crude oil accounted for 59.2 percent and foreign crude oil for 40.8 percent (May 1978) of the input to U.S. refineries.

The stark reality is that, if our crude oil and product supply from foreign sources were denied to this country, our supply of gasoline, fuel oil, and other refinery products needed to run our daily commerce would be about half of present demands. During the "Arab Embargo," a reduction in crude supply of only about 6 percent was experienced, yet almost everyone felt the impact of even that small impairment. It takes little imagination to project the potential chaos with a crude oil shortage of 40 to 50 percent in the event we must depend solely on domestic production.

Farming, transportation, and personal needs are highly dependent on an adequate supply of gasoline, jet, and diesel fuel. Our heating requirements and industrial uses of petroleum products for power generation, manufacturing operations, and commerce of other types add to this demand.

In the unlikely event of an international situation in which our supplies of crude oil from South America and Mexico were entirely cut off, our navy would be challenged to keep sea lanes open, for such oil is moved by tanker. During World War II, the small German submarine fleet essentially stopped domestic tanker movements in Gulf Coastal and Atlantic waters.[4] Because our eastern refineries are totally supplied by tanker and there is no crude oil pipeline serving these plants with oil from the major fields of the Gulf Coastal areas of Louisiana and Texas, a failure of tanker service could shut down these operations.

In the event of the loss of foreign oil supply, our economy could be expected to be immediately reduced to half of current levels. There is serious doubt in the writer's mind that we could long endure under such reduction in energy supply, especially if the country were under direct attack by a strong foreign power. This bleak scenario would be further exacerbated by "bombings" of our refineries, crude oil supply, and product-distributing facilities by concentrated efforts of terrorists and sabotage groups.

Peacetime Conditions

The main focus of this discussion is not on wartime conditions but on sabotage and possible terrorist activities during peacetime. Such actions would attack present and future existing petroleum facilities that daily meet the energy demands of our commerce and personal lives.

The energy flow is discussed in considerable detail in a report to the Committee on Energy and Natural Resources.[5] A review of the maps supplied with that report clearly show the movement of all types of energy used in the country. Crude oil moves from the field to the refineries. Refined products move from the refinery areas to market. There is no physical protection of these facilities, except those supplied for operational safety by the owners of the system. Although this situation may soon be corrected, there is no government agency with the mandate to furnish protection to these energy operations, except after damage has occurred.

Refineries

Our refining facilities have been concentrated in a few areas of the country.[6] This trend continues. National defense planning should decree that some de-concentration of such facilities occur and that many small, strategically located plants be built to make it impossible to wipe out such operations with only a few properly placed nuclear bombs.

Figure 3 shows the general distribution of major U.S. refineries. In 1978,[7] there were 285 refineries having a capacity of 16,848,684 barrels of crude oil per calendar day (allowing for normal shut-down for repair). Table 1 shows that over 69 percent of our refining capacity is concentrated in six states and the plants are usually close together in the refining areas.

Although a rocket, mortar shell or heavy rifle fire, or the destruction of electric power supply can cause extremely serious damage to a refinery, the fact that employees are always on the premises and that many emergency procedures are practiced daily makes the refinery less vulnerable to the work of a saboteur than other more remotely located petroleum facilities. One should not underestimate the costly damage that is possible to an

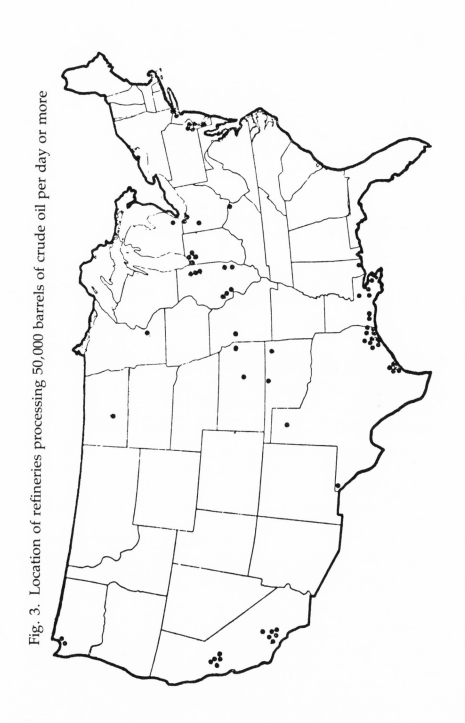

Fig. 3. Location of refineries processing 50,000 barrels of crude oil per day or more

TABLE 1

REFINING CAPACITY BY STATES

State	Number of plants	Barrels per calendar day	Percentage of total
Texas	53	4,597,075	27.3
California	40	2,373,933	14.1
Louisiana	23	2,097,616	12.4
Illinois	12	1,181,250	7.0
Pennsylvania	10	801,620	4.8
New Jersey	4	644,000	3.8
Others	143	5,153,190	30.6
U.S. total	285	16,848,684	100.0

oil refinery, but the temporary loss of the products from one or several plants would not be greatly detrimental to total energy flow, except in the local market. Often, extra capacity at other plants can be put into use to handle the shortage. Of course, a concerted attack on a number of plants would reverse this conclusion.

Widespread damage to the oil supply, product transportation, or power supply to a refinery group could cause greater concern. The average refinery operates on only a three- to five-day supply of crude oil. The plant "dies on the vine," so to speak, with this supply cut off, and in a relatively short time all downstream products from the plant cease to flow.

Oil Operations

Offshore   There are two general types of oil and gas production operations—offshore and onshore. Although, in general, the methods of drilling and oil production are essentially the same, offshore operations, exposed to the open sea, offer an attractive target to the well-equipped saboteur. Many of these offshore structures serve forty or so wells and, in recent times, production has occurred in over 1,200 feet of water. One structure can have a value in excess of fifty million dollars. A fire on these structures is disastrous to the company owning the platform and, if several were started, great economic stress could be placed on the companies involved. These impressive structures appear to be open invitations to terrorists. Fortunately, their vast number (over 3,000 in the Gulf of Mexico) serve as some protection. Most dissident groups look for extensive television and press coverage, which would most likely be minimal in offshore destruction because of a lack of easy press accessibility. It is more probable that the larger, or politically motivated, groups would choose these structures as targets.

No government agency has a clear mandate, in time of peace, to give protection to offshore wells. In war time, the navy could be assigned surveillance responsibilities. Kessler[8] discusses the lack of protection for offshore structures. Each company must do what is necessary to protect its own interest. There is essentially no protection of offshore oil platforms against intrusion. Sensitive equipment is available that would offer intrusion surveillance and even remedial protection. At present, most companies have not found interest in the use of such installations. There is a hope that the federal government will address itself to this problem, if only to avoid ship collisions.

Onshore   Domestic oil fields are scattered over thousands of miles. No one area supplies a major portion of our nation's supply. Outside of causing local harassment, there seems little point in attacking these areas, except, possibly, in time of war. Even then, the widespread nature of our oil and gas production makes a meaningful effort somewhat futile.

Oil Production Distribution   Oil is produced in thirty-one states of this country from approximately a half-million wells averaging about sixteen barrels per day. While very high grade crude is produced in Pennsylvania, West Virginia, Ohio, Kentucky, and New York, most oil comes from the southern states. California and Alaska stand out in the West as major oil sources. Table 2 shows that Texas and Louisiana produce about half of the nation's domestic crude oil. Offshore production predominates in Louisiana. Only one-eighth of total production comes from offshore wells.[9]

Seven widely separated states produce seven-eighths of the nation's oil. But the oil produced by the other states becomes of great significance in time of war, for most such areas supply local

TABLE 2

OIL PRODUCTION BY STATES
(May 1978)

State	Montly total (barrels)	Daily average (barrels)	Percentage of total
Texas	91,912,000	2,964,200	33.6
Louisiana	44,757,000	1,443,800	16.4
Alaska	39,649,000	1,279,000	14.5
California	29,365,000	947,300	10.8
Oklahoma	13,185,000	425,000	4.8
Wyoming	11,958,000	385,700	4.3
New Mexico	7,102,000	229,100	2.6
Others	34,909,000	1,126,100	12.8
U.S. total	272,837,000	8,800,200	99.8

refineries. These in turn furnish products for a specific area that might otherwise be cut off by major pipeline interruption.

VULNERABLE ASPECTS OF NATURAL GAS OPERATIONS

Much of the above discussion on oil relates also to the natural gas industry. The pattern of product flow differs in that the natural-gas processing plants serve this industry as does the refinery to the oil industry (see Figure 1). The oil/gas fields have identical problems. In fact, about one-fifth of domestic natural gas comes from oil wells as associated gas.

Natural gas is produced in thirty-two states of the country.[10] As shown in Table 3, about 71 percent of the nation's natural gas production comes from Louisiana and Texas. But the strategic position of these states changes when one considers the amount of interstate gas produced in Louisiana. In 1976,[11] of its marketed production of 7,191,859 millions of cubic feet (MMcf), Texas used 4,403,942 MMcf and exported into interstate lines a net of only 2,762,110 MMcf. Louisiana, which produced and marketed

TABLE 3

NATURAL GAS PRODUCTION BY STATES
(Millions of Cubic Feet at 14.73 PSIA)

| State | Gross withdrawals (1976) | | Total | Percentage of total |
	From gas wells	From oil wells		
Texas	6,213,395	1,452,537	7,665,932	36.6
Louisiana	6,365,774	777,266	7,143,040	34.1
Oklahoma	1,491,165	351,024	1,842,189	8.8
New Mexico	939,491	300,161	1,239,652	5.9
Kansas	704,197	127,467	831,664	4.0
California	174,477	253,163	427,640	2.0
Wyoming	262,692	74,141	336,833	1.6
Others				7.0
U.S. total	17,190,655	3,753,123	20,943,778	100.0

almost as much gas as Texas, used only 2,216,289 MMcf intra-state, exporting a net of 4,785,602 MMcf of its production into interstate lines, or almost twice that of Texas. A high percentage of this gas goes to the eastern portion of the country to supply the residential, commercial, industrial, and utility demands. About 53 percent of the net deliveries of interstate gas comes from Louisiana. Another 30.6 percent comes from Texas. Together, these two states furnish 83.6 percent of the gas used in states other than where the gas was produced. Much of the gas from Texas flows in pipelines through Louisiana on its way to eastern and Atlantic coastal markets. From the standpoint of the natural gas supply, Louisiana is the most strategically located state in the country.

Clearly, disruption to the flow of natural gas from Louisiana could cause major chaos to the vast number of consumers in heavily populated and commercial areas of the East. The eastern United States is almost totally dependent on this gas. In time, gas should be available to the East from Alaska, but the reality of a trans-Canadian pipeline is years away. For the next five to ten years at least, Louisiana and Texas are destined to be the major natural gas suppliers to the eastern consumer (see Figure 4).

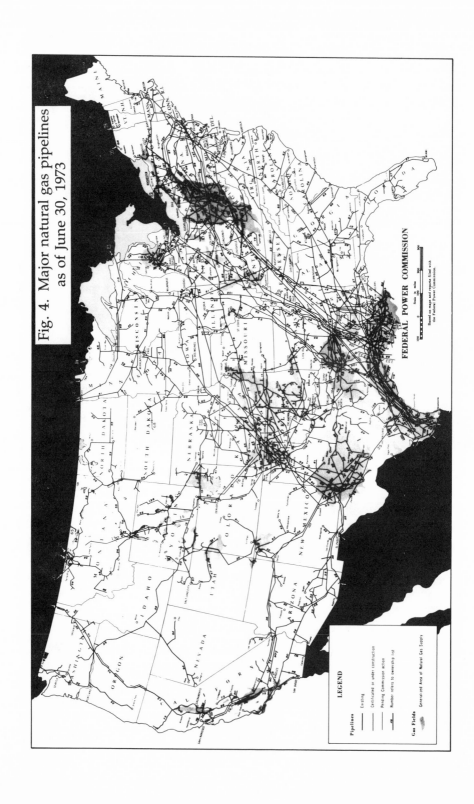

Fig. 4. Major natural gas pipelines as of June 30, 1973

FEDERAL POWER COMMISSION

Scale in miles

Based on maps and reports filed with the Federal Power Commission.

LEGEND

Pipelines

——— Existing

——— Certificated or under construction

——— Pending Commission action

68 Number refers to ownership list

Gas Fields

Generalized Area of Natural Gas Supply

Since much of this interstate gas moves through a relatively few major transmission lines, and many of these lines concentrate in certain geographical areas, it seems warranted to give some protective surveillance to major river crossings and compressor stations of these major systems. At present, there is essentially no protection of these critical areas, except for that provided for normal safe operation by individual companies that own the lines.

The natural gas system does not have the redundancy that electric power has. Once the gas enters the main transmission line of a company, there are few places, if any, where gas can be exchanged with another company. This is not true within the state of origin of the gas. Serious damage to a main line could cause a prolonged interruption of the natural gas supply to consumers served by the damaged system. Natural gas imported to the country in a liquid state is augmenting the gas supply on the East Coast. Since liquid natural gas (LNG) is transported in specially insulated tankers and stored in similar equipment at minus 270 degrees Fahrenheit, there is a substantial risk involved, not usual in natural gas operations. The LNG ports and terminals are sensitive areas.

Segments of major natural-gas transmission lines should therefore stand out as attractive targets to the saboteur. Damage at strategic places could shut down operations for months before repair and full flow could be restored. Fortunately, there is at present an overbuilding of transmission lines. Some unused, or partly used, lines exist. But in construction, when a line is looped (that is, several parallel lines laid together to form the system), it is popular to place the parallel lines along the same, or nearby, right-of-way. This policy is for the convenience of servicing, but it heightens the vulnerability of the total system to destruction.

Lines in wetland areas and the crossings of major rivers are places most difficult to repair quickly. Of course, since the equipment in large compressor stations, which boost line pressures to keep gas flowing on its way to market, is not usually an "off the shelf" item, damage to such equipment takes time to repair and necessitates special replacement.

The uninterrupted flow of natural gas is economically essential to the country. Since eastern refineries could be denied tanker service during an embargo or blockade, natural gas could become even more essential in a national emergency.

VULNERABILITY OF PIPELINE SYSTEMS

The vulnerability of natural-gas transmission lines was discussed above. The natural gas system, except for lines serving both oil and gas production in the field, is independent of petroleum operations.

Crude Lines

Oil is "gathered" from individual wells or a cluster of wells of a platform and brought to central points. Here, crude oil enters larger trunk pipelines in its flow to petroleum refineries. Crude oil, as mentioned above, is not usable in its natural state (except in case of a few engines made especially for crude oil use).

Oil is moved to the refinery by pipeline, barge, tanker, truck, and rail. Oil products are moved from the refinery by the same combination of transportation facilities. Tables 4 and 5 show the percentage of crude oil and products moved by various carriers.

The Department of Energy indicates that in 1977 there were 77,972 miles of crude trunklines, 81,296 miles of product trunklines, and 67,798 miles of gathering systems. This last figure is usually reported to be higher by the American Petroleum Institute. A total of 227,066 miles of pipeline serves the domestic industry of the country. Gathering lines are usually of small diameter, ranging from 2 inches to 12 inches. A few larger lines, up to 26 inches, exist. Crude trunklines are usually 8 to 12 inches in diameter, although 48-inch lines are in service. Product trunklines are commonly 6 to 20 inches in diameter, but some 40-inch lines are in use.

Although each line is of importance to its local system, several major trunklines are of significance. The recently completed Alaskan pipeline, moving oil from Prudhoe Bay to the ice-free port of Valdez, Alaska, is well known. There are a number of very critical sections along this line that, in time, could be of interest to

TABLE 4

TOTAL CRUDE PETROLEUM CARRIED IN DOMESTIC TRANSPORTATION AND PERCENTAGE
OF TOTAL CARRIED BY EACH MODE OF TRANSPORTATION
(in Tons of 2,000 Pounds)

Year	Total Crude Petroleum Carried	Pipelines		Water Carriers		Motor Carriers[a]		Railroads	
		Tons Carried	Percentage of Total	Tons Carried	Percentage of Total	Tons Carried	Percentage of Total	Tons Carried	Percentage of Total
1938	180,508,947	128,175,000	71.01	46,173,283	25.58	2,115,000	1.17	4,045,664	2.24
1943	240,730,423	176,835,000	73.46	31,129,833	12.93	7,875,000	3.27	24,890,590	10.34
1948	322,991,312	221,198,250	68.48	75,126,140	23.26	12,450,000	3.86	14,216,922	4.40
1953	376,860,595	283,379,400	75.19	70,585,701	18.73	19,012,642	5.05	3,882,852	1.03
1958	402,173,215	307,059,000	76.35	67,965,254	16.90	25,953,401	6.45	1,195,560	0.30
1963	468,083,466	351,876,969	75.17	83,235,525	17.78	32,189,676	6.88	781,296	0.17
1968	574,814,400	425,837,300	74.08	107,010,300	18.62	40,900,000	7.11	1,066,800	0.19
1970	615,273,800	457,156,700	74.30	116,300,900	18.90	40,900,000	6.65	916,000	0.15
1971	616,257,000	459,860,200	74.62	114,720,700	18.62	40,800,000	6.62	876,100	0.14
1972	643,739,000	487,606,700	75.75	103,672,800	16.10	51,000,000	7.92	1,459,500	0.23
1973	640,391,700	492,382,300	76.89	90,518,500	14.13	55,590,000	8.68	1,900,900	0.30
1974	620,599,600	464,272,400	74.81	83,580,000	13.47	70,043,000	11.29	2,704,200	0.43
1975	611,616,700	454,690,000	74.34	77,887,000	12.74	76,207,000	12.46	2,832,700	0.46
1976	608,630,800	458,508,800	75.33	75,210,000	12.36	72,625,500	11.93	2,286,500[b]	0.38

SOURCE: Association of Oil Pipe Lines, Washington, D.C.

[a] The amounts carried by motor carriers are estimates.
[b] Preliminary.

TABLE 5

Total Petroleum Products Carried in Domestic Transportation and Percentage of Total Carried by Each Mode of Transportation
(in Tons of 2,000 Pounds)

Year	Total Petroleum Products Carried	Pipelines[a]		Water Carriers		Motor Carriers[b]		Railroads	
		Tons Carried	Percentage of Total	Tons Carried	Percentage of Total	Tons Carried	Percentage of Total	Tons Carried	Percentage of Total
1938	173,911,713	11,045,962	6.35	91,555,208	52.65	18,423,060	10.59	52,887,483	30.41
1943	233,003,200	19,556,443	8.39	84,865,592	36.42	68,596,500	29.44	59,984,665	25.75
1948	363,282,518	41,254,281	11.36	162,390,189	44.70	108,447,800	29.85	51,190,248	14.09
1953	485,834,799	75,762,935	15.59	202,890,739	41.76	165,612,789	34.09	41,568,336	8.56
1958	615,006,000	125,968,566	20.48	230,690,771	37.51	226,071,342	36.76	32,275,321	5.25
1963	727,919,323	169,272,168	23.25	252,376,335	34.67	280,393,430	38.52	25,877,390	3.56
1968	988,583,300	300,606,600	30.41	253,992,300	25.69	408,800,000	41.35	25,184,400	2.55
1970	1,070,468,000	333,085,000	31.12	286,367,000	26.75	425,200,000	39.72	25,816,000	2.41
1971	1,103,555,900	346,810,800	31.43	302,071,300	27.37	429,900,000	38.96	24,773,800	2.24
1972	1,199,710,500	388,641,400	32.39	322,930,400	26.92	462,500,000	38.55	25,638,700	2.14
1973	1,282,527,200	419,827,600	32.74	330,687,300	25.78	504,177,000	39.31	27,835,300	2.17
1974	1,253,462,500	420,375,600	33.54	323,868,200	25.84	481,993,000	38.45	27,225,700	2.17
1975	1,219,899,100	424,759,300	34.82	326,077,900	26.73	444,398,000	36.43	24,663,900	2.02
1976	1,336,604,000	475,600,300	35.58	349,947,400	26.18	486,615,700	36.41	24,440,600[c]	1.83

SOURCE: Association of Oil Pipe Lines, Washington, D.C.

[a]Products pipelines move only light petroleum products—gasoline, heating and fuel oils, liquid petroleum gas, kerosene, and jet fuel.
[b]Estimated amounts.
[c]Preliminary.

the saboteur. This line will carry in excess of one million barrels of crude oil per day to enhance crude supply to western markets. At present, Alaskan crude is "landlocked" in California, except for that which moves by tanker to eastern refineries. A pipeline is planned from the Los Angeles area to the Texas area of El Paso, Midland, and Big Springs, but environmental interests have long delayed the completion and operation of this line. Such a system will play an important role in moving the excess crude oil supply from California to Texas and will relieve dependence on tankers. It is estimated that it will not function, however, until 1980–1981.

Capline, on the Mississippi River, at St. James, Louisiana, moves oil northward to Patoka, Illinois, and, hence, to refineries of St. Louis and Chicago and those in the central states. This line will serve the "Superport" now under construction in the Gulf of Mexico, near Grand Isle, Louisiana. It will carry in excess of one million barrels of crude oil per day.

As mentioned above, there are no crude trunklines serving the eastern refineries. Oil is moved to these plants almost totally by tanker.

Figure 5, though not updated to show all present construction, does indicate the prevailing trend of crude movement by pipeline. "Capline" needs to be added to the map.

Product Lines

After the crude oil is processed at the refinery, it is moved to the consumer market by pipeline, tanker, barge, rail, and truck. Trucks have become most important in the final movement of gasoline and fuel oil from terminals outside large metropolitan areas to automobile service stations and truck stops, or to dealers making deliveries of fuel oil to homes and commercial users. Long haul of products is accomplished, for the most part, by pipeline or tanker, as shown in Table 5.

Pipelines carry only the light ends of the refined product, that is, gasoline, jet fuel, kerosene, and light fuel oil. Heavy oil for industrial use must move by other modes of transportation.

Since there are no crude oil lines from Texas and Louisiana to the eastern refineries, product lines to these areas become of considerable significance. Reference to a pipeline map (Figure 6)

Fig. 5. Crude oil pipeline capacities

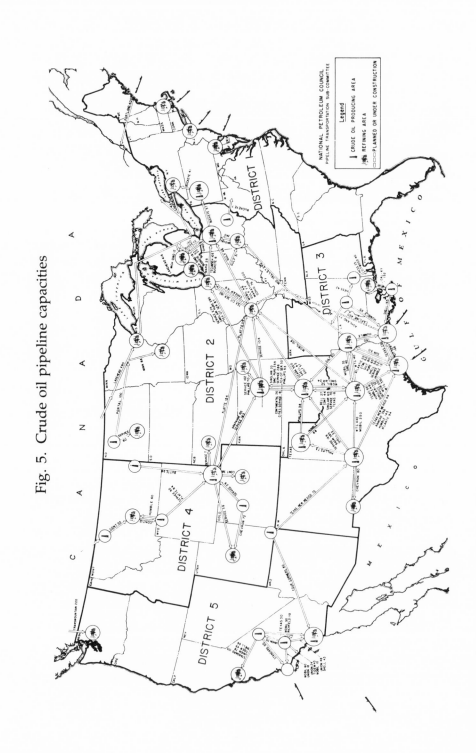

will show a general trend of flow of products from Texas, Louisiana, and some midcontinent areas to the east central and eastern states. Of special interest are the Colonial, Plantation, Texas-Eastern, and, perhaps, the Dixie lines. Over two and one-half million barrels (42 gallons per barrel) of light products are moved daily through these systems. Certainly, damage to any of these major lines will have significant economic impact on the eastern areas. Plantation and Colonial move products into Pennsylvania, New Jersey, and New York City.

As with other lines, damage to the special equipment of large pumping stations and, in particular, major river crossings, can cause long delays to product movement. Since the systems are computer-controlled and have little manual capability, destruction or damage could become a major problem, taking months to correct. It seems important that certain sensitive areas be given added protection as threats of sabotage increase.

VULNERABILITY OF STORAGE AREAS

Natural Gas

There are numerous gas underground storage areas strategically placed throughout the country. These are like condensers on the lines and take up seasonal surge in demand. In summer, these "pools" are filled to whatever extent natural gas is available. Withdrawals of gas occur when winter demands increase above the field ability to supply the required extra volume.

The input and withdrawal into the storage pools varies from state to state and from year to year, depending upon the field supply and the demand of consumers. In 1976, studies by the American Gas Association's Committee on Underground Storage showed input to storage to be 1,918,541,256 thousand cubic feet (14.73 PSIA @ 60°F.), output from storage to be 2,059,897,948 Mcf, or a net loss to storage of 165,327,189 Mcf, after certain adjustments and revisions in data were made. This was the first time withdrawals exceeded the quantity put into storage in a calendar year. Warm winters, or extra discoveries, allow the replenishing of underground storage reservoirs.

Fig. 6. Product pipeline capacities

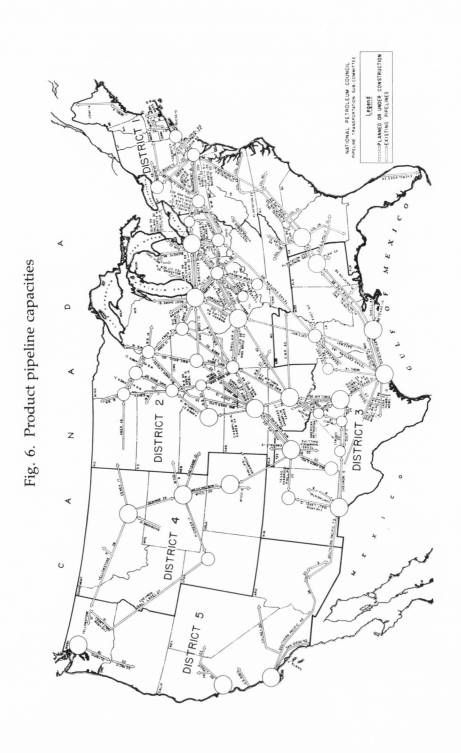

NATIONAL PETROLEUM COUNCIL
PIPELINE TRANSPORTATION SUB-COMMITTEE

Legend

PLANNED OR UNDER CONSTRUCTION
EXISTING PIPELINES

By the end of 1976,[12] there were 380 underground storage reservoirs capable of holding 6,579.7 billion cubic feet of natural gas. Pennsylvania has 61 such reservoirs, West Virginia has 38, and Michigan and Illinois have 37 and 34, respectively.

Of course, underground storage projects are of interest to the individual saboteur but, as in the case of natural gas storage, the loss of one project would not be likely to have serious national impact. Here again, the number of such projects and their geographical distribution make their destruction only of local interest and, of course, harassing to the owners.

The United States departed from self-sufficiency in oil supply in 1967. Since that time, dependence on foreign oil has increased to its present level. In the "exercising" of the Emergency Petroleum and Gas Administration, the "Star Group" of the Federal Preparedness Agency, and the Defense Civil Preparedness Agency, and in studies by the writer and others, it became evident that the storage of crude oil at strategic places in the country was important to national security. The recommendation for such storage is now being implemented.

The country is faced with the problem of having oil where and when it is needed. Crude stored in salt domes of the Gulf Coast will not be available to eastern refineries during a national emergency. A more sensible plan is to have storage available to eastern refineries, an area now totally dependent on tanker service. The writer finds no problem with the government's salt-dome storage program of Louisiana if the objective is to have oil available during some future, brief "Arab Embargo." But, to have greater national security significance, oil storage needs to be concentrated in areas likely to be denied tanker service.

CONCLUSION

The targets selected by terrorist groups, or even by lone saboteurs, will usually depend on their objectives. A dedicated revolutionary group usually does expect that its attack will serve a specific purpose. Such need not be so in the case of a disgruntled former employee or a psychologically disturbed individual. Some sabotage studied by the writer seems to have little purpose except to cause harassment of the company involved.

It is well known that politically motivated groups try to create problems that will cause embarrassment to local authorities and to demonstrate the inability of authorities to give protection. And if a dissident group is seeking publicity and national recognition of its cause, then an objective causing spectacular interest and wide press coverage is likely to be chosen.

The oil and gas industry is highly efficient in that it brings a continuous supply of petroleum products and natural gas to the consumer in almost any quantity demanded. But the facilities of this industry are designed for most economic service and not maximum security. Most plants, offshore platforms, central oil and gas processing facilities, pipelines, and refineries are totally exposed and are highly vulnerable. River crossings, which, if destroyed, could take months to repair, are, by law, identified by large roadway signs, as if to invite destruction. Power units, serving a refinery complex, are usually located along main highways and protected by nothing more than a chainlink fence. Although such substations are usually "looped" and alternate service can usually be routed to replace destroyed transformers, still there are numerous places where it is not always possible to restore electric service before an emergency plant shutdown becomes necessary. As for our pipeline system, if a group were seriously trying to affect the economy of the United States, attacks on critical segments of this system could be surprisingly devastating.

The federal and state governments have taken little or no interest in the possibility that petroleum and gas facilities can be victims of sabotage or the focal point of terrorists. But most companies do not wish direct government security supervision for fear of encroachment on their managerial rights. There is a degree of impasse on this subject between government and company management.

Our domestic oil and gas production will be our total supply in case of an all-out war, naval blockade, or embargo. At present, it supplies only about half of our peacetime needs. Anything that affects the smooth operation of that industry directly affects the national and local economy. Our national security and ability to protect ourselves depends on the free flow of petroleum products and natural gas. Segments of the systems need some degree of facility protection from potential attack by terrorists.

NOTES

1. Maynard M. Stephens, *Vulnerability of Total Petroleum Systems*, Report prepared for the Defense Civil Preparedness Agency, DAHC 20-70-C-0316 (Washington, D.C.: U.S. Department of the Interior, May 1973), p. 2.

2. OOJ Statistics, "OOJ Production Report," *Oil & Gas Journal*, October 16, 1978, p. 126.

3. U.S. Department of Energy, Office of Energy Data and Interpretation, "Energy Data Reports, May 1978" (Washington, D.C., September 18, 1978), p. 1.

4. This is fully discussed in Stephens, *Vulnerability of Total Petroleum Systems*, p. 43.

5. Committee on Commerce, Science and Transportation, "Report Prepared for the Committee on Energy and Natural Resources and Committee on Commerce, Science and Transportation," Publication 95-15, *National Energy Transportation*, Vol. 1: *Current Systems and Movements* (Washington, D.C., May 1977).

6. Maynard M. Stephens, "Minimizing Damage to Refineries from Nuclear Attack, Natural and Other Disasters" (Washington, D.C.: U.S. Department of the Interior, Office of Civil Defense, February 1970).

7. Ailleen Cantrell, "Annual Refining Survey," *Oil & Gas Journal*, March 29, 1978, p. 108.

8. Christian J. Kessler, "Legal Issues in Protecting Offshore Structures," Professional Paper No. 147 (Arlington, Va.: Center for Naval Analysis, June 1976).

9. U.S. Department of Energy, "Energy Data Reports."

10. Leonard L. Fanelli, "Natural Gas Production and Consumption—1976," Natural Gas Annual, Energy Data Reports (Washington, D.C.: U.S. Department of Energy, February 7, 1978).

11. Ibid.

12. Ibid.

Crisis Management: Some Opportunities

ROBERT H. KUPPERMAN, RICHARD H. WILCOX, and HARVEY A. SMITH

Many alarming trends of our present culture share common roots. Worldwide inflation, worldwide resource shortages, extensive famine, and the inexorable quest for more deadly weapons may very well reach crisis proportions if these trends continue. They serve already as examples of national and international failures of efficient resource allocation and communications. It is important that we understand the possible future implications that these failures hold and, more important, that we develop means for dealing with them.

In discussing the crisis management demanded by such situations it is tempting to start by defining what is meant by a crisis, but this is a difficult matter. Crises are matters of degree, being emotionally· linked to such subjective terms as calamity and emergency. In fact it is not necessary to define crises in order to discuss problems generally common to their management, including the paucity of accurate information, the communications difficulties that persist, and the changing character of the players as the negotiations for relief leave one or more parties dissatisfied.

In a sense, crises are unto the beholder. What is a crisis to one individual or group may not be to another. However, crises are generally distinguished from routine situations by a sense of urgency and a concern that problems will become worse in the absence of action. Vulnerability to the effects of crises lies in an inability to manage available resources in a way that will alleviate

SOURCE: Reprinted from *Science* 187 (February 7, 1975), pp. 404–410, by permission of the authors and the American Association for the Advancement of Science. Copyright © 1975 by the American Association for the Advancement of Science.

the perceived problems tolerably. Crisis management, then, requires that timely action be taken both to avoid or mitigate undesirable developments and to bring about a desirable resolution of the problems.

Crises may arise from natural causes or may be induced by human adversaries, and the nature of the management required in response differs accordingly. Thus the actions required to limit physical damage from a severe hurricane and to expedite recovery from it differ substantially from the tactics needed to minimize the economic effects of a major transportation strike and to moderate the conditions which caused it. Yet each also exhibits some characteristics of the other. For example, recovery from the devastation wrought by the hurricane's wind and floodwaters brings competition among different managers whose conceptions of recovery differ: Is the goal to reestablish the status quo, including slums, or to seize upon the opportunity for urban renewal? Similarly, a transportation strike may cause such economic chaos that the Congress—535 crisis managers—might threaten to pass laws that are detrimental to a union leadership's prestige and control over its members.

It is useful to note the characteristics common to most crisis management. Perhaps the most frustrating is the uncertainty concerning what has happened or is likely to happen, coupled with a strong feeling of the necessity to take some action anyway "before it is too late." This leads to an emphasis on garnering information: military commanders press their intelligence staffs, and civil leaders try to get more out of their field personnel and management information systems. Unfortunately, few conventional information systems are equal to the task of covering unconventional situations, so managers in a crisis must frequently fall back upon experience, intuition, and bias to make ad hoc decisions (1).

The problems of uncertainty are exacerbated by the dynamic nature of many crises. Storms follow unpredictable courses; famine is affected by vagaries in the weather; terrorists perform apparently irrational acts; and foreign leaders, responding to different value systems or simply interpreting situations differently, select unexpected courses of action. Thus, with limited information and resources the manager may find it difficult just to keep up with rapid developments, let alone improve the overall picture of the situation.

During a crisis, not only does an involved manager suffer from poor information, but he has the problem of identifying the objectives he wishes to accomplish and ordering them by priority in accord with his limited resources. The order in which his objectives are placed may be quite controversial, and his priorities may change as he learns of the success or failure of his prior actions and the sharply vocalized opinions of his supporters and detractors. There is generally no single acceptable course of events for him to follow; rather, there is a wide selection which can be ordered more or less by their relative economy and political difficulty of accomplishment.

To illustrate this phenomenon, consider the plight of the Federal Disaster Coordinator during a major natural disaster. There is limited manpower, equipment, and time. Few would disagree that the saving of lives and providing of food and initial shelter is the first order of business; and few would disagree that reconstruction of public parks can be postponed. But when one considers the multiple and relatively incommensurate questions of the restoration of utilities, the securing of mobile homes for temporary housing, and the clearance of major debris, the manager has his hands full in setting priorities. The widespread effects of Hurricane Agnes of 1972 provide an example: extensive damage, severe resource shortages, and a lot of political heat.

Under crisis conditions the manager has relatively little time to analyze available alternatives (his own or those of an adversary) or to develop new capabilities. His flexibility depends primarily upon the extent to which he has forecasted for the situation and made the investment to prepare for it. If he has foreseen the potential emergency adequately, he may be able to avoid it entirely. Although this is, in principle, the ideal form of crisis management, in practice it can be a thankless achievement, for few can recognize what has been accomplished. Glamour and a sense of heroism accompany the "crisis resolver," not the "crisis avoider."

If domestic and international tensions are to be mitigated with greater success, the important role of the "crisis avoider" must be recognized. Because some of the problems facing the world today are sufficiently serious, their amelioration may be prerequisite to the avoidance of major world conflict. Included in this category are famine, particularly in Africa and the Indian subcontinent; inadequacy of available world energy supplies and related distribution systems that cannot support even the present rate of growth, let alone the emergence of developing nations; and the spreading trend of terrorism by extremist groups.

The Process of Managing Crises

We will use the term "crisis management" to mean any process which a manager exercises to meet his goals within a potentially deteriorating situation at an acceptable cost to him, persuading those with whom he is interacting that the costs of opposing him are greater than the costs of allowing him to attain his objectives.

This definition of crisis management is broad and admittedly something of a straw man. It implicitly involves resource allocation, urgency, and various forms of communications. It admits the possibilities of programmed conflict as well as of situations offering minimal feedback. The management of economic problems, disasters, famines, and the termination or avoidance of war are includable within the definition.

In international relations, the process of crisis management can be regarded as having the objective of convincing an opponent that the immediate and long-run costs of opting for, continuing, or increasing hostilities exceed the immediate costs of accepting an offer to resolve conflict that minimally promises face-saving opportunities to the leaderships of the more powerful nations.

New initiatives in international crisis management in military policy—and, hence, arms control—are prompted by the present thrusts of U.S. strategic doctrine (2). As the United States proceeds to modify its nuclear deterrence policy from mutual assured destruction alone to one involving a wider set of options, we are forced to examine carefully the likely reactions of our opponents. Such a broader policy, in fact, requires the most involved crisis management efforts. Without refined analyses and communications techniques we would be left with little more than the prior binary strategy, albeit prolonged in execution; there would still be missing any planned military activities of less than catastrophic magnitude. Controlled warfighting remains a game-theoretic exercise. Though nuclear war lurks in the shadows, we hardly understand the nature of the game that an adversary may perceive himself to be playing—in fact, we do not even seem to do very well at understanding ourselves.

Negotiations with an adversary in an international crisis rest, at bottom, on conveying to him the costs of opposition in terms of his own value system. (In many cases these may be opportunity costs, that is, costs attributable to lost or deferred opportunities.) Moreover, for our position to be credible to an opponent he must perceive that the costs we propose to meet in gaining our objectives are actually acceptable to us in terms of our value system. There are a number of hazards in this task. One of the hazards implicit in conveying costs is that the tactics themselves are a part of the value system. An opponent may, for instance, have a cultural bias toward noncooperative behavior, such as playing zero-sum games—that is, treating all bargaining as though a gain for one side must represent a loss for the other (3).

Another hazard is connected with the conceptual problems of exploring fully an adversary's measures of utility (quantitative indicators of desire or goodness), as well as our own. Nations foster economic and political institutions that are imperfect images of differing implicit value systems. At best we can discern preferences among alternatives, and these preferences need not be internally consistent nor temporally constant. It may be that reluctance to depart from familiar practices has daunted us from responding effectively to the challenges posed by the more difficult communications and control problems between nations, because we have engaged in dialogues that are predicated on our differing value systems.

These difficulties appear to become more tractable, fortunately, as the economic and political interdependencies among nations increase. Such interdependence does not necessarily entail losses in natural or cultural identities. Rather, each party is forced into mutual manipulation of the different socioeconomic structures of the others as each attempts to understand relative preferences among policy options and consequent areas of mutual benefit. This is just as true for competitive trade relations as for cooperative ventures like dealing with international terrorism.

A number of difficulties have been noted here as being common to the management of crises: uncertainty, poor data-handling methods, too little data, too much data, inadequate communications, differing value systems, changing management objectives, political harassment, little planning, and insufficient time in which to learn. To this long list of conceptual difficulties must be added the psychological and physical problems of confusion and fatigue. Clearly, the successful crisis manager must be a versatile person—a resource allocator, a communicator, and an artful negotiator with a tough hide.

As we begin to recognize the enormously complex problems that threaten every nation with disaster, can we continue to trust the ad hoc processes of instant reaction to muddle through? If not, "crisis management" must be inseparable from "crisis preparedness" and must consist of concerted international efforts to jointly develop tools of communications, management, and analysis in order to better deal with each other. With natural resource and food shortages as well as the threats of atomic terrorism rapidly coming upon us, little will be solved by reviving the Cold War in any form. In order to institutionalize a more harmonious structure of relationships, a modern international planning process must aid in encouraging further communications leading to economic and political interdependencies.

Of all the planning concerns that must be addressed, the most difficult is the measurement of utility, especially among comparative value systems, Here we face what might appear to be limiting conceptual problems. How can two nations with radically different outlooks and perceptions engage in a meaningful dialogue involving respective value systems not well understood by either? In what follows we present an approach to treating the problems of comparative value systems in a manner that capitalizes on a vital class of analytical and data management activities.

A Metalanguage for Peace

The prior sections of this article emphasize the data management and communications problems that are present during crises. If we can establish our objectives, our inventory of resources, and the time and cost constraints, we can allocate scarce materials and services efficiently. This is the essence of any planning function.

In practice, however, planning tends to be ignored. It is most difficult for top executives to give up the immediate services of their more valuable people to do planning. The natural tendency is to call on them every time there is the slightest sense of urgency, and "minicrises" occur in staccato fashion in the top levels of every large institution, including nations.

Let us now consider the potential of computer-assisted conferencing systems as a means for eventually developing planning and operational bases for international crisis management (4). The application of computers themselves to such subjects is, of course, not new. Both in research institutions and in government agencies there is a long-standing tradition of politico-military gaming. Scholars from many nations have developed models for economic and military planning (5). Military leaders in the United States have often ended up adopting the results of models they have severely criticized initially, and it would not be surprising to discover the same phenomenon in other nations. They do so for a very simple reason: there appear to be no better alternatives for justifying their specific weapons and budgetary requests. Thus, we are led to propound an analog of the "Peter Principle" (6): computer models are expanded until they become accepted surrogates of an unattainable reality.

But if modeling efforts are to overcome the limitations of narcissistic mirror-imaging or other forms of myth fulfillment, there must be developed a means for nations to share their images of and correct the other's perceptions. The marriage of computer conferencing with computer modeling offers a concept for the international use of models as constructive progenitors for common "metalanguages" to serve as communications bridges.

In a conventional conference the participants follow certain rules in an effort to provide each a chance to air his views and all a chance to hear them. Formal conferences rigidly adhere to highly institutionalized parliamentary procedure, but even small informal groups usually accept tacitly—perhaps even unconsciously—much simplified but still analogous sets of rules. These codes of communication behavior impose a synchronous regimen on the proceedings: only one person speaks at a time, and all participants who wish to address a given topic do so in turn. In general, participants must be present in order to take part in the proceedings effectively. Conferences are of course held over the telephone to overcome geographic separation, but all participants must still take part during the same time interval, and special procedures such as roll calling or unceasing speaker self-identification must usually be invoked to avoid chaos.

In a computer-assisted conference the participants do not need to gather at a common table, or even at a common time by their separate telephones. Their participation is asynchronous. That is, each sits at times of his own choosing at a typewriter-like device which is connected by telephone to a common computer. He receives automatically all written proposals and reactions thereto originated by other participants since his last session at the terminal. He then composes his own comments and new proposals and enters them into the system for distribution to the others. The participant may vote on various proposals placed before the group or request a vote on his own proposals. After doing all this without interruption, he may wait for immediate reactions from others, or he may "sign off" to turn his attention to other pressing matters, returning later without fear of missing anything because all statements generated elsewhere in the interim will be held for his return. In fact, he may never personally sit at the computer terminal, relying instead upon aides to bring him new conference business arriving at his terminal from other participants and giving his aides his own input in the form of comments and proposals. The role of the computer is to store and identify all inputs, forward them to each other participant whenever he or his agent is "on-line," record and tally votes, and provide various editing and sorting services to facilitate the organization of lucid information.

Use of Descriptive Models

In addition to the convenience and economy afforded by simple computer conferencing, as described above, the embedding of a dynamic model in the conference could assist the participants materially in understanding the real import of each other's statements. (By a model is meant a description, either mathematical or verbal, of the essence of the subject under discussion. Well-known models of the economy, for example, could be easily embedded for analysis.) Because of the power and speed of the computer, a participant could illustrate his proposals for change by demonstrating those changes in the model dynamically and producing results which all could witness identically. Similarly, "what if" questions could be explored with the model by individuals or the group, without problems of their misunderstanding either the options tried or the effects obtained.

A fundamental difficulty during an international crisis is that of conveying accurately to an adversary the essential nature and intent underlying proposals intended to lessen tensions. If these proposals could be made partly in terms of sophisticated socioeconomic models available identically to all discussants, then definitional issues could be more readily resolved, relevant parameters adjusted, and the implications of foreign policy or military decisions mutually tested.

Whether or not the models available to such a conferencing system are initially considered to offer a "true" picture of reality is relatively unimportant; the value lies not in the original basis, but rather in the system's ability to support evolving bases for planning and dialogue among nations (7). As the dialogue continues interactively, the phrases and descriptions in the conference—the models—will be modified extensively and grow in number, both from feedback by the principals and as a result of intensive scholarly attention. Eventually a class of models will evolve to the point of being accepted as reality, for the assertion of any other reality must bear the test of mutual interaction and acceptance into the system in order to be believed. The system thus would eventually become the arbiter of reality.

It may be argued by the more operationally oriented, with considerable justice, that present behavioral science models are not sufficient for the level of descriptive and predictive analysis needed to make computer conferencing useful. The often intangible problems of measuring utility are at the root of the conceptual difficulties of socioeconomic modeling. Nevertheless, analytic tools can at least help in establishing relative preferences among alternatives. And in an interactive conferencing context, the invariant properties among differing value systems of the negotiants can be discerned. Although accurate prediction is always important, computer conferencing provides an experimental basis for improving human communication, and the value of such collective judgment in the long run will be considerable. The objective is computer augmentation of human reasoning (8), reasoning that is cooperative and involving many nations. By definition, this represents communication, and this is a kind of communication that is much needed.

Computer-supported conferencing is now a reasonably well-established technique in its own right (9). Its deliberate use in conjunction with analytical models to achieve an increased level of understanding of differing value systems is, however, decidedly unconventional. Thus it should be expected that the remarkable improvements promised by such an arrangement would be accompanied by several serious problems to resolve. In particular, if adversaries are coupled through a computer conference and are using shared analytical models, the nature of the communication interface between man and machine can become critical.

This problem is perennial in the computer business, and it becomes considerably more difficult when the participants are not "computer people." The results of model calculations must be conveyed effectively to those who make policy and their staffs, and so must the explicit parameters and implicit assumptions behind those calculations. Such people are subject matter specialists, and to be useful to them a computer terminal should be no more difficult to use than an automobile. Just as one need not be a mechanical engineer to use an automobile as an effective mode of transportation support, so one should not have to be a computer engineer to use a remote terminal as an effective mode of cognitive support (10).

Current Status, Remaining Problems

Fortunately, there is a growing history of successful experience to draw upon in designing computer conferencing systems for use by "noncomputer people" in poorly defined contexts. Some dramatic results were achieved by the former Office of Emergency Preparedness in 1971 (11), from which some very effective extensions grew (12). These systems were devised and developed for use in domestic crisis situations characterized by rapidly expanded operational staffing, little advance knowledge of the information which would be needed, and rapidly changing perceptions.

To the casual observer, the distinctive features of these computer conferencing systems for crisis use would appear to be ease of use, breadth of applicability, and extreme flexibility. Rather than requiring knowledge of a computer language, they actively present the user with a "menu" of things which he can do, so that he needs only to select the appropriate items. Through interactive steps, he can refine his selections or correct his mistakes. The nature of the choices presented to users, and the form and content of information obtained or accepted as a result, can be changed relatively rapidly to suit the conditions of a specific crisis and the preferences of the specific decision-makers managing it.

An even more significant feature of these systems, for our purposes, is the underlying concept of perennially evolving design which makes the breadth and flexibility of use possible. It is a fundamental design concept that the specific information requirements placed upon the systems cannot be known ahead of time, so that detailed "final design" has to be transient, taking place during actual operation and based upon feedback from the operators. Thus design is never considered final; the systems continue to evolve throughout each crisis in which they are implemented. The users not only interact with the computer system in addressing the problem of interest, they also interact with the designer in modifying the system to better address the problem (13).

Although this approach to computer conferencing has been successful in managing domestic crises, severe problems remain. In particular, the processes of including more sophisticated models, embedding the models overtly into the conferencing system to facilitate computer support, and extending the combination effectively into the sphere of multilanguage international discussions remain to be completed (14).

One important concern to be addressed, and to be resolved carefully, is the fundamental psychological difference between nontechnically inclined professional managers and computer specialists. The managers are concerned that they are losing control of the situation to machines they don't understand. On the other hand, the computer specialists' isolation from the pragmatic world sometimes creates in them the private suspicion that perhaps the machines really could do the job better. It is absolutely essential that the computer output be effectively conveyed to, and controlled by, the humans participating substantively in the discussions. Among the leaders of all advanced nations of the world there is recognition that nuclear war must be avoided; but machines might not be so constrained.

The communications barriers between crisis managers using a model and the computer specialists who would normally design and operate it could be bypassed to a large extent by embedding the model directly into the conference system. The "menu approach" already used to facilitate lay use of computer-based information systems could be used similarly to enable a conferring crisis manager to modify the model himself. That is, a list of model parameters described in conventional language could be presented to the conferee, from which he could select the change he wished to explore and the specific values he wished to try. Other crisis managers in the conference could view the results he obtained, and might try the same or other changes for themselves. Even if the conferees did not fully understand the inner workings of the model, their common observation of its responses resulting from their own stimuli would provide the metalinguistic bases being sought.

It is obvious, of course, that if our own crisis managers could capitalize upon the model-oriented, computer-assisted conferencing system to try out ideas on the side, then an adversary could do the same. In fact, multiple adversaries could use adjunct conferences to form coalitions. But countercoalitions could also be formed, so that in the long run there would be no net loss in plotting capability. Obviously, it will behoove crisis managers to acquire as much skill as possible in the use of conferencing systems, but that is true of any tool or technique used for communications among cooperating adversaries. A computer-assisted conference can facilitate the communications by improving the likelihood that an adversary correctly understands the concepts we intend to convey (and vice versa), but it cannot unilaterally enhance our capability to generate superior concepts, any more than it can improve our physical means to defend ourselves—we must still think intelligently, and we must still have minimally adequate resources available to manage. Computer-assisted conferencing can only assist in communicating and analyzing available information, and in efficiently allocating available resources (15).

Possible Future Applications

In keeping with our definition of international crisis management, it seems appropriate to speculate about some of the ultimate uses computer-assisted conferencing can offer. We assume that it will take a decade or so for such systems to develop internationally in such a way that many nations of the world gain sufficient planning experience to engage in computer-assisted crisis management. Nations will then be able to enjoy rich methods of communications that will offer them deep understanding of each other's socioeconomic institutions. A host of cooperative ventures will then become possible.

The conferencing system could simulate foreign exchange between nations, for example. At present, domestic price ratios are used as measures of value in calculating foreign exchange rates. These price ratios, however, do not accurately reflect "value" because most market economics are no longer "free." Price ratios do not even exist in any comparable form in controlled economies. Thus currency exchange rates based on price ratios present accuracy problems. The conferencing system could augment the present system for valuing trade by accommodating a large variety of barter deals.

Also in the economic realm, when changes in internal economies lead individual nations to consider import tariffs, quotas, or other disruptions to existing trade patterns, a model-oriented conference among interested nations could permit relatively unemotional exploration of the international effects of implementing the proposed move. If an economic crisis did occur, perhaps because of unanticipated side effects, the conference would greatly facilitate a cooperative approach to its amelioration and would permit "tuning" the response through successive small actions tailored to the developing situation.

The use of computer conferencing to address economic problems obviously need not be restricted to international forums. For example, a model developed to exhibit the interaction of a corporation and its employees with the community, the industry, and the regional economy could be used in a labor-management conference to explore the implications of demanded or proposed contract provisions and, conversely, of a strike if agreement were not reached. Even if the disputants disagreed concerning the appropriate model parameters to describe some of the effects, representative values chosen by both factions could be used in order to generate alternative predictions which should acceptably bracket the range of expected effects.

A case of particular interest is that of safeguarding nuclear material against terrorists and guerrillas. The proliferation of nuclear weapons and the materials with which to make them may be alarming within the decade. The nations of the world must be able to account for the stockpiles of nuclear materials, safeguard them, and cooperate fully when one or more of them is threatened. For example, in order to coerce the United States, a dissident terrorist group capable of having fabricated a nuclear weapon might threaten Paris with atomic demolition if the French did not place adequate pressures on the United States to meet the radicals' demands. Conferencing could provide an analysis of the repercussions of alternative actions for the United States and France; perhaps even more important, it would enable settlement of an equitable (or at least acceptable) allocation of costs, risks, and losses between the two nations. The crisis is more likely to be mitigated with minimum harm to both nations in such a controlled situation.

An analogous problem comes from the field of strategic warfare. If entire populations were no longer to be used as hostages in order to deter strategic confrontation, then specific economic pressure points, such as key industrial, power, and transportation sites, might become hostages instead. These pressure points would have to be clearly understood by the opponent but kept secret from the public because of their potential vulnerability to terrorists. Optimal investments in redundancy and physical protection could be determined so that cost thresholds could be set that would be low enough to provide opposing nations unimpeded opportunity for effective retaliatory attack but high enough to deter terrorists from attacking these points.

Finally, consider a case of economic aggression, such as an oil embargo imposed by the Organization of Petroleum Exporting Countries (OPEC). The utility of such behavior is often questionable in both the short and the long run. Do embargoes promote fear and thus support for the aggressor's policies or do they promote outrage and a determination to resist more tenaciously? A greater flow of information among nations, with accompanying appreciation for each other's socioeconomic values and institutions, would lead potential aggressors to better recognize unproductive or self-damaging programs. An interactive conferencing system could let OPEC nations discover the limits beyond which belligerent behavior would become counterproductive; such a system would also help threatened nations coordinate efforts to defend themselves should a crisis occur. Under such controlled circumstances the likelihood of mutually destructive embargoes would be mitigated, as would political and economic chaos should an embargo occur.

A Humanitarian Beginning

Although it was convenient to assume in the last section that use of international computer conferencing systems would be commonplace within a decade or so, such widespread adoption will not come about automatically. Indeed, many factors against rapid adoption have already been identified, including bureaucratic inertia and administrative mistrust of quantitative science and technology—particularly the "fearsome" computers. Thus we turn now to the question of how to introduce the proposed techniques successfully into the international arena.

The surest road to failure would be a lavishly funded crash program to address some delicate and highly controversial issue. With so many aspects of application remaining to be developed, the inevitable failure of such a headlong approach would stifle any further attempts for a long time. What is needed is a situation which is international in scope, noncontroversial in the overall goal sought, nontrivial, inherently interdisciplinary, and sufficiently long-term in nature that there is opportunity for substantial development in both the system and its use while a solution to the problem is being pursued.

Of all the looming world problems, the one which seems best to fit this prescription is famine. The increasingly serious situation in the Sahel region of northern Africa forms a current multination example of growing international concern (16). No one seems to favor starvation, although effective relief may perturb other food supplies, compete for transportation, and disturb domestic economies. Despite the long history and widespread nature of the problem, little seems to be known about the quantitative dynamics of famine. Successful attack calls for natural and social science, mathematics and experiment, technology and economics, government and industry. We know, for instance, that at some point seed corn and domestic animals are eaten, and that this complicates the recovery from famine, but useful quantitative models of the process do not appear to exist. Evolving models for the famine process, for world food resources, and for the relevant processing and transportation facilities via a computer-assisted international conference might allow agreement on an objective plan of action and a coherent long-term relief effort, rather than sporadic and ineffective attempts to feed the hungry. Feedback to model designers from field operations would provide checks on the validity of the models. The implementation and management of such a plan would both develop and test the crisis-management potential of the system.

Human lives would, of course, be at risk, and the pressure to make life and death decisions could become increasingly intense. Conceivably, as in the triage system of battlefield medical treatment, the "right" decision may turn out to be counterinstinctual. Although we expect that everyone would favor famine relief in principle, we would expect some divergence based on differing national outlooks when really difficult choices had to be made. When chaos reigns it is easy to fall back on the belief that "nothing can be done" and so avoid responsibility. But when it becomes clear that something can be done, although the choice is among a number of direly unpleasant options each involving numerous fatalities, then the burden of responsibility cannot be avoided.

The challenge to resolve such disputes and allay the resulting passions, growing out of such a worthwhile objective as alleviating famine, would make a first-rate preliminary test of the possible usefulness of model-oriented computer conferencing systems in the larger arena of maintaining world peace. But how can the development of the necessary system be organized and financed? To ask an operational agency with crisis management responsibilities to fund the development would be inappropriate. The international Food and Agriculture Organization (FAO), for instance, would expect to spend its money on distributing food for the hungry and could be severely criticized for investing in a speculative crisis management system instead. Some more broadly chartered organization, such as the United Nations Educational, Scientific, and Cultural Organization, should probably be the custodial sponsor of the activity, in much the same way as such organizations now sponsor more conventional conferences. Initial funding could be sought from foundations, governments, and international agencies and, after the system reached a certain point of development, a user organization such as FAO might join in. As the system began to demonstrate its utility, subsequent beneficiaries could be expected to pick up more of the cost.

To start the ball rolling a working conference of scientists, technologists, and government resource managers addressing the quantitative and management problems of famine relief would be organized, perhaps on an urgent basis. In order to include the necessary experts with their frequent schedule conflicts, the conference would be held on a decentralized basis, use being made of the present forms of computer assistance that would evolve according to needs perceived by the participants and model designers as the conference proceeded. Because of the nature of these systems, the conference participants would be able to take part at their own convenience. Records, training materials, and summaries of proceedings could be maintained automatically and referred to or augmented as needed. If the nature of the problems being discussed requires that conference be prolonged, a participant's embarkation on a field trip or other engagement would not have to prevent his continued active participation in the conference because he could carry a portable terminal that could be linked to the conference by telephone line or even by satellite communications.

At some point the transition between a scientific conference and a crisis management operation would have to begin. This could probably best be effected by having the responsible crisis managers in the role of both sponsors and leading participants in the conference, with the intent of guiding it toward pragmatic rather than (or in addition to) academic ends. The hoped-for end product of such guidance would be a smooth transition from an academic conference to a planning group to a crisis management team as knowledge was sifted and applied. Essentially, the conference would never have to adjourn until the crisis was surmounted. Meanwhile, the custodial sponsor would gain considerable experience with this type of operation and could begin to think about applying it to more controversial areas—another bonus for having a United Nations-affiliated custodian. But the role of the custodian itself would remain one of promoting scientific development, international exchange, and application of technology to world problems by supplying the (computer-based) conferencing facilities.

Although we propose famine relief as an appropriate area for introducing cooperative international crisis management, there are several other areas that are also suitable for the initial application of these techniques, such as control of the illegal international drug traffic and the management of world trade, energy, and monetary problems. Regardless of the area chosen, however, it will be essential to establish during this primary endeavor the effectiveness of computer-based conferencing in bringing scientific, technical, and executive colleagues and adversaries together on one particular problem. If this can be demonstrated, then the system will be more readily adopted in other areas and the point will be reached where it will routinely be used as an adjunct to planning before matters reach crisis proportions.

Summary

Modern crises present decision-makers with many agonizing management choices. Very often a crisis manager is confronted with a plethora of conflicting information and given very little time to choose an appropriate course of action. Although contemporary methods of systems analysis have been used in attempts to organize data and clarify options, they have generally been of little use in presenting an accurate picture of an opponent's values and perceptions. Thus it is clear that we must now make use of the improved communications and technological devices at our disposal if crises are to be avoided or resolved with minimum damage.

Our proposal to establish international model-oriented computer-assisted conferences is designed to promote greater cooperation and understanding among scientists and crisis managers of differing nations by enabling them to share images of themselves and one another. With better information and more rational options available, the chances of catastrophic misunderstanding or miscalculation can be meaningfully reduced. We have proposed a possible scenario for the initial implementation of such a system to combat famine, and hope that the same approach might be used in other areas over time. The ultimate goal is a system by which specialists of all persuasions cooperate so that international crises will be resolved on the bases of mutual benefits without resort to armed conflict.

NOTES

1. See, for example, W. R. Reitman, in *Human Judgments and Optimality*, M. Shelly and G. Bryan, Eds. (Wiley, New York, 1964), pp. 282–315.

2. R. H. Kupperman, R. M. Behr, T. P. Jones ["The Deterrence Continuum" *Orbis*, Fall 1974.]

3. For example, see H. S. Dinerstein, *Fifty Years of Soviet Foreign Policy* (Johns Hopkins Univ. Press, Baltimore, Md., 1968), particularly chap. 3.

4. R. H. Kupperman and R. H. Wilcox, *Proc. 2nd Int. Conf. Computer Communications* (Stockholm, 12 to 14 August, 1974), pp. 469–471.

5. V. Rock, Ed., *Policy-Makers and Model Builders: Cases and Concepts* (Gordon & Breach, New York, 1969). For an even earlier expression of interest by a Soviet academician, see A. J. Ivakhnenko, in *Computer and Information Sciences*, J. Tou and R. Wilcox, Eds. (Spartan Books, New York, 1964), pp. 501–518.

6. L. J. Peter, *The Peter Principle* (Morrow, New York, 1969).

7. The creation of initial models acceptable to both sides can present somewhat of a problem. We are indebted to Professor Oskar Morgenstern for proposing a practical way to start a conference. Each side would design two models, one describing its own national goals and institutions and the other its image of the opponent's goals and institutions. The models would then be exchanged, and an iterative "preconference" would ensue to develop better models. (In addition to analyzing physical, economic, and political models to

improve dialogue among nations, one should also note that computer conferencing can deal with a wide variety of psychological and sociological models.)

8. M. A. Sass and W. D. Wilkinson, *Computer Augmentation of Human Reasoning* (Macmillan, New York, 1965), particularly chap. 9.

9. M. Turoff, *Proc. 1st Int. Conf. Computer Communications* (Washington, D.C., 1972), pp. 161–171. For a discussion of the policy implications of the "Era of Forced Choice," see C. R. Price, in *11AP/PPSST Special Report* (Innovative Information Analysis Project, Program of Policy Studies in Science and Technology, George Washington Univ., Washington, D.C., 1974), particularly pp. 1 and 2. For a recent paper that deals with conferencing for the Project on Global Systems Analysis and Simulation of Energy, Resources and Environmental Systems, see T. Utsumi, Report No. 1 (Mitsubishi Research Institute, Tokyo, February 1973).

10. M. Turoff, *Ekistics* 35, 337 (June 1973).

11. R. H. Kupperman and R. H. Wilcox, *Proc. 1st Int. Conf. Computer Communications* (Washington, D.C., 24 to 26 Oct. 1972), pp. 117–120.

12. N. Macon and J. D. McKendree, *Proc. 2nd Int. Conf. Computer Communications* (Stockholm, 1974), pp. 89–92.

13. Some recent Russian work appears to permit direct user-computer interaction to improve the "fit" of the problem with the system without requiring the user to participate in the design of the system; see, for example, S. Samoylenko, *Proc. 2nd Int. Conf. Computer Communications* (Stockholm, 1974), pp. 477–483.

14. Computerized language translation is not suggested here. Rather, human interpreters should be included as conference participants, so that a message entered in the originator's language would quickly appear in other participants' languages also. Where participants use different alphabets (for example, Roman, Arabic, Cyrillic), separate printer terminals would be needed.

15. Initially, there would probably be mutual suspicions concerning an opponent's use of deceitful models and data. Each might build—and suspect the others of building—"private" models to aid in his own policy formulation. Although this would impede international acceptance of computer conferencing, the traditional uses for covert intelligence would tend to lessen this difficulty by making the "private" models intelligence targets, thus providing feedback for the conference.

16. C. Sterling, *Atlantic Monthly* 233 (No. 5), 98 (May 1974); condensed in *Reader's Digest* 104 (No. 626), 80 (June 1974). For an extended discussion of inadequate development planning in the Sahel region, see N. Wade, *Science* 185, 234 (1974).

(Our thanks to R. M. Behr, J. Everett, S. C. Goldman, D. Kulikowski, R. Osgood, P. J. Sharfman, and E. Shaw for substantive and editorial contributions. The views expressed in this article are the authors' and do not necessarily reflect the views of the United States Government or any of its agencies or departments.)

Terrorism: Patterns for Negotiation A Case Study Using Hierarchies and Holarchies

JAMES P. BENNETT and THOMAS L. SAATY

INTRODUCTION

Many forms of political terrorism confront the authorities with a complex, multiparty negotiating problem. Typically, individuals or objects of value are taken hostage. Terrorists demand concessions designed to accomplish objectives such as to publicize and legitimate the terrorists' movement, to compromise the ruling authorities' legitimacy, to increase operating freedom for subsequent operations, to acquire resources, such as by gaining the freedom of imprisoned supporters, and to persuade or coerce third parties to undertake policy shifts similarly designed to benefit the terrorists' other objectives.

As part of a larger study (Bennett and Saaty 1977) we have investigated the use of analytic hierarchies and holarchies (which are hierarchies with "feedback") to guide negotiating strategies for authorities confronted by terrorists holding hostages. We examined the cases of the Hanafi Muslims' seizure of three buildings in Washington, D.C., in 1977, the campaign of Tupamaro guerrilla terrorism in Uruguay from 1970 to 1972, and Black September's bloody attempt to disrupt peace negotiations during the Olympic Games in 1972.

The three cases span many facets that have been identified with modern political terrorism (see Jenkins 1975, Thornton 1964, Handman 1937). Several themes run through all three cases. The terroristic activities were employed by relatively weak or endangered groups as instruments for the achievement of radical objectives unattainable by other means. In the three cases, groups used terrorism instrumentally; they sought to avoid terrorizing indiscriminately. In all three cases there were important cooperative as well as conflictive elements in the interactions among terrorists, hostages, authorities, and others relevant to determining outcomes. In complex, multiactor, mixed-motive situations, the clarification of the structure of the situation achieved by modeling it as a hierarchy or as a holarchy, or even through a more general method, is an essential first step to demarcate the constraints upon the several actors' choice of strategies. Ultimately, it may aid the authorities' initiative to resolve the crises upon relatively favorable terms.

Analytic hierarchies have been used in several contexts in which cooperative motives have predominated (ADAR 1975, Saaty and Rogers 1976, Saaty and Khouja 1976, Saaty and Bennett 1977). In conjunction with metagame theory, it has been applied to primarily conflictive situations (Alexander and Saaty 1977). In the cases of terrorism, we encounter negotiating situations in which the objectives of some participants are strongly cooperative, those of others are strongly opposed, and those of still others are mixed.

This paper recounts only briefly one of the three cases—the Munich massacre of 1972. In the following section we outline the construction of an analytic hierarchy based upon the events of that incident. Subsequently, we quantitatively describe the configuration of objectives and influence among the parties most centrally involved. The final section distills from the major themes of the Munich and other cases some policy guidance for individuals responsible for negotiating with terrorists holding hostages. It emphasizes the interdependence between terrorists and hostages on the one hand, and terrorists and authorities on the other.

We suggest as a first cut for bargaining with terrorists the use of a six-stage procedure to integrate the hierarchical analysis with negotiations on the scene. This procedure attempts to avoid concessions as long as possible in a coordinated effort to alter crucial segments of the terrorists' hierarchy of expectations. It provides for collapse of negotiations and the ultimate resort to force. But it also attempts to shape the unfolding situation to effect trade-offs on terms favorable to the authorities. Our prescriptions are ultimately based in the belief that control over pace and procedure can engender control over the substance of outcomes.

THE MUNICH MASSACRE

When the XX Olympiad opened in early September 1972 in Munich, elements of the Black September terrorists had already taken accommodations and were preparing for the action ahead. They had come separately to the Games to escape notice by the relatively light security checks prepared for the Olympics. Two of them had apparently found employment within the athletes' compound.

Early on the morning of September 5, the group climbed a fence into the compound that segregated, and presumably protected, the athletes. No alarm was raised, in part because athletes frequently sneaked into camp to avoid curfew. Once inside the compound, the terrorists readied their weapons—grenades and machine pistols—and moved toward the Israeli team's apartments. By 5:30 A.M. the terrorists had seized two of the five Israeli suites, killed two Israelis who resisted, and taken nine others hostage. Escaping athletes warned the Munich police, who set up a "crisis center" near the compound. Several hundred police sealed off the immediate area, but spectators and newsmen were able to get within shouting range of the terrorists. The Munich Chief of Police approached the apartment but was told that demands would be forthcoming shortly.

About 9:00 A.M. a message in English was thrown out of the apartment window. It listed 236 Arabs held in Israeli jails. The Black September group demanded release of the prisoners and safe passage of both terrorists and hostages out of West Germany to any Arab country except Lebanon or Jordan. If these demands were not met within three hours, the terrorists threatened to kill two hostages every half hour.

Bonn had already been alerted by the time the demands were received. A hot line between Bonn and the Israeli cabinet was set up. Almost immediately the Israeli Government informed the Germans of three principles governing the Israeli response:

1. Israel would neither release prisoners nor negotiate with the terrorists;
2. Israel considered that the German Government bore full responsibility for resolving the kidnapping; and, therefore,
3. the Israeli Government would not object to the German Government's giving the terrorists safe passage if the German Government could assure the safety of the hostages.

The German Minister of the Interior personally took charge of the negotiations. He countered the terrorists' demands with the offer:

1. the terrorists could receive an unlimited amount of money;
2. German volunteers would substitute for the Israeli hostages.

The terrorists refused both points. The German Minister stalled negotiations by claiming that communication with Israel was under way. Many present in Munich believed the hostages already to be dead. The Minister demanded to see the hostages. To shore up their credibility, the terrorists permitted the Minister to visit the apartment and witness the bound hostages. During these negotiations the terrorists postponed the deadline for beginning to kill hostages, first to 3:30 P.M., then to 5:00 P.M., and subsequently twice more through the evening. During the afternoon several police marksmen were placed around the building, although they had orders not to fire unless the terrorists tried to escape.

Crowds gathered and taunted the guerrillas. Prime Minister Meir asked that the Games be suspended—they were, at 4:00 P.M.—freeing the sports television crews massively to cover the incident. Within the German Government a decision on negotiating strategy was reached late in the afternoon. Chancellor Brandt publicly accepted responsibility for the fate of the hostages and enunciated the principle that the terrorists would not be allowed to leave the country with hostages. With some reason, the authorities feared that the terrorists would kill hostages once they were airborne. Thus, both terrorists demands had been rejected, one by Israel and one by Germany. Brandt did decide to free two fedayeen in German jails. This, he claimed, was all he had power to do (Groussard 1975: 88).

Various Arab states were asked by the German and other governments to use their good offices to resolve the impasse. Understandably, the Arabs did not want to be involved in what they viewed as a no-win situation. Behind the crisis in Munich lay delicate negotiations with Israel, whose disruption was the most plausible ulterior target of the terrorists. If the Arabs appeared to be saving the lives of Israelis and compromising the lives of Palestinians, they would be vulnerable both to broader Arab condemnation and to specific acts of violence from Black September and other extremists. If, on the other hand, they appeared to abet Black September, they risked loss of financial support from the conservative Gulf states and possibly the West, and might be drawn closer to Palestinian extremism than compatible with their political preferences. One exception to the Arab response was the Tunisian Ambassador to Bonn who—although he might be ideologically suspect to Black September—offered to participate in the negotiations.

Two Arab officials did participate in the negotiations: A. D. Touny, Egyptian member of the International Olympic Committee, and Mohammed Khalif, head of the Arab League in Bonn. Both men were careful not to compromise the position of the terrorists. As honest intermediaties they were useful to the German authorities, for the terrorists' leader came to trust Khalif in particular. The Tunisian Ambassador was also welcomed by the terrorists, who later tried to contact a mysterious accomplice in Tunis (Groussard 1975: 254).

When Black September members tried to telephone a guerrilla headquarters in Lebanon, the call was not accepted. The Palestinian movement, especially the official leadership of the PLO, tried to distance itself from the events in Munich without seeming to criticize the operation or to offer sympathy for the Israelis. Rejection by other Palestinian groups may have induced a feeling of desertion and isolation among the terrorists at the hour of what, they believed, should be their greatest honor. For the negotiators a key decision had to be made about the consequences of the terrorists' psychological isolation: Would they grow more desperate and self-sacrificial, or would they be induced to compromise and surrender? One tragedy of the incident is that the negotiators never waited long enough to find out.

Worldwide attention put great pressure on the German Government to resolve the crisis quickly. The Games were adjourned; the terrorists were receiving massive television coverage; the terrorists threatened to kill hostages if delayed. Politically the German Government faced two directions of criticism akin to that which dissuaded Arab states from intervention. First, domestic public opinion was known to be opposed to compromising law and order except for tactical expediency to save lives. Second, opinion in the United States and much of Western Europe could be expected to criticize Germans for permitting Jewish deaths and for failing to support the Israeli antiterrorist policies. Together the governments of Germany and Israel foreclosed any effective flexibility for the negotiators on the scene.

Two important options remained to the negotiators. They might try to wait out the siege, see if the terrorists would, in fact, begin to execute hostages, and begin a war of psychological attrition. Or they might try somehow to release the hostages by force, perhaps through fraudulent negotiations.

Believing the terrorists could no longer be stalled, the German negotiators opted for the latter approach. They realized the hostages could not be forcibly freed as long as they remained in the Israeli team's quarters. To place the terrorists in a more vulnerable position, the German Minister conveyed his Government's offer to fly the terrorists and their hostages anywhere in the world. The concession was not genuine. From brief communications with the leader of the terrorists, the authorities came to believe that if the leader could be assassinated, his followers would surrender. The authorities' plan called for ambushing the terrorists as they approached the aircraft intended to take them from the country. The terrorists announced that they would go to Cairo, perhaps selecting the destination intended to induce greatest dissension in the Arab World.

The logistics of transfer were accomplished with difficulty, and at 10:00 P.M. the terrorists with their hostages boarded a bus. The bus drove a few blocks to a helicopter pad. The police, who were prepared to ambush the terrorists at any point in their itinerary, found no opportunity to open fire. The terrorists and their hostages reached the airport in two helicopters. By the time they arrived at a prepared jet, the airport was surrounded by police and five marksmen transferred from the Olympic Village. The police were untrained in using infrared sights; thus they had to rely upon conventional telescopic sights despite the darkness. As the helicopters arrived at the airport, the terrorists demanded a crew of eight to fly them to an unannounced destination, perhaps not after all to Cairo.

The marksmen were ordered to fire at will when the terrorists became visible. However, the terrorists were careful never to reveal more than three of their number at once. The marksmen opened fire, killing three; but in return fire that lasted most of an hour, one policeman was killed and a helicopter pilot was wounded. At the end of the battle, all the Israeli hostages, five terrorists, and one policeman had died. The surviving terrorists surrendered.

Constructing a Hierarchy Pertinent to the Munich Case

Five actors possess substantial importance to determination of outcomes: the Black September terrorists, the hostages, the German Government, the Israeli Government, and the Arab World.

Black September acquired its name from the harshest of the Arab repressions of Palestinians, that by Hussein's Bedouin army. A number of Palestinian leaders became disenchanted with what they saw as an ineffective official PLO, and they secretly created a more action-oriented suborganization whose members usually also participated overtly in the "official" Palestinian groups within the PLO.

Experts disagree to what extent Black September acted under the control of the central leadership of the PLO. Some of its acts prior to 1972 appear to have subverted or neutralized official PLO policy. Its operations were paid for wittingly in part by radical Arab governments, such as Libya's, and perhaps unwittingly in part by support to "official" Palestinian groups within al-Fatah.

The relationship between the PLO and the terrorists is described by Jureidini and Hazen (1976:85):

> . . . the actors for these operations belong to many groups, ranging from the PFLP to Fatah. Usually they belong to the militant segments of the organizations. They are dedicated to the Palestinian revolution and believe strongly in the use of force to resolve the Palestinian dilemma. In most cases they are prepared to become martyrs for the Palestinian cause.

Despite the terrorists' undoubted commitment, before they began to strike inside Israel in 1974 most of their operations had clearly announced objectives of releasing prisoners. Exceptions include the revenge-slaying of Jordanian officials involved in the suppression of 1970 and 1971, the May 1972 attack on the Tel Aviv airport (which was undertaken by Japanese terrorists acting on behalf of the PFLP), a single aircraft hijacking for ransom, and an attack in Rome on an American aircraft. Among the terrorists, Black September itself had a clearer record of intent in its choice of terroristic activities.

Before Black September receded from prominence in 1973 after being taken under the operational control of Fatah, its activities against non-Jordanian targets fell into a distinct pattern. On the one hand were operations of sabotage, bombings, and letter bombings, intended as punishment against particular individuals. In these no negotiations were involved. On the other hand, a smaller number of more spectacular operations were intended to take hostages to bargain for the release of Palestinian prisoners. Such operations make little sense unless the terrorists can establish credibility as serious negotiators. Israel's counterterror strategy has consistently sought to deny this credibility in part by avoiding setting a precedent for negotiations.

Black September operations were frequently launched for two ancillary purposes. One was the establishment of recognition by the movement—the objective of publicity common to almost all terrorism. The second was to sabotage discussions by other Palestinians and Arabs about solutions to the Palestinian problem rejected by the militants. This objective, which has been termed "defense of militancy," is often crucial for understanding the timing of incidents but of less relevance to determining outcomes. Once an operation is launched, peace initiatives may be sabotaged; the operation's disruptive effects are less contingent upon the type of resolution.

We believe that the terrorists at Munich could have altered their planned operation; that is, they were relatively autonomous once the operation got under way. Thus, they must be considered a separate actor. The "official" PLO leadership, on the other hand, was incapable of influencing events after the hostages were taken. It could not afford to moderate the terrorists' demands; nor could it politically afford close association with the unfolding violence at Munich.

A second actor proved relatively powerless: the set of hostages of the Israeli Olympic team. Because the hostages all died in the incident, it is of course not possible to obtain much information about their objectives and preferences. We must, therefore, apply evidence of hostages' reactions as acquired in other incidents, such as the several Arab hijackings and the South Moluccan activities. (Groussard [1975] is an exhaustive account, but it is difficult to determine his sources for much of the detail.)

The German Federal Government, especially in the persons of Chancellor Brandt and Interior Minister Genscher, was the third actor. The government exercised general control over the Munich police and took charge of, and responsibility for, the negotiations. Although constitutionally the German federal system grants a wide margin of local autonomy in police matters, in this incident of international significance the federal executive stepped in. Details of the operation, such as arrangements for the ambush, eluded Bonn's control. The effectiveness of command and control from the center was vitiated by the federal structure.

The Israeli Government was an important fourth actor. As noted above, its early decision not to negotiate severely constrained other actors' attempts at resolution. Our quantitative analysis will clarify just how little room for maneuver remained.

To simplify the analysis, we construct a fifth actor from the governments of Arab states, excluding the conservative Gulf states, Jordan, and Lebanon. This "Arab World" as perceived by the terrorists constitutes both a potential constituency of support for their action and a target of their pressure for more active involvement in the Palestinian struggle. The Arab World is also important as a possible negotiator or mediator in Munich. We need not presume that it represents a single coherent policy toward the Munich crisis, nor that it had a united Palestinian policy. Nevertheless, despite the differences in preferences and objectives of individual governments of the Arab World, one can make reasonably valid judgments about this actor's collective or aggregated views on aspects of the terrorist incident.

Figure 1 locates the actors within the hierarchy with which we characterize the negotiating situation.

Fig. 1. An analytic hierarchy of the Munich incident

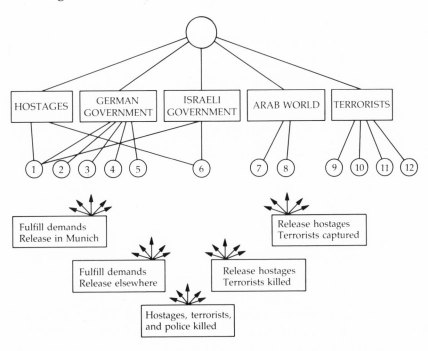

OBJECTIVES:

1. Release of hostages
2. Good relations with Israel
3. Good relations with Arab World
4. Avoidance of police casualties
5. Preservation of reputation
6. Prevention of future terror

7. Good inter-Arab relations
8. Good relations with non-Arab world
9. Publicity for Palestinians
10. Release of comrades
11. Unification of struggle against Israel
12. Escape from Germany

We briefly enumerate twelve major objectives. Not every objective is relevant to each actor. Indeed, the degree of qualitative overlap, diagrammed in Figure 1, is a first approximation to the degree of shared interests.

1. Release of the hostages. This was important to the German and Israeli Governments and, of course, to the hostages. Release might occur in Germany or abroad.

2. Good relations with Israel, and indirectly, with the United States. An important objective of the German Government was avoidance of the criticism of trifling with Jewish lives. Maintenance of good relations with Israel was linked, through relations with the United States, to European security generally.

3. Good relations with the Arab World. The German Government could not lose sight of its sources of petroleum and important export markets.

4. Avoidance of police casualties. In approaching the crisis, the German Government preserved the strong priority of the Munich government that police lives be protected. This objective dominated the planning of the ambush attempts.

5. Preservation of international reputation. The German Government was concerned, especially during the Olympics, with its international image. Because the Olympics were delayed, at Israeli request, world attention was drawn to German problems with maintaining order during a major international event.

6. Prevention of future terrorism. Both the hostages and the German Government wished to avert future incidents of this kind.

7. Good inter-Arab relations. The Arab World found inter-Arab relations to be challenged by Black September. Disputes among hard- and soft-liners on the Israeli question threatened to disrupt the semblance of Arab unity.

8. Good relations with the non-Arab world. The Arab image was also of concern to the Arab World. This consideration led in part to the governments' refusal to become overtly involved.

9. Publicity for the Palestinians' cause. A major purpose of the attack was Black September's desire to publicize the Palestinian plight, Israeli intransigence, and Arab waffling. Munich was chosen for its publicity value; operations elsewhere would have less impact upon world news media.

10. Release of comrades. The terrorists were doubtlessly genuinely intending to free their comrades in Israeli jails.

11. Unification of Arab peoples in the struggle against Israel. Both governments and competing Palestinian factions might be unified in violent struggle if a decisive blow were struck against Israel and its foreign allies.

12. Escape from Germany. The terrorists hoped to leave Germany in freedom.

The objectives constitute the second level of the hierarchy of Figure 1. Before discussing the method of appraising the importance of objectives, we complete the hierarchy with the enumeration of elements on a third level of outcomes.

One can distinguish marginally different outcomes in large number. However, five outcomes are particularly important because they reflect decisively different end states of negotiations among the actors.

1. The terrorists' demands are fulfilled. The hostages are released in Munich and the terrorists escape Germany.

2. The terrorists' demands are fulfilled. The terrorists take the Israelis with them as hostages to another Arab country. This outcome might begin a second negotiating process in which an Arab government attempts to gain the hostages' freedom. Or the hostages might be released unharmed.

3. The hostages, terrorists, and some German police are killed in an attempt to forcibly end the stand-off.

4. The hostages are released and the terrorists killed in successful police action. Casualties to police and hostages are relatively minor.

5. The hostages are released as the terrorists surrender.

The lists of actors, objectives, and outcomes constitute the principal structure of the hierarchy. One should note that additional categories can be added at any level. Further, additional levels can engender finer distinctions, say, by inserting a level of agents subordinate to that of actors, or by inserting a level of tactics between the objectives and the outcomes. The practitioner of analytic hierarchies will tailor the structure of the hierarchy to the purpose of his analysis; here we are content to illustrate the principles and procedures of this modeling. To demonstrate the application of hierarchies to structuring negotiations, we must demonstrate how elements of the hierarchy can be ranked by priority.

A THEORY OF HIERARCHIES

The thrust of hierarchically structuring decisions is to permit disaggregation of problems, produce—perhaps through a process of trial-and-error iterative attempts at disaggregation—a number of unidimensional scales, and then reaggregate the decision problem to enable quantitative comparison of the relative importance of its several components.

A hierarchy is a nonempty set H with a partition into disjoint subsets (called the levels of the hierarchy) such that:

1. H is a partially ordered set that is a chain (a set whose elements are completely ordered) with respect to a simple order on its strata (so that we can refer to "upper" and "lower" strata in this order). Note that H is not a lattice because any two elements in one stratum do not have a unique least upper bound in the immediately higher stratum.

2. Each element of each stratum that is not the sup is dominated by at least one element in the immediately upper stratum.

3. Each element of an upper stratum dominates at least one element of the immediately lower stratum.

Any stratum may be partitioned into (not necessarily disjoint) subsets, each consisting of all those elements dominated by a single element of the adjacent upper stratum. On each such subset we have a total order (relating to the dominating element of the adjacent upper level) that is reflexive and antisymmetric (but not necessarily transitive). We call a hierarchy *complete* if each element of a given stratum is dominated by every element of the adjacent upper stratum.

The meaning of the relation joining adjacent strata in a hierarchy will vary with the nature of the decision-problem being studied and with the stratum in the hierarchy. In many applications an element on a lower stratum can be thought of as "contributing to" or "possessing" some property of an element in an upper stratum. In such applications, the element in the upper stratum serves as a criterion for evaluating the relative "contributions" of elements in the lower stratum. For instance, if elements of the lower stratum are particular industries and they are being evaluated with respect to an element "public health" on the upper stratum, then one would expect informed respondents to indicate the "food industry" as highly dominant over the "tobacco industry." If the elements of the lower stratum are individuals and the relevant element in the upper stratum is a character trait, the individuals can naturally be compared as to their relative possession of that trait. Discovering a hierarchical structure in a concrete decision must, of course, make explicit what relations exist among strata as well as how order within a stratum is evaluated.

Given a subset of elements, $x = (x_1, \ldots, x_n)$ of a hierarchy stratum dominated by the set, $y = (y_1, \ldots, y_m)$, if w_i is the priority of x_i, $i = 1, \ldots, n$ in x and w_j is the priority of y_j, $j = 1, \ldots, m$ in y, then we assume that the following set of linear relationships holds:

$$w_i = a_{i1} w_1' + \ldots + a_{im} w_m' \qquad\qquad i = 1, \ldots, n.$$

Here a_{ij} is the ith entry of the jth column of a matrix whose columns are eigenvectors of judgmental matrices at the lower stratum with respect to the jth element of the adjacent upper stratum.

To generalize this relation to a complete hierarchy of h levels with n_k, $k = 1, \ldots, h$ elements in the kth level, where obviously $n_1 = 1$, we write:

$$w_{i_k} = a_{i_k,1} w_{1_{k-1}} + a_{i_k,2} w_{2_{k-1}} + \ldots$$
$$+ a_{i_k,n_{k-1}} w_{n_{k-1}} \qquad i_k = 1, \ldots, n_k.$$

In a complete hierarchy H let W_k be the vector of priorities of the kth stratum and let V_k denote the corresponding matrix of coefficients expressing linear dependence on W_{k-1}. We state without proof the theorem:

$$W_k = V_k V_{k-1} \cdots V_{m+1} W_m \qquad k > m.$$

In particular we have $W_h = V_h \ldots V_2 W_1$.

The following observation holds for a complete hierarchy but is applicable more generally. The priority order of an element in a stratum is the sum of its priorities in each of the subsets to which it belongs, each weighted by the fraction of elements of the stratum which belong to that subset and by the priority order of that subset. The resulting set of priorities is then normalized by dividing by its sum. The priority of a subset in a stratum is equal to the sum of the priorities of the dominating elements in the next stratum.

An Eigenvalue Approach to Setting Priorities

The eigenvalue approach transforms pair-comparison judgments into a scale, which is interpretable as the relative priorities of the activities being compared. In comparing complex activities, one normally has difficulty in translating feelings and experiences to numbers that say exactly how much more impact one activity has on a given objective than another. In order to assign numerically meaningful numbers when comparing two activities, one needs a thorough understanding of both activities and the extent of the properties they have relevant to the criterion being considered. The model requires that judgments be supplied by questioning experienced people who know the activities and the criteria and their interactions. These judgments indicate the relative importance of one activity over another for each criterion.

In constructing a scale of relative importance of several activities, one customarily asks a decision-maker to state: (a) which of two activities, in his opinion, is more important, and (b) his perception of the magnitude of difference in importance, expressed as a number on a given scale. Only *direct* effects of activities on the criterion are considered in the judgment process. One method for dealing with *indirect* effects is to consider input-output types of relations between the activities.

A scale constructed from pair-comparison judgments should have several properties. It should reflect accurately the feelings embodied in the judgments. It should allow for a moderate uncertainty in judgments without substantially changing the judgment value on the scale. Strong change in judgment should be reflected in appropriate variations up or down the scale. Moreover, the results of the model should not change drastically overall by making small changes in judgment values.

As a preliminary step toward the construction of a scale of importance for activities, we have broken down the numerical values as follows:

Intensity of Importance	Definition	Explanation
1	Equal importance	Two activities contribute equally to one objective.
3	Weak importance of one over another	There is evidence favoring one activity over another, but it is not conclusive.
5	Essential or strong importance	Good evidence and logical criteria exist to show that one is more important.
7	Demonstrated importance	There is conclusive evidence as to the importance of one activity over another.

9	Absolute importance	The evidence in favor of one activity over another is of the highest possible order of affirmation.
2,4,6,8	Intermediate values between the two adjacent judgments	Compromise is needed.
Reciprocals above nonzero numbers	If activity i has one of the above nonzero numbers assigned to it when compared with activity j, then j has the reciprocal when compared with i.	

Note that the integers are used to estimate a scale of values $(w_1, \ldots, w_n)$ of the activities. Each value a_{ij} assigned in the matrix of pairwise comparison A may be regarded as an estimate of the ratio w_i/w_j taken to the nearest integer after appropriate scaling to make values between the (unknown) underlying scale and the approximation scale appropriately correspond through ratios (Stevens 1972).

If we assume that the values are estimated precisely, i.e., $a_{ij} = w_i/w_j$, it is sufficient to require consistency of the judgment matrix to obtain such equality. Consistency means $a_{ij}a_{jk} = a_{ik}$ from which we have for the main diagonal entries $a_{ii} = 1$ and the reciprocal relations $a_{ji} = 1/a_{ij}$. In general, we do not expect consistency to hold everywhere in the matrix because people's feelings do not conform to an exact formula such as the one just given. However, to improve consistency in the numerical judgments, it is recommended to those who supply the judgments that whatever values a_{ij} they may assign in comparing the ith activity with the jth one, they should consider assigning the reciprocal value to a_{ji}, thus puttling $a_{ji} = 1/a_{ij}$. It follows that $a_{ii} = 1$.

It can easily be seen that when we have consistency, the matrix has unit rank and it is sufficient to know one row of the matrix to construct the remaining entries. For example, if we know the first row, then $a_{ij} = a_{1j}/a_{1i}$ (a rational), assuming, of course, the $a_{1i} \neq 0$ for all i. We do not insist that judgments be consistent and, hence, they need not be transitive. If the relative importance of C_1 is greater than that of C_2 and the relative importance of C_2 is greater than that of C_3, then the relative importance of C_1 need not be greater than that of C_3, a common occurrence in human judgment.

The easier and more elegant case of consistency is a special case. We shall assume that our judgmental inputs are all provided by a single individual expert or are the collective view of several individuals in situations in which no single person knows enough to supply all the judgments. We further assume that the individual has time to supply the $n(n-1)/2$ judgments required for each objective, where n is the number of activities and reciprocals are used.

With inconsistency we no longer have $a_{ij}w_j/w_i = 1$, $i,j = 1,\ldots,n$. We seek a condition on each row of the matrix. We note that with consistency

$$\sum_{j=1}^{n} a_{ij}w_j/w_i = n, \quad i = 1, \ldots, n,$$

where the right side is the same constant n, the largest eigenvalue of A, whose other eigenvalues are all zero since the rank of A is unity and the sum of the eigenvalues is equal to the trace $\Sigma a_{ii} = n$.

It is possible to argue for the general case that the desired scale $w = (w_1, \ldots, w_n)$ must satisfy the eigenvalue problem $Aw = \lambda_{max}w$, where λ_{max} is the largest eigenvalue of A, which, by Perron Froebenius's theory, turns out to have an essentially unique nonnegative solution w if A is nonnegative and irreducible.

In the consistent case, if we take a typical row $a_{i1}, a_{i2}, \ldots, a_{in}$ and multiply a_{i1} by w_1, a_{i2} by $w_2, \ldots, a_{in}$ by w_n, we will obtain $w_i, \ldots, w_i$. In this case all these values are exact and, therefore, when we perform the operation Aw, we obtain the vector nw, solving $Aw = nw$. We normalize the vector w by dividing each of its entries by

$$\sum_{i=1}^{n} w_i$$

to obtain the desired scale. In the general case the process of multiplying the ith row as above does not yield exact values $w_i, \ldots, w_i$ but deviations about them that amount to perturbations of the exact values. It is known in matrix theory (Franklin 1968) that the eigenvalues of a matrix are continuous functions of the coefficients. If we perturb the coefficients of a consistent matrix, the largest eigenvalue will remain near n and the remaining ones near zero. Thus our problem becomes: find w which satisfies $Aw = \lambda_{max}w$ and the results will be the more valid the closer λ_{max} is to n as indicated by an index of consistency $(\lambda_{max}-n)/(n-1)$. We can show that $\lambda_{max} \geq n$ always for reciprocal matrices.

It is worth noting that we have a ratio scale (invariant under positive similarity transformations) because the scale is derived from the solution to the (linear) eigenvalue problem.

Once ratio judgments are elicited from the subjects to form one row or column, the use of pair-comparisons can make further contributions to locating the stimuli by possibly enhancing stability where the data are nearly, but not quite, perfectly consistent. More importantly, requiring each subject to rate each pair of stimuli separately permits tests of dimensionality to be undertaken.

CONFIGURATIONS OF OBJECTIVES AND INFLUENCE AMONG ACTORS

From a variety of accounts of the Munich massacre we have made provisional judgments about the relative importance of each of the actors to the determination of an outcome. As a first approximation, we evaluate the actors pairwise with regard to their general influence over all plausible outcomes. These judgments, with the corresponding largest eigenvalue and eigenvector, are given in Table 1. Below we shall sharpen the analysis by evaluating actors' influence with regard to specific outcomes.

With reference to the first row of the matrix of judgments in Table 1, one sees that the terrorists and German Government are judged to be of equal importance in determining outcomes. The terrorists are, however, weakly more important than the Israeli Government. This conclusion stems primarily from the latter's

TABLE 1

PAIRWISE JUDGMENTS AND DERIVED PRIORITIES OF ACTORS

	T	G	I	A	H		
Terrorists	1	1	3	7	8	.369	
German Government		1	2	8	8	.369	
Israeli Government			1	5	8	.176	$\lambda = 5.13$
Arab World				1	5	.050	
Hostages					1	.034	

capability to preclude satisfaction of the terrorists' major demand for the release of prisoners. Israel nevertheless fails to constrain the terrorists' treatment of the hostages or to control the content of other agreements reached between the terrorists and the German Government. The terrorists are substantially more important than either the Arab World or the hostages.

The second row of the matrix gives the relative influence of the German Government and other actors. Because the German Government deferred to the Israelis on decisions for a negotiated settlement, the former is only marginally more influential. Neither the Arab World nor the hostages are of even remotely comparable importance.

Judgments elsewhere in the matrix show the Israeli Government to be strongly more important than the Arab World, and the hostages matter almost not at all. The maximum eigenvalue is slightly greater than five, indicating that the matrix is highly consistent. The column at far right presents the priorities assigned to the actors. Not suprisingly, the German Government and terrorists appear equal in importance, with the Israeli Government being the only other actor of note.

The judgments in Table 1 are not meant to be definitive. Indeed, one of the practical advantages of the method of analytic hierarchies is to encourage debate among experts on a field to engage in highly focused debate over specific evaluations. One might apply different judgments, compute the scale of priorities, and iterate the process of discussion and evaluation until a group of experts reached consensus that a set of judgments were the most satisfactory currently attainable.

In a parallel manner, the several objectives are evaluated pairwise for each of the actors to which they pertain. Here a judgment represents the actor's imputed relative preference among objectives. In Table 2 we present only the computed priorities with their respective eigenvalues at the base of the columns. Entries omitted from the table have weights of zero.

The terrorists' principal objective, we believe, was to publicize the Palestinian cause. The Arab World is seen to be more interested in its relations with the non-Arab world than with internal relations. The Israeli Government overwhelmingly chose deterrence of future terrorism to saving the hostages' lives. The German Government was most vitally concerned with future relations with Israel. In its scale of priorities, the hostages were less important than the German reputation but more important than minimizing police casualties. Finally, the hostages naturally found their own release to be the dominant consideration.

If one takes the matrix of normalized eigenvectors of Table 2

TABLE 2

PRIORITIES OF OBJECTIVES

	Hostages	German Govt.	Israeli Govt.	Arab World	Terrorists
Release of hostages	.833	.140	.143		
Relations with Israel		.537			
Relations with Arab World		.074			
No police killed		.042			
German reputation		.207			
Prevention of future terror	.167		.857		
Internal Arab relations				.333	
Arab relations with rest				.667	
Publicity for Palestinians					.519
Release of comrades					.150
Unification against Israel					.194
Escape from Germany					.137
λ_{max}	2	5.51	2	2	4.07

and postmultiplies it by an appropriately ordered column vector of actor priorities from Table 1, the product is an assignment of overall priorities to objectives in the Munich events. This is shown as Table 3. It is evident that the safety of the hostages is not one of the jointly most important objectives. Of more importance are the incompatible pair, good German relations with Israel and publicity for the Palestinian cause. In this case compromise between authorities and terrorists is not precluded by their respective priorities directly, but by the Germans' espousal of Israeli priorities as instrumental to good relations with Israel. This, no doubt, was strategic to Black September's selection of the Munich Olympics as a forum for terror.

The five outcomes enumerated above have differential impact upon the attainment of the twelve objectives. The analyst must compare the five outcomes pairwise with respect to their contribution to each objective. Two matrices of judgments, chosen more or less at random, are given in Table 4. On the left, the outcomes are evaluated by their impact upon the German Government's relations with Israel. It is readily apparent from this matrix that outcome 4, hostages released and terrorists killed, plays a dominant positive role. Least helpful are outcomes 1 and 2, fulfillment of the terrorists' demands and release of the hostages either in Germany or in another country.

The matrix of judgments on the right of Table 4 shows the

TABLE 3

OBJECTIVES WEIGHTED BY ACTORS' INFLUENCE

1.	Release of hostages	.105
2.	Relations with Israel	.198
3.	Relations with Arab World	.027
4.	No police killed	.015
5.	German reputation	.076
6.	Prevention of future terror	.157
7.	Internal Arab relations	.017
8.	Arab relations with rest	.033
9.	Publicity for Palestinians	.191
10.	Release of comrades	.055
11.	Unification against Israel	.072
12.	Escape from Germany	.051

TABLE 4

Typical Matrices of Judgments Relating Outcomes to Objectives

Criterion:	German relations with Israel				Criterion:	The Arab World's external relations			
1	1	1	1/5	1/9	1/7	1	1	5	1/3	1/5	1/9
2		1	1/5	1/9	1/7	2		1	1/5	1/7	1/9
3			1	1/8	1/7	3			1	1/3	1/7
4				1	3	4				1	1/5
5					1	5					1

contribution to the Arab World's external relations of the five outcomes. The first two rows indicate that the terrorists' "victory" is seen as detrimental. Outcome 5, the hostages' release and terrorists' capture, dominates each of the other outcomes, even outcome 4, hostages released and terrorists killed. Whatever the role of other considerations, the Arab World apparently viewed its relations with the non-Arab countries as improved by the terrorists' suppression with as little bloodshed as possible.

Table 5 presents the priorities of each of the outcomes as columns for the twelve objectives. The format parallels Table 2: eigenvalues are shown at the base of each column.

Because actors' preferences for outcomes ultimately determine their strategies, we should like to designate the priority of outcomes for each actor. By taking the matrix of Table 5 (which lists outcomes by objectives) and postmultiplying by that of Table 2 (which lists objectives by actors), we derive Table 6, actors' preferences for outcomes. In Table 6 one finds, not surprisingly, that the terrorists most sought that their demands for the prisoners' release be fulfilled and the hostages be released outside Germany—the two conditions specifically rejected by Israel and Germany. The German Government, by contrast, most preferred that the hostages be released and the terrorists captured. The Israeli Government preferred that all be killed, since that would presumably contribute most to the prevention of future acts of terrorism. A close second Israeli preference was consonant with that of the German Government.

TABLE 5

RELATIVE CONTRIBUTIONS OF OUTCOMES TO OBJECTIVES

	OBJECTIVES											
	1	2	3	4	5	6	7	8	9	10	11	12
1. DEMANDS FULFILLED Hostages released in Munich	.332	.031	.496	.358	.095	.041	.200	.057	.300	.429	.085	.418
2. DEMANDS FULFILLED Hostages released in Arab country	.180	.031	.060	.269	.033	.040	.200	.025	.314	.429	.132	.418
3. HOSTAGES, TERRORISTS, AND SOME POLICE KILLED	.024	.095	.183	.034	.022	.381	.200	.110	.037	.048	.280	.039
4. HOSTAGES RELEASED Terrorists get killed	.079	.517	.149	.034	.282	.353	.200	.222	.035	.048	.466	.039
5. HOSTAGES RELEASED Terrorists taken into custody	.384	.326	.102	.305	.566	.185	.200	.586	.314	.048	.036	.085
λ_{max}	5.62	6.02	6.05	5.05	5.50	5.26	5.00	5.69	5.01	5.00	5.26	5.11

TABLE 6

ACTORS' PREFERENCES FOR OUTCOMES

	Hostages	German Govt.	Israeli Govt.	Arab World	Terrorists
1. DEMANDS FULFILLED Hostages released in Munich	.283	.135	.083	.105	.290
2. DEMANDS FULFILLED Hostages released in Arab country	.157	.064	.060	.083	.310
3. HOSTAGES, TERRORISTS, AND SOME POLICE KILLED	.084	.074	.330	.148	.090
4. TERRORISTS KILLED Hostages released	.125	.360	.314	.215	.120
5. TERRORISTS TAKEN INTO CUSTODY Hostages released	.351	.366	.214	.457	.190

Outcomes are determined jointly, and to determine joint outcomes one must weight the preferences in Table 6 by the relative "power" of the actors to generate outcomes, as given by Table 1. This is admittedly a naive way to compute "joint" effects, but it points to an interesting result. Outcomes weighted by contributions to objectives and actors' influence to attain objectives are ranked in Table 7. The *least* "jointly preferred" outcome is that which eventuated: hostages, terrorists, and some police killed.

How, then, did things go so wrong? We shall briefly explore two possibilities. First, our analysis has not taken into account the differential capabilities of the actors to effect different outcomes. To incorporate this element we shall evaluate separately the actors' influence on particular outcomes, that is, we shall "cycle" the hierarchy into a more general structure called a *holarchy*. Subsequently, we shall investigate strategic aspects of the actors' choice of policies leading to outcomes. In this regard, the examination of effective "vetoes" proves illuminating.

The Munich Massacre as a Holarchy

We have analyzed the Munich massacre using a hierarchy that looks like Figure 2a: a level L0 represents the overall situation,

TABLE 7

OUTCOMES WEIGHTED BY CONTRIBUTIONS TO OBJECTIVES
AND ACTORS' INFLUENCE

1. Terrorists' demands are fulfilled, hostages are released in Munich	.187
2. Terrorists' demands are fulfilled, hostages are released somewhere else	.158
3. Hostages, terrorists, and some police are killed	.132
4. Terrorists are killed, most hostages are not killed	.246
5. Nobody is killed, hostages are released, terrorists are taken into custody	.277

Fig. 2. Hierarchy and holarchy of actors, objectives,
and outcomes

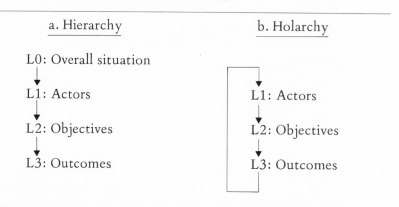

with sequentially subordinate levels of actors, objectives, and outcomes. In this hierarchy, the impact of L1 on L0 was a generalized measure of "power" or influence to determine outcomes. However, it is clear that the power of an actor to bring about an outcome varies over the set of outcomes considered. For instance, the Government of Israel possessed power to obstruct outcomes 1 and 2, although it had minor means to bring about outcomes 3, 4, or 5.

By treating the conflict system as a loop, as pictured in Figure 2b, we produce a holarchy. The arrow drawn from L3 (outcomes) to L1 (actors) indicates that every pair of actors must be evaluated with regard to their relative ability to effect *each* of the five outcomes.

Let $A_{i+1,i}$ be the matrix of eigenvectors giving the impact of level $i+1$ upon level i, where $A_{i+1,i}$ has n_{i+1} rows and n_i columns. Following our practice above, the columns are normalized. A supermatrix to describe the system in Figure 2b can be written

$$A = \left\{ \begin{array}{ccc} 0 & 0 & A_{13} \\ A_{21} & 0 & 0 \\ 0 & A_{32} & 0 \end{array} \right\}$$

where the A_{ij} matrices contain eigenvectors describing the impacts between levels, or subsystems. Because there is "feedback" each subsystem will impact upon itself. The system being a simple closed cycle with three elements, the matrix A^3 yields the first order feedback effect

$$A^3 = \left\{ \begin{matrix} A_{13}A_{32}A_{21} & 0 & 0 \\ 0 & A_{21}A_{13}A_{32} & 0 \\ 0 & 0 & A_{32}A_{21}A_{13} \end{matrix} \right\}$$

It holds that $\lim_{k \to \infty} A^{3k}$ gives the overall impact of the elements of the subsystems on the whole system:

$$\lim_{k \to \infty} A^{3k} = \lim_{k \to \infty} \left\{ \begin{matrix} (A_{13}A_{32}A_{21})^k & 0 & 0 \\ 0 & (A_{21}A_{13}A_{32})^k & 0 \\ 0 & 0 & (A_{32}A_{21}A_{13})^k \end{matrix} \right\}$$

Each of the diagonal blocks in the limiting matrix will have identical columns because the system is nondecomposable. In other words, in the limit a given element of a subsystem will impact in the same way on all other elements of the same subsystem. To use the analog of a stochastic process, each of the diagonal blocks in A^3 corresponds to the matrix of transition probabilities of a discrete stochastic process. Because every element impacts on all other elements—including itself—the process will be ergodic, and therefore the columns of the limiting matrix will be identical.

We let the columns of each of the diagonal blocks in the limiting supermatrix be w_1^* (actors), w_2^* (objectives), and w_3^* (outcomes). Judgments (not shown) were obtained for actors under criteria of outcomes, and the limiting supermatrix was computed. Table 8 presents a comparison of weights obtained for actors, objectives, and outcomes under the initial hierarchical and subsequent holarchical design.

TABLE 8

COMPARISON OF WEIGHTS OBTAINED BY HOLARCHY AND HIERARCHY

	Holarchy	Hierarchy
Actors	w_1'	w_2
Hostages	0.041	0.034
German Government	0.331	0.369
Israeli Government	0.223	0.176
Arab World	0.062	0.050
Terrorists	0.342	0.369
Objectives	w_2'	w_3
Release of hostages	0.112	0.105
Relations with Israel	0.178	0.198
Relations with Arab World	0.025	0.027
No police killed	0.014	0.015
German reputation	0.069	0.076
Prevention of future terror	0.198	0.157
Internal Arab relations	0.021	0.017
Arab relations with world	0.041	0.033
Publicity for Palestinians	0.178	0.191
Release of comrades	0.051	0.055
Unification against Israel	0.066	0.072
Escape from Germany	0.047	0.051
Outcomes	w_3'	w_4
Demands fulfilled, hostages released in Munich	0.182	0.187
Demands fulfilled, hostages released in Arab country	0.153	0.158
Hostages, terrorists, and some police killed	0.140	0.132
Hostages released, terrorists killed	0.249	0.246
Hostages released, terrorists in custody	0.277	0.277

The most striking feature of Table 8 is the similarity between the two designs. The small differences that do appear are attributable largely to the relatively greater importance accorded Israel in the holarchical structure. As a consequence, the relative weight for outcome 3 (hostages, terrorists, and some police killed) increases slightly. Outcome 3 remains, however, the least "jointly preferred" outcome.

The extension to a holarchy does little to explain the outcome at Munich. It illustrates how one can, within the general approach of analytic hierarchies, rearrange characterization of decision problems to permit "loops" and still more general configurations.

Yet to better understand the outcome at Munich we shall have to explore strategic interdependencies among the actors' choices of policies.

What Were the Prospects for a Negotiated Settlement at Munich?

In the traditional fashion of terrorists, the initial aim of Black September was to gain control over the situation by seizing hostages and making threats credible by killing two of the Israelis in the beginning. Did this imply that their ultimate intention was to kill the remainder of the hostages? Both Israelis and Germans came to believe so, thus precluding extended attempts to negotiate a settlement. The data in Table 6 presents some justification for this conclusion.

The magnitude of priorities in this table varies enormously. We shall focus only on the largest elements of each column. The hostages are primarily concerned with outcomes 1 and 5. The German Government seeks 4 and 5; the Israeli Government, 3 and 4; the Arab World only 5; and the terrorists, 1 and 2. To simplify exposition, consider for a moment that the small priorities are zero. One sees then a rather clear pattern: in similarity of preferences for outcomes, the actors are arranged roughly circularly.

The terrorists share a concern with the hostages for outcome 1. The hostages share a concern with the German Government for outcome 5. The German Government and Israeli Government share 3. No party gives high priority to both outcomes 2 and 3. For a pictorial comprehension of the relations in this table, we used a nonmetric scaling algorithm (Lingoes 1968) to display the priorities over actors and outcomes simultaneously. A two-dimensional solution of adequately small error is shown in Figure 3. Without undue distortion one can imagine an oval through the points corresponding to actors and a second oval through points corresponding to outcomes.

Points in the space are located such that actors with relatively more similar preference profiles over the outcomes are nearer than actors with less similar profiles. Furthermore, outcomes are located relatively closer to actors that prefer them highly than to

Fig. 3. Two-dimensional solution to actors' relationships
with other actors and to outcomes

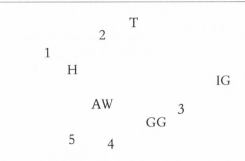

actors that have little preference for them. If two actors are widely separated with a single outcome lying between them—as roughly describes the locations of Black September and the Israeli Government—they will tend to share only the single, central outcome and to disagree on the desirability of other outcomes. If they are forced to reach a joint solution, the central outcome may result, even if it is highly prized by neither. This appears to have happened when the deaths of hostages and terrorists formed the only "common ground" in the Israelis' and terrorists' positions.

The terrorists are closest to outcome 2, but outcomes 1 and 3 might also lie within some range of tolerance. The Israeli Government is closest to outcome 3; the others are quite distant. Although the terrorists do not savor outcome 3, it appears in the figure as the sole outcome on which the terrorists and Israel, if left alone, might agree. We believe that the negotiating process at Munich resulted in granting both terrorists and Israelis effective vetoes over terms of any solution. Consequently, the result was— if one considers the weighted preferences of all actors in the aggregate—that least jointly desirable. The tragedy of Munich was that negotiations failed to transform the situation from a sort of Prisoners' Dilemma.

This interpretation does not address why the ambush attempt failed in implementation. Had the ambush succeeded as planned by the authorities, outcome 4 (terrorists killed; hostages released) would have resulted. Outcome 4 was anathema only to Black September. But perhaps the ambush had little real chance of success. As one German official was quoted after the disaster:

The hostages were as good as dead from the minute the Israeli Government refused to hand over prisoners. We only tried to free some of the hostages, or possibly all of them, in the event that the terrorists made a mistake.

The terrorists made no mistake. They took extreme precautions on the trip to the airport and turned on the hostages once the police opened fire.

Rather than critique the tactics of the German police, it is more useful to suggest a six-stage bargaining procedure whose design is based on the Munich and other cases we have studied. As condensed here, the prescriptions must appear somewhat didactic and Machiavellian. They are intended to exploit the authorities' usual advantage in controlling the tempo of negotiations and altering the psychological as well as material context of terrorists holding hostages. There are historical and hypothetical situations to which the prescriptions cannot apply. We hope the reader will be stimulated to expand this outline as well as to revise and substantiate it.

TOWARD POLICY GUIDANCE FOR NEGOTIATING WITH TERRORISTS HOLDING HOSTAGES

The negotiating procedure has six major stages. The rate at which the stages unfold and their particular thrust must respond to characteristics of the terrorist organization and the content of its demands. We label the stages as follows:

1. Exploratory contacts
2. Coordinated delay
3. Introductory negotiations in earnest
4. Psychological shaping and trade-offs
5. Bargaining in bad faith
6. Storming of the hostages' locations

The sequence of stages is not invariant. The micro-processes of the negotiations must responsively guide the design and evaluation of a hierarchy of the situation. The construction of an initial hierarchy will typically be followed by revision and reevaluation during each of the first four stages.

Stage 1: Exploratory Contacts

Three principles govern the authorities' initial contacts with the terrorists: (1) place the burden of communication upon them; (2) avoid a show of overwhelming force at the outset unless there is a good possibility of actually storming the hostages' location with acceptable loss; (3) attempt to deflate the terrorists' expectations of imminent decisive action.

At the outset terrorists must establish their demands and the credibility of their threat. Reliance on a single channel of communications with the authorities invites the distortion or loss of demands and endangers credibility. Black September tossed a written message of demands from the occupied apartment, but this did nothing to allay suspicions that the hostages were already dead. The authorities can usually delay by claiming either that they never received a message or that it is not clear.

The authorities should exert every effort—even to the point of exposing the hostages to greater risk—to attain effective control over the terrorists' communications with other terrorists (if they occupy separated sites), with their parent organization, with the public or special constituencies, and with the authorities. This does not mean that the authorities should necessarily disrupt the terrorists' communications. That decision must be integrated into the larger bargaining strategy. Yet it should be left to the authorities' discretion to permit or prevent particular communication with the outside world, particularly with the media.

Demands by the terrorists can be ignored, reached on a low level, or taken with utter seriousness. We believe the authorities will usually gain by initially downplaying the seriousness of the demands or deliberately interpreting them ambiguously. Some delay is advantageous to the authorities who must establish command and control over their agents. To force the pace of events, terrorists will generally make threats against their hostages with specific sanctions and a designated time limit for compliance. Initial efforts by authorities to avoid a premature showdown should thus attempt to involve the terrorists' energies in communicating demands and clarifying threats.

Premature showdown can often be averted by minimal show of force. To capture control over communications, the authorities must isolate the terrorists together with their hostages. Unless this can be achieved, efforts to control negotiations will likely to prove futile, as in the Moro kidnapping. Police cordons should be unobtrusive. The authorities should maintain the façade of minimal disruption of civic life. The Black Septembrists might have become more relaxed in their commitment as well as in their security precautions had the police been less manifestly threatening at the outset.

Insofar as possible the terrorists should be led to believe that their act is isolated, inconsequential, and, above all, not worth dying to consummate. Thus the third component of the first stage is to deflate the terrorists' egos by impressing them that they *can* expect to advance their demands but *only* by waiting patiently while the authorities "get their act together."

Terrorists are most primed for decisive action at the beginning of their operation. They appear usually to be most willing to sacrifice themselves at this time. Delay of six to eight hours may not dissipate their initial enthusiasm. Longer delay gives time to question a commitment to the objectives they have set. One cannot, of course, expect that highly motivated "professional" terrorists will abandon their commitment merely by reflecting upon it any more than that mercenaries will be converted by the propaganda of their adversaries. A more realistic expectation is that the authorities can take the edge of excitement off the operation in the terrorists' minds, to let them reconsider priorities as fatigue and boredom arise. There is a fine line between resignation and desperation: the authorities must insightfully couple real or imaginary concessions with strategic immobility.

Stage 2: Coordinated Delay

The second stage of negotiations consists basically of the authorities protracting the discussion of terms, making minimal concessions to motivate the talks. Prolongation of the negotiations is useful in itself and to facilitate collection of additional information about the terrorists' expectations and vulnerabilities in their beliefs. Information is acquired directly in talks, through third parties with access to the terrorists or hostages, through debriefing of released hostages, and (as achieved in the Moluccan train hijacking) by eavesdropping devices planted within the terrorists' redoubt.

Concessions are used to mitigate terrorists' demands and to gain confidence to permit the dialogue to emerge. Two kinds of needs may be satisfied through concessions: the long-range substantive goals and the immediate instrumental needs, such as food and security. Satisfaction of the latter is inexpensive for the authorities and may reap benefits. Frustration of immediate needs that leads to discomfort may backfire by making terrorists treat hostages more harshly. They are also likely to become more anxious and to diminish discrimination among bargaining options, perhaps aborting the authorities' attempts to broaden the discussions.

Once the terrorists give evidence of accepting the likelihood that they can obtain their substantive goals only after prolonged negotiations, the authorities should diminish the scope and modify the promptness of concessions already granted. They should also gradually strangle the terrorists' lines of communication with the media, if such exist. Official negotiators—who begin communications in the image of low-level, ill-prepared, harassed bureaucrats, frequently compromised by superiors in their duties—gradually impose the image of individuals with greater efficiency and resolve.

By the end of the second stage, the authorities should be well informed about the terrorists, and the terrorists' patience close to exhaustion. The authorities now require a transition to a new mode of negotiation without appearing either irresponsibly conciliatory or alarmingly militant. Their goal in the third stage is to create additional room for maneuver, perhaps by offering a complex package of counteroffers.

Stage 3: Introductory Negotiations in Earnest

To conduct meaningful negotiations, the authorities must choose negotiators with care. One tactic is to alter contact with a hard-liner, as a fulfillment of the terrorists' preconceptions of an authoritarian martinet, and a soft-liner, who attempts to appear to be under pressure from the hard-liner to obtain concessions from the terrorists, but who also wishes to *make* concessions *to* the terrorists. Alternative interrogations by hard- and soft-liners are a time-honored police tactic of potential applicability to communicating with terrorists. We suspect these roles were approximated by official negotiators in the Hanafi incident.

The soft-liner cannot appear to be too closely attached to the terrorists, or they will attempt to use him as their own negotiator. It is equally damaging to permit a hostage to serve as negotiator or as the sole intermediary. Hostages, depending on how they are treated, may have a tendency to identify with the terrorists or with fellow hostages, at least to the extent of accepting the terrorists' demand for safe conduct. The terrorists must be led to think that the soft-liner is "in a bind like us" but not "one of us."

The same individual negotiator cannot act multiple roles. He must be consistent and the psychological dialectic must be methodically pursued. If there must be significant revision of the authorities' position once negotiations have started, the new position should be represented by an official of greater authority than the exponent of the abandoned position. Authorities must take care to portray any change in stance as the result of forces or considerations beyond the influence of the terrorists. Such portrayal supports the authorities' oft-repeated contention that the terrorists are fundamentally too weak to expect fulfillment of their objectives.

Confusion about the negotiator's character—such as occurred at Munich when he was variously a potential hostage, hard-liner, and soft-liner—gives the terrorists an impression of inconsistency and lack of resolve by the authorities. It encourages the terrorists to try to impose their own version of how the authorities should behave and how their demands are to be met. This makes it doubly difficult to use control over time to change their idea about what is required and what is possible.

In the course of negotiations, if major symbolic or substantive concessions are granted, these should occur in an orchestrated fourth stage in which concessions are coupled with the authorities' own demands. A *quid pro quo* should accompany each concession as it is discussed.

Stage 4: Psychological Shaping and Substantive Trade-offs

The fourth stage is undoubtedly the most difficult to execute. The negotiators try to maximize to the terrorists the psychological significance of concessions accorded to avert harm to hostages while simultaneously minimizing the real value to the terrorists of the same concessions. Three themes are intertwined at this stage: counteroffers, psychological pressure, and evolutionary influence over the terrorists' organization. To each theme we propose a maxim:

1. Counteroffers, which may subsequently be revoked, should be sufficiently attractive to tempt the terrorists' consideration but sufficiently complex to entail substantial delay;
2. A safe, quick "easy way out" for the terrorists should recur with increasing frequency in the discussions;
3. The terrorists should be conceded what they can least advantageously use.

A counteroffer should be attractive upon first glance. No matter how committed to specific objectives the terrorists are, they are unlikely to reject out of hand an offer that appears almost as good as (or better than) their initial demands. Because discussions deadlocked in stage 3, counteroffers become the vehicle for a transformed agenda in stage 4.

The authorities should make counteroffers privately. They may subsequently have to renege, so public airing of positions can prove costly. The authorities should make the counteroffer complex. Its function to alter the negotiating format is enhanced if it also motivates the terrorists to serious thought about its relations to their original demands. The authorities' chances for creating divisions among the terrorists rests upon involving them in discussion of alternative "goods": there is more room for differences among friends over obtaining alternative "goods" than over avoiding alternative "bads."

It is sometimes politically feasible—when the value of the hostages is substantial and when the terrorists have not already inflicted unacceptable damage—to offer the terrorists a means of escape as the sole concession. When this offer is first made, it will probably not be attractive to them. Nevertheless, as the impasse wears on, the negotiators should continually raise the possibility of escape and focus upon the mechanics of its execution. Even trained terrorists may succumb, as did members of Black September who seized hostages in Thailand but released them in return for freedom.

If the authorities decide that some substantive concessions are necessary, they should offer those items of least value to the terrorists' organization over the long haul. The authorities may thus choose to deny symbolic concessions but grant material ones. Life itself may have to be conceded. No modeling technique can supplant individual responsibility for such decisions. But the authorities would ideally like to drive the terrorists' organization into an evolutionary cul-de-sac.

To this end, the authorities should offer concessions that tend to make the terrorists appear to be ordinary criminals (e.g., the German Government's monetary ransom to PFLP hijackers), acceptable participants in the political process (e.g., the attempts to defuse Moluccan terrorism by creating joint Dutch-Moluccan commissions to review Moluccan status in the Netherlands), or completely pathological cases (e.g., the District of Columbia's payment of Khaalis's legal expenses in a previous trial, and the German Government's broadcasting hysterical and incoherent demands of the Baader-Meinhof Gang in one incident).

To exploit control over the terrorists' evolution requires a deep understanding of factors that motivate and direct their activity, a topic far beyond our present paper (see, for instance, Jenkins 1972). The central idea is, however, simple: the hostage relationship should be reversed—only if the terrorists possess something that is vulnerable and that they value can the authorities threaten to reverse roles. Kupperman (1977) has applied to counterterrorism the traditional tactic of rulers to give dissidents a "stake" in the existing order that can be held hostage against their subsequent "good behavior." Nihilistic terrorists cannot, of course, be so deterred. The particular developmental prospects of a terrorist organization demand appropriately matched strategies of containment.

The fourth negotiating stage terminates either with an agreement acceptable to both parties or with a renewed impasse. It marks the end of possibilities for trade-offs accomplished by each party "rationally" appraising what it can exchange or concede. The next stage may occasionally lead to a breakthrough, but this results from unilateral concessions by terrorists. At the end of stage 4 the authorities have offered all the concessions they can afford.

Stage 5: Bargaining in Bad Faith

By this stage the impasse over at least one of the terrorists' major demands appears unbridgeable. The authorities have exhausted their negotiating repertoire. To the point at which mental and physical harm to the hostages becomes overbearing, the authorities generally have little to lose in prolonging the situation. There are conditions in which social disruption is itself unbearable and, of course, the terrorists may terminate negotiations.

Because discussions are carried on patiently by the authorities with hope of favorable resolution only by unforeseen events, we use the label "bargaining in bad faith." The "bad faith" is compounded when preparations for storming the terrorists' redoubt go along at the same time. The nature of preparations for an assault lies beyond the scope of this study. Although it is not likely that preparations can be made at very short notice, the authorities should avoid the more obvious preparations as long as possible.

Stage 6: Storming of the Hostages' Locations

We offer no analytic advice for assaults. Three important considerations pertain to the postassault stage, when it may be necessary for authorities to minimize the damage.

Insofar as possible, captured terrorists should be held in isolation, especially from the media. There is no point in according terrorists cheap publicity after the incident if costly measures were required during the incident to deny publicity.

Whether the freed hostages contribute to pro-terrorist propaganda depends upon their treatment, casualties during the assault, and the like. Publicity from hostages and their relatives is difficult to control. The authorities might find expeditious assistance to liberated hostages, whether injured or not, to be a good investment in a long-term struggle against terrorism. If, during the period of captivity, the terrorists were solicitious of hostages' needs, the authorities could hardly afford to be less so after the hostages' release.

Some concessions, such as freed prisoners, are beyond the power of authorities to retract. Other apparent concessions are revocable. These may include statements sympathetic to or propaganda distributed on behalf of the terrorists. Authorities cannot rely upon ordinary disclaimers to negate the effect of their earlier acts or statements. A carefully arranged public relations campaign will be more effective if it avoids claims of low credibility, such as "never again shall we make concessions" or "humanitarian concerns predominated in our calculations."

THE ROLE OF ANALYTIC HIERARCHIES IN CONFRONTING TERRORISM

With this tentative case study we believe analytic hierarchies have begun to make four contributions to the policy-oriented study of terrorism. First, they show how to exploit room for maneuver in a terrorist-hostage incident. Second, they suggest how to augment possibilities for resolving the incident by expanding its stakes, the number of participants, or duration. Third, the method enables the analyst, who may be a mediator or participant, to isolate those judgments or values of the actors most crucial in bringing about a change in negotiating positions. Fourth, the strongest contribution of analytic hierarchies and holarchies is to offer an open-ended procedure for representing the conflict. The method of analytic hierarchies permits unlimited expansion of detail and internal complexity to enable the policy-maker to explore consequences of induced changes in the participants' evaluations. Thus it forms an effective planning vehicle in the long-term struggle against political terrorists of various ideologies and purposes.

BIBLIOGRAPHY

ADAR Corporation (1975) *Sudan transport study: the use of hierarchies in the design of transport systems.* T. L. Saaty, Project Director. 5 vols.

Alexander, J. M. and T. L. Saaty (1977) "The forward and backward processes of conflict analysis," *Behavioral Science* 22, 2.

Bennett, J. P., and T. L. Saaty (1977) "Terrorism: patterns of negotiations; three case studies through hierarchies and holarchies." Unpublished manuscript prepared for the Arms Control and Disarmament Agency.

Dobson, C. (1974) *Black September.* Macmillan.

Franklin, J. N. (1968) *Matrix theory.* Prentice-Hall.

Groussard, S. (1975) *The blood of Israel: the massacre of the Israeli athletes, the Olympics, 1972.* Trans. J. J. Salemson. William Morrow.

Handman, J. B. S. (1937) "Terrorism," *Encyclopedia of the social sciences,* vol. 14.

Jenkins, B. (1975) *International terrorism: a new mode of conflict.* Crescent Publications.

Jureidini, P. A., and W. E. Hazen (1976) *The Palestinian movement in politics.* Lexington Books.

Kupperman, R. H. (1977) "Treating the symptoms of terrorism: some principles of good hygiene," *Terrorism* 1, 1.

Lingoes, J. C. (1972) "A general survey of the Guttman-Lingoes nonmetric program series." In R. N. Shepard et al., eds., *Multidimensional scaling,* vol. 1. Seminar Press.

New York Times, September–October 1972.

Saaty, T. L. (1977) "A scaling method for priorities in hierarchical structures," *Journal of Mathematical Psychology* 15.

——, and M. W. Khouja (1976) "A measure of world influence," *Journal of Peace Science* 2, 1.

——, and P. C. Rogers (1976) "The future of higher education in the United States (1985–2000)," *Socio-economic Planning Sciences* 10, 6.

——, and J. P. Bennett (1977) "A theory of analytical hierarchies applied to political candidacy," *Behavioral Science* 22, 4.

Stevens, S. S. (1972) *Psychophysics and social scaling.* General Learning Press.

Thornton, T. P. (1964) "Terror as a weapon of political agitation." In H. Eckstein, ed., *Internal war.* Free Press.

Torgerson, W. S. (1958) *Theory and method of scaling.* Wiley.

Time, 18 September 1972.

Heuristic Modeling Using Rule-Based Computer Systems

D. A. WATERMAN and BRIAN M. JENKINS

ABSTRACT

This paper discusses a recent effort at The Rand Corporation to apply heuristic modeling techniques to the topic of international terrorism. By heuristic model we mean an information processing model described in terms of heuristics (rules of thumb) which define the operation of the model. This joint project by computer scientists and social scientists is designed to provide researchers working on the problem of terrorism with a tool, in the form of computer programs, which will aid them in their analysis of terrorist activities. As a first attempt at developing such a tool, we have precisely defined the basic concepts needed for a model of terrorism and have used these concepts in the implementation of a program that extracts information about terrorist activities from a terrorism analyst and automatically represents it in a form that facilitates machine analysis of the information. This analysis consists of applying rules to the data extracted from the analyst in order to infer new data. We have found that the exercise of extracting information from an analyst in terms of precisely defined concepts not only sharpens the analyst's skills but also provides a basis for constructing programs to process the information.

SOURCE: This paper (number P-5811) was originally published in March 1977, by The Rand Corporation, Santa Monica, California 90406. It is here reprinted by permission.

I. INTRODUCTION

This paper describes work in progress on the task of applying heuristic modeling techniques to ill-defined problems in the social sciences. The ultimate goal of the project is to explore ways in which current computer technology, in the form of rule-based systems, can be used to help an expert understand the domain he is working in and assist him in decision-making, particularly in crisis situations. Our approach is to provide the expert with a set of computer programs that constitute a model of his domain of expertise and that enable him to store information explicitly as rules and data. He can then use the model as a tool that guides and stimulates decision-making by its ability to explain the lines of reasoning it uses to arrive at each decision it makes.

The heuristic model is a model of a situation stated in terms of heuristics (rules of thumb) which describe the dynamics of the situation. It is particularly useful for problem domains that are not well formalized and for which no generally agreed upon axioms or theorems exist. The domain we have chosen for investigation—international terrorism—is just this type of domain. By studying the techniques needed to develop a heuristic model of international terrorism we hope to gain insight into how these methods can be applied to other ill-defined domains in the social sciences.

In this study we outline the objectives of the project, describe how information can be represented in rule-based form, describe some preliminary attempts to create programs that help the expert input information into the computer system, and, finally, discuss the usefulness of providing an expert with this type of tool.

Background

This project is defined by the intersection of two separate research efforts at Rand—one involving the application of computer science techniques to the problem of helping people who are not computer experts interact with computers, and the other involving the study and analysis of international terrorism. The immediate goal is to provide terrorism analysts with computer programs specifically designed to aid them in their analysis of terrorist activities. These programs are designed so that they can be carefully tailored to the individual needs of each analyst.

The computer science project, initiated in July of 1974, is based on the premise that a good way to aid a computer user is to provide him with his own personal computer, one that is sensitive to his needs and desires. This can be accomplished in many ways (via timesharing, intelligent terminals, etc.) but the underlying theme is to have the software designed to accommodate the skills of the user, with more sophisticated software for the less advanced users. The system developed for this is called RITA, Rule-directed Interactive Transaction Agent (Anderson and Gillogly, 1976a, 1976b). An interactive transaction agent is simply a program (piece of software) that can perform some task for the user. Examples of typical tasks are (a) filing, retrieving, and editing of data on local storage files, (b) handling interactive dialogues with external information systems, (c) providing a local tutorial facility, and (d) heuristic modeling of subjective or judgmental information (Waterman, forthcoming). The most distinctive feature of the RITA architecture is the use of rules to describe judgments, where a rule is defined to have the form "IF condition THEN action," meaning "if the given condition is true in the current situation then perform the recommended action." This is called a rule-based or production system approach to heuristic modeling.

Since 1973, The Rand Corporation, sponsored jointly by the Defense Advanced Research Projects Agency and the Department of State, has been engaged in research on the phenomenon of international terrorism. The theory of terrorism, terrorist tactics, and terrorist groups has been examined, and data on over a thousand incidents of political violence have been amassed. Several hundred of these have been the subject of more detailed examinations. During the course of the research, the participants in the project came naturally to make "expert judgments" or to develop "hunches" regarding various aspects of terrorist activity, such as the responsibility for incidents where credit was not claimed, the objectives of a particular action, and the probable outcome of certain types of episodes. Though often unarticulated, and sometimes unrealized by the participant, these hunches were often based on a series of individual "rules" derived from an understanding of the logic behind the use of terrorist tactics, the observed modi operandi of various terrorist groups, and the outcome of similar episodes in the past. Thus the domain of terrorism is a reasonable area in which to use rule-directed systems.

The heuristic modeling project is beneficial to both the computer scientists involved in the intelligent terminal project and the social scientists working on the terrorism analysis project. The computer scientists benefit by gaining access to a problem domain which can be used to evoke and test ideas about the design and implementation of heuristic models. The feasibility of using a rule-based system like RITA for constructing a large complex model of decision-making in an ill-defined domain has already been demonstrated by the MYCIN system (Shortliffe, 1974; Davis et al., 1975). MYCIN is a computer model composed of over 200 rules which provide the basis for medical consultations on the task of selecting antibiotic therapy for patients with bacterial infections.

Heuristic modeling is also beneficial to the analysts studying terrorism. It provides a requirement and a means for articulating the series of steps that lie behind the "intuitive" judgments made by the analysts in reaching a particular conclusion. In the process of explaining each step, they find themselves asking questions not asked before, simply because the rapid process of thought does not demand such detailed explanations. Previously, in describing why they felt something to be so, it was explained simply as an intuitive judgment, or a hunch. The requirements of machine analysis impose a new degree of rigor on the analysts, lead to new questions, extract articulations about the theory and logic of terrorism, and point to new areas of exploration. In sum, it not only provides a useful tool for the analysts to use but also aids them in formalizing their domain of study.

When fully operational the heuristic model or "intelligent agent" will continue to demand of the analyst that he examine each incident in a comprehensive manner, and that he explain each judgment. On the basis of rules provided by the analyst the agent will reach conclusions with which the analyst may disagree. In this case, the analyst will be compelled to reexamine the basis for his own deduction, and this may lead to the formulation of new rules for the agent. In this way the system will enable analysts to preserve their own judgments and those of others in a form that is easily retrievable and can be made available to decision-makers faced with real crisis situations.

Basic Assumptions

This project is based on three major assumptions. The first is that terrorist activities can be analyzed in a formal, rigorous fashion. The violence of political extremists, for the most part, is not viewed as a collection of mindless, irrational, and thus totally unpredictable events. It follows certain rules of logic that can be discerned by the experienced analyst. Patterns emerge which can be translated into "rules." For example, a study of political kidnappings and hostage incidents shows that political extremist groups that operate in their home territory and have the support of an underground organization generally prefer standard kidnappings as a means of taking hostages. (In a standard kidnapping, the victim is held at an unknown location while the kidnappers bargain by means of telephone or mail with the targets of their demands. This enables them to hold their hostage for months if necessary to increase pressure for concessions.) Groups operating abroad or lacking an underground tend to become involved in barricade-and-hostage incidents (captors seize their hostages in a public place, allowing themselves to become hostages; they bargain for escape along with other demands). This is not always true, but it is generally true. Some of the patterns are based on group characteristics or modi operandi. For example, the Irish Republican Army has shown no inclination to seize hostages for bargaining purposes. Many of the Palestinian and Latin American groups frequently do so.

The second assumption is that although the domain of terrorism is obviously complex with each group and each incident highly unique, it is nonetheless believed that even a limited number of rules that prod thinking and formalize the domain will enhance analysis of the topic.

The third assumption is that heuristic models of terrorist activities can be formulated as rule-directed models. We have already justified the use of the rule-based architecture through reference to the work done with MYCIN. The limiting constraint here is the number of rules needed to adequately model the domain. This can be avoided to a certain extent by attempting to model only a small portion of the domain of international terrorism. In this initial effort we have restricted our attention to the problem of terrorist bombings.

Objectives of the Project

The primary objective of the heuristic modeling project is to determine the feasibility and utility of developing heuristic models within the rule-directed framework and to help the user make complex decisions in ill-specified domains containing large amounts of information that must be coordinated and used in a short amount of time. The secondary objective is to develop a demonstration model that performs interesting and useful deductions within the domain of international terrorism. Other objectives are:

1. to provide a method or procedure to stimulate new ideas and provoke new questions about the domain;
2. to provide a framework within which a high degree of analytic rigor can be imposed;
3. to provide a framework for decision-making that structures thinking and guides problem solving during a crisis situation;
4. to assist in the analysis and understanding of terrorist activities and groups;
5. to ultimately provide a predictive tool, one that can infer what will happen in the near future or what the immediate effect of certain actions will be.

Characteristics of the Heuristic Model

The heuristic model currently under development is a collection of RITA agents that the terrorism analyst will have at his disposal. These agents will constitute a tool that the analyst can use to aid in decision-making or problem-solving tasks. The model will have the following primary characteristics:

1. A deductive inference capability. This means that the agents will be capable of not only retrieving information stored in the

data base but of using that information to make deductions that can cause new information to be added to the data base. This capability is a direct result of using a rule-based model, since the rules are, in effect, procedures defining how new information can be deduced from existing data.

2. Dynamic growth. In the domain of international terrorism both data and judgments (or policy) are subject to constant revision. The modularity imposed by the rule-based organization of the agents facilitates such dynamic growth, i.e., it is easy to add, delete, or modify both the data and the rules that constitute the judgments.

3. Integrated collection of knowledge. The agents that constitute the model can represent judgments of many experts from various parts of the world. This expertise is stored at one location for later use by experts and nonexperts alike. However, the real utility of such a system is that it will permit a constant exchange of data and judgments by leading experts, and this will lead to the formation of new rules and ideas about the domain.

II. REPRESENTATION OF INFORMATION IN PRODUCTION SYSTEM FORM

A production system is a collection of rules of the form condition → action (Newell and Simon, 1972), where the conditions are statements about the contents of a data base and the actions are procedures that alter the contents of that data base. RITA is a specialized production-system architecture, that is, a programming language within which one can write specific programs that are production systems or RITA agents. Production-system architectures have been developed to facilitate adaptive behavior (Waterman, 1970, 1975; Waterman and Newell, 1976), to model human cognition and memory (Newell, 1972, 1973), and to create large systems that represent heuristic models of the judgments of a collection of experts (Feigenbaum et al., 1970; Shortliffe and Buchanan, 1975; Davis et al., 1975; Lenat, 1976). RITA was designed with the latter task in mind and accordingly has two types of production rules: those called rules and those called goals. The rules are left-hand-side driven, i.e., when all the conditions of a rule are true relative to the data base, the rule "fires," causing the associated actions to be taken. The goals, however, are right-hand-side driven. This means that the system is given a condition to make true, or, in effect, a question to answer through deductive inference. The right-hand sides of rules are examined to find one that could make the desired condition true. When such a rule is found, its left-hand side is examined to see if all its conditions are true. If they are, the rule is fired; if not, the process continues in the same manner in an attempt to make each condition in the left-hand side of the rule true.

Data Representation in RITA

In RITA the data are represented as objects that can have any number of attribute-value pairs. Thus, to represent a person whose name is John Smith, whose age is 32, and whose salary is in the $33,789 to $43,923 range, the object PERSON would have associated with it three attribute-value pairs: NAME = JOHN SMITH, AGE = 32, and SALARY RANGE = $33,789 TO $43,923. This would be written in RITA as:

> OBJECT person
> name is "John Smith",
> age is "32",
> salary-range is $33,789 to $43,923";

The fact that John Smith, Mary Jones, and Tom Brown are all government service employees and are all part of a group of such employees called GS level 15 can be represented as:

> OBJECT group
> name is "GS Level 15",
> type is "government service employees",
> members is ("John Smith", "Mary Jones", "Tom Brown");

Note that the value of an attribute can be either an item like "John

Smith" or a list like "John Smith", "Mary Jones", "Tom Brown"). Also, more than one object of the same type can exist simultaneously in the data base. The data base can contain many distinct persons and groups, each with different attribute-value pairs. Thus Mary Jones might also be in the data base as:

>   OBJECT person
>   name is "Mary Jones",
>   age is "22";

Goal and Rule Representation in RITA

Judgments and procedures in RITA are represented as goals and rules. The goals are more generally used for judgments and the rules for procedures, but either can be used for judgments or procedures. The format for a goal is shown below.

>   GOAL goalname
>   IF   premise AND premise . . . AND premise
>   THEN action AND action . . . AND action.

A few examples will make this format clear. Figure 1 shows judgments in English and below them the corresponding RITA goals. The format for rules is very similar to that for goals as shown below.

>   RULE rulename
>   IF   premise AND premise . . . AND premise
>   THEN action AND action . . . AND action.

Some examples of RITA rules are given in Figure 2. These tend to describe processes or procedures more than judgments. The "deduce" action in rule 2 is a signal to RITA to process the goals in an attempt to infer the desired information.

The data, goals, and rules just described can be combined to form a RITA agent which will tell the user the name and salary range of each person in the data base if that range is known or can be deduced. The agent is shown in Figure 3.

Fig. 1. Examples of RITA goals

1. "The salary range of a government service group can be determined by the salary range of any of its members."

   or

   "If you don't know the salary range of a government service group but you do know the salary range of a member of that group, then the salary range of the group is just the salary range of that member."

GOAL 1

   IF: there is a group whose type is
         "government service employees"
   and whose salary-range is not known
   and there is a person whose salary-range
         is known
   and the name of the person is in the members
         of the group

   THEN: set salary-range of the group to the
         salary-range of the person;

2. "The salary range of a member of a government service group can be determined by the salary range of the group."

   or

   "If you don't know the salary range of a member of a government service group but the salary range of the group is known, then the salary range of the person is just the salary range of the group."

GOAL 2

   IF: there is a person whose salary-range is not known
   and there is a group whose salary-range is known
   and the name of the person is in the members
         of the group

   THEN: set the salary-range of the person to the
         salary-range of the group;

Example of a Deduction by a RITA Agent

When the agent in Figure 3 is executed, rule 1 is tested against the data base and found to be true, since John Smith's salary range is known but nothing is known about John Smith's status. Since all the premises of rule 1 are true, rule 1 "fires," i.e., the associated action is taken and the agent writes "John Smith $33,789 to $43,923" at the user's terminal and sets John Smith's

Fig. 2. Examples of RITA rules

---

1. "Send the name and salary range of each person to the user."

   or

   "If the salary range of a person is known and it has not yet been sent to the user then send both the name and salary range of the person to the user."

RULE 1

   IF: there is a person whose salary-range is known
   and whose status is not known

   THEN: send the name of the person to the user
   and send the salary-range of the person to the user
   and set the status of the person to "accounted for";

2. "Infer the salary range of every person whose salary range is not known."

   or

   "If there is a person whose salary range is not known then infer that salary range."

RULE 2

   IF: there is a person whose salary-range is not known

   THEN: deduce the salary-range of the person;

---

status to "accounted for." Again rule 1 is tested against the data base but now fails to fire for John Smith, since the second premise, concerning John Smith's status, is no longer true. It also fails to fire for Mary Jones, since the first premise concerning her salary range is not true.

Since the premises in rule 1 are not true, it cannot fire and rule 2 is tested. The premise in rule 2 is true for Mary Jones so the rule fires and the salary range of Mary Jones is deduced. This deduction involves just the goals. The right-hand sides (action parts) of the goals are checked to see if they could determine the salary range of a person. Only goal 2 can do this, so its premises are checked to see if they are true so the goal can be fired.

The first premise of goal 2 is true for Mary Jones but the second premise is not, since the salary range of the group is not known. Now the system does a clever thing. Instead of giving up and deciding that goal 2 is not true, it tries to deduce the second premise of goal 2, i.e., the salary range of the group. The only applicable goal is goal 1, so its premises are checked. The first

Fig. 3. A RITA agent that attempts to deduce the salary range of all persons in the data base

OBJECT person <1> :

name	IS	"John Smith",
age	IS	"32",
salary-range	IS	"$33,789 to $43,923";

OBJECT person <2> :

name	IS	"Mary Jones",
age	IS	"22";

OBJECT group <1> :

name	IS	"GS Level 15",
type	IS	"government service employees",
members	IS	("John Smith", "Mary Jones", "Tom Brown");

RULE 1

IF: THERE IS a person WHOSE salary-range IS KNOWN
　　AND WHOSE status IS NOT KNOWN

THEN: SEND the name OF the person TO user
　　& SEND the salary-range OF the person TO user
　　& SET the status OF the person TO "accounted for";

RULE 2

IF: THERE IS a person WHOSE salary-range IS NOT KNOWN
THEN: DEDUCE the salary-range OF the person;

GOAL 1

IF: THERE IS a group
　　WHOSE type IS "government service employees"
　　AND WHOSE salary-range IS NOT KNOWN
　　& THERE IS a person WHOSE salary-range IS KNOWN
　　& the name OF the person IS IN the members OF the group

THEN: SET the salary-range OF the group TO the
　　salary-range OF the person;

GOAL 2

IF: THERE IS a person WHOSE salary-range IS NOT KNOWN
　　& THERE IS a group WHOSE salary-range IS KNOWN
　　& the name OF the person IS IN the members OF the group

THEN: SET the salary-range OF the person TO the
　　salary-range OF the group;

premise of goal 1 is true, since the group is government service employees and its affiliation is not known. The second and third premises of goal 1 are true for John Smith and the group, so all the premises are true and the goal fires, setting the salary range of the group to "$33,789 to $43,923." This makes the second premise of goal 2 true, and, since the third premise of goal 2 is true for Mary Jones, all the premises are true and goal 2 fires, setting the salary range of Mary Jones to "$33,789 to $43,923."

The deduction is now complete and control returns to the rules. Rule 1 is checked and this time is true for Mary Jones. It fires, printing "Mary Jones $33,789 to $43,923" at the user's terminal and setting the status of Mary Jones to "accounted for." Now rule 1 is checked again but is not true, nor is rule 2, so the agent halts. The data base after the deductions are made is shown below.

```
OBJECT person < 1 > :
        name            IS   "John Smith",
        age             IS   "32",
        salary-range    IS   "$33,789 to $43,923",
        status          IS   "accounted for";
OBJECT person < 2 > :
        name            IS   "Mary Jones",
        age             IS   "22",
        salary-range    IS   "$33,789 to $43,923",
        status          IS   "accounted for";
OBJECT group < 1 > :
        name            IS   "GS Level 15",
        type            IS   "government service
                             employees",
        members         IS   ("John Smith", "Mary Jones",
                             "Tom Brown"),
        salary-range    IS   "$33,789 to $43,923";
```

Note that not only was the desired information about the salary range of Mary Jones deduced and added to the data base but as a side effect information concerning the salary range of the group was also deduced and stored in the data base.

III. HEURISTIC MODELING USING RITA AGENTS

Building a heuristic model for a domain like terrorism is a complex task independent of the method chosen for constructing the model. The method used here centers on extracting data and rules from an expert on terrorism in a form that focuses on the essential and relevant information in the domain.

Data and Rule Extraction

The first step involved in building a heuristic model in an ill-defined domain is the job of formalizing the domain. This critical step consists of deciding what elements in the domain are relevant to the problem at hand, how they should be categorized, and how they should be defined. It imposes the degree of organization on the data that is needed for later development of relationships between the data elements. The key to formalizing the domain is data extraction—the process of extracting data or knowledge about the domain from an expert. This was accomplished, in our case, by a series of dialogues between the expert and the model-builders, in which the model-builders played the role of protocol analysts (Waterman and Newell, 1973, 1976). Typically the protocol analyst will ask pertinent questions of the expert which reveal assumptions and attitudes the expert may not have been conscious of having. These ideas are then expanded by the expert and the protocol analyst into a characterization of the domain.

Rule extraction proceeds in exactly the same manner as data extraction, through an extended dialogue between the expert and the protocol analysts. We have found that trying to extract rules out of context, i.e., posing the question, "Give me all the rules you know about bombings by the Palestinian Groups," leads to vague generalities that are seldom useful. The most successful approach has been to focus on particular events, analyze them in great depth, and then classify the rules generated during the analysis as either specific to a particular context or as a special case that is generally true—one that almost occupies the status of an axiom or tautology in the system. We thus end up with two types of rules: axiomatic ones that are true with near 100 percent probability, and heuristic ones that are true with a lesser probability. While both types of rules can be used to infer new information, the axiomatic rules can also be used to check the validity of the information being extracted.

Data extraction or domain formalization is not something that is done in a single step that is followed by the step of rule extraction. In actuality these steps proceed in parallel, progress in each affecting the status of the other. Thus many iterations must be made through the cycle of defining and organizing relevant data, generating rules that relate data elements to each other, and then revising the definitions and organization to accommodate new components of new rules. Eventually we would like to have the job of rule extraction automated, performed perhaps by a RITA agent capable of asking the right questions and using the answers to build RITA rules.

Focal Points for Terrorism

It appears to us that there are three important focal points around which we can build a system for modeling terrorist activities. These are focal points around which information can be gathered and rules can be formulated. They are "event," "group," and "context." The term "event" stands for a terrorist incident: a bombing, hijacking, kidnapping, etc. The term "group" means a terrorist group, that is, a group that has used terrorist tactics. "Context" is a somewhat less precise label that encompasses local political and economic developments, effectiveness of internal security, etc. In a specific situation, it may include the circumstances external to the actual incident or event, for instance, the response of a government to the specific terrorist activity.

A useful analogy is to consider these focal points as hubs of wheels; one wheel for group, one for event, and another for context. Radiating from the hublike spokes are the "attributes" that are associated with each wheel. Radiating from the hub labeled "event" are attributes pertaining to its date, time, type, location, target, victim, and so on. Protruding from the hub labeled "group" are attributes such as size, ideology, composition of membership, etc. Around "context" would be attributes like the effectiveness of police, etc. The answer or item of information associated with each attribute, the "value," is located at the rim of the wheel (see Fig. 4).

Fig. 4. Example of object-attribute-value
relationship for the object "event"

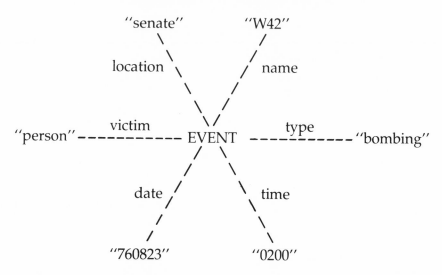

Rules can relate one attribute or spoke to another on the same focal point or wheel. For example, the answer (or value) to a specific question (that derives from an attribute) will determine the answer to another question. To illustrate, let us use a bombing (an event). One of its attributes is the "target." By having the target stated (specific individual, political property, corporate headquarters or offices, etc.), the machine may be led to a deduction about the tactical objective of the event. For example, if the target is "vital systems," the tactical objective may be "disruption."

The rules may also nullify certain questions on the basis of answers to previous questions. For example, if the bomb is identified as a "Molotov cocktail," the machine does not need to ask how the bomb was delivered. Molotov cocktails are thrown. It does not need to ask about the size of the bomb, since it knows it must have been small. These rules do not represent sophisticated judgments for which experts are required. They are virtually axiomatic. They are included only to expedite the interrogation process by dropping irrelevant or repetitious questions.

Rules may also relate attributes from one focal point to another. For example, if we are talking about bombings, the type of bomb and type of target regularly chosen by a particular group may tell us something about the educational background of its members or about its ideology. Such rules are not likely to be axiomatic. The judgments here are likely to be quite complex and based upon several or even many answers to specific questions.

The possible combinations are endless. Rules may be built upon several attributes in each focal point. To arrive at a judgment of what members of the Japanese Red Army who are holding hostages in the French Embassy are most likely to do if their demands are not met requires a very complex chain of reasoning. However, it is important to point out that the deduction does not have to be correct so long as the user can follow the chain of logic used by the machine to arrive at its conclusion. The user then can agree with certain parts or disagree to reach his own conclusion. In the process, he will have been compelled to review his own reasoning and examine his own assumptions. The machine will have assisted, not replaced, the analyst or decision-maker.

IV. CURRENT STATE OF DEVELOPMENT

At this point we have made one iteration through the cycle of formalizing the domain of terrorist bombings and refining the associated rules. Table 1 shows a small representative sample of the information that represents our concept of the domain. The entire formalization is given in Addendum 1.

To aid the terrorism expert in construction of the domain, a RITA agent called MODIFY has been implemented. This agent queries the expert, permitting him to add, modify, or delete information from the data base that represents the formalization of the domain. The expert uses MODIFY first to create the data base and then to update and modify it as his conception of the domain becomes more clear. A protocol of an expert interacting with the MODIFY agent to add a new attribute called STAGE to the object GROUP is shown below. The expert's answers are given in italics.

What is to be modified . . . *group*
What attribute of group is to be modified . . . *stage*

TABLE 1

SAMPLE OF FORMALIZATION OF TERRORISM DOMAIN FOR TERRORIST BOMBING INCIDENTS
(See Addendum 1)

event . . . .

    name
    [give the event to be defined an identifying name]

    type
    [type of the terrorist event; e.g., bombing, kidnapping]
        bombing
        barricade-and-hostage
        kidnapping

    date
    [use the format yymmdd; e.g., 760330]

    target
    [who or what was the immediate object of the attack?]
        specific individual
        representative individual
        random individual
        political property
        corporate headquarters or offices
        other commercial property
        private property
        vital systems
        head of state

    instigator
    [name of person(s) or group who planned the event]

    perpetrator
    [name of person(s) or group carrying out the event]

group . . . .

    name
    [type the full proper name used by the group and the acronym, if any]

    objective
    [what are the strategic objectives of the group?]
        enlarge the group
        expansion
        overthrow of government
        discredit the system
        territorial independence
        limited reforms or concessions
        vigilante-like defense

TABLE 1 (Cont.)

tactics
[the typical types of events perpetrated by the group]
    bombing
    barricade-hostage
    kidnapping
    assassinations
    hijackings
    armed assaults
    robbery
    dissemination of propaganda
    sabotage

person . . . .
    name
    [name of the person]

    sex
    [male or female]

    age
    [approximate age in years]

    group-membership
    [organizational affiliation]

Now defining the stage of the group:
What is the type number?   ?
Let me rephrase the question . . .
Do you want to enumerate some of the stages of the group?
yes
Can any single group have more than one stage? *no*
Give a prompt for the stage of the group
the current stage of the development of the group (1 through 5)
Now enter new values and prompts
[Type only a carriage return to terminate]
A new value for the stage of the group is . . . *1*
The prompt for "1" is . . .
violent propaganda stage: sporadic bombings of symbolic targets
A new value for the stage of the group is . . . *2*
The prompt for "2" is . . .
organizational growth stage: attacks with specific tactical objectives

A new value for the stage of the group is . . . 3
The prompt for "3" is . . .
guerrilla offensive stage: attacks on real rather than symbolic targets
A new value for the stage of the group is . . . 4
The prompt for "4" is . . .
mobilization of masses stage: attack on judiciary to provoke repression
A new value for the stage of the group is . . . 5
The prompt for "5" is . . .
urban uprising stage: mass uprising, full-scale urban warfare
A new value for the stage of the group is . . .
What attribute of group is to be modified . . .
What is to be modified . . .
Objects saved on file bomb objects

After the expert has created the data base that represents the domain he has at his disposal, another RITA agent, called BUILD, uses the domain just defined to help him enter new data about terrorist events or groups into the computer. BUILD uses the domain data base to formulate questions about the object to be described. For example, the questions BUILD would ask as a result of the definition given to the MODIFY agent are shown below in an actual protocol of an expert interacting with BUILD. Again the expert's responses are shown in italics.

Is the stage of the group :
    1?   ?
[violent propaganda stage: sporadic bombings of symbolic targets]
    1? *no*
    2? ?
[organizational growth stage: attacks with specific tactical objectives]
    2? *no*
    3? ?
[guerrilla otfensive stage: attacks on real rather than symbolic targets]
    3? *no*
    4? ?

[mobilization of masses stage: attack on judiciary to provoke repression]
  4? *no*
  5? *?*
[urban uprising stage: mass uprising, full-scale urban warfare]
  5? *yes*

In this protocol the expert responded to each question of the agent by first typing a question mark to obtain a definition of the term being used and then answering with either "yes" or "no." This feature of being able to ask the agent to explain itself is of critical importance, since the definitions of terms are somewhat arbitrary and not easily inferred. After the expert answered "yes" to the last question, BUILD created the object shown below.

    OBJECT group <1> :
        stage   IS   "5";

The BUILD agent is designed to help the user enter information about terrorist activities into the computer in a form that can be accessed by other RITA agents. However, BUILD does more than just query the user and map the user's replies into RITA data. Before it asks each question it attempts to deduce the answer itself based on the information it has gathered up to that point. If it can deduce the answer it notifies the user of that fact and does not ask him the question. Only when it is unable to deduce the answer does it query the user. Some typical RITA goals that BUILD uses to make deductions about bombing incidents are shown in Figure 5. These goals have the status of axioms in the system, i.e., the probability of their being true is very close to 1. A complete protocol of an expert entering data about a hypothetical bombing incident is shown in Addendum 2. An informal description of the hypothetical incident plus the resulting RITA description of it are shown in Figure 6.

BUILD is an agent for acquiring data from the user. What is also needed is an agent for acquiring judgments or rules from the user. Such an agent would query the user in much the same manner as BUILD and use the information gathered to construct rules or goals about terrorist activities. To present a clearer idea

Fig. 5. Some of the goals used by the BUILD agent to deduce information about terrorist bombings

---

GOAL 1

    IF: the time-of-day OF the event IS less THAN 0600
      & the bomb-size OF the event IS "small"

  THEN: PUT "property damage-no casualties" INTO the tactical-objective OF the event AS the LAST MEMBER;

GOAL 2

    IF: "no warning" IS IN the recipient-of-warning OF the event

  THEN: SET the warning-time OF the event TO 0;

GOAL 3

    IF: the bomb-type OF the event IS "Molotov-cocktail"

  THEN: SET the bomb-delivery OF the event TO "thrown"
      & SET the bomb-detonation OF the event TO "impact"
      & SET the secondary-detonation OF the event TO "no detonation"
      & SET the bomb-sophistication OF the event TO "low"
      & SET the detonation-source OF the event TO "self-detonating"
      & PUT "home-made" INTO the explosive-source OF the event AS the LAST MEMBER
      & SET the bomb-size OF the event TO "small";

GOAL 4

    IF: the bomb-type OF the event IS "letter or parcel"

  THEN: SET the bomb-delivery OF the event TO "delivered"
      & SET the bomb-size OF the event TO "small"
      & SET the risk-to-perpetrator OF the event TO "low";

GOAL 5

    IF: the bomb-type OF the event IS "land mine"

  THEN: SET the bomb-delivery OF the event TO "planted"
      & PUT "no warning" INTO the recipient-of-warning OF the event AS the LAST MEMBER;

---

of how such an agent might work a hypothetical user-agent dialogue is shown below.

  QUESTION 1: What do you want to know about the event that you do not already know?

    ANSWER 1: I want to know the tactical-objective of the event and the political-ideology of the group.

Fig. 6. A hypothetical bombing incident and the corresponding RITA description

The event took place in Washington, D.C., at about 1:26 P.M. in the Senate Office Building on August 23, 1976. As Secretary of State Henry Kissinger was exiting the front door a lone individual hurled a Molotov-cocktail at him and then fled on foot. The bomb failed to explode and no one was hurt. Two minutes before the attempted bombing a woman who identified herself as a member of the New World Liberation Front called the *Washington Post* and claimed credit for the act. She said the reason for the incident was the failure of the government to free SLA political prisoners. The bomb itself was estimated to have weighed about 4 pounds.

OBJECT event < 2 > :

name	IS	"Washington Incident",
type	IS	"bombing",
date	IS	"760823",
time-of-day	IS	"1326",
location	IS	"Senate",
locale	IS	"Washington",
region	IS	"urban",
host-country	IS	"United States",
announced-claimant	IS	("New World Liberation Front"),
when-claimed	IS	("before-bombing"),
announced-purpose	IS	("retaliation against government"),
target	IS	("specific individual"),
target-symbolic-value	IS	"inherently obvious",
target accessibility	IS	"medium",
victim	IS	("person"),
bomb-weight	IS	"4",
bomb-type	IS	"Molotov-cocktail",
bomb-size	IS	"small",
bomb-delivery	IS	"thrown",
bomb-detonation	IS	"impact",
secondary-detonation	IS	"no detonation",
detonation-source	IS	"self-detonating",
explosive-source	IS	("home-made"),
bomb-sophistication	IS	"low",
audacity	IS	"high",
risk-to-perpetrator	IS	"high",
recipient-of-warning	IS	("no warning"),
warning-time	IS	"0",
outcome	IS	"malfunction/no detonation",
tactical-objective	IS	("publicity/group", "murder"),
strategic-objective	IS	("publicity"),

Fig. 6 (Cont.)

number-killed	IS	"0",
number-wounded	IS	"0",
primary-damage	IS	"no damage",
secondary-damage	IS	"no damage",
instigator	IS	("New World Liberation Front"),
perpetrator	IS	("New World Liberation Front"),
unused	IS	("disclaimant", "bomb-composition");
OBJECT target <1> :		
name	IS	"Kissinger";

QUESTION 2: What do you think the tactical-objective might be? ("I don't know" is not acceptable.)

ANSWER 2: Extortion.

QUESTION 3: What do you think the political-ideology might be? ("I don't know" is not acceptable.)

ANSWER 3: New left.

QUESTION 4: What pieces of information would you need in order to validate or negate your answers?

ANSWER 4: I would want to know the locale of the event, the target of the event, and the announced-purpose of the event.

QUESTION 5: What is a possible locale for extortion and new left?

ANSWER 5: California.

QUESTION 6: What is a possible target for extortion and new left?

ANSWER 6: Vital systems.

QUESTION 7: What is a possible announced-purpose for extortion and new left?

ANSWER 7: Reduce utility rates for the poor.

RESPONSE: On the basis of your answers, I have constructed the following rule:

RULE 1

IF: the locale of the event is "California"
& the target of the event is "vital systems"

& the announced-purpose of the event is "reduce utility rates for the poor"

THEN: set the tactical-objective of the event to
"extortion-specified philanthropic"
& set the political-ideology of the group to
"new left";

QUESTION 8: Does this rule strike you as being irrelevant
or inaccurate? If so, rewrite it as one or
more rules which you believe are more
accurate.

This type of rule acquisition capability would be similar to the
one developed for MYCIN (Davis, 1976). The agent and the user
would work together to develop and refine the rules, with the
user always having the final say in the matter. Figure 7 shows
what some goals acquired this way might look like. Note that
these goals are more complex than the axiomatic-type goals used
by BUILD (see Fig. 4). They would be used, in conjunction
with many other similar goals, to deduce information about
bombing campaigns.

V. WHAT HAVE WE LEARNED THUS FAR?

The process of formalizing the domain by identifying the important concepts or objects, their attributes, and the associated
values is of major importance in the construction of a heuristic
model. This is because these basic components are all that are
available for describing the complex heuristics or rules that define
activity in the domain. If these basic building blocks are too
narrow in scope there will be relevant relationships that cannot be expressed. If they are too wide, the system will tend
to be inefficient, spending much time processing irrelevant
information.

The task of eliciting from analysts judgments that the system
can use as "rules" is far more difficult and complex than originally anticipated. "Experts," it appears, have a tendency to state
their conclusions and the reasoning behind them in general
terms that are too broad for effective machine analysis. It is

Fig. 7. Goals for deducing information about bombing campaigns

---

GOAL 1

    IF: the public-opinion OF the current-event
        IS "anti-terrorist"

  THEN: SET the government-response OF the current-event
        TO "harsh crackdown on terrorists";

[If the public is strongly against the terrorists, then the government will take harsh measures to suppress the terrorists.]

GOAL 2

    IF: the casualty-level OF the current-event IS "high"
        OR THERE IS a campaign WHOSE event-list IS KNOWN
    & the name OF the current-event
        IS IN the event-list OF the campaign
    & the frequency OF the campaign IS "escalating"
        OR the time-between-attacks OF the campaign IS "short"

  THEN: SET the public-opinion OF the current-event
        TO "anti-terrorist";

[If the current event caused many casualties or is part of a campaign whose frequency is escalating or which has a short time between attacks, then the current event will affect public opinion, i.e., the public will become anti-terrorist.]

GOAL 3

    IF: the number-killed OF the current-event IS greater THAN 0

  THEN: SET the casualty-level OF the current-event TO "high";

[If 1 or more people are killed the casualty level is considered high.]

GOAL 4

    IF: the attacks-per-month OF the campaign IS NOT less THAN 1

  THEN: SET the time-between-attacks OF the campaign TO "short";

[If the attacks average 1 or more per month they are considered frequent.]

---

advantageous to have the machine work at a more basic level, dealing with clearly defined pieces of basic information that it can build into more complex judgments. In contrast, the analyst seldom operates at a basic level. He makes complex judgments rapidly, without laboriously reexamining and restating each step in his reasoning process. The pieces of basic knowledge are assumed and are combined so quickly that it is difficult for him to describe the process. When he examines a problem, he cannot easily articulate each step and may even be unaware of the individual steps taken to reach a solution. He may ascribe to intuition or label a hunch that which is the result of a very complex reasoning process based upon a large amount of re-membered data and experience. In subsequently explaining his conclusion or hunch he will repeat only the major steps, often leaving out most of the smaller ones, which may have seemed obvious to him at the time.

Knowing what to consider basic and relevant and not requiring further reevaluation is what makes an analyst an "expert." An economic forecast does not begin with an explanation of why 2 plus 2 equals 4. A political forecast in the United States does not begin with a statement that there are three branches of govern-ment and presidential elections every four years. An intelligent discussion about terrorism does not start with the fact that Palestinians are Arabs or that aerial hijacking means taking over an airplane. And when arguing what a particular group might do in a specific situation the analyst seldom states that he is basing his conclusion perhaps in part on the personality of a particular leader, in part on the modus operandi of a particular group, and in part on his recollection of outcomes in similar episodes in the past. This type of information is considered "basic" by the expert. Nor does he discuss why he chose certain past episodes as relevant and discarded others that the non-expert might have chosen, or what specific aspect of the modus operandi is perti-nent to the current circumstances. The analyst is not deliberately mysterious about his process of reasoning, nor is his analysis sloppy or incorrect. He simply does not state every single piece of information and every small component part of every judgment he makes. Thus we discovered that the judgments the analysts considered simple and basic were actually complex, often com-posed of many individual steps that could be elicited only by the annoying process of repeatedly asking him to justify each state-ment, including the statements used to clarify previous state-ments. Obtaining the basic rules the machine needs in order to mimic the reasoning process of the analyst is a difficult and some-times painful task.

Attempts to extract rules from terrorist experts in the abstract simply by asking them to write all the rules they could think of pertaining to a particular domain did not prove successful for two reasons. First, experts don't usually think of their judgments as being based on a set of "rules," and have trouble putting their ideas into rule form. Second, the rules elicited by this method varied in level of abstraction but generally were all too abstract or complex for the machine to use. They had to be broken down into their component parts, which is something the experts had not been required to do and normally were not accustomed to doing.

We discovered that it was far more useful to elicit rules during or immediately after an actual event in which the analysts were interested and wanted to discuss anyway. The event provided the stimulus for a lively discussion. During the discussion the analysts were asked to offer their opinions or judgments or hunches about some particular aspect of the event. Then they were asked why they felt this to be true. This generally produced a train of rather complex judgments. They were asked to explain how they had made each individual judgment. Each of these produced a train of somewhat less complex judgments which were "pulled apart" by the interrogators, and the process was continued until the critical attributes were identified and basic rules about them articulated.

This by itself was a major achievement. In effect, the extraction process compelled the analyst to examine his own train of thought with an unprecedented degree of rigor. The first and most obvious result was the identification of the attributes of an event or group that were generally agreed upon to be the relevant things to examine. These were the basis for most judgments. The second result was the emergence of some rules about how these attributes interact. But the final result was more than this—and most important: the process itself, the extraction of basic rules, sharpened the experts' analytical skills. Regardless of whether these rules could ever be assembled into a system that could in any way approach human reasoning in dealing with complex and ill-defined subjects, being forced to articulate every step along the way to a problematical conclusion was a useful calisthenic for the analysts. It made them more aware, and hence more critical, of their own reasoning; it caused them to examine closely how they arrived at conclusions; and it taught them to look carefully at the spaces between the steps they described. Also, it conditioned them not to overlook things that otherwise might have been ignored, especially in crisis situations where they would be compelled to make snap judgments without time for reflection.

This would seem to indicate a potential utility of this effort that transcends the feasibility of being able to represent the entire domain of terrorism by rules in a minicomputer. It is not necessary for the machine alone to duplicate human thought. Nor is it necessary for the analyst alone to derive from his subject area a set of judgments that can be stored in a computer. It is the interaction of the two that causes an improvement in the analyst's analytical capabilities, in both ordinary and crisis situations, and results in a tool for the analyst to use.

It is now anticipated that it will require a large number of rules to deal with a small portion of the domain of international terrorism. This problem could be alleviated to some extent by creating many relatively small agents (300 rules or less), each a specialist in some restricted area of the domain. They could all have access to a large agent containing general information about terrorism and would make use of this agent when necessary. Because of the complexity of the task we will need as much computing power as the state of the art can provide. Thus as the power of minicomputers increases, so will the feasibility of modeling complex domains using interactive transaction agents.

VI. APPLICABILITY AND FUTURE DEVELOPMENTS

In addition to the usefulness of heuristic models in improving the skills of analysts working with the problem of international terrorism, it appears that minicomputers with heuristic modeling systems built into them may be extremely useful in the management of crisis situations. Terrorist actions, such as the hijacking of an airliner or the takeover of an embassy, frequently create a crisis situation to which the government must respond. The usual response is to assemble a task force or several task forces at different locations to deal with the crisis. The members of the task force represent different skills (intelligence, public affairs, negotiations, area specialists) and the different agencies and departments that are somehow involved in the episode. The task force decides or offers options to the official who must decide the course of action to take. In dealing with these episodes, particularly hostage situations where lives are at stake, a crisis atmosphere often prevails. Time is critical. (An average barricade-and-hostage incident lasts around 36 hours although some may drag on for days.)

Assembling information about the individuals and groups involved is difficult, but this problem can be alleviated with conventional data retrieval systems. Assembling the data that are particularly relevant to a given situation is more difficult. A data retrieval system would not know which special circumstances call for certain actions and which do not. No one has time to read lengthy reports on the group and skilled specialists themselves might not know which reports to look at first. Moreover there is the problem of decision-making by committee. It is difficult to sit around a table for any period of time in silence. People tend to fill the gaps with conversation or discussion about things that may or may not be particularly relevant to the problem at hand. These result in distractions that slow or divert the decision-making process.

The system envisioned here first of all provides a straight-forward way of proceeding toward a solution. It does this by asking questions about the episode already determined relevant by the experts. In other words, it produces demands for the most relevant information. It summons from its own memory the relevant judgments that have been made about similar groups or events in the past. Furthermore, it enables the committee to explore various options by creating in the machine similar artificial events and changing various responses. The machine can then display likely outcomes to these events. Interaction between the members of the committee and the machine will cause them to examine their own conclusions and decisions in the same manner that it does for the analyst. In sum, the machine imposes a degree of discipline on the course of the discussion, asks the most relevant questions, provides the best judgments of expert analysis, and allows the committee to explore viable options. It also sharpens the committee's skills during the process. It is not essential that the system be entirely accurate or that its performance be flawless. Again, it is the interaction that leads to good sharpened answers, not the machine revealing them from a stored memory.

Remote interactive transaction agents with a capability for examining terrorist incidents would be especially useful in a crisis if they linked together several task forces in a manner similar to the ARPAnet. This would enable the individuals or groups at different locations to see and participate in each aspect of the decision-making. Everyone would see the same video display at the same time. They could intervene with questions or opinions and their interventions could be seen by all of the others.

Such a system also has utility as a storehouse of judgmental information compiled by many expert analysts over a period of time. Indeed, it may be seen as a judgment retrieval system as opposed to a data retrieval system. This would add to the overall amount of expert opinion that is available, would allow interaction between experts at different times and in different locations, and would tend to ameliorate the effect of lost capabilities that result from rotation or unavailability of personnel.

There are many directions in which this research can progress in the future. First, we can introduce the notion of certainty factors, probability measures on all the rules and goals that give a subjective estimate of their accuracy. This would provide us with a way of more accurately evaluating the results of our deductions. Second, we can expand the scope of the analysis to other terrorist activities, such as kidnappings or barricade-and-hostage events. The scope can also be widened by including data on more groups and incidents. Third, we can develop agents to help the user recognize and define new rules, as described in Sec. IV. Fourth, we can develop agents that are capable of making predictions about future terrorist activities and use them to test the accuracy of our current formalism. Finally, we can attack the problem of inductive inference, recognizing regularities in the data and automatically forming rules to describe these regularities.

FORMALIZATION OF A DOMAIN
FOR TERRORIST BOMBINGS

event ....
   name
   [give the event to be defined an identifying name]
   type
   [type of the terrorist event; e.g. bombing, kidnapping]
      bombing
      barricade-and-hostage
      kidnapping
   date
   [use the format yymmdd; e.g., 760330]
   time-of-day
   [a four-digit number; e.g., 0830, 1635]
   location
   [an object; e.g., embassy, airplane]
   locale
   [a place; e.g., Paris, Madrid]
   region
   [environs in which the event occurred]
      urban
      rural
      water
      air
   host-country
   [name of country in which event occurred]
   announced-claimant
   [name of person(s) or group claiming credit for the event]

when-claimed
[when were claims announced taking credit for the event?]
   before-bombing
   before-publicity
   before-casualty-report
   after-casualty-report

announced-purpose
[announced reason for carrying out event]

disclaimant
[name of person(s) or group disclaiming credit for the event]

target
[who or what was the immediate object of the attack?]
   specific individual
   representative individual
   random individual
   political property
   corporate headquarters or offices
   other commercial property
   private property
   vital systems
   head of state

target-symbolic-value
[what symbolic value did the object of the attack have?]
   inherently obvious
   specified by perpetrator
   none apparent

target-accessibility
[how accessible was the object of the attack to the perpetrators?]
   low
   medium
   high

victim
[who or what was the event intended to affect?]
   person
   organization
   government
   ideal

bomb-weight
[estimated weight in pounds; e.g., 10]

bomb-type
[which type of bomb was used in the event?]
   Molotov-cocktail
   other incendiary
   letter or parcel
   pipe
   small explosive charge
   shopping bag
   grenade
   car
   land mine

bomb-size
[estimate the size of the bomb: small, medium, or large]
   small
   medium
   large

bomb-delivery
[how did the bomb arrive at its destination?]
   planted
   delivered
   thrown

bomb-detonation
[what method was used to detonate the bomb?]
   command-line
   command-radio
   impact
   time
   mechanical
   electrical
   chemical
   fuse
   x-ray
   photoelectric
   altitude

secondary-detonation
[what type of backup detonation device did the bomb have?]
   no detonation
   command-line
   command-radio
   impact
   time

    mechanical
    electrical
    chemical
    x-ray
    photoelectric
    altitude

detonation-source
[who detonated the bomb?]
    victim
    perpetrator
    self-detonating

bomb-composition
[what type of explosive material was used in the bomb?]

explosive-source
[source of the explosive material: commercial, military, etc.]
    commercial
    military
    home-made

bomb-sophistication
[give a subjective estimate of the sophistication of the bomb]
    low
    medium
    high

audacity
[give an appraisal of how brazen and audacious the incident was]
    low
    medium
    high

risk-to-perpetrator
[assess the risk to the perpetrators of capture or death]
    low
    medium
    high

recipient-of-warning
[who received prior warning of the bomb?]
    media
    target
    police
    no warning

warning-time
[minutes before the expected detonation the warning was received]

outcome
[what happened to the bomb?]
  detonated
  discovered/defused
  malfunction/no detonation

tactical-objective
[what was the immediate goal of the bombing?]
  murder
  punishment/retaliation
  property damage-no casualties
  property damage-casualties
  extortion-payoff to perpetrator
  extortion-unspecified philanthropic
  extortion-specified philanthropic
  disruption
  publicity/group
  publicity/commemorative

strategic-objective
[what was the more global objective of the instigator?]
  increase-pain-level
  halt-operation
  publicity
  discredit-government
  political-victory
  military-victory
  defense of the group/movement
  intergroup rivalry

number-killed
[number of people killed during incident]

number wounded
[number of people wounded during the incident]

primary-damage
[what was the damage resulting directly from the bomb itself?]
  no damage
  low
  medium
  high

secondary-damage
[what was the damage caused in the aftermath of the bomb?]
   no damage
   low
   medium
   high

instigator
[name of person(s) or group who planned the event]

perpetrator
[name of person(s) or group carrying out the event]

group   ....

   name
   [type the full proper name of the group and the acronym, if any]

   political-ideology
   [political persuasion or connections of group]
      fascist
      right-wing
      Moscow-line communist
      independent communist
      Trotskyite
      Maoist
      anarchist
      new left

   nationality
   [country of origin or primary base]

   age
   [how many years has the group been in existence?]

   objective
   [what are the strategic objectives of the group?]
      enlarge the group
      expansion
      overthrow of government
      discredit the system
      territorial independence
      limited reforms or concessions
      vigilante-like defense

action-frequency
[the approximate number of incidents perpetrated per year]

past-incidents
[type the names of the past incidents instigated by the group]

affiliations
[names of allied groups]

stage-of-development
[stages 1 to 5 allowed]

ethnic-composition
[major nationality or ethnic composition represented in the group]

educational-composition
[what kind of education do the group members have?]
   uneducated
   high school
   university

supporters
[groups, sectors, and organizations that aid and abet the group]
   other terrorist groups
   university-educated population sectors
   working-class sectors
   minority groups
   foreign governments
   nobody

level-of-sophistication
[sophistication of the group in terms of planning and execution]
   low
   medium
   high

tactics
[the typical types of events perpetrated by the group]
   bombing
   barricade-hostage
   kidnapping
   assassinations
   hijackings
   armed assaults
   robbery
   dissemination of propaganda
   sabotage

type
[characterize the goal of the group in terms of the given categories]
   separatist/irredentist
   national revolutionary
   international revolutionary

activity-span
[how many years has the group been active at terrorism?]

targets
[the types of objects or persons typically attacked]
   specific individual
   representative individual
   random individual
   government property
   political property
   corporate headquarters or offices
   other commercial property
   private property
   vital systems

members
[type names of members: first name (alias) last name]

headquarter location
[where the decision-makers are located, e.g., Berkeley, Beirut]

territory-of-operations
[the territorial area over which the group spreads its operations]
   international
   national
   regional
   state
   local

level of support
[extent of support for the group: e.g., local, regional]
   insignificant
   local
   regional
   national
   international

type-of-support
[expressions of support for the group]
   passive sympathy

    limited help
    total commitment

person ....

    name
    [name of the person]

    nationality
    [name of country of national origin]

    sex
    [male or female]

    age
    [approximate age in years]

    occupation
    [what does the person do for a living?]
      police/military
      government
      corporate official
      political-figure
      private-citizen

    group-membership
    [organizational affiliation]

    terrorism-role
    [how is this person connected with terrorist activities?]
      target
      perpetrator
      instigator
      hostage

Addendum 2

PROTOCOL OF AN EXPERT USING THE BUILD AGENT

% rita use.build.goal
use.build.goal:

Fill-in-the-blanks questions can be answered with either a single reply such as "Fred Jones", or with a list of replies each separated by a comma followed by a space, i.e., "Fred Jones, Mary Smith, John Doe". To indicate that you don't know just type <carriage return>.

For questions of the form: "The <a> of the <b> is . . .", typing "unknown" is equivalent to typing <carriage return>. For questions of the form: "Other <a>s of the <b> . . .", typing "none" is equivalent to typing <carriage return>.

Yes-or-no questions can be answered with either "y", or "yes" for yes; "n", "no", or carriage return for no; or a single answer, such as "school building" for a qualified yes.

You may type "?" in response to any question to elicit information about the type of answer required.

To terminate the session type "nothing" in response to the "What is to be defined . . ." question. Then to see the data base that was just created type "display all objects".

The most current event took place in Washington, D.C., at about 1:26 P.M. in the Senate Office Building on August 23, 1976. As Secretary of State Henry Kissinger was exiting the front door a lone individual hurled a Molotov-cocktail at him and then fled on foot. The bomb failed to explode and no one was hurt. Two minutes before the attempted bombing a woman who identified herself as a member of the New World Liberation Front called the *Washington Post* and claimed credit for the act. She said the reason for the incident was the failure of the government to free SLA political prisoners. The bomb itself was estimated to have weighed about 4 pounds.

What is to be defined . . . event

The name of the event is: Washington Incident

Is the type of the event: bombing? yes

The date of the event is: ?
[use the format yymmdd; e.g., 760330]

The date of the event is: 760823

The time-of-day of the event is: ?
[a four-digit number; e.g., 0830, 1635]

The time-of-day of the event is: 1326

The location of the event is: Senate

The locale of the event is: Washington

Is the region of the event: urban? yes

The host-country of the event is: United States

The announced-claimant of the event is: ?
[name of person(s) or group claiming credit for the event]

The announced-claimant of the event is: New World Liberation Front

Is the when-claimed of the event: before-bombing? ?
[when were claims announced taking credit for the incident? Give one
   answer for each announced claim]
      before-bombing? yes
      before-publicity? no
      before-casualty-report? no
      after-casualty-report? no

Other when-claimed(s) of the event . . .

The announced-purpose of the event is: retaliation against government

The disclaimant of the event is:

Is the target of the event:
   specific individual? Kissinger
   representative individual? no
   random individual? no
   political property? no
   corporate headquarters or offices? no
   other commercial property? no
   private property? no

vital systems? no
head of state? no

Other target(s) of the event . . .

Is the target-symbolic-value of the event:
  inherently obvious? yes

Is the target-accessibility of the event:
  low? no
  medium? yes

[I deduce that the victim(s) of the event includes:
  ("person")]

The bomb-weight of the event is: ?
[estimated weight in pounds, e.g., 10]

The bomb-weight of the event is: 4

Is the bomb-type of the event:
  Molotov-cocktail? yes
[I deduce that the bomb-size of the event is "small"]
[I deduce that the bomb-delivery of the event is "thrown"]
[I deduce that the bomb-detonation of the event is "impact"]
[I deduce that the secondary-detonation of the event is "no detonation"]
[I deduce that the detonation-source of the event is "self-detonating"]

The bomb-composition of the event is:
[I deduce that the explosive-source(s) of the event includes:
  ("home-made")]
[I deduce that the bomb-sophistication of the event is "low"]

Is the audacity of the event:
  low? no
  medium? no
  high? yes

Is the risk-to-perpetrator of the event:
  low? no
  medium? no
  high? yes

Is the recipient-of-warning of the event:
  media? no
  target? no
  police? no
  no warning? yes

Other recipient-of-warning(s) of the event . . .
[I deduce that the warning-time of the event is "0"]

Is the outcome of the event:
   detonated? no
   discovered/defused? no
   malfunction/ no detonation? yes
[I deduce that the tactical-objective(s) of the event includes:
   ("publicity/group", "murder")]
[I deduce that the strategic-objective(s) of the event includes:
   ("publicity")]
[I deduce that the number-killed of the event is "0"]
[I deduce that the number-wounded of the event is "0"]
[I deduce that the primary-damage of the event is "no damage"]
[I deduce that the secondary-damage of the event is "no damage"]
[I deduce that the instigator(s) of the event includes:
   ("New World Liberation Front")]
[I deduce that the perpetrator(s) of the event includes:
   ("New World Liberation Front")]

Finished with the event

What is to be defined . . . nothing

The following data were added to file bomb data in your file area:

[OBJECTS:]

OBJECT event < 2 > :

name	IS	"Washington Incident",
type	IS	"bombing",
date	IS	"760823",
time-of-day	IS	"1326",
location	IS	"Senate",
locale	IS	"Washington",
region	IS	"urban",
host-country	IS	"United States",
announced-claimant	IS	("New World Liberation Front"),
when-claimed	IS	("before-bombing"),
announced-purpose	IS	("retaliation against government"),
target	IS	("specific individual"),
target-symbolic-value	IS	"inherently obvious",
target accessibility	IS	"medium",
victim	IS	("person"),
bomb-weight	IS	"4",
bomb-type	IS	"Molotov-cocktail",

bomb-size	IS	"small",
bomb-delivery	IS	"thrown",
bomb-detonation	IS	"impact",
secondary-detonation	IS	"no detonation",
detonation-source	IS	"self-detonating",
explosive-source	IS	("home-made"),
bomb-sophistication	IS	"low",
audacity	IS	"high",
risk-to-perpetrator	IS	"high",
recipient-of-warning	IS	("no warning"),
warning-time	IS	"0",
outcome	IS	"malfunction/no detonation",
tactical-objective	IS	("publicity/group", "murder"),
strategic-objective	IS	("publicity"),
number-killed	IS	"0",
number-wounded	IS	"0",
primary-damage	IS	"no damage",
secondary-damage	IS	"no damage",
instigator	IS	("New World Liberation Front"),
perpetrator	IS	("New World Liberation Front"),
unused	IS	("disclaimant", "bomb-composition");

OBJECT target <1> :

name	IS	"Kissinger";

exiting.
%

BIBLIOGRAPHY

Anderson, R. H., and J. J. Gillogy (1976a). Rand Intelligent Terminal Agent (RITA): Design Philosophy. The Rand Corporation, R-1809-ARPA, February.

Anderson, R. H., and J. J. Gillogly (1976b). Rand Intelligent Terminal Agent (RITA): Reference Manual. The Rand Corporation, R-1808-ARPA.

Davis, Randall (1976). Applications of Meta Level Knowledge to the Construction, Maintenance, and Use of Large Knowledge Bases. Stanford University, Artificial Intelligence Laboratory, Memo AIM-283.

Davis, Randall, et al. (1975). Production Rules as a Representation for a Knowledge-Based Consultation Program. Stanford University, Artificial Intelligence Laboratory, Memo AIM-266.

Feigenbaum, E. A., et al. (1970). On Generality and Problem Solving: A Case Study Using the DENDRAL Program. In B. Meltzer and D. Michie (eds.), *Machine Intelligence 6*. Edinburgh University Press. (Also in Stanford University, Artificial Intelligence Laboratory, Memo AIM-131, August 1970.)

Lenat, Douglas, B. (1976). AM: An Artificial Intelligence Approach to Discovery in Mathematics as Heuristic Search. Stanford University, Artificial Intelligence Laboratory, Memo AIM-286, Ph.D. dissertation.

Newell, A., and H. A. Simon (1972). *Human Problem Solving*. Prentice-Hall, Englewood Cliffs, N.J.

Newell, A. (1972). A Theoretical Exploration of Mechanisms for Coding the Stimulus. In A. W. Melton and E. Martin (eds.), *Coding Processes in Human Memory*. Winston and Sons, Washington, D.C.

Newell, A. (1973). Production Systems: Models of Control Structures. In W. G. Chase (ed.), *Visual Information Processing*. Academic Press, New York.

Shortliffe, E. H. (1974). MYCIN: A Rule Based Computer Program for Advising Physicians Regarding Antimicrobial Therapy Selection. Stanford University, Ph.D. dissertation.

Shortliffe, E. H., and B. G. Buchanan (1975). A Model of Inexact Reasoning in Medicine, *Mathematical Biosciences*, 23, pp. 351–379.

Waterman, D. A. (1970). Generalization Learning Techniques for Automating the Learning of Heuristics, *Artificial Intelligence*, 1, pp. 121–170.

Waterman, D. A., and A. Newell (1973). Preliminary Results with a System for Automatic Protocol Analysis. Carnegie-Mellon University, Computer Science Department.

Waterman, D. A. (1975). Adaptive Production Systems, *International Joint Conference on Artificial Intelligence-4 Proceedings*, Vol. 1, September, pp. 296–303.

Waterman, D. A., and A. Newell (1976). PAS-II: An Interactive Task-Free Version of an Automatic Protocol Analysis System, *IEEE Transactions*, April.

Waterman, D. A. (1976). Serial Pattern Acquisition: A Production System Approach, *Proceedings of the 1976 Workshop on Pattern Recognition and Artificial Intelligence*, August.

Waterman, D. A. Rule-Directed Interactive Transaction Agents: An Approach to Knowledge Acquisition. The Rand Corporation, draft report, R-2171 (forthcoming).

Terrorism, the Media, and the Police*

YONAH ALEXANDER

Terrorism, as an expedient tactical and strategic tool of politics in the struggle for power within and among nations, is not new in the history of man's inhumanity to man. From time immemorial opposition groups, functioning under varying degrees of stress, have intentionally utilized instruments of psychological and physical force—including intimidation, coercion, repression and, ultimately, destruction of lives and property—for the purpose of attaining real or imaginary ideological and political goals. That is, as agitational and disruptive civil violence, terrorism has been employed by sub-national groups either seeking to effect limited changes within the existing political structure, or desiring to abolish completely the established system, principally, but not exclusively, as part of a parochial or transnational revolutionary strategy.

Unlike older historical precedents, non-state terrorists, sanctified by their precipitators in the name of higher principles, have introduced into contemporary life a new breed of violence in terms of technology, victimization, threat and response. The brutalization and globalization of modern violence makes it amply clear that we have entered a unique "Age of Terrorism" with all its formidable problems and frightening ramifications. To be sure, it is generally recognized that extra-legal terrorism poses many threats to contemporary society and is likely to have a

SOURCE: Reprinted from the *Journal of International Affairs* 32, no. 1, 1978. Published by permission of the *Journal of International Affairs* and the Trustees of Columbia University in the City of New York.

*Originally prepared for the 19th Annual Meeting of the International Studies Association, Washington, D.C.

serious impact on the quality of life and on orderly civilized existence. Perhaps the most significant dangers are those relating to the safety, welfare and rights of ordinary people, the stability of the state system, the health and pace of economic development and the expansion, or even the survival, of democracy.[1]

But, in spite of various national and international efforts to deal with the dangers of terrorism, the level of non-state violence remains high. The reasons for these conditions are diverse but include at least ten factors: disagreement about who is a terrorist, lack of understanding of the causes of terrorism, the support of terrorism by some states, the existence of an international network of terrorism, the politization of religion, double standards of morality, loss of resolve by governments, weak punishment of terrorists, flouting of world law and the roles of the mass media.[2] While all these factors deserve serious and thorough study, this essay will focus on the interaction of terrorism and the media, specifically as related to current criminal justice processes.

Clearly, modern technology has provided terror groups with a critical communications instrument—the media—which willingly or unwillingly serve their specific or general propaganda and psychological warfare needs.[3] More specifically, the strategy of terrorism followed by sub-national groups does not prescribe instant victories over established regimes or states. On the contrary, the struggle for intended ends is seen as complicated and protracted. Terror groups, by their very nature, are too small and too weak to achieve an upper hand in an eyeball-to-eyeball confrontation on the battlefield. Since sheer violence can accomplish little or nothing in terms of ultimate goals, an extension of the duration and impact of the violent deed is therefore mandatory in the terrorist strategy. As Walter Laqueur stated, "The media are the terrorist's best friend. The terrorist's act by itself is nothing; publicity is all."[4]

It is because of this realization that terrorist operations have been broadly symbolic rather than physically oriented. In relying on immediate and extensive coverage of television, radio and the press for the maximum amount of propagandizing and publicizing, terrorists can rapidly and effectively reach watching, listening and reading audiences at home and abroad and thereby hope to attain essentially one or two of the following communications purposes: First, to enhance the effectiveness of their violence by creating an emotional state of extreme fear in target groups, and, thereby, ultimately alter their behavior and dispositions, or bring about a general or particular change in the structure of government or society; and, second, to draw forcibly and instantaneously the attention of the "whole world" to themselves in the expectation that these audiences will be prepared to act or, in some cases, to refrain from acting in a manner that will promote the cause they presumably represent.

Terrorism, then, like advertising, increases the effectiveness of its messages by focusing on spectacular incidents and by keeping particular issues alive through repetition. Carlos Marighella, in his much publicized *Minimanual of the Urban Guerrilla*, gave a better insight into this strategy:

> The coordination of urban guerrilla action, including each armed action, is the principal way of making armed propaganda.
>
> These actions, carried out with specific and determined objectives, inevitably become propaganda material for the mass communications system.
>
> Bank assaults, ambushes, desertions and diverting of arms, the rescue of prisoners, executions, kidnappings, sabotage, terrorism, and the war of nerves, are all cases in point.
>
> Airplanes diverted in flight by revolutionary action, moving ships and trains assaulted and seized by guerrillas, can also be solely for propaganda effects.

He further elaborates:

> The war of nerves or psychological war is an aggressive technique, based on the direct or indirect use of mass means of communication and news transmitted orally in order to demoralize the government.
>
> In psychological warfare, the government is always at a disadvantage since it imposes censorship on the mass media and winds up in a defensive position by not allowing anything against it to filter through.
>
> At this point it becomes desperate, is involved in greater contradictions and loss of prestige, and loses time and energy in an exhausting effort at control which is subject to being broken at any moment.[5]

The utilization and manipulation of the media, as directed by Marighella and other proponents of political and ideological violence, have been followed by practically all terrorist movements. They have sought not only to spread fear among the primary target, but also to publicize their discontent as well as their ideologies with a view of making their violent deeds appear heroic.

One dramatic instance of media manipulation is the Patricia Hearst—SLA episode. Her kidnapping in February 1974 was used as a form of propaganda for the revolution of the SLA. The terrorists insisted that the media carry in full their messages—both tapes and printed material—lest the safety of the prisoner be jeopardized. For several years the media have continued to magnify the case out of proportion to its real significance, thus providing sensational mass entertainment and serving the publicity needs of the SLA and its successors as well. What is most disturbing about this case is the fact that the media have given a small group of criminal misfits a "Robin Hood" image and transformed it into an internationally known movement possessing power and posing an insurmountable problem to the authorities.

Also, overseas terrorist operations have not been carried out for the sake of immediate results or for the purpose of violence itself. Thus, in November 1975 the Montoneros in Buenos Aires kidnapped the industrial director of Germany's Mercedes-Benz there and released him after the company *inter alia* published advertisements in newspapers in Europe, Washington, D.C., and Mexico denouncing the "economic imperialism" of multinational corporations in developing countries.

In another episode, which occurred in February 1975, the Baader-Meinhof terrorists kidnapped a West Berlin politician in order to secure the release of their imprisoned comrades and also "hi-jacked" a local television network. Describing this incident, one West German editor related that "for 72 hours, we lost control of the medium. We shifted shows to meet their timetable. [They demanded that] our cameras be in position to record each of the prisoners as they boarded a plane, and our news coverage had to include prepared statements of their direction."[6]

In light of the foregoing, it can be concluded that, in the final analysis, the communications purposes which at least revolutionary terror groups seek through the media are attention, recognition and legitimacy. As Weisband and Roguly succinctly observed,

> For the terrorist, the path to legitimacy is through one's reputation for resilience, for self-sacrifice and daring, for brutality, and, above all, for effective discipline over words and actions. The terrorist is his own torch and bomb; he ignites the flames of national passion and, if possible, of political sympathy, and he does it by violating universal human sensibilities. It is the credibility that violence produces, whenever it appalls, that renders terrorism horrifying yet powerful and, if successful, self-legitimating.[7]

To what extent does the media's extensive coverage of terrorism have an impact on public attitudes? Although there is no definite answer to this question, according to nationwide public opinion polls conducted by Yankelovich, Shelly & White, Inc. with regard to American public attitudes towards the Palestine Liberation Organization (PLO),[8] there seems to be a close relationship, at least in terms of a greater awareness.[9]

The first poll in January 1975 was taken shortly after widespread media coverage of Yasir Arafat's triumphal appearance before the U.N. General Assembly in November 1974 with all the pomp and circumstance surrounding a head of state. The second poll was conducted a year later, toward the end of January 1976 after the U.N. Security Council had invited the PLO to participate in its debate on the Middle East. In the intervening period, the PLO had succeeded in gaining admission to other U.N. sponsored conferences and had opened offices in many countries in Europe and the third world. But the PLO was also becoming more and more embroiled in the Lebanese civil war which was increasingly in the news at the time.

As one might expect, the continuing attention given to the PLO by the mass media over the year was reflected in increased public awareness of the group's existence. In January 1975 only about one-half of the American public (52 percent) said that it had heard of the PLO. By January 1976 the figure had gone up to 63 percent. Again, as might be expected, the higher the educational level of the respondents, the greater the likelihood that they are aware of the PLO, with 88 percent of college graduates answering in the affirmative.

Another major consequence resulting from extensive media coverage of terrorism is the exportation of violent techniques which, in turn, often triggers similar extreme actions by other individuals and groups. As Richard Clutterbuck asserted, "ideas travel . . . through the normal news media . . . people watching and listening to the reports get ideas about doing the same things themselves."[10] That is, the more publicity given to bomb scares, the more bomb scares there are likely to be, and reports about plane hijacking lead to more plane hijackings.

The excessive media coverage of the two attempts on President Ford's life in 1975 caused deep concern that this publicity might set off similar actions by other would-be assassins. As the then Vice President Rockefeller stated, "Let's stop talking about it. Let's stop putting it on the front pages and on television. Psychiatrists say every time there is any publicity, it is stimulating to the unstable." A similar view was expressed by the then Secretary of the Treasury, William E. Simon: "It's the responsibility of the press, certainly, to tell the American people indeed what is happening. . . . But when these people are glamorized on the front pages of our national magazines, I think that this has to be thought of as doing great harm."[11]

The Hanafi Muslim takeover of three buildings in Washington, D.C., in March 1977 also became a major media event with similar implications. "The media," Charles Seib of *The Washington Post* wrote, "were as much a part of it as the terrorists, the victims and the authorities. The news business did what it always does when it deals with violence, bloodshed and suspense: It covered it excessively."[12] Ambassador Andrew Young, expressing concern about the contagious effect of such coverage, stated that it is tantamount to "advertising to neurotic people" who are inspired to attempt "suicidal and ridiculous" acts.[13]

An estimate of such an impact on the mass audience was provided recently by an academic observer. He explained:

Typical reporting of a terrorist event here in the United States might reach an audience of, say, conservatively, 40 million people. What's the chance that it may come to the attention of some borderline psychopath who may be stimulated to take part in some future episode? If we were to consider that just one-tenth of one per cent of the audience were borderline psychopaths, that would be 40,000 potential maniacs. If we took one one-thousandth of one per cent we've still got 400. If we took 1/100,000 of one per cent, we would still have the four that are necessary to carry out a typical terrorist episode.[14]

To be sure, because terrorism, however local, is by its very nature a world-wide theatrical attraction, it tends to encourage angry and frustrated groups beyond a particular country to undertake similar acts as a way out of their helplessness and alienation. For example, several weeks after Argentina's Montoneros removed the body of ex-President Pedro Aramburu to secure the return of Eva Peron's body from Spain, Burmese terrorists stole the body of U Thant for the purpose of using it in negotiations with the Burmese government.

Another major issue related to the problem of terrorism and the media is the particular interaction of both with police agencies. In every terrorist incident an inevitable critical relationship develops between the media responsible for reporting the episode and the law enforcement personnel handling the incident. Not infrequently, the media, especially broadcasters, hinder effective police responses to terrorist activities. The media can, for instance, have three detrimental effects in siege-management situations: interfere with on-going operations; exacerbate the pressure on the responsible authorities and contribute to impaired decision-making; and harass relatives of victims by pressing for interviews.

During the Hanafi episode the media unknowingly worked at cross purposes with official action. They furnished the terrorists with direct intelligence information by continuing on-site television coverage, thus adding to their feeling of power. The media also made direct telephone calls to the terrorists for interview purposes and thereby tied up communication between the police negotiators and the criminals.

Some details concerning this case were provided by Charles Fenyvesi, a reporter who had been a hostage at the B'nai B'rith building during the siege. He related:

The most damaging case concerned the TV reporter who caught sight of a basket, lifted up by rope, to the fifth floor, where, the

world later learned, some people evaded the round-up and barricaded themselves in a room. Their presence apparently was not
known to the gunmen, who held their prisoners on the eighth
floor but patrolled the lower floors until late Wednesday afternoon.
The gunmen were probably informed of the TV reporter's scoop by
their fellow Hanafis who monitored the news media outside the
captured buildings. Fortunately the gunmen did not break through
the door.

Another case of a reporter endangering lives occurred when
Khaalis was asked, during a live telephone interview with a leading
local radio station, 'Have you set a deadline?' The police and all
the other experts have thought that the absence of a deadline was
one encouraging sign. Fortunately, Khaalis was too engrossed in
his rhetoric to pay any attention to the question.

A third example: One prominent Washington newscaster called
Khaalis a Black Muslim. Khaalis, whose family was murdered by
Black Muslims, flew into a rage and stormed into the room where
we hostages were held. He declared that he would kill one of us in
retaliation for the newsman's words. The police, meanwhile,
advised the newscaster to promptly issue an apology, and Khaalis
was eventually mollified.[15]

Robert L. Rabe, Assistant Chief of Police, Metropolitan Police
Department, who was personally involved in handling the incident, complained about another instance of media irresponsibility
during the Hanafi siege: " . . . a local reporter took it upon
himself to report live over the radio and television what appeared
to him to be boxes of ammunition being taken into the B'nai B'rith
building in preparation for an all-out police assault, when, in fact,
what was being taken were boxes of food for the hostages. Just
imagine what the repercussions could have been if the terrorists
had been monitoring their radios and televisions at that precise
moment."[16]

It is noteworthy that, after the Hanafi hostages were freed, they
were warned by the police not to give interviews to the media lest
the prosecutor's task in dealing with the case become more
difficult and complicated. According to complaints by the hostages, some members of the media were insistent on obtaining
interviews. In one particular case, a network representative
justified his request for an interview by asserting that "the public

has the right to know." The harassed hostage declined to grant the interview, replying "Is it in the Constitution that the public has the right to invade my privacy, to insist on exposing people already humiliated, to wallow in their pain and misery?"[17]

Finally, it is also evident that the media have jeopardized the authorities' management of terrorist incidents abroad. In the October 1977 hijacking of the Lufthansa jet, for instance, the media directly contributed to the death of a hostage because they did not realize that certain information, especially in regard to tactical operations, had to remain outside public knowledge. In this case, the terrorists on board the jet heard over the public radio broadcasts to which they had access that the German captain was passing valuable intelligence information to the authorities on the ground through his normal radio transmissions. Subsequently, the terrorists executed the captain.

To be sure, the roles of the media are not always detrimental. There are situations where the media, by publicizing an incident, have, in the words of Special Agent of the FBI Conrad Hassel, "relaxed the pressure of the terrorist finger."[18] Also, Harold Coffman, Professor of Law and Psychiatry at Georgetown University, has stated ". . . that coverage of such events is helpful. It allows these people to have some method of ventilating their anger and frustration, in making known their grievances. The more coverage given, the more they are likely to see themselves part of, rather than outside, the system."[19]

One such example is the Croatian TWA case of September 1976. Here, the hijackers insisted that specific demands be accomplished as the price for terminating the hijacking, including, *inter alia*, that two propaganda tracts be published on the front page of a number of newspapers. *The New York Times, The Washington Post* and *The Chicago Tribune*, to mention a few, complied and thereby contributed to a satisfactory management of the incident.

The media also played a helpful role in establishing a vital link between authorities and the public-at-large in connection with the May–June 1977 South Moluccan incident in Holland. During that episode daily news releases containing bits of information on details not crucial to developing strategy and tactics satisfied the public appetite for information, as well as conveyed an image of official responsibility and effective crisis management.

In light of these ramifications, the question is, what role should the media in democratic systems have in combating terrorism? Two major problems must be considered in this connection. First are the facts that, to terrorists, an extensive coverage by the media is the major reward and that "establishment" communications channels willingly or unwillingly become tools in the terrorist strategy, and that advertising terrorism increases the effectiveness of its message through repetition and imitation. The second concerns the vital importances of protecting "people's right to know" and of a free press in open societies. A closely critical issue is the relationship between the media and law enforcement agencies. Although each has a duty to perform and a right to perform that duty, the legitimate roles of both entities are seemingly diametrically opposed.

In sum, how can the media in a democratic society devise new methods of fair and credible reporting of terrorist activities without jeopardizing their responsibilities to the public and without adversely affecting the current criminal justice processes?

It is obvious that there are no easy answers to these vital concerns but most difficult choices. Indeed, the various issues have been highly controversial. For example, in April 1977 a Gallup poll found that Americans were divided about whether the media should give complete, detailed coverage of terrorism.[20] More definitive in their responses are the administrators of justice personnel. Thus, among the results of a survey of the police chiefs in some thirty American cities, the following views are emphasized:

1. Ninety-three percent of the police chiefs believed live TV coverage of terrorist acts encourages terrorism.

2. None of the big-city police chiefs surveyed believed that coverage of terrorist acts should be televised live. Sixty percent thought such TV coverage should be delayed or video taped, and 27 percent believed terrorist acts should not be covered by television.

3. Forty-six percent of police chiefs consider live television coverage of terrorist acts "a great threat" to hostage safety

and 33 percent considered it "a moderate threat." Only 7 percent considered it a minimal threat.

4. More than half of the police chiefs had generally unfavorable judgments of on-the-scene television reporters covering terrorists. Twenty percent of the police chiefs believed television reporters covering terrorist acts were "poor" and 33 percent believed they were "average." Only 20 percent believed that TV journalists covering terrorists were good.

5. Sixty-seven percent of the police chiefs said TV journalists should only communicate with terrorists with official consent. Another 33 percent believed that under no circumstances should TV journalists communicate with terrorists while they are engaged in criminal activity.[21]

Although this survey is limited in scope, it is reasonable to assume that, in general, law enforcement agencies, which now lack both the legal authority and the practical ability to control coverage of terrorist activities, look upon the media "as a powerful force, sometimes more influential than government itself,"[22] which should somehow be restrained. This apparent attitude was underscored by Ambassador Andrew Young's assertion that "the First Amendment has got to be clarified by the Supreme Court in light of the power of the mass media," and that they should censor themselves.[23]

To be sure, some newsmen seem to realize that the media have much too much influence in domestic and international affairs.[24] A few are even prepared not to cover terrorism at all. One television news director in Cleveland explained, "We feel that the coverage we give such incidents is partly to blame, for we are glorifying lawbreakers, we are making heroes out of non-heroes. In effect we are losing control over our news departments. We are being used."[25]

While most journalists recognize the perils involved in covering terrorist incidents, the media in general reject as unthinkable any suggestion that would curtail their reporting. The National News Council, for example, warned that "the dangers of suppression should be self evident: doubts over what the media have withheld and the motives for such a blackout; questions about other types of news which might also have been withheld ostensibly in the public interest; and the greater possible risks involved in wild and reckless rumors and exaggerated, provocative word-of-mouth reports."[26]

To some journalists even the suggestion that guidelines be adopted as one way to prevent excesses in terrorist-incident-coverage implies censorship and, ultimately, suppression. This sentiment was expressed by A.M. Rosenthal, executive editor of *The New York Times:* "The last thing in the world I want is guidelines. I don't want guidelines from the government and I don't want any from professional organizations or anyone else. The strength of the press is its diversity. As soon as you start imposing guidelines, they become peer-group pressures and then quasi-legal restrictions."[27]

In light of these and similar concerns, it is highly unlikely that governments in Western democracies, believing that free and dynamic media are vital to the success of their systems, will institute any form of official management of news. It has been reported, for instance, that President Carter "has no desire to seek legislation or to otherwise impose a solution and hopes those who make news decisions will themselves determine definable boundaries of legitimate coverage."[28]

A rare example where a democratic government has requested a news ban occurred in connection with the Schleyer kidnapping and the Lufthansa hijacking in October 1977. In this case the threat of terrorism was so grave that the West German government, for the first time ever, appealed to the media to impose a strict silence on themselves. This request was almost universally accepted. Subsequently, the government published, as originally promised, a detailed account of the events and decisions related to these specific terrorist incidents.[29]

In spite of this unique experience, the complex question of the role of the media as influencing terrorist results and societal initiative behavior remains largely unresolved. Admittedly, the interaction between the media and domestic violence has been a subject of serious discussion and substantial research since 1968. The various studies produced have, indeed, provided insightful data and a basis for further investigation in this important field.[30] Yet, the problem of how the media should function under terrorist-crisis conditions, particularly as they affect incident-management situations, has not, thus far at least, been suitably explored and systematically studied. Only isolated initiatives have been undertaken in this connection. Several conferences and limited research activities have dealt with some aspects of the problem.

In June 1976 the City University of New York (The Ralph Bunche Institute on the United Nations) and the State University of New York (The Institute for Studies in International Terrorism) co-sponsored a Conference on "Terrorism" in New York City supported with a grant from the Rockefeller Foundation. The conference brought together scholars and authorities from universities, institutes, the United Nations, the media, and the legal and diplomatic professions. Important personages participating included Senator Jacob Javits, former Attorney General Ramsey Clark, Correspondent Pauline Frederick, and many others of comparable status. One spin-off result from this meeting was the publication of a book, *Terrorism: Interdisciplinary Perspectives*, which includes a chapter on the role of the media.[31]

Both universities, in cooperation with *The Courier-Journal, The Louisville Times* and The American Jewish Committee (Institute on Human Relations) also organized a Conference on "Terrorism and the Media," in November 1977. Among those participating in the program were Robert H. Kupperman (U.S. Arms Control and Disarmament Agency), Peter Schlem (Assistant U.S. Attorney, Brooklyn), Captain Thomas M. Ashwood (Airline Pilots' Association, International), Dr. Frank M. Ochberg (National Institute of Mental Health), Professor Arthur M. Schlesinger, CBS correspondent Richard C. Hottelet, Robert Kleiman of *The New York Times*, Norman Isaacs of The National News Council, and many others. The meeting dealt with the tension between two major concerns—the media as a tool in the terrorist strategy and the importance of protecting "people's right to know." . . .

Another meeting on "The Media and Terrorism" was organized in Spring 1977 by James Hoge, editor-in-chief of *The Chicago Sun-Times* and *Chicago Daily News*, and Marshall Field, publisher of Field Enterprises, Inc. The day-long seminar included local and national experts from the fields of law enforcement, criminal law and the media. A report was subsequently published and the sponsors also developed standards for *The Sun-Times* and *Daily News* coverage of terrorist acts, especially those involving hostages.[32]

Similarly, The Oklahoma Publishing Company (*The Daily Oklahoman-Oklahoma City Times*) co-sponsored a Seminar on "Terrorism: Police and Press Problems." Held in April 1977, this workshop aimed at dealing with the problems and causes of terrorism and at stimulating an exchange of needs and concerns between the press and the official sector. The overall purpose of this meeting was, in the words of Charles C. Bennett, executive editor of *The Oklahoman* and *Times*, "to create the highest level of preparedness in Oklahoma City in the event of future terrorist activity."[33]

In May of the same year, the Maryland Chapter Society of Professional Journalists sponsored a panel session on "Police Relations with Press" at the meeting of the Maryland-Delaware-D.C. Press Association, held in Ocean City, Maryland.[34] Another meeting on "Terrorists and Hostage Coverage," held in Washington, D.C., in Fall 1977, was organized by the Radio-Television News Directors' Association (RTNDA).[35]

These gatherings, as well as similar initiatives, have generated useful suggestions for responsible reporting of terrorist incidents. Moreover, some news organizations even adopted specific policies with a view of better managing such situations. In addition to *The Chicago Sun-Times* and *Chicago Daily News* already mentioned, *The Courier-Journal* and *The Louisville Times*, United Press International and CBS News have also unilaterally determined internal guidelines for coverage.[36] Other media entities such as *The Washington Post* and WMAL-TV of Washington, D.C., have established temporary rules to handle specific incidents as, for instance, the Hanafi episode.[37]

Finally, the research conducted by scholars on this subject is rather fragmentary, consisting of portions of reports,[38] occasional articles[39] or several chapters in books.[40] Perhaps the most comprehensive study is *Disorders and Terrorism*, published by the National Advisory Committee on Criminal Justice Standards and Goals.[41] While the task force examines some aspects of news coverage during commission of acts of terrorism, contemporaneous coverage and follow-up reporting,[42] it fails to assess fully the role of the media as they affect the management of terrorist activities by the authorities.

While the foregoing activities over the past several years are, indeed, commendable for contributing preliminary relevant material in this important area of public concern, there exists no multidisciplinary data-base of past efforts, no serious analysis of success and failure of handling specific terrorist incidents from the perspectives of the media and law enforcement officials themselves, and no acceptable and tested models of media and policy management of terrorist situations. In view of this condition, there is an immediate need to undertake a rigorous study on the interaction of terrorism, the media and police, and thereby fill the gap in scholarship pertinent to current criminal justice processes. A new urgency is given to this need by the warning of Walter Scheel, President of West Germany: "Unless this flame [of terrorism] is stamped out in time, it will spread like a brush fire all over the world."[43] Indeed, this message forces us to ponder the future with grave concern and to determine appropriate courses of action.

In conclusion, any research undertaken in connection with terrorism and the media should take into account the following major observations and considerations: First, terrorism is essentially violence for effect and is directed not only at the instant victims of it and their family members but, by extension, also at a wider audience. Second, terrorism is a theater, at least in its embryonic stages, and, consequently, terrorists are making a conscious and deliberate effort to manipulate the media for their intended ends. Third, as the media are an industry based on competition and profit, it is inevitable that they become an integral part of any terrorist act, providing star actors, script writers and directors. Fourth, by providing extensive coverage of incidents the media give the impression that they sympathize with the terrorist cause, thereby creating a climate congenial to further violence. Fifth, the media often hinder the work of law enforcement agencies, thus jeopardizing successful outcomes of incidents. Sixth, the media have occasionally been helpful to the authorities in managing incidents without abandoning their responsibilities to the public's right to know. Seventh, the media should objectively, accurately and credibly report about terrorist acts lest the public panic and lose trust and confidence in both the press and government. Eighth, any attempts to impose media blackouts are likely to force terrorists to escalate the levels of violence in order to attract more attention. Ninth, since a major goal of terrorism is to undermine authority and cause anarchy, an unjustifiable limitation or even destruction of free media will ultimately result in the victory of terrorism. Tenth, the media, without surrendering their prerogatives, should help criminal justice processes in dealing with terrorism, and, conversely, the administration of justice officials should turn to the media for professional assistance in handling incidents and in limiting their derivative societal repercussions. Eleventh, given the nature and complexity of modern terrorism, the determination of a proper role for the media should not be left to their judgment alone, nor is it desirable that law enforcement agencies should unilaterally develop policies on this matter. And, twelfth, the threat of contemporary terrorism requires the openness, understanding and cooperation of both the media and criminal justice authorities, as well as many other segments of society, so that we can deal with this important area of public concern more hopefully and realistically.

NOTES

1. For details see Yonah Alexander, ed., *International Terrorism* (New York: Praeger Publishers, 1976); Yonah Alexander and Seymour M. Finger, *Terrorism: Interdisciplinary Perspectives* (New York and London: John Jay Press and McGraw-Hill, 1977); and Yonah Alexander and Herbert M. Levine, "Prepare for the Next Entebbe," *Chitty's Law Journal*, Vol. 25, No. 7 (September 1977); and Yonah Alexander, Editor-in-Chief, *Terrorism: International Journal*, Vol. 1, Nos. 1 (November 1977) and 2 (February 1978).

2. The mass media in a broad context includes newspapers, magazines, books, radio, television and films. For the purposes of our discussion we are concerned with the news media. Hereafter we shall use the term "media."

3. For a case study of the interaction between communications instruments and politics see, for example, Yonah Alexander, *The Role of Communications in the Middle East Conflict: Ideological and Religious Perspectives* (New York: Praeger Publishers, 1973).

4. "The Futility of Terrorism," *Harper's*, Vol. 252, No. 1510 (March 1976), p. 104.

5. Carlos Marighella, *Minimanual of the Urban Guerrilla* (Havana: Tricontinental, n.d.), p. 103. For a similar discussion see: Jerry Rubin, *Do It!* (New York: Simon and Schuster, 1970).

6. Quoted in Neil Hickey, "Terrorism and Television," *TV Guide*, July 31, 1976, p. 4.

7. Edward Weisband and Damir Roguly, "Palestinian Terrorism: Violence, Verbal Strategy, and Legitimacy," in Alexander, *International Terrorism*, supra, note 1, pp. 278–279.

8. One may regard the PLO as a terrorist organization or as guerrillas according to the measures of one's identification with the cause involved in this particular case. The U.S. Government, thus far at least, considers the PLO a terrorist movement.

9. Remarks by George E. Gruen delivered before the Conference on "International Terrorism" organized by the City University of New York and the State University of New York, June 10, 1976.

10. "Terrorism Is Likely to Increase," *London Times*, April 10, 1975.

11. Quoted in *The New York Times*, October 8, 1975.

12. Charles B. Seib, "The Hanafi Episode: A Media Event," *The Washington Post*, March 18, 1977, p. A27.

13. *The New York Times*, March 15, 1977.

14. Michael T. McEwen's statement before a Seminar on "Terrorism: Police and Press Problems" sponsored by the Oklahoma Publishing Company and the University of Oklahoma, April 14, 1977. Unpublished Proceedings, p. 32.

15. Quoted in "The Media and Terrorism," Proceedings of a Seminar sponsored by *The Chicago Sun-Times* and *The Chicago Daily News* (Spring 1977), pp. 28–29.

16. Remarks by Robert L. Rabe presented at the Conference on "Terrorism and the Media" sponsored by the Ralph Bunche Institute on the U.N. (The City University of New York) and the Institute for Studies in International Terrorism (State University of New York) and held at the Graduate Center of The City University, November 17, 1977.

17. Quoted by Charles Fenyvesi in remarks presented at the Conference on "Terrorism and the Media." See supra, note 16.

18. Stated by Conrad Hassel at a Seminar on "Terrorism and Business" sponsored by the Center for Strategic and International Studies (Georgetown University) and the Institute for Studies in International Terrorism (State University of New York), held in Washington, D.C., December 14, 1977.

19. Quoted at the Seminar on "Terrorism: Police and Press Problems," see supra, note 14, p. 65.

20. Reported in *Editor and Publisher*, August 27, 1977, p. 12.

21. *Ibid.*

22. Robert L. Rabe statement at the Conference on "Terrorism and the Media." See supra, note 16.

23. *The New York Times*, March 15, 1977.

24. See, for example, Barry Sussman, "Media Leaders Want Less Influence," *The Washington Post*, September 29, 1976, p. A-1.

25. Philip Revzin, "A Reporter Looks at Media Role in Terror Threats," *The Wall Street Journal*, March 14, 1977, p. 16.

26. The National News Council, "Paper on Terrorism," March 22, 1977, unpublished document.

27. David Shaw, "Editors Face Terrorist Demand Dilemma," *The Los Angeles Times*, September 15, 1976, p. 14.

28. *The New York Times*, March 15, 1977.

29. *The German Tribune*, November 13, 1977.

30. The list of research in this area includes, for instance, U.S. National Advisory Commission on Civil Disorders, *Report* (Washington, D.C.: U.S. Government Printing Office, 1968); thirteen volumes of reports from the U.S. National Commission on the Causes and Prevention of Violence, especially D. L. Lange, R. K. Baker, and S. J. Ball, *Mass Media and Violence: A Staff Report to the National Commission on the Causes and Prevention of Violence*, Vol. 9 (Washington, D.C.: U.S. Government Printing Office, 1969); U.S. Surgeon General's Scientific Advisory Committee on Television and Social Behavior, *Television and Social Behavior: Technical Reports to the Committee*, 5 vols. (Washington, D.C.: U.S. Government Printing Office, 1972); Otto Larsen, ed., *Violence and the Mass Media* (New York: Harper and Row, 1968); and Charles U. Daley, ed., *The Media and the Cities* (Chicago: University of Chicago Press, 1968).

31. Yonah Alexander and Seymour M. Finger, *Terrorism: Interdisciplinary Perspectives*, supra, note 1, pp. 141–206.

32. *The Media and Terrorism*, A Seminar sponsored by *The Chicago Sun-Times* and *Chicago Daily News* (Chicago: Field Enterprises, 1977).

33. Charles L. Bennett's letter of invitation to invited participants, March 18, 1977.

34. *Editor & Publisher*, September 17, 1977.

35. *Broadcasting*, September 26, 1977.

36. For a text of these guidelines see The National News Council, supra, note 26.

37. For other policy positions of news organizations see, for example, Ina Meyers, "Terrorism in the News," *The Daily Times* (Mamaroneck, N.Y.), April 2, 1977.

38. See, for example, Robert J. Jackson et al., *Collective Conflict, Violence, and the Media in Canada* (Ottawa, Ont.: Carleton University, n.d.).

39. See, for instance, Yonah Alexander, "Communications Aspects of International Terrorism," *International Problems*, Vol. 16, Nos. 1–2 (Spring 1977), pp. 55–60, and H. H. A. Cooper, "Terrorism and the Media," *Chitty's Law Journal*, Vol. 24, No. 7 (1976), pp. 226–232.

40. See, for example, Alexander and Finger, supra, note 31, and Cherif Bassiouni, *Terrorism and Political Crimes* (Springfield, Ill.: Charles C. Thomas, 1975), pp. 43–46.

41. *Disorders and Terrorism*, Report of the Task Force on Disorders and Terrorism (Washington, D.C.: National Advisory Committee on Criminal Justice Standards and Goals, 1976).

42. *Ibid.*, pp. 366, 387–388, 401–402.

43. Quoted in *The New York Times*, October 25, 1977.

The Medical Survival of Victims of Terrorism

MARTIN E. SILVERSTEIN

I. INTRODUCTION

The common elements in all terrorist attacks are threats to the lives of innocent noncombatants or actual injury and death of such victims. A second element is the inducement of fear and panic in large segments of unprotected citizenry, by association an implied threat. Government has an ethical, moral, and legal responsibility to minimize permanent injury and death to citizens while accomplishing other antiterrorist goals. When, despite the best intelligence, attack cannot be prevented, the public will feel somewhat secure if it believes that individuals have an excellent chance of rescue and survival intact. Thus, a practical subsystem for medical rescue and medical care for the victims should be an essential part of a national counterterrorist system.

Because the medical problem is in many ways unique, the basis of such a subsystem, if it is to be optimum, requires an analysis of the environmental and pathological definition of injury. Investigation indicates that, despite the devastating and dreadful effects on victims of expected terrorist weaponry, there are common elements in the pathological process of such early injury that lend themselves to a practicable and fairly economic system of medical rescue and medical care.

An antiterrorist rescue system will require intelligence, education and reeducation of medical personnel, preparatory planning, resource deployment, and a nationwide management system.

II. PROBLEM DEFINITION

The medical aspects of counterterrorism can be divided into two problems. The initial one involves modes of overcoming kidnappers while protecting and providing for delivery of their victims. The second and greater problem embraces the means of extricating multiple civilian casualties from a target site and providing for the full cycle of their medical care.

Since a medical system for the successful treatment of such mass casualties is not yet generally in operation in our country, this paper will be directed primarily toward setting up such a system. A study of civilian wartime casualties and, in particular, analysis of the victims of Provisional IRA attacks in Great Britain, provide indications of the type of casualties and the type of injuries. The British studies also suggest the inadequacy of existing systems of rescue and emergency care.

Problem elements:

A. Victim elements

1. *Demography*—Densely packed population of broad age spectrum.

    The range of terrorist weaponry and the psychological goals of the terrorists have directed attacks to crowded public places typified by pubs, shopping centers, busy streets, and sectors of airline terminals. The size of the population subject to intermediate attacks in urban guerrilla warfare can be expected to range from twenty to two hundred persons. Larger groups typified by the "Superbowl population" can be expected from the delivery of larger weapons. The Malta bombing experiences of World War II indicate that larger population size presents a larger, roughly linear problem.

    Typically, the victims are shoulder to shoulder so that blast weaponry produces secondary missiles consisting of the victims and their amputated members. The population density, to some extent, may protect some of the victims, particularly those farthest from the center of the blast. But in enclosed structures, when secondary missiles consisting of wood, steel, glass, cement, and other structural elements strike a densely packed target area, every fragment finds a victim. The typical population density is also harmful because the uninjured trample the injured in a panic-stricken escape attempt. Among dense urban subpopulations the needs for search and rescue are diminished, but the victims themselves provide physical obstacles to extrication. The composition of a civilian target population can be expected to consist of both sexes of all ages, presenting the special problems of pediatric, geriatric, and gynecologic care.

2. *Epidemiology*—Wide spectrum of preexisting disease.

Unlike the military casualty group that can be expected to consist of healthy, hardened, young persons, the civilian target population will contain many persons with preexisting disease and in varying states of fitness. The fatigued, the obese, the elderly, and the malnourished do not have optimum physiological resources to stave off the onset of shock and infection, whereas the potential military casualty may not suffer hemorrhagic or other shock states for thirty minutes to two hours. Preexisting cardiac disease produces a potential victim whose cardiac pump is less than adequate to cope with blood volume loss. The sprinkling of pregnant females may be subject to miscarriage and hemorrhage, and in this instance there are two potential victims rather than one. Existing psychoneuroses can be expected to be aggravated by victim status.

3. *Psychological effects*—Fear effects in peripheral population and observers.

Beyond those persons directly injured by the weapon, the observers of those injured and those who fear a potential attack on themselves provide an additional set of casualties and obstacles. Panic causes well people to injure one another during stampedes, during loss of control of motor vehicles, and by latent aggression. Excitement with its attendant change in pulse rate is known to produce heart attacks (myocardial infarction) at sports events. The same can be expected to occur in the region of an attack or at a remote distance from the attack as a result of "scare" rumors.

B. Site elements

1. *Configuration of the site*

Victims trapped in closed spaces receive higher doses of noxious gases or of aerosol-delivered microorganisms. Closed rooms, cellars, and caves have a greater implosion and explosion blast effect on the victims than unenclosed areas. The surrounding building structure tends to produce secondary missiles, as has been noted. In all, a civilian locale tends to be a more lethal target site than a field or a jungle site of military operation.

2. *Traffic patterns: access and egress*

Since delay in the initiation of resuscitation is likely to be the most common cause of failure to salvage the most seriously injured, ground and air access and the capability to extricate the patient from entrapping buildings become the key to survival. Urban mass-casualty victims are often lost because of traffic congestion, blocking rescue personnel from the target site. In addition to normal traffic problems, the "spectator phenomenon" in which uninvolved persons rush to the scene out of sheer curiosity, is a major factor in closing traffic arteries to rescue personnel and equipment. The same obstacles hinder the removal of injured personnel from the site to areas of safety and treatment. For this reason, vertical air transport is an intrinsic part of all mass casualty rescue. It is the best way of bringing medical personnel in and removing those victims who have to be transferred during the early part of treatment.

3. *Geographical relationship of nearby hospitals*

The principal source of rescue personnel, and particularly medical care personnel, is the area's hospitals. The speed with which they can mobilize teams to be moved to the site of the strike, the facilities and vehicles that exist for moving such personnel, and the available garages and helicopter pads materially determine the speed with which early care can be delivered. It should be noted that hospitals are not at this time prepared to dispatch mobile care teams except in a few locations. The proximity of hospitals does not guarantee early and adequate care to multiple-casualty sites.

C. Weaponry problem elements—specific patterns of early injury

1. *Bomb blast and small arms missile injuries*

   Bullet and explosive devices produce mechanical trauma to the human body by the disruption of tissue and by the transfer of kinetic energy to tissues and organs, injuring or destroying cells and causing failure of the complex interactive organ systems that determine life. From the standpoint of care, mechanical trauma can be divided into blunt or closed injuries, in which there is no tear of the enveloping skin, and open injuries, in which internal tissues are exposed to the external environment.

   An analysis of the injuries produced in the Birmingham pub bombings of November 1974 provides a realistic categorization of urban blast and missile injuries:

   a) *Burns*

      All degrees of burns occur, although flash burns tend to predominate. First- and second-degree burns, that is, skin reddening and blisters, do not (as a solitary injury) tend to produce shock. Third-degree burns with significant charring of large areas of body surface invariably produce shock, but within limits amenable to early intravenous fluid replacement therapy.

   b) *Open thoracic wounds*

      Multiple small penetrations of the chest by wooden splinters and larger bomb casing fragments occur in approximately one-fourth of the patients. Hemothorax and pneumothorax result. Larger wounds shatter the thoracic cage and literally blow the victim apart. This second type of victim is not, of course, amenable to rescue.

c) *Closed or blast injuries of the thorax, lung, and heart*

A very large proportion of patients will suffer the classic changes of "blast lung" with minute hemorrhages in the walls of the air passages and under the pleural lining of the lung. It has been established that this is a result of the "Spalling phenomenon" caused by the blast wave passing through the chest wall and the high-density lung substance to the low-density air within the lung. The surface between these two media are disrupted by water molecules forcibly ejected into the air space. A momentary maximal compression of air within the cavity may reach 100,000 atmospheres. The air bubble implodes and further damage is caused. Under present modes of care, a large number of patients with this form of injury die, but there is strong suspicion that early resuscitative care could save these individuals. A lesser percentage of victims of closed-blast injury develop tears in the main vessels as they leave the heart, or disruption of these vessels as they leave the heart. These patients, too, have constituted the dead-on-arrival category, although experience has shown that they are salvageable by early appropriate medical care.

d) *Intra-abdominal injuries*

Blast and missiles produce ruptured spleens and lacerated livers with intraperitoneal or internal hemorrhage. In some victims, the small and/or large intestine are perforated by bomb splinters or by the bursting effect of blast. Early care of shock and operative surgery will prevent death from these injuries.

e) *Head and neck injuries*

About half of blast victims can be expected to have fractures of the skull. The Birmingham experience indicates that only a small percentage have massive brain destruction with inevitable death. The neck is minimally subject to blast injury, with swelling of the larynx and suffocation. Missile injuries to the neck, particularly fragments of the surrounding building, produce early hemorrhage and require prompt surgical care.

f) *The limbs*

A little under half of the British casualties suffered traumatic amputation of a leg or an arm. Both open or compound and closed fractures were common.

g) *The skin*

Various nonlethal injuries to the skin occur, ranging from tattooing to large laceration. None of these should be, in themselves, fatal.

h) *Blast injury to the ear*

A large number of surviving patients can be expected to have perforated eardrums and/or a buzzing tinnitus as result of blast. In most explosions, solid substances are suddenly changed into a gas with enormous increase in volume and pressure. The blast wave ripples outward from the site of explosion. At its center, the blast wave exceeds the speed of sound and consists of a short positive phase followed by a much longer but less distinct negative phase. The duration of the positive phase is mere seconds. The negative wave is less than atmospheric pressure, but its duration is in tenths of milliseconds. Blast trauma to the ear is quite different from noise-induced trauma caused by high-intensity occupational noises, or the so-called report or artilleryman's deafness that is due to short, repeated stimuli. Occupational noise produces eventual damage to the inner ear, but little to the middle ear.

In March 1972, a five-pound bomb exploded in a restaurant in Belfast, Northern Ireland. In addition to the other injuries, most of the eighty victims were deafened by the relatively small blast in a small confined space. They were studied retrospectively and found to have widespread sensorineural or perceptive deafness. One-third showed high-frequency deafness in one or both ears on a long-term basis, and

10 percent lost the frequencies necessary to hear speech. Buzzing or tinnitus was a common symptom, but vertigo existed in only a few victims. Most victims had perforation of the eardrum, and in most cases these healed spontaneously with simple protection against infection. It is doubtful that a perforated eardrum protects the more delicate middle and neural inner ear. Later surgery is necessary in a few cases to remove fragments of the ruptured drum from the inner ear. The inner ear may be protected by intravenous infusions of low-molecular-weight dextran, although this remains unproven.

i) *Hemorrhage, shock, and tissue oxygen deprivation—common elements*

In the early phase of injury, whether it be by bullet, bomb fragment, or blast, damage to individual organs is usually less significant than the resulting injury to the whole body. Hemorrhage and shock deplete the body of blood volume and blood components. Injury to the airways and to the lungs interferes with the intake of oxygen. Blood pressure drops, pulse rises, oxygen conveyance to the brain and other vital organs is impaired, and the state known as "shock" intervenes. Death may occur in as short a time as seven minutes, although the shock period is usually considerably longer. Whatever organ is injured, the approach is the same. The wound should be covered with a pressure dressing, bleeding should be arrested, and blood volume should be replaced by commercial electrolyte solutions, plasmas, or artificial plasma substitutes. The airway is kept open by cleansing and removal of obstruction, placement of an artificial airway of some type, supply of oxygen, and, if necessary, mechanical ventilation.

2. *Fire bombs and fire storms*

Fire is such a common accompaniment of disasters that the effects of thermal energy upon the human body must be considered as an independent entity. The absorption of this energy to tissues results in injury to two major systems. The first is the skin and its immediately underlying tissues, resulting in loss of the body's "raincoat," and a maldistribution of body water and the blood volume. The second system affected is the respiratory system, with smoke injury to the trachea, bronchi, and, to a lesser extent, the smallest breathing tubes with resulting suffocation. Replacement of blood components and oxygen will sustain most of these patients until they can be transferred to definitive treatment centers.

3. *Microbiological weapons—bacteria, viruses, and toxins*

Almost any infectious disease easily cultured can be considered as a weapon (Tables 1 and 2). The viruses require fairly sophisticated techniques, and are probably denied to the urban guerrilla engaged in terrorism. They

TABLE 1

NUMBER OF PERSONS AT RISK FROM AN ATTACK WITH CHEMICAL OR BIOLOGICAL WEAPONS ON THE MOST DENSELY POPULATED AREAS OF TYPICAL URBAN TARGETS

Population of town	Industrially developed country Type of area[a]			Industrially developing country Type of area[a]		
	I	II	III	I	II	III
500,000	50,000	75,000	120,000	180,000	200,000	250,000
1,000,000	60,000	100,000	180,000	100,000	160,000	250,000
5,000,000	150,000	300,000	500,000	60,000	150,000	250,000

SOURCE: Adapted from *Health Aspects of Chemical and Biological Weapons* (Geneva: World Health Organization, 1970).

[a] The types of area selected are the most densely populated areas of the sizes specified below in the different kinds and sizes of town:

AREA I extends from an attack line 1 km upwind of the town center to 2 km downwind of the town center, and is 2 km wide.

AREA II extends from 1 km upwind of the town center to 9 km downwind of the town center, and is 2 km wide.

AREA III extends from an attack line 10 km upwind of the town center to 10 km upwind of the town center and is 2 km wide.

TABLE 2

Some Potential Biological Weapons Against Man

	Protection by vaccination against currently known strains	Effectiveness of serotherapy or chemotherapy
VIRUSES		
Adenoviruses (some strains)	±a	–a
Arthropod-borne viruses (eastern, western and Venuzuelan equine encephalitis; Japanese B; Russian spring-summer group. dengue; yellow fever; etc.)	+ to –	–
B virus and related herpes viruses	–	–
Enteroviruses (some members)	–	–
Influenza	±	–
Marburg virus (vervet monkey disease)	–	–
Sandfly (phlebotomus) fever	–	–
Smallpox	+	±
RICKETTSIAE AND BEDSONIAE		
Psitacosis (ornithosis)	–	+
Q fever	?	+
Rickettsialpox	–	+
Rocky Mountain spotted fever	±	+
Scrub typhus (tsutsugamushi fever)	–	+
Typhus (epidemic)	+	+

BACTERIA		
Anthrax	±	±
Brucellosis	±	±
Cholera	±	+
Glanders	−	?
Meliodosis	±	?
Plague	?	+
Shigellosis	+	+
Tularaemia	±	+
Typhoid fever	±	+
FUNGI		
Coccidioidomycosis	−	?
PROTOZOA		
Schistosomiasis (bilharziasis)	−	±
Toxoplasmosis	−	±

SOURCE: Adapted from *Health Aspects of Chemical and Biological Weapons* (Geneva: World Health Organization, 1970).

[a] + = suitable or good
± = moderately effective
− = unsuitable or poor
? = marginal or of questionable value, either because of the nature of the agent or because of insufficient knowledge.

include arthropod-borne viruses carrying yellow fever, tick-borne diseases and Japanese encephalitis, dengue fever, Venezuelan equine encephalitis, Chikundunya Rift Valley fever, and similar diseases. Water- and airborne infections such as the influenza virus, smallpox, and the related rickettsial infections of typhus, Rocky Mountain Spotted fever, Q fever, and others are, to a large degree, difficult to culture without complicated equipment.

Any number of bacterial infectious diseases are easily cultured and some, because of their past history, have a pronounced psychological effect. The related diseases of plague, tularemia, and brucellosis are endemic in Western United States. Typhoid fever is always with us. The great secondary danger of bacteriological weapons is the ease with which they create epidemics. The victims become the vectors. Since highly infective agents can be used against target populations without national immunity, it can be shown mathematically by standard epidemiologic formulae that both the chance of epidemics and the size of the epidemic are likely to be much greater than an ordinary disease epidemic, and consequently much more difficult to control.

Since there are a vast number of microorganisms available to the terrorist, it is impossible to lay out more than a general schema for this type of attack. Microorganisms are easily airborne, disbursed by aerosol, or vectored by reservoir water. A few will produce a very early fever and shock states not unlike traumatic shock. Most will have a longer incubation period so that case finding by epidemiologic means rather than rescue from a specific target area will be the basis of salvage. The public will have to be educated to recognize specific symptoms once an attack organism is identified. Epidemiological intelligence or police work will be required to trace contacts. Since anthrax, caused by the *Bacillus anthracis* is considered a likely attack weapon, its manifestations are worth considering. Three routes of infection of humans are known: through the skin, through the respiratory tract, and through the alimentary tract. One acquires it by touch, by breathing, or by drinking. The skin form is manifested by a localized boil or abcess. The most dangerous, the pulmonary form, appears as a pneumonia and fatal blood poisoning and is an unlikely route for terrorist attack. The treatment of all forms is penicillin and tetracycline, with support for the pulmonary form by way of mechanical ventilation via a tracheostomy or an endotracheal tube.

The exotoxin of a related organism, *Clostridium botulinum*, is an archetypal toxic weapon. Unlike the living anthrax organism, the botulism toxin is a pure crystalline poison produced by a living organism. The toxin itself cannot multiply and reproduce itself as does the anthrax organism, but is produced in culture and remains after the producing organism dies. Thus, the parent organism is a self-reproducing factory of poison, and the poison itself, a very powerful substance. Indeed, seven ounces of crystalline *botulinum* Type A toxin is sufficient to kill the entire human population of the world. Human botulism results from the ingestion of the toxin in food or water. The toxin blocks transmission from nerve fiber to nerve fiber (principally the cholinergic nerve fibers) and neural impulses are interrupted, producing a muscle paralysis much like poliomyelitis. The clinical illness may vary from mild indisposition to a rapidly fatal disease that eventuates in death within 24 hours. The symptoms begin characteristically some 12−36 hours after ingestion. Nausea and vomiting may occur, but weakness, lassitude, and dizziness are usually the earliest signs. There is severe dryness of the mouth and pharynx, and in 12−72 hours blurred vision, inability to swallow, and muscle weakness leading to the inability to move the respiratory muscles and, therefore, to breathe. Unlike symptoms resulting from live bacterial weapons, mentation remains intact and fever is usually not observed. The pupils are dilated and fixed, and the eyes paralyzed, resembling some head injuries. Identification of the disease depends upon a high index of suspicion and good intelligence. Positive identification depends on injection of a sample of the toxin or a sample of the patient's blood into small animals with and without the protection of specific antisera. Unfortunately, there are six strains of *Clostridium botulinum* and at least three strains of antisera. Aside from treatment with the antisera, the key to survival of patients with botulism is mechanical support of their respiratory systems and fluid replacement of the blood volume. In this regard, they resemble the trauma patient, the burn patient, and the microbiologically infected victim.

Botulinum toxin is lethal. A simpler toxin which is easily grown in the home kitchen is that of the *Staphyloccus aureus*. This substance is really a mixture of four toxins which act upon the gastrointestinal tract, characterized as the A, B, C, and D protein substances. The one most commonly discussed as a weapon is the B toxin, hence the designation SEB. The enterotoxin is most commonly found in bacterial contaminated foods such as cheddar cheese mixtures, macaroni and cheese, and similar mass-prepared meals. Unwashed salad components and custards are common carriers. Since this substance is much more heat resistant than botulism, ordinary cooking cannot be relied upon to render heavily contaminated foods harmless. Thirty minutes of boiling will not necessarily destroy the B toxin, but longer periods and higher heat such as heat under pressure will. The *Staphyloccus aureus* gastrointestinal toxicity is a common civilian disease. The toxin must be ingested, and within a short period no greater than four hours produces severe nausea and vomiting sometimes accompanied by diarrhea. The nausea and vomiting may be so severe that the patient goes into shock. The therapy is support of the blood volume by intravenous fluids. The disease is self-limiting if support is provided. Debilitated persons will, however, be in danger of death.

4. *Nuclear Weapons*

The blast and thermal effects of weapons we have discussed above. The early effects of nuclear weaponry are caused principally by the highly penetrating gamma rays inhaled and inhaled beta rays produced by the explosion, and secondary gamma and beta rays produced when neutrons strike the earth's surface. The bone effects of alpha rays are not seen early. For the living, after such an exposure, radiation produces persistent severe vomiting, followed by high fever, diarrhea, and severe dehydration. The vomiting and dehydration rapidly reduce the blood volume in the interfacing body water compartments. The immediate treatment is supporting that blood volume by the administration of water-electrolyte solutions, plasma, and plasma substitutes. The need for blood and blood cellular products such as leukocytes and platelets is a later phase of treatment, and can be attended to in the hospital. Vomiting and diarrhea can be reduced by sedation, and specifically by the use of anti-emetic drugs such as Bonine (meclizine hydrochloride), chlorpromazine, and prochlorperazine. Unlike the missile and the explosive bomb victim, individuals exposed to nuclear radiation require immediate removal from the area (since the site is likely to remain "hot"), rapid removal of their clothing, and water-wash decontamination.

5. *Airborne or air-disbursed noxious chemical agents: three groups*
   a) *Lethal agents*—those intended to cause death when the victim is exposed to concentrations well within the capability of hostile delivery (Table 3).
      (1) Nerve gases exemplified by such chemicals as sarin and VX have an LD/50 of approximately 100 mgm. per minute per meter cubed. Doses of greater than 5 mg. per minute per meter cubed are regarded as casualty producing for sarin. No more than 0.5 mg. per minute per meter cubed are regarded as casualty-producing by VX. They act by inhibiting tissue cholinesterase, blocking nerve transmission. In the absence of these sophisticated military agents, terrorists can be

TABLE 3

Some Properties of Selected Chemical Warfare Agents

	Sarin	VX	Hydrogen cyanide	Cyanogen chloride	Phosgene
1					
2	Lethal agent (nerve gas)	Lethal agent (nerve gas)	Lethal agent (blood gas)	Lethal agent (blood gas)	Lethal agent (lung irritant)
3	Vapor, aerosol, or spray	Aerosol or spray	Vapor	Vapor	Vapor
4	All types 6f chemical weapons		Large bombs	Large bombs	Mortars, large bombs
5	1,000 kg	1,000 kg	1,000 kg	1,000 kg	1,500 kg
6	100%	1–5%	100%	6–7%	Hydrolyzed
7	12,100 mg/m^3	3–18 mg/m^3	873,000 mg/m^3	3,300,000 mg/m^3	6,370,000 mg/m^3
8(a) (b)	Liquid Liquid	Liquid Liquid	Liquid Liquid	Solid Vapor	Liquid Vapor
9(a) (b) (c)	1/4–1 h 1/4–4 h 1–2 days	1–12 h 3–21 days 1–16 weeks	Few minutes Few minutes 1–4 h	Few minutes Few minutes 1/4–4 h	Few minutes Few minutes 1/4–1 h
10	>5 mg-min/m^3	>0.5 mg-min/m^3	>2,000 mg-min/m^3	>7,000 mg-min/m^3	>1,600 mg-min/m^3
11	100 mg-min/m^3	10 mg-min/m^3	5,000 mg-min/m^3	11,000 mg-min/m^3	3,200 mg-min/m^3
12	1,500 mg/man	6 mg/man			

1	Mustard gas	Botulinal toxin A	BZ	CN	CS	DM
2	Lethal and incapacitating agent (vesicant)	Lethal agent	Incapacitating agent (psycho-chemical)	Harassing agent	Harassing agent	Harassing agent
3	Spray	Aerosol or dust	Aerosol or dust	Aerosol or dust	Aerosol or dust	Aerosol or dust
4	All types of chemical weapons	Bomblets, spray-tank	Bomblets, spray-tank	All types of chemical weapons		
5	1,500 kg	400 kg	500 kg	750 kg	750 kg	750 kg
6	0.05%	Soluble	?	Slightly soluble	Insoluble	Insoluble
7	630 mg/m^3	Negligible	Negligible	105 mg/m^3	Negligible	0.02 mg/m^3
8(a)	Solid	Solid	Solid	Solid	Solid	Solid
(b)	Liquid	Solid	Solid	Solid	Solid	Solid
9(a)	12–48 h	—	—	—	—	—
(b)	2–7 days				2 weeks for CS1; longer for CS2	
(c)	2–8 weeks				—	—

TABLE 3 (Cont.)

1	Mustard gas	Botulinal toxin A	BZ	CN	CS	DM
10	>100 mg-min/m^3	0.001 mg (oral)	100 mg-min/m^3	5–15 mg/m^3 concentration	1–5 mg/m^3 concentration	2–5 mg/m^3 concentration
11	1,500 mg-min/m^3	0.02 mg-min/m^3	?	10,000 mg-min/m^3	25,000–150,000 mg-min/m^3	15,000 mg-min/m^3
12	4,500 mg/man					

SOURCE: Adapted from *Health Aspects of Chemical and Biological Weapons* (Geneva: World Health Organization, 1970).

KEY: 1. Common name
2. Military classification
3. Form in which the agent is most likely to be disseminated
4. Types of weapon suitable for disseminating the agent
5. Approximate maximum weight of agent that can be delivered effectively by a single light bomber (4-ton bomb load)
6. Approximate solubility in water at 20°C
7. Volatility at 20°C
8. Physical state: (a) at −10°C; (b) at 20°C
9. Approximate duration of hazard (contact, or airborne following evaporation) to be expected from ground contamination: (a) 10°C, rainy, moderate wind; (b) 15°C, sunny, light breeze; (c) −10°C, sunny, no wind, settled snow
10. Casualty-producing dosages (for militarily significant injuries or incapacitation)
11. Estimated human respiratory LCt$_{50}$ (for mild activity: breathing rate approx. 15 litres/min)
12. Estimated human lethal percutaneous dosages

expected to look to commercially available insecticides, organophosphorous pesticides that will produce the same effects in much larger doses and are commercially available. Systemic absorption causes tightness in the chest, dyspnea, cough, pulmonary edema, and cyanosis. Nausea, abdominal pain, diarrhea, and involuntary defecation occur. Less disabling signs and symptoms include anxiety, headache, tremor, apathetic withdrawal, ataxia, Cheyne-Stokes respiration, convulsions, pinpoint pupils that may sometimes be unequal, sweating, occasional elevation of the blood pressure, and bradycardia. The end points are collapse and depression of respiratory and circulatory centers. Treatment consists of countering the toxic effects with anticholinergic drugs such as atropine that will counter almost—but not all—of the paralytic effects. Reactivators such as Pralidoxime iodide supplement the anticholinergic atropine. In addition to these specific antidotes, maintenance of a clear airway by an endotracheal tube or tracheostomy and mechanical ventilation with a supply of oxygen will sustain respiration and the perfusion of body tissues with oxygen.

(2) Chemical agents that block cell respiration (blood gas agents): Hydrogen cyanide and cyanogen chloride typify such agents. Hydrogen cyanide can produce percutaneous intoxication, but is generally an inhalant. It produces sudden loss of consciousness and death from respiratory arrest. In smaller doses, there is an immediate and progressive sensation of warmth, which is due to vagal dilation, accompanied by flushing. Prostration follows with nausea, vomiting, and headache. The key is difficulty in breathing or dyspnea. Late asphyxial convulsions follow. Cyanogen also has a respiratory irritant effect. Casualty-

producing dosages are much higher than the nerve gases, ranging from 2000 mg. per minute per meter cubed to 7000 mg. per minute per meter cubed. Proven antidotes for hydrogen cyanide are the rapid administration of nitrites such as amylnitrite and thiosulfates, which break up the circulating hydrogen cyanide. Supportive therapy consists of maintenance of respiration by mask and mechanical ventilation.

(3) Lung irritants: Phosgene, a sweet colorless gas, typifies this group. Since it is used commercially, it is readily available. This heavy gas causes an irritation of the eyes and the respiratory tract that, in the presence of a large dose, proceeds to acute pulmonary edema and bronchiolar constriction with potential asphyxia. There is also an effect on the blood-clotting mechanism causing hemolysis. The symptoms are breathlessness, cough, dyspnea, thirst, vomiting, and chest pain. Unclassified literature indicates no successful antidote, and the treatment must be supportive pulmonary care such as the supply of oxygen and mechanical ventilation and support of the cardiovascular system by maintenance of blood volume by intravenous fluids.

(4) Vesicants: Epitomized by mustard gas, the vesicants are also used as incapacitating agents. Mustard gas is minimally soluble in water, but dissolves in organic solvents and fat. It produces acute toxic effects only at supralethal dosages. At these levels there is central nervous system excitation with convulsions and rapid death. At lower dosages there are no immediate effects on exposure except for possible sneezing and smarting of the eyes. Hemorrhage from the nose is apparently a fairly common early symptom. The earliest recognizable sign is grittiness, pain, and redness of the conjunctiva. Sore throat, coughing,

and hoarseness then appear. After four to sixteen hours there is nausea and vomiting with abdominable pain, followed by diarrhea. Skin itching is followed by a dark erythematous rash of the exposed parts of the body and the axilla and genitals that proceeds to blistering. Death almost never occurs in the first day after exposure. More systemic symptoms appear after twenty-four hours with a severe tracheitis and mucopurulent secretion. The injured lungs become infected and death tends to occur between the second day and the fourth week. In patients who survive, the blisters may heal in two or three weeks, or ulcerate or become infected. Treatment consists of water decontamination of the skin and support of respiration, as in any erosion of the lining of the tracheobronchial tree with infection. The sequence is, therefore, injury to the tracheobronchial tree and pneumonia. Skin lesions are treated as second-degree skin burns with cleansing and protection against infection.

(5) Ricin is easily available in large doses as a result of extraction in treatment of castor beans. It is basically a crude plant toxin of heavy molecular weight. Its potentiality as a homemade poison aerosol is of significance in urban guerrilla warfare.

b) *Incapacitating agents*—those designed to cause temporary disease or to induce temporary mental or physical disability for a duration well beyond a period of exposure.

(1) BZ, a psychochemical agent, is an anticholinergic agent substance that exists as a white crystalline solid deliverable as an aerosol. Its prime organ target is the respiratory system, although it is also absorbed through the skin. It produces tachycardia, dry skin, dry mouth, wide pupils, blurred vision, ataxia, and confusion. Sufficient doses can

lead to stupor and coma. Drowsiness should be considered a predominant symptom, especially when accompanied by an elevated skin temperature. Since its action is that of cholinergic blockade, it resembles atropine, although it is much more potent. The specific antidote is the anticholinesterase physostigmine.

(2) Lysergic acid derivatives (LSD 25) is a crystalline-free base, insoluble in water. This well-known psychochemical is fortunately destroyed by oxidizing agents, including the chlorine in super-chlorinated water. LSD is highly active when administrated orally or by vein. It is probable that it is administratable by inhalation. The symptoms fall into three categories: (a) systemic or visible body symptoms include dizziness, weakness, tremor, nausea, drowsiness, and blurred vision; (b) perceptual symptoms produce hallucinations of altered shapes and colors; and (c) psychic symptoms are represented by alterations in mood from happiness to sadness or irritability. Victims have dreamlike feelings and a distorted time sense. Since physical effects are few, reliance must be placed on dilated pupils, incoordination, and ataxia for recognition. All doses of 0.2 to 0.4 mg. in nontolerant persons are sufficient to incapacitate the victim. There is no specific antidote, and treatment consists of confining the patient with a course of sedation while the effects wear off.

c) *Harassment agents*—those short-term incapacitating agents that are capable of causing a rapid disablement and are designed to last for a little longer than the period of exposure.

(1) Chloroacetophenone (CN) is a solid that can be disbursed by aerosol, and is basically a lachrimator or tear gas. In low doses, 0.5 mg. per meter cubed, a copious flow of tears is produced within

a minute. This is one of the fastest acting of the useful gases. Higher concentrations or prolonged exposure cause intense irritation of the nose and upper respiratory tract, followed by itching and burning of moist areas of the skin such as the axilla and genitalia. A significant number of persons are allergic to this substance, with a potential for death from anaphylactic shock. Recovery is swift on exposure, but serious lung damage may have occurred from large doses. Death from pulmonary edema is quite possible. Wiping of the eyes constitutes the primary treatment. If the lungs are injured, oxygen, airway clearance, and mechanical ventilation are indicated. Should allergic or anaphylactic shock intervene, adrenal steroids and support of blood volume are indicated.

(2) Chlorobenzalnalononitrile (CS) is a substance that resembles CN, has even more rapid onset, and brings about symptoms at lower concentration. Significant harassment occurs at 1 mg. per cubic meter. The symptoms are basically the same as those of CN. The respiratory effects, like those of CN, are likely to be lethal if there is allergy to the drug, or if the victim suffers from asthma, chronic bronchitis, emphysema, or other pre-existing pulmonary disease.

(3) Adamsite (DM) is an unusual gas that irritates the upper respiratory tract and is primarily a sternutator, causing severe sneezing as a result of irritation to the peripheral sensory nerves in the respiratory tract. There is a lesser irritation of the skin. At high doses it attacks the tracheobronchial tree with the resulting pulmonary-edema pneumonia. However, in ordinary doses the symptoms are that of a bad cold followed by severe coughing and choking. Unbearable headache occurs and may be accompanied by severe chest pains, shortness of breath, and nausea and vomiting. The

patient is liable to be weak and trembling. Effect occurs about two or three minutes after exposure and recovery occurs in one to two hours. Unless the dosage is very high, there is not likely to be lung damage or death.

D. Secondary population elements—fear and anxiety

Fear is the normal emotional response to consciously recognized and external sources of danger. Anxiety is apprehension and tension resulting from the anticipation of danger, the source of which is largely unknown or unrecognized. It has a large, if not, total intrapersonal, intrapsychic origin. Terror weaponry need not necessarily be used to produce damage among the population beyond the periphery of the target zone. Unsubstantiated rumor that a fearsome weapon has been used and potentially threatens this population is sufficient to cause loss of life and property and paralysis of social institutions. If the actual target has been hit, rational means for protection and prevention may disappear because of anxiety and fear syndromes. Indeed, counterproductive behavior may result. Suicide, obstruction of rescue, and attacks on normally supported institutions can occur. It is important that these secondary effects be countered by accurate information promptly supplied. It is particularly important that the peripheral public be reassured that government is in control of the situation, and is protecting them and optimally caring for the victims of the incident. The role of the public media is obvious in this instance. In addition, rescue personnel and responsible authority must avoid the normal defensive mechanism technically known as denial. This is a term applied to the various degrees of nonperception, misperception, nonrecognition, or nonacceptance of reality in order to cope with otherwise unacceptable intrapsychic conflicts, feelings, or memories. There is some reason to believe, based on the experience of the traumatologist and other observers of disaster scenes, that public authorities themselves tend to manifest denial in this technical sense. This may be a manifestation of a feeling of guilt that they have allowed a public disaster to happen, or frustration that they are unable to cope with it or lack a protocol or routine for coping with it. This form of denial is manifested by a great desire to "clear the scene" without respect to the goal of maximum salvage of lives, as if by sweeping away the debris one can deny that the accident happened. Similarly, frustration with a massive problem of rescue and care, as well as the desire to avoid the overtly gory scene, leads to the concept that nothing can be done—that all of the victims must die in a major disaster and only those capable of walking away or requiring a minimum care can be saved. It is quite possible that denial added to ignorance and lack of planning have led to the conventional wisdom that this is indeed true. This attitude will be dealt with below.

E. Intermediate and long-term problem elements

Discussion thus far has been directed toward immediate problem elements, early effects on victims, and the elements of early care. These are, of course, the crucial elements in rescue. If the patient can be removed from the scene alive, and life is prolonged for a few days, the chances of survival are much greater. Mechanically traumatized patients may require repeated surgeries, long periods of intensive care, rehabilitation, and retraining for occupation. Their families may require support during this period. The victim of bacteriological and gas attack requires several weeks of antibiotic therapy and supportive hospital care. A large number of patients requiring multiple, high-level hospital service over a concentrated time period can be expected to cause confusion and threaten the breakdown of medical services in any single area. Civilian hospitals rarely contain more than 15 percent reserve bed capacity. The capacity of intensive care units is usually minimal; the same is true of operating theaters. Hospital personnel of all types are usually carried at a roster level sufficient to deal with this capacity. There is very little elasticity in staffing patterns, and the only way to increase staff is to bring in personnel from unaffected regions or to transfer patients out of the immediately affected target area. Secondary psychological effects have been mentioned, and among these are the long-term effects of loss of faith in authority and social institutions. A breakdown of occupational capability of the peripheral population occurs and dehumanization is manifested by the sense of loss of personal responsibility and a feeling of powerlessness. Irresponsible rumor and the news media tend to be preoccupied with morbidity and mortality statistics and evince relatively slight concern for the victims.

III. PHILOSOPHY OF RESCUE:
FEASIBILITY OF MAXIMUM PRESERVATION OF LIFE

There is a widely held, if nonanalytic, belief that mass casualties are doomed by the dreadful nature of the event and the inaccessibility of the many victims. The acceptance of this traditional "wisdom" represents a preconditioning of both authority and potential victim that enhances exponentially the effects of terrorism and constitutes a weapon needlessly placed in the urban guerrilla's arsenal.

It is the thesis of this report that mass casualty victims are salvageable if dealt with by a health delivery system appropriately designed for immediate, on-site rescue and resuscitative measures and logically phased medical care.

Documented experience from two disparate areas support this view. The first is the theater of war. Mortality and morbidity from almost every aspect of military warfare have decreased steadily from World War I through Vietnam as a result of probable analysis, therapeutic research, and the organization of health delivery.

Infectious disease, the scourge of the Napoleonic, Crimean, and Civil Wars, is now a negligible cause of death. Fatalities from smallpox and tetanus decreased to zero by World War II. From World War I to Vietnam the understanding of hypovolemic shock (hemorrhagic and traumatic shock) increased steadily and the derived therapy and management led to progressively greater life expectancy. The World War I period produced physiological descriptions of the mechanism of this universal killer. Shock in World War II responded to field resuscitation with intravenous fluids administered by corpsmen. The Korean conflict demonstrated that later death from kidney failure was not inevitable. The Vietnamese experience introduced recognition and prevention of the even later pulmonary shock syndromes.

Thermal burns, an increasing factor in casualties after the advent of high-altitude bombing, jet engines, and nuclear weaponry, were attacked vigorously during the Korean War. Burn shock, a dread, rapid killer, was found to be treatable by formula administration of colloid and electrolyte solutions. With most intermediate-burn victims now surviving the shock phase, death from sepsis has been found preventable by early wound and antibiotic treatment.

Sound research and innovative management techniques have eliminated the centuries-old concept that arterial wounds mean inevitable death or amputation. Field use of the tourniquet has been abandoned, as has destructive amputation surgery. Replacement with early surgical repair has salvaged lives and limbs.

A second source of evidence that analysis, planning, and research can materially increase the number of survivors of a terrorist attack is to be found in recent advances in civilian emergency medicine. The last four years have seen an attitudinal and methodological revolution in the care of highway and other accident patients. New systems of care have been derived from the fruits of research in anesthesiology and pulmonary physiology, military medicine, and experiments in new health delivery systems.

Aerospace-originated physiologic electronic sensing and massive improvement in computer communications have changed not only the mode of care but the very definition of death. These technological advances would not have become embedded so rapidly in actual medical practice if Congress had not become aware of a gap in American medical practice and stimulated new systems with the Emergency Medical Services Act of 1973.

IV. SOME EVIDENCE OF INADEQUACY OF EXISTING SYSTEMS OF RESCUE

In the preparation of this paper a large number of recent military, civil, and terrorist-initiated disasters were reviewed. Among the available, most carefully documented are the civil "Summerland Disaster" on the Isle of Man, the Malta Cave Bombing, and the Birmingham Pub Bombings attributed to the Provisional IRA.

On the evening of August 2, 1973, 3,000 holiday makers were enjoying the facilities of the Summerland leisure complex on the Isle of Man. An accidental fire began in an adjacent kiosk and spread to the adjoining building complex. During the panic rush to the exits, a large number of victims were injured by being crushed or trampled upon. Others were injured when they attempted to jump to safety. Still other victims were burnt when attempting to leave the building or inhaled smoke when returning to the building to find lost relatives, particularly children. The area is served by Noble's Hospital in Douglas, a standard, 200-bed general hospital on the Isle of Man that serves a seasonal population of 556,000 persons. The area is equipped with ambulances for transportation. During the disaster, these ambulances were supplemented by taxis and private cars. There is little evidence of organized or professional rescue except that carried out by the police and fire departments in the course of their duties. Neither had encountered a major fire disaster on the Isle of Man in recent years. The approach used was the standard one of removing the victims from the disaster site to the hospital as fast as possible. No major attempt was made to provide on-site resuscitation. The patients arrived at the hospital from twenty minutes to one hour after the first alarm. Forty-eight patients were dead on arrival from suffocation, carbon monoxide poisoning, burns, or mechanical traumatic injuries to the head, trunk, and limbs suffered when jumping from windows or being trampled. At the opposite pole of the injury spectrum were the survivors. None of the burn patients were in shock. Thirty-two patients were admitted to the hospital; fourteen had a variety of injuries to the chest, abdomen, and limbs accompanied by burns. Hart el al., in studying this disaster, reported that none of those admitted were seriously injured. Three cases required respiratory intensive care; two of these had serious preexisting pulmonary disease. It is a fair judgment that since none of the victims required resuscitation, those who did would have required it prior to arrival at the hospital, and therefore are grouped under those listed as DOA. How many could have been saved by on-site treatment is purely speculative.

Targets on the Island of Malta were under military bombing attacks in 1943. During a heavy dive-bombing attack a 500-kgm. bomb fell near the entrance of a crowded rock cave. The shelter was in deep rock and entered by a stairway at either end—leading downward into a main tunnel. There were several right-angle turns and the tunnel contained many sleeping cubicles. Witnesses in the shelter reported a loud explosion, tongues of fire, and gusts of wind of tremendous force. Although rescuers entered the site within five minutes, care was apparently limited to first aid and removal to general hospitals. Wilson et al. reported on the autopsy findings of eleven victims considered dead on arrival. Analysis of these cases indicates the widespread evidence of blast injury to the lung with only moderate additional injuries. It seems reasonable to speculate that these cases might have survived with pulmonary mechanical ventilation and support of their blood volume.

Two of the best-studied urban guerrilla attacks occurred after two bombs exploded in two separate public houses in the center of Birmingham on November 21, 1974. Again, traditional rescue and removal techniques were used. However, the interval between blast and initial emergency department resuscitation was materially shorter than in most cases. The Birmingham General Hospital, in the heart of industrial England, and its staff have had a long experience and interest in traumatic cases. Eighteen victims were dead on arrival; three died later in the hospital; sixty-one suffered minor injuries sufficient to be discharged after ambulatory treatment; and nineteen were admitted and successfully managed. A number of the last group received early resuscitation in the emergency department for shock. Nevertheless, a postmortem analysis of the DOA victims as reported by Waterworth and Carr suggests that a portion of the DOA patients died of respiratory failure secondary to blast injury. Less than 10 percent of those who survived and were admitted had injuries to the chest and the abdomen. Of the twenty-one who died, eighteen suffered from blast lung with relatively minor anatomical disruption. These injuries should be salvageable by early maintenance of blood volume and mechanical support of respiration. In the last ten years and particularly since the Vietnam War, great strides have been made in the care of respiratory failure in the United States. Retrospective analyses are at best speculative, but there seems to be considerable evidence that a system of phased care beginning as soon as possible should produce a higher yield of preserved lives.

V. THESIS: COMMONALITY OF INJURY INDICATES A LOGICAL UNIFIED RESUSCITATIVE MODEL

An in-depth analysis of pathophysiological effects on the human body of expected terrorist weaponry and a logical investigation of the requirements of wounded victims indicate a commonality of early injury effects that lend themselves to a simple, unified resuscitative approach to all casualties and are modified only slightly by the nature of the weaponry. The resuscitative approach can, fortunately, be temporarily phased from the simple to the complicated. This allows early resuscitation to be performed by the paramedical rescuer preserving the patient for definitive phases of treatment by advanced medical teams.

The common physiological response consists of a failing cardiovascular system secondary to blood component loss, impairment of respiratory ventilation with inadequate perfusion of the tissues of organ systems by oxygen, and neurological failure of the control systems of the cardiorespiratory complex leading to death from within seven minutes to one hour.

These effects are managed by two major steps teachable to any paraprofessional with a mere 200 hours of rescue medical training and a modicum of equipment.

A. Maintenance of oxygen flow to the tissues:
   1. Provide an unobstructed airway by position and cleansing of the mouth and tongue and placement of an artificial airway (tube) in the pharynx or trachea by non-operative means.
   2. Supply oxygen at 20 percent concentration (air) or greater.
   3. Provide mechanically induced and controlled ventilation. This can be accomplished by a simple rubber bag and mask apparatus until mobile equipment is available.

4. Release extra-pulmonary thoracic air or blood via needle thoracic paracentesis and use of the Heimlich valve.

B. Maintenance of blood circulation (transportation of oxygen):

1. Use pressure applications and dressings to control bleeding wounds.

2. Support the blood volume by intravenous infusion of electrolytes and/or colloid solutions.

3. Maintain the chemical environment of the cardiac pump by intravenous doses of sodium bicarbonate, calcium chloride, and rhythm controlling drugs such as lidocaine and atropine.

4. Provide combined vasomotor control and inotropic "tuning" by additions to the intravenous infusion of dopamine or norepinephrine.

VI. GENERAL MEDICAL-RESCUE MODEL SYSTEM

A. Introduction

It is evident that the present-day terrorist threat to American lives is too sophisticated, too well organized, and too potentially harmful to be dealt with by archaic efforts dependent on volunteer community effort for planning and execution. The time element required for preserving life prohibits relegating principal planning and response to postattack periods. The magnitude of the threat requires provisions of an agency comparable in organization and skills to the federal law enforcement agencies dealing with the same problem.

B. Objective

By utilizing the best in available technology and methodology, we should establish a national system capable of rapid medical rescue response to single or multiple intermediate terrorism attacks in such a manner that there is a maximum preservation of victim life and a minimum of fear and panic.

C. General operation of the system—scenario

Response may best be generalized in scenario form. Consider a midwestern or southwestern city of 450,000 in which a bomb and small-arms attack is made upon the local airport at the height of a holiday season. The region will have a preestablished command post, a team of highly mobile paramedical personnel within the organization of the police department, fire department, or other agency. The geography, traffic access and egress patterns, and structural characteristics of the potential targets, including the airport, will exist within the file. Early adequate local hospitals will contain pretrained in-house triage teams, resuscitation teams, intensive care teams, and field surgical, biological, and nuclear teams and their equipment within their existing staffs of physicians, nurses, and technicians. A city of this size can be expected to have different specialty teams and thus avoid overly depleting its base force.

If the rescue system is operating well, local law enforcement and the local rescue force will have been alerted to the potential target and expected weaponry by the intelligence section of the network in liaison with federal security agencies.

Upon notification by local sources or the national information network, the paramedic team will be dispatched and immediately begin rescue and Phase I resuscitation efforts under the protection of local security forces. The command and communications center will be fully manned; the region's hospitals will begin mobilizing their off-duty forces and deploying their reserve beds. All approved American hospitals have existing in-house disaster plans. Triage officers and Phase II definitive medical resuscitation teams will be dispatched to take over selected patients from the paramedics and begin this phase of medical care (see Fig. 1).

If the number of casualties approaches twenty, field intensive care and field surgery teams and their equipment will be sent to the scene to establish their units on site. Nearby regional depots will be alerted by the management information system for the deployment of additional

Fig. 1. Sequence of care

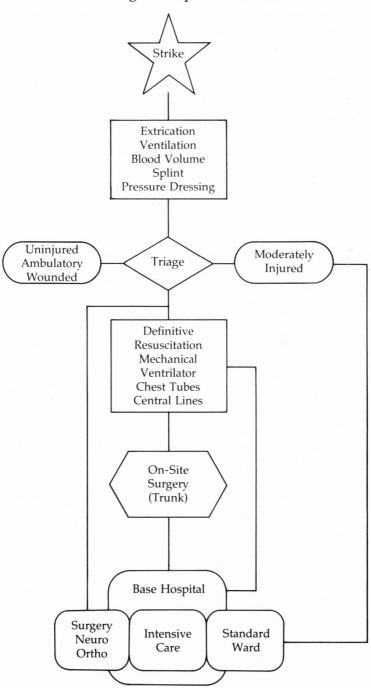

transportation vehicles, chauffeurs, and pilots, and medical supplies ranging from pharmaceuticals to splints and disposable surgical equipment. The duties of the additional paramedic group will consist of extraction of trapped individuals, splinting and maintenance of oxygenation and circulating blood volume by the use of airway tubes, bag respirators, and intravenous solutions. They will also apply identity tags and preserve and identify clothing and effects for law enforcement purposes. The triage officers will sort the casualties, dispatch the miminally injured from the scene, and determine which patients are to receive definitive resuscitation and/or intensive care or immediate surgery. In conjunction with traffic control they will decide whether patients can withstand transportation to base hospitals for thoracic and abdominal surgery or whether the degree of hemorrhage requires on-site intervention. At least one triage officer will be charged with the rapid diagnosis and disposition of the hitherto neglected psychiatric casualty. Phase II resuscitation will consist of skilled diagnostic examination, placement of chest tubes, initiation of large central venous lines, and application of central venous pressure, electrocardiographic, and other monitoring equipment. Patients receiving such care will require extensive and long-term life support.

Phase III care will consist of ongoing on-site intensive care—an extension of Phase II—or transfer to an on-site or base surgical theater. Although research will be required to determine optimum equipment, present investigations have indicated that trailer truck units serve as the nucleus of adequate Phase II resuscitation efforts (field intensive care and surgery facilities).

When patients are stabilized on site they will be removed to the expanded areas of base general hospitals for further trunk surgery, neurosurgery, orthopedic surgery, and other specialty procedures and to base hospital intensive care units. Analysis of civilian emergency medicine and disasters indicates that most orthopedic and neurosurgical patients will not require on-site surgery unless injury to these organ systems are combined with trunk injuries or severe multiorgan system breakdown.

Since the medical force in any region is likely to be over-whelmed and exhausted within a short time, this factor will be monitored by command control and additional personnel will be transferred to the target region from uninvolved regions by the national emergency management system.

The essentiality of a national management system that can mobilize personnel and facilities from the entire country can be envisioned in the event of a strike against multiple targets in the same region or in several regions simultaneously.

Atomic, biological, and gas strikes will require additions to the central core of this scenario.

D. Development of a national network system for mass casualties

1. *Establishment of regions*

    The country may be logically divided into emergency regions distinguished by population and geography. In addition to state governments, existing regions have been described by the Bureau of the Census, Military Districts, HEW, and the like.

    Factors in the definition of an Emergency Region will include logical local and federal preexisting governance, geography that admits the ready transfer of personnel and supplies, and, especially location of targets and base hospitals.

2. *A national management information network*

    It is obvious that economy forbids a large standing force awaiting a disaster. A frugal system can be developed by the training of a reserve personnel force that can be readily mobilized and by the optimal national deployment of supplies, vehicles, and those reserve personnel. In situations in which time is of the essence and multiple targets can be expected, both information and management of the system must be on-line and in real-time. Not only will the National Emergency Management and Information Service be charged with activity during a strike, but it will be responsible for the transfer of intelligence information, management of the supply depots, and transportation of personnel and supplies for readiness states.

It is evident that a modular communications capability is the heart of such a system. Precedent for such a system exists in the Resource Interruption Monitoring System (RIMS) and the Emergency Management Information System and Reference Index (EMISARI) used during the wage-price freeze and the oil crisis. The computer-based communications system permitted on-line, real-time communication—interactive and control capability between widely separated geographical centers. They had an extraordinary advantage of being operable by first-time users at both professional and clerical levels, being adaptive and having a modicum of commands. For an emergency management system the system would require the capability for real-time update of target and depot supplies.

It is essential that an emergency system subject to aggression have the option of communication by both ground line and secure radio. The system would require terminals in national offices, depots, local command and control centers, and portable terminals available for the target sites. Such a system would be much larger than RIMS.

3. *National command and control personnel*

Counterterrorism and the management of mass casualties requires skilled permanent management personnel. Although these need not be numerous they should be capable of handling secure intelligence information, medical rescue response, law enforcement response, and the logistics of a large communication, transportation, and supply system.

4. *Supply depots*

Even a minor medical disaster absorbs an enormous amount of pharmaceutical, food, and transportation resources. These must be instantaneously available and rapidly transportable. The custom established during civil defense preparations against atomic disaster and continued today under federal law of crated equipment in relatively inaccessible depots has no place in an emergency medical system. Depots must be of sufficient number and strategically located. Their status must be known to the system's information files at all times. Research will be required to determine optimum deployment and modes of rapid mobilization.

5. *Liaison with the Secret Service, FBI, the National Institutes of Health, and other related forces*

To be effective the medical system must have adequate information as to possible weaponry, their effects, and modes of treatment. The ability to set up partial states of readiness in response to intelligence will contribute to the economy and effectiveness of the system. Research will be required to determine modes of therapy and decontamination.

6. *Communication*

Reliable communication is an essential part of the computer communication complex. It must have the qualities of security and the capability of carrying resource management information as well as emergency command and control.

7. *Transportation*

An economical system demands the capability of transferring both personnel and equipment to the target site from a nationwide depot system. Since target sites are almost always congested and rail and highway access subject to aggressive strike, much reliance will be placed on air and particularly on vertical lift transportation for the delivery of personnel and supplies and the removal of patients. Specially equipped aircraft can be used for the transportation of patients and as mobile care centers.

8. *A network of hospitals and expert personnel*

After immediate care, many patients will require special facilities for the care of burns, radiation injury, and the effects of other special weaponry. It would be inefficient, uneconomical, and impracticable to establish such skills and facilities on a widespread basis. Centers for such injuries presently exist in certain military and civilian hospitals. The patients can be airlifted to these hospitals after preliminary care. Similarly, specialist physicians and teams exist that can be airlifted into each region to take command of previously established protocols for such treatment and determine new therapeutic strategies for new weapon situations.

9. *Protection for essential nodes in the system*

The system itself must be protected against terrorist strike. An example may be seen in biological or toxic attacks against regional water supplies. Chlorination alone does not provide optimum protection. However, special techniques such as activated carbon and/or ozone can be used exclusively for water supplies to hospitals and food preparation plants.

10. *Disaster status on the Presidential level for a strike or a potential strike*

Experience in civilian emergency medicine and disasters has demonstrated the lag time involved in mobilizing disparate but cooperating agencies. For example, thirty or forty minutes involved in mobilizing military aircraft via channels negates the utility of the speed of modern flight in emergencies.

Many civil defense efforts place greater emphasis on nonprofessional community participation than on effectiveness. All medical organizations must be dedicated to the patient rather than the organization. Everyone desires to help in a crisis, but again, it is the patient's needs and not the volunteer's needs that must come first.

E. *Development of the regional network*

If the federal system were to supply the appropriate equipment, hospital staffs could be expected to form and train reserve teams in Phase II resuscitation, intensive care, triage, or field surgery.

1. *Paramedic forces, personnel, and vehicles*

Many fire departments and municipal and county organizations are now establishing emergency medical forces. Paramedics are receiving training varying from 81 to 1,000 hours. These paramedics have integrated into systems that include radio-controlled rescue ambulances, telemetry to base hospitals, and special emergency departments. The cost of these systems has been inadequately borne by the federal government under the Emergency Medical Systems Act of 1973. Equipment supplied under the Federal Civil Defense Act of 1950 has often been present in the community but unavailable to the emergency medical systems organizations. As in the case of the hospitals, it is expected that vehicular, communication, and direct care equipment will have to be supplied on a federal basis.

2. *Regional command and control post*

Most communities have a civilian defense or police command and control post available for local disasters. These posts will require integration into the national system and appropriate communication links. Suitable terminals will be required.

3. *Field medical personnel*

Although reliance can presumably be placed on reserve volunteer medical teams and components of regional public safety forces, some full or post-time personnel will be required to manage the system. Surgical intensive care and resuscitative field forces will be drawn from volunteer units associated with local community hospitals. Equipment will be supplied by the national network.

F. *Education and training*

All personnel components of the system and, particularly hospital medical teams and paramedical teams, will require initial and continuing education and training. This training is not presently available outside of the system, but can be offered by the system directly or on contract via the country's medical schools.

VII. APPLICABILITY TO ALL DISASTERS AND MASS CASUALTY SITUATIONS

It is evident that the system described here has applications beyond terrorism. With a moderate expansion in training and equipment the unified force required to cope with cyclones, floods, earthquakes, large fires, and other mass casualty situations could be developed. The prevention of death by emergency medical rescue is today as much a right of the American citizen as police protection. With the urbanization and growing population of the country, emergency medical rescue and resuscitation can no longer be looked upon as within the scope and capability of local volunteer efforts.

VIII. SUMMARY AND CONCLUSIONS

1. Terrorist attacks represent a significant medical threat to life and limb of large numbers of American citizens.
2. The belief that victims of terrorist and other mass casualty disasters are totally unsalvageable is in conflict with current military and civilian emergency medical experience. The health profession and the federal government have a responsibility for preparation and provision of optimum rescue and medical care for the victims of terrorist attack.
3. The public knowledge that American victims of terror will be cared for by an expert organization that can be rapidly mobilized will contribute to negation of the essential weapon of terror—public fear and panic.
4. Analysis indicates that the medical consequences of widely disparate modes of terrorist weaponry are amenable to relatively standardized, straightforward rescue and resuscitation algorithms. Care can be initiated by inexpensively trained paramedic personnel utilizing on-shelf equipment and materials. Radiotelemetry control by hospital-based emergency department physicians provides immediate command and control that guarantees the level of medical care.
5. A program to prevent and cope with the individual effects of terror will require a real-time management information system, appropriate national resource allocation, utilization of existing civilian emergency medical systems and proliferation of such systems, stockpiles of material, and a national training program for paramedic and other medical personnel.

BIBLIOGRAPHY

Adgey, A. A. J., et al. "Acute Phase of Myocardial Infarction." *Lancet* 2:501 (1971).

Ayres, S. M.; Giannelli, S., Jr.; Mueller, H. S.; and Buehler, M. D. *Care of the Critically Ill.* 2nd ed. New York: Appleton-Century-Crofts, 1974.

Baker, George W., and Chapman, Dwight W. *Man and Society in Disaster.* New York: Basic Books, 1962.

Ballinger, W. F., Rutherford, R. B., and Zuidema, G. D. *The Management of Trauma.* 2nd ed. Philadelphia: W. B. Saunders Co., 1973.

Beeson, P. B., and McDermott, W. *Cecil-Loeb Textbook of Medicine.* 12th ed. Philadelphia: W. B. Saunders Co., 1967.

Bendixen, H. H.; Egbert, L. D.; Hedley-Whyte, J.; Laver, M. B.; and Pontoppidan, H. *Respiratory Care.* St. Louis: C. V. Mosby Co., 1965.

Black, E. A., ed. *The Study of Injured Patients: A Trauma Conference Report.* DHEW NIH 74-603. February 1973.

Blakely, J. *The Care of Radiation Casualties.* Springfield, Ill.: Charles C. Thomas, 1968.

Blakemore, W. E., and Fitts, W. T., Jr., eds. *Management of the Injured Patient.* New York: Harper and Row, 1969.

Boesch, F. T., ed. *Large-Scale Networks: Theory and Design.* New York: IEEE Press, 1976.

Bower, W. F., and Hughes, C. W. *Surgical Philosophy in Mass Casualty Management.* Springfield, Ill.: Charles C. Thomas, 1960.

Burrows, W. *Textbook of Microbiology.* Philadelphia: W. B. Saunders Co., 1973.

Cameron, M., Wilkinson, F., and Hampton, J. R. "Follow-Up of Emergency Ambulance Calls in Nottingham: Implications for Coronary Ambulance Service." *British Medical Journal* 1:384 (1975).

Care for the Injured Child. By the Surgical Staff, The Hospital for Sick Children, Toronto. Baltimore: Williams and Wilkins Co., 1975.

Cave, E. F., Burke, J. F., and Boyd, R. J. *Trauma Management.* Chicago: Year Book Medical Publishers, 1974.

Clemesdon, D. J. "Blast Injury." *Physiology Review* 36:336 (1956).

Coppel, D. L., and Gray, R. C. Scientific Abstracts. *First World Congress on Intensive Care,* 1974.

Crockard, H. A., Coppel, D. L., and Morrow, W. F. K. "Evaluation of

Hyperventilation in Treatment of Head Injuries." *British Medical Journal* 4:634 (1973).

Dewar, H. A., McCullom, J. P. K., and Floyd, M. "A Year's Experience with a Mobile Coronary Resuscitation Unit." *British Medical Journal* 4:226 (1969).

Disaster and Emergency Medical Services for Infants and Children. Evanston, Ill.: American Academy of Pediatrics, 1972.

Early Care of the Injured Patient. By the Committee on Trauma, American College of Surgeons. Philadelphia: W. B. Saunders Co., 1972.

Flint, T., Jr., and Cain, H. D. *Emergency Treatment and Management.* 4th ed. Philadelphia: W. B. Saunders Co., 1970.

Fox, C. L. "The Role of Alkaline Sodium Salt Solutions in the Treatment of Severe Burns." *Annals of the New York Academy of Sciences* 150:823 (1968).

Fox, C. L., et al. "Silver Sulfadiazine—A New Topical Therapy for Therapy of Pseudomonas Infection Burns." *Archives of Surgery* 96:184 (1968).

Frank, H., and Frisch, I. T. "Network Analysis." *Scientific American* 223: 94 (July 1970).

Fu, W. R. *Angiography of Trauma.* Springfield, Ill.: Charles C. Thomas, 1972.

Goldin, M. D. *Intensive Care of the Surgical Patient.* Chicago: Year Book Medical Publishers, 1971.

Gordon, D. S. "Missile Wounds of the Head and Spine." *British Medical Journal* 1:614 (1975).

Grah, R. C., and Coppel, D. L. "Intensive Care of Patients with Bomb Blast and Gunshot Injuries." *British Medical Journal* 1:502 (1975).

Greenwalt, T. J., ed. *General Principles of Blood Transfusion.* Chicago: American Medical Association, 1970.

Hall, A. D. *A Methodology for Systems Engineering.* Princeton, N.J.: D. Van Nostrand Co., 1962.

Hart, R. J.; Lee, J. O.; Boyles, D. J.; and Batey, N. R. "The Summerland Disaster." *British Medical Journal* 1:256 (1975).

Health Aspects of Chemical and Biological Weapons. Geneva: World Health Organization. 1970.

Healy, Richard J. *Emergency and Disaster Planning.* New York: John Wiley and Sons, 1969.

Hieronimus, T. W. *Mechanical Artificial Ventilation.* 2nd ed. Springfield, Ill.: Charles C. Thomas, 1971.

Hindle, J. F.; Plewes, L. W.; and Taylor, R. G. "Accident and Emergency

Services in Russia." *British Medical Journal* 1:445 (1975).

Huckstep, R. L. *A Simple Guide to Trauma.* Baltimore: Williams and Wilkins Co., 1970.

Kennedy, T. L., and Johnston, G. W. "Civilian Bomb Injuries." *British Medical Journal* 1:382 (1975).

Kerr, A. G., and Byrne, J. E. T. "Blast Injuries of the Ear." *British Medical Journal* 1:559 (1975).

Livingstone, R. H., and Wilson, R. I. "Gunshot Wounds of the Limbs." *British Medical Journal* 1:667 (1975).

Lowbury, E. J., et al. "A Cabinet for the Detection of Fluorescent Bacterial Cultures." *Journal of Clinical Pathology* 15:339 (1962).

Lowbury, E. J., et al. "Alternative Forms for Local Treatment for Burns." *Lancet* 2:1105 (1971).

McCaughey, W., Coppel, D. O., and Dundee, J. W. "Blast Injuries to the Lungs: A Report of Two Cases." *Anaesthesia* 28:2 (1973).

McNair, T. J., ed. *Hamilton Bailey's Emergency Surgery.* Baltimore: Williams and Wilkins Co., 1972.

Macon, N., and McKendree, J. D. "Emisari Revisited: The Resource Interruption Monetary System." Proceedings of the Second International Conference on Computer Communication, August 1974, Stockholm.

Madding, G. F., and Kennedy, P. A. *Trauma to the Liver.* 2nd ed. Philadelphia: W. B. Saunders Co., 1971.

Miller, R. H., and Cantrell, J. R., eds. *Textbook of Basic Emergency Medicine.* St. Louis: C. V. Mosby Co., 1975.

Moore, F. D.; Lyons, J. D., Jr.; Pierce, E. C., Jr.; Morgan, A. P., Jr.; Drinker, P. A.; MacArthur, J. D.; and Dammin, G. J. *Post-Traumatic Pulmonary Insufficiency.* Philadelphia: W. B. Saunders Co., 1969.

Moseley, H. F., ed. *Accident Surgery.* New York: Appleton-Century-Crofts, 1962.

Mushin, W. W.; Rendell-Baker, L.; Thompson, P. W.; and Mapleson, W. W. *Automatic Ventilation of the Lungs.* Philadelphia: F. A. Davis Co., 1969.

Orkin, L. A. *Trauma to the Ureter.* Philadelphia: F. A. Davis Co., 1964.

Phillips, R. E., and Feeney, M. K. *The Cardiac Rhythms.* Philadelphia: W. B. Saunders Co., 1973.

Rutherford, W. H. "Disaster Procedures." *British Medical Journal* 1:443 (1975).

Sandler, G., and Pistevos, A. "Mobile Coronary Care: The Coronary Ambulance." *British Heart Journal* 34:1283 (1972).

Schwartz, S. I. *Principles of Surgery*. New York: McGraw-Hill Book Co., 1969.

Shires, G. T., Carrico, D. J., and Canizaro, P. C. *Shock*. Philadelphia: W. B. Saunders Co., 1973.

Smith, C. A. *The Critically Ill Child*. Philadelphia: W. B. Saunders Co., 1972.

Stephenson, H. D., Jr. *Cardiac Arrest and Resuscitation*. 4th ed. St. Louis: C. V. Mosby Co., 1974.

Stevenson, H. M., and Wilson, W. "Gunshot Wounds of the Trunk." *British Medical Journal* 1:728 (1975).

Thal, A. P.; Brown, E. B., Jr.; Hermreck, A. S.; and Bell, H. H. *Shock*. Chicago: Year Book Medical Publishers, 1971.

Turoff, M. "Computerized Conferencing," "Party Line," and "Discussion," Proceedings of the First International Conference on Computer Communication, October 1972, Washington, D.C.

Waddell, G.; Scott, P. D. R.; Lees, N. W.; and Ledingham, I. M. C. A. "Effects of Ambulance Transport in Critically Ill Patients." *British Medical Journal* 1:386 (1975).

Walt, A. J., and Wilson, R. F. *Management of Trauma: Pitfalls and Practice*. Philadelphia: Lea and Febiger, 1975.

Waterworth, T. A., and Carr, M. J. T. "An Analysis of the Post-Mortem Findings in the 21 Victims of the Birmingham Pub Bombings." *Injury* 7:89, 1975.

Waterworth, T. A., and Carr, M. J. T. "Report on Injuries Sustained by Patients Treated at The Birmingham General Hospital Following the Recent Bomb Explosions." *British Medical Journal* 2:25 (1975).

Weil, M. H., and Shubin, H. *Critical Care Medicine Handbook*. New York: John N. Kolen, 1974.

White, N. M., et al. "Mobile Coronary Care Provided by Ambulance Personnel." *British Medical Journal* 3:618 (1973).

Whittenberger, J. L., ed. *Artificial Respiration*. New York: Harper and Row, 1962.

Wilson, I. V., and Tunbridge, R. E. "Pathological Findings in a Series of Blast Injuries." *Lancet* 257 (1943).

Zuckerman, S. "Experimental Study of Blast Injuries to the Lungs." *Lancet* 2:219 (1940).

Zuckerman, S. "The Problem of Blast Injury." *Proceedings of the Royal Society of Medicine* 34:171 (1943).

Hostage Confrontation and Rescue

FRANCIS A. BOLZ, JR.

In the years since that fateful day of September 5, 1972, in Munich, Germany, many hostage situations have occurred, but none so indelibly inscribed as the "Olympic Tragedy." During the course of the eighteen and a half hours this event encompassed, eleven Israeli athletes, five Black September Arabs, and one Munich policeman lost their lives. Three other Arab commandos were captured; as the result of another airplane hijack, they were later released. This episode, as it unfolded, was destined to become the classic hostage confrontation, one that would be the basis for the formulation of plans and guidelines by the New York City Police Department for dealing with this new form of criminality.

At 4:00 A.M. on September 5, 1972, eight Arab terrorists, armed with automatic weapons as well as ten hand grenades packed in athletic bags, gained entry to the Olympic Village by scaling a small fence. The civilian security guards were accustomed to "not seeing" athletes who might be out beyond the training curfew, climbing over these fences. The commandos split up into two groups and proceeded to enter the building that housed the Israel Olympic team. Four entered through the basement and four via the front door. A confrontation took place at the apartment door where a coach was shot as he attempted to slam the door and an athlete was shot as he tried to escape. Nine athletes were taken hostage and kept prisoners in several rooms. The rest of the team managed to escape and sound the alarm that "four" terrorists were holding the nine athletes hostage.

Selection of this location was apparently not by chance. During the Olympic games, news writers from all over the world, numbering in excess of 3,000, were in Munich to ensure global coverage. By 8:00 A.M. on that September day the entire world was aware of the events unfolding and the resultant deaths.

Between 8:00 and 10:00 A.M. various attempts at negotiation were made by the local police and the German Government, as well as many foreign diplomatic personnel at the highest levels, to effect the release of the hostages. Each of these efforts was fruitless as were the offers of money, alternate hostages, and safe conduct out of Germany. The Arabs demanded the release of some two hundred Arab prisoners who were being held in Israeli prisons. Israel, considering itself in a state of war, would not consider it. The Arabs also warned the Federal Republic that if the Israeli athletes were taken from Germany, their lives would probably be lost. For this reason the officials were requested not to permit Israelis to be taken from Germany. At this time one of the Israelis who had escaped noted that the Arab who was negotiating was, in fact, an additional man and not one of the "four" he remembered. Attributing the miscount to the excitement at the time, the police updated their intelligence information to prepare for five perpetrators.

The only remaining solution was liberation by force. Deadlines were set and passed, but the possibility of more deaths constantly loomed. Because the building was constructed like a fortress, direct assault would surely cost police lives. In addition, it was unlikely that they would be able to rescue the hostages before their captors executed them, so plans for direct assault were scrapped. (There was no chemical agent that would work so fast that the captors would be deterred from killing their hostages.)

A plan had to be devised that would bring the Arabs and their hostages out of the building to a location that would afford the police a better tactical advantage. It was decided that an airplane would be brought to the old NATO airport at Fürstenfeldbruck and passage would be given the captors and the athletes to the airport. At that location, marksmen would then be used to neutralize the Arabs and bring about the safe release of the hostages. A second airport nearby had to be covered in the event the Arabs diverted to that location.

German law at that time was not specific as to whether an

order to shoot to kill could be given. At the end of World War II the Federal Republic of Germany abolished capital punishment. The necessity to direct the sharpshooters to kill the terrorists created a strong psychological problem among the police personnel. Each airport was covered by five sharpshooters, as the new intelligence had indicated there were five captors.

At approximately 9:00 P.M., the hostages and their captors were moved from the Israeli compound by bus to the makeshift helipad near the Olympic Village, then by two helicopters to the Fürstenfeldbruck airport. At this time the deficiency of the police intelligence first came to light. It was ascertained that instead of five perpetrators, there were actually eight.

Because of the quick succession of events, the police were unable to increase the number of sharpshooters at the airports to coincide with the number of terrorists. A plan was quickly developed whereby it was assumed that the leaders themselves would probably want to check out the airplane while the hostages were still in the helicopters. As soon as possible they were to be neutralized and then the rest would probably capitulate. Two captors did check out the aircraft. As they returned to their helicopter the order was given and they were shot by police sharpshooters. One was killed almost instantly, the second only wounded.

But the other terrorists did not capitulate. Instead a hand grenade was thrown into one helicopter and the other helicopter was machine-gunned. When the shooting stopped, all nine hostages, five Arabs, and one Munich policeman were dead. Three Arabs were captured.

And so the tragic events ended, but not the memory or the lessons learned that day.

Because of these events and the possibility of similar confrontations taking place in New York City, the United Nations capital of the world, a plan was needed to cope with such criminality.

Chief Simon Eisdorfer, the Commanding Officer of the Special Operations Division of the NYCPD, called together representatives of the Police Academy, the Patrol Division, the Emergency Service Unit, the Detective Bureau, and Dr. Harvey Schlossberg of the Psychological Services Section. (The author had the privilege of representing the Detective Bureau.) A set of guidelines for dealing with barricaded felons and hostage situations was developed that sought to eliminate any impulsive or uncoordinated actions which might unnecessarily cost human life. Various specific responsibilities and functions based on past experience and ability fell to the Patrol Division, Emergency Service Section, and the Detective Bureau.

Patrol Division

The Patrol Officers are usually first on the scene. Their duties are the initial confrontation and containment of the perpetrator, the evacuation of innocent bystanders and neighbors, and the gathering of the initial intelligence of the operation. In addition, in New York City, in order to ensure unity of command, clear-cut authority, and responsibility, the Patrol Borough Commander is in charge of the entire situation, with Specialty Units acting as staff personnel. The reason for this command framework is that the senior officer, who is most familiar with the locality involved, will be able to make more knowledgeable decisions. He will also be left to deal with the community when the Specialty Units pack up their "hardware" and move on. Thus, the borough commander makes the decisions as to whether or not deadly physical force will be used in a controlled and contained situation. Of course, this does not preclude the use of force in a personal emergency involving self-defense. (Note: Good cover and a "display of force" will usually discourage any charge by the perpetrator.)

Emergency Service

The Emergency Service Division is the firearms battalion of the New York City Police Department. Over two hundred men and women are specially trained in rescue techniques and are charged with bringing the trucks and rescue equipment as well as the heavy weaponry of the department to the scene of hostage confrontations.

Well-trained and disciplined, they come equipped with bullet-resistant garments and body armor, shotguns, scoped rifles, machine guns, tear gas, and sufficient walkie-talkie radios on a dedicated frequency to ensure clear and unimpeded communication within the inner perimeter of the operation. The Emergency Service personnel relieve the Patrol Forces who initially contained the perpetrator, so that they may assume control of the outer perimeter and crowd control.

Detective Bureau

Detectives traditionally have been charged with investigation, interrogation, and interviews. This experience gives them certain lay psychological insights that, coupled with extensive clinical training, make them extremely well qualified to act as negotiators in hostage confrontations. They are also charged with the establishment of liaison with other departments and agencies and with the control and operation of the mobile portion of the plan if movement from one location to another is required to gain tactical advantage.

Phases of the Plan

The plan, based upon what was learned in Munich, was structured in three parts, which are called phases. Patrol, Emergency, and Detective Units respond and carry out specifically delineated duties and responsibilities.

Phase I is the location of the site at which the hostage is held. This is where the captor and his hostage are contained and police personnel and resources are consolidated. This is also where the all-important gathering of intelligence must start and continue throughout the entire operation. The effect of this operation upon the community is greatly influenced by the initial response and the control and discipline of firepower on the part of Patrol and Emergeny Service Units. Communication via a dedicated special radio frequency enables all police personnel directly involved to be informed as to what is taking place. By eliminating any ignorance of the situation, we eliminate fear. By eliminating fear, we cut down on the possibility of uncontrolled gunfire on the part of the police. This phase is parallel to the Israeli compound in Munich.

Phase II is the mobile portion of the operation. If a demand is made for a vehicle or transportation to another location that would afford a tactical advantage, removing the operation from a fortress-like location, as in Munich, to another location, we would accomplish this in a controlled operation on wheels. The same discipline and coordination are carried out from the Phase I location to the destination. The Detective Bureau is responsible for and in command of the caravan as it moves from one location to another. Should the captor alight from the vehicle and take up a new location, the detectives escorting the procession would take up containment positions and lock the perpetrator into this new location, pending the moving up of the Emergency Service Unit, which we would consider Phase III.

Phase III is for all intents and purposes a duplication of Phase I in that containment, consolidation, and intelligence are commenced again, with the Emergency Service moving up to relieve the detectives on containment positions. It is not inconceivable that a situation could leapfrog to three or four locations before it was concluded. During each of these moves, though it is tricky for the police and we would prefer not to move, it is also difficult for the perpetrator and we are constantly ready to seize the advantage if he makes a mistake.

Courses of Action

There are, in hostage situations generally, four courses of action that can be may followed:

1. Direct Assault   At any time, with personnel equipped with body armor and cut-down shotguns, we can assault the location where the perpetrator is holding hostages. However, we must know many things before we attempt this: the layout of the building or apartment, the number of perpetrators and their armament, whether or not they may have changed clothing, and so on. A premature charge could cost the lives of police officers as well as the hostages.

2. Selected Sharpshooters   We have the capability of staying long distances from the captor and, with rifles equipped with 9-power scopes, of shooting the captor without exposing ourselves. Again, intelligence is extremely important. On one occasion, in another jurisdiction, a hostage was used as a shield for the perpetrator to look out of a window and a rifle appeared to be protruding from under the arm of the hostage. A sharp-shooter saw the weapon and fired, killing the hostage in the window. Other possible barriers exist. If we shoot one perpetrator, a second or third might feel all is lost and kill the hostage and himself.

3. Chemical Agents   We have the capability and equipment to flood an area with tear gas in order to hamper the captor, but no gas is so fast working that it will immobilize the him, preventing him from killing hostages before we can rescue them. In addition, we must know if a hostage suffers from any respiratory ailment that might be adversely affected by tear gas. We must also consider the atmosphere in the location where we contemplate using the gas. The most effective chemical agent projectiles are the "hot" burning type that produce a gas, yet these have been known to start fires. All of this must be considered from an intelligence point of view.

4. Contain and Negotiate   This is the format of the plan used in New York. Note that the first three courses of action are violence-oriented, and once committed to an action, it is unlikely that we will be able to deescalate. But if containment and negotiation fail, we can move up the scale of our tactics, fortified with more intelligence than we would have had at the outset.

Why Negotiate?

The locking in of a perpetrator will generally stop the action in a given situation. This cessation in and of itself will help the situation somewhat. We utilize negotiators to buy time from the perpetrators, thereby permitting transference to take place between the captor and his hostages.

The term "transference" and the phenomenon might best be explained by example. Did you ever notice when traveling by air how extremely friendly the other passengers are? They will start up a conversation with a total stranger, tell him where they are going, whom they are going to see, and so on, and even show photos of their kids or grandchildren. Why? Because they are afraid of flying. They are in a crisis and they seek other human beings with whom to share this crisis. On the other hand, if a fellow starts talking to a young lady on the local subway or bus, she is apt to hit him on the head with her pocketbook or call a cop to have him stop bothering her.

This transference, or crisis adjustment, is the phenomenon that keeps hostages, perpetrators, and negotiators alive in these life-and-death situations. The more time spent together, the less likelihood that the captor will take the hostage's life.

Negotiation actually treats these people in crisis situations and engages them in a form of therapy to alleviate the anxiety and tensions that the captor is experiencing. This training and experience are based upon the theories and program established by Dr. Harvey Schlossberg, who was a full-time detective in the New York City Police Department, as well as the director of the department's Psychological Services Bureau. Working with other members of the NYCPD, Dr. Schlossberg developed profiles of the hostage-taker type. They fall into three (oversimplified) categories:

1. The Professional Criminal   He is the man who robs banks or stores for a living. While committing a holdup, his escape is blocked and he takes a hostage as a "ticket to freedom." He is, perhaps, the easiest to deal with. He is rational, and after a given period of time will generally see the futility of getting further involved or, perhaps, getting killed over a simple holdup. Weighing the odds, he will come to terms with the police.

2. The Psychotic: A Person with Psychological Problems This type presents a difficult and more complex problem. He tends to be irrational and is, therefore, less predictable in his action. An inadequate personality, he now finds himself in a position of great power and generally unable to handle this new-found authority. He is usually highly charged and emotionally tense. By treating this anxiety we expend a great deal of his physical and psychological energies, bringing him down to a position where he can rationalize and accept help.

3. The Terrorist Group   These persons are the most difficult to deal with. Many rationalize their behavior as necessary to put forward their "cause" Many are charged up, as were the kamikaze pilots of World War II, ready to die for their cause. Time influences their decisions, and the resolve to die deteriorates as time passes. It also permits them to make mistakes that we must always be ready to capitalize on.

We will negotiate almost anything, with two exceptions:

1. Weapons If the subject has a bogus weapon or no ammunition, giving him a weapon would create a real danger.

2. Additional Hostages We do not exchange hostages: whoever the captor has in the beginning is who he will keep throughout. We especially would not exchange police personnel. This would change an objective operation to a subjective operation if one of the "police family" were being held. This is much like a doctor operating on his own children. It is not done because of the emotional problems involved.

Credibility must be maintained. You cannot be caught in a lie to the perpetrator, otherwise you will be useless as a negotiator. The negotiator is the semiauthority figure between the captor and the ultimate authority.

Why Detective Negotiators?

It takes a singular type of individual to deal unarmed, face-to-face with an armed felon holding a hostage. He must be cool, resourceful, mature, and, above all, effective in verbal communication. Successful detectives have developed these attributes through their experience in dealing with the public, interviewing witnesses, and interrogating suspects.

Selection of Negotiators

Following are some of the criteria used to select the members of the Hostage Negotiating Team:

Volunteers only
Good physical condition, psychologically sound
Mature appearance
Good speaking voice, outgoing

Skilled interrogators

Representatives of various ethnic and racial groups with, if possible, the ability to speak a foreign language, college education, and other special qualifications

Over seventy members of the Detective Bureau have been selected and trained as hostage negotiators, two of whom are women, twelve blacks, twelve Hispanics, and the balance Caucasians. The languages spoken by the group include Italian, Spanish, German, Hebrew, Yiddish, Greek, Polish, Portuguese, Russian, Ukrainian, and Croatian. In addition, other members of the department who are not members of the group speak Arabic, Chinese, and Japanese and are available as translators.

Training of Negotiators

The group underwent an intensive four-week training course conducted at various locations throughout the city as well as in the classroom. Training consisted of the following subjects:

Psychology   The greatest emphasis was placed on intensive psychological training to prepare team members to analyze various situations and develop strategies using psychological techniques rather than force to obtain the safe release of hostages. The point of this training was to provide a basis for understanding and anticipating the hostage-taker's moves as well as his possible reactions to police tactics. Role-playing and the use of crisis intervention therapy were learned.

Physical Training   This encompassed general upgrading of physical condition as well as weapon-disarming methods and techniques of unarmed self-defense.

Firearms   Firearms training included the qualification with .38 caliber revolver, 9mm submachine gun, .223 caliber sniper, scope rifle, shotgun (double barrel and pump), 37mm tear gas launcher, .25 caliber automatic, and .22 caliber Derringer. Candidates wore bullet-proof vests during the firing of all weapons.

Electronic Equipment   All members were familiarized with and had to qualify in the use of a miniphone wireless transmitter and recorder and in the use of electronic tracking devices that utilize range and relative-bearing features, which can be quite valuable in Phase II.

Emergency Rescue Ambulance   Each team member learned to operate the emergency rescue ambulance, a full-track armored personnel carrier. This training also included the use of its auxiliary equipment; that is, the public address system, intercom, radio equipment, fire-fighting system, and first-aid gear. The ERA has been used to establish contact with heavily armed, barricaded hostage-takers.

Vehicle Operation   Instruction was given in the operation of escape and chase vehicles. Special attention was paid to those streets and routes from various locations in the city to airports or other destinations that would offer the team the best tactical advantage.

Liaison   Hostage-team candidates received two days of training on jurisdictional matters and cooperation with other agencies, including the FBI and the Federal Aviation Administration. One day of training was held at John F. Kennedy International Airport and LaGuardia Airport with the Port of New York and New Jersey Authority Police, where the team integrated its plan with their emergency programs.

Retraining   In addition to this initial program, debriefings are scheduled to critique every significant hostage situation that takes place anywhere in the world. During such critiques, "Monday morning quarterbacking" and speculations are encouraged. From the situations under study, officers gain new insights and learn new techniques.

Working Detectives

Members of the Detective Bureau Hostage Negotiating Team are working detectives who are assigned to various squads throughout the city. Once their training as hostage negotiators is completed, they return to their permanent commands, resume their normal investigative duties, and are called to respond to situations as they occur.

Since no two hostage situations are alike, there can be no standardized format, only guidelines. Each situation is treated as it unfolds, but the discipline of firepower and communication seems to permit the subsequent portions of the program to take effect. The one overriding principle that permeates the entire program is that life is sacred—the life of the hostage, of the police officer, and even of the captor.

The "New York Plan," as it has been labeled by law enforcement agencies that have been trained by Dr. Schlossberg and me, has been used effectively in many jurisdictions in the United States and Canada. Our department has shared its experience with other departments and other countries. The program has been applied successfully throughout the world. Since the program's inception in 1973, we have never lost a hostage, police officer, or even a perpetrator.

We are aware that we could at some future time lose a hostage, but this does not mean we will shelve the program. We have saved lives and shall continue to try to save lives. This is no accident. The overriding principle of our program is "The life of the hostage is the most important consideration of this program."

Contributors

YONAH ALEXANDER is Professor of International Studies and Director of the Institute for Studies in International Terrorism at the State University of New York, and concurrently directs that university's Seminars on Terrorism held in London, Geneva, and Jerusalem. He is also a research associate of the Center for Strategic and International Studies (Georgetown University) and a member of the International Institute for Strategic Studies (London). Holder of degrees from Columbia University (Ph.D.) and the University of Chicago (M.A.), Dr. Alexander has taught and done research in Europe, Asia, the Middle East, and Latin America, as well as in the United States and Canada. He is editor-in-chief of *Terrorism: An International Journal*, and is author, editor, or co-editor of ten books, including *Terrorism: Interdisciplinary Perspectives; International Terrorism*; and *Terrorism; Theory and Practice.*

JAMES P. BENNETT is Assistant Professor of Regional Science and Co-director of the Peace Science Unit at the University of Pennsylvania. Dr. Bennett has also taught at the University of North Carolina (Chapel Hill) and was a Peace Corps volunteer in Turkey. He has written a number of articles on political affairs, national security, and international relations. He holds a B.A. degree with honors from Harvard College and a Ph.D. from the Massachusetts Institute of Technology.

FRANCIS A. BOLZ, JR., is a captain in the New York City Police Department and has been the coordinator of the department's Hostage Negotiating Team since its inception in early 1973. He has personally and successfully negotiated almost a dozen cases and responded to over 75 percent of the hostage call-outs in New

York City (an average of twenty-two a year), gaining the safe release of more than two hundred hostages. With Dr. Harvey Schlossberg, Captain Bolz devised a training method for negotiators; and they have now trained, in addition to over seventy members of the NYCPD's Hostage Negotiating Team, representatives from more than fifteen hundred domestic and foreign law-enforcement agencies, including the U.S. Secret Service, the U.S. State Department, and the FBI. Captain Bolz received a B.S. degree from the John Jay College of Criminal Justice.

BRIAN JENKINS is a senior staff member at the Rand Corporation in Santa Monica, California. Since 1973 Mr. Jenkins has been engaged in research on international terrorism. He has written extensively on the subject, his works including *International Terrorism: Trends and Potentialities; International Terrorism: A New Mode of Conflict; Will Terrorists Go Nuclear?; Hostage Survival: Some Preliminary Observations*; and "International Terrorism: A Chronology 1968–1974." Mr. Jenkins is a consultant for the Nuclear Regulatory Commission and for the Military Department of the State of California. He has appeared as an expert witness before Congressional committees investigating international terrorism and currently directs several studies dealing with various modes of political violence and contemporary conflict.

BOWMAN H. MILLER is a research analyst in the Directorate of Counterintelligence of the Air Force Office of Special Investigations in Washington, D.C. He has studied at Georgetown, Cornell, and George Washington Universities, and in West Germany at the Universität Bonn and at the Universität Tübingen, where he was a Fulbright-Hayes Scholar. In collaboration with Dr. Charles A. Russell, he has written several articles, including "Profile of a Terrorist," "Out-Inventing the Terrorist," and "Transnational Terrorism: Terrorist Tactics and Techniques." Mr. Miller is currently a captain in the U.S. Air Force.

CHARLES A. RUSSELL is an associate of Risks International in Alexandria, Virginia. Dr. Russell has written and lectured extensively on the subject of terrorism, his publications including "The Urban Guerrilla," "The Urban Guerrilla in Latin America: A Select Bibliography," and several articles in collaboration with

Bowman H. Miller. Dr. Russell is a member of the Bar of the U.S. Court of Appeals and of the U.S. Court of Military Appeals, and holds advanced degrees from Georgetown University (J.D.) and American University (Ph.D.).

THOMAS SAATY is a professor at the Wharton School of the University of Pennsylvania, his subjects being operations research, social systems science, applied mathematics, energy management and power, peace science, civil engineering, and decision science. He is currently Director of the Sudan Transport Study. Dr. Saaty has served as a consultant for numerous foundations, government agencies and departments, and private corporations, and has published more than one hundred research articles and books. He received a Ph.D. from Yale University and also did postgraduate work at the University of Paris.

MARTIN E. SILVERSTEIN is Chief of the Section on Trauma in the Department of Surgery at the University of Arizona College of Medicine. Dr. Silverstein has served as a consultant for a variety of government and other public service organizations and was an associate dean of the New York Medical College. He is a leading researcher in the field of trauma medicine and has published some thirty articles on that subject. In 1978 he jointly patented both a noninvasive, ultrasonic means of measuring cardiac blood flow and a bypass intraluminal occlusion device. He received his M.D. from New York Medical College.

HARVEY A. SMITH is Chairman of the Department of Mathematics at Arizona State University. Holder of advanced degrees from the University of Pennsylvania (M.S., M.A., and Ph.D.), Dr. Smith has taught at Oakland University, the University of Pennsylvania, the Drexel Institute of Technology, and the University of Maryland. He has worked for both government and industry and during 1968–1970 was the Chief Deputy of the Systems Evaluation Division of the President's Office of Emergency Preparedness. Dr. Smith has written extensively on applications of mathematics to complex social problems and has served as a consultant for the Arms Control and Disarmament Agency, the Executive Office of the President, and several private corporations.

MAYNARD STEPHENS is Professor of Petroleum Engineering and Director of Special Projects in the Department of Mechanical Engineering at Tulane University. Dr. Stephens has had more than forty years of experience as a hard- and soft-rock geologist, earth scientist, and registered professional engineer (petroleum and mining). Currently the principal scientist for energy projects of the Gulf South Research Institute, he has for the past five years conducted studies of the Gulf Coastal area on the vulnerability, operations, economics, and environmental problems of the petroleum and natural gas industry. He received a Ph.D. from the University of Minnesota and a P.E. (postgraduate degree in petroleum engineering) from Pennsylvania State College.

DONALD A. WATERMAN is a computer scientist at the Rand Corporation in Santa Monica, California, where he is engaged in work on the design of a rule-based language for exemplary programming. Before joining the staff at Rand, he was associated with Carnegie-Mellon University, where he performed research in both cognitive psychology and artificial intelligence. He is the author of many articles and monographs, particularly on the subject of artificial intelligence. Dr. Waterman holds an M.S. degree from the University of California at Berkeley and M.S. and Ph.D. degrees from Stanford University.

RICHARD H. WILCOX is Special Assistant for Information Systems in the Weapons Evaluation and Control Bureau of the U.S. Arms Control and Disarmament Agency. Before assuming this position, Mr. Wilcox established and directed the ACDA Arms Transfer Division, participating directly in the federal government's review of proposed foreign military sales from the United States and in the development of national policy concerning such sales. Mr. Wilcox has also held a variety of management positions in the President's Office of Emergency Preparedness and for ten years was on the staff of the Office of Naval Research, receiving a patent on a microwave correlator based on his original work there. He holds the professional degree of Electrical Engineer from Lafayette College and a Master of Engineering degree from George Washington University.

Notes

FOREWORD

1. Their publications include M. Funke, ed., *Terrorismus: Untersuchungen zur Struktur and Strategie revolutionärer Gewaltpolitik* (Kronberg: Athenum-Verlag 1977); H. Luebbe, *Endstation Terror* (Stuttgart: Seewald, 1978); Bergedorfer Gesprächskreis, *Terrorismus in der demokratischen Gesellschaft* (Hamburg, 1978); H. Geissler, ed., *Der Weg in die Gewalt* (Munich: Olzog, 1978); H. Glaser, "Die Diskussion über den Terrorismus," *Aus Politik und Zeit Geschichte*, June 24, 1978.

2. Robert S. Frank, *The Prediction of Political Violence from Objective and Subjective Social Indicators* (Edinburgh: International Psychoanalytical Congress, 1976).

3. *Die Zeit*, September 16, 1977.

4. *Die Neue Gessellschaft* 7, 1978.

5. J. Habermas et al., *Gespräche mit Herbert Marcuse* (Frankfurt am Main: Surkamp, 1978), p. 150.

6. Geissler, *Der Weg in die Gewalt*, p. 65.

7. G. Schmidtchen, *"Bewaffnete Heilslehren,"* in ibid., p. 39; and Luebbe, *Endstation Terror*, passim.

8. W. Middendorff, in Giessler, *Der Weg in die Gewalt*, p. 182.

INTRODUCTION

1. The Harris Survey, Chicago Tribune-New York News Syndicate, December 5, 1977.

2. Brian Michael Jenkins, *Terrorism: Trends and Potentialities* (Santa Monica, Calif.: Rand Corp., 1977).

3. Walter Laqueur, *Terrorism* (Boston: Little, Brown and Co., 1977).

CHAPTER 1

1. David Fromkin, "The Strategy of Terrorism," *Foreign Affairs*, July 1975, p. 693.

2. Quoted in Walter Laqueur, *Terrorism* (Boston: Little, Brown and Co., 1977), p. 28.

3. Ibid., p. 25.

4. We are indebted to David Fromkin's thought-provoking analysis, "Strategy of Terrorism," for many of the insights in the discussion that follows.

5. See Laqueur, *Terrorism*, pp. 46–48.

6. For a discussion of the factors cited here, see David Milbank, "International and Transnational Terrorism: Diagnosis and Prognosis," Research Study, PR 76 10030 (Washington, D.C.: Central Intelligence Agency, Office of Political Research, April 1976).

7. Ibid., p. 22.

8. See Brian M. Jenkins, "International Terrorism: A New Mode of Conflict," in David Carlton and Carlo Schaerf, eds., *International Terrorism and World Security* (New York: John Wiley and Sons, Halsted Press, 1975), p. 29.

9. For a full, unclassified overview of terrorist trends, see Historical Evaluation and Research Organization, "The Terrorist and Sabotage Threat to United States Nuclear Programs" (Dunn Loring, Va., August 1974).

10. Quoted in Albert Parry, *Terrorism: From Robespierre to Arafat* (New York: Vanguard, 1977), p. 541.

11. Claire Sterling, "The Terrorist Network," *The Atlantic*, November 1978, pp. 37–38.

12. Ibid., p. 41.

13. Jenkins, "International Terrorism," p. 29.

14. R. W. Apple, "A Loose Alliance of Terrorists Does Seem to Exist," *New York Times*, October 23, 1977, sec. 4, p. 1.

15. Ibid.

16. Sterling, "Terrorist Network," pp. 41, 43.

17. Ibid., p. 42.

18. For good general discussions of international support for terrorism, see David Anable, "Terrorism: How a Handful of Radical States Keeps It in Business," *Christian Science Monitor*, March 15, 1977, pp. 14–15; Parry, *Terrorism*, pp. 536–544; and Laqueur, *Terrorism*, pp. 112–116. For a carefully reasoned presentation of the evidence suggesting extensive Soviet involvement, see testimony of Brian Crozier, "Transnational Terrorism," in U.S. Congress, Senate, Committee on the Judiciary, Subcommittee to Investigate the Administration of the Internal Security Act and Other Internal Security Laws, *Terrorist Activity: International Terrorism, Hearings*, 94th Cong., 1st sess., May 14, 1975, Part 4, pp. 179–212.

19. Parry, *Terrorism*, p. 541.

20. Sterling, "Terrorist Network," p. 42.

21. Charles Babcock, "Suspected German Terrorist Arrested Crossing US Border," *Washington Post*, July 21, 1978, p. 1.

22. Brian Jenkins, *International Terrorism: Trends and Potentialities* (Santa Monica, Calif.: Rand Corp., 1977), pp. 8–16.

23. Ibid., p. 53.

24. Ibid., p. 26.

25. Statement of Richard Preyer, in U.S. Congress, House, Committee on Internal Security, *Terrorism, Hearings*, 93rd Cong., 2nd sess., February 27, 1974,

Part 1, p. 2970; and Jerry Rubin, in ibid., p. 4190: "You can't be a revolutionary today without a color TV set—it's as important as a gun."

26. Statement of Dr. Frederick Hacker, in ibid., August 14, 1974, Part 4, p. 3039.

27. David Binder, "Cuban Exile Admits Bombing an Airliner, Killing 73 Aboard," *New York Times*, October 19, 1976, p. 2.

28. Milbank, "International and Transnational Terrorism," p. 18.

29. Henry Tanner, "Terrorist Bombs Severely Damage Rome Power Plant," *New York Times*, June 15, 1978, p. 8.

30. "Israel Cuts Export of Oranges to Europe," *New York Times*, February 10, 1978, p. 7.

31. Walter Laqueur, quoted in "Terrorism: Old Menace in New Guise" (interview), *U.S. News & World Report*, May 22, 1978, p. 35.

CHAPTER 2

1. Ovid Demaris, *Brothers in Blood: The International Terrorist Network* (New York: Charles Scribner and Sons, 1977).

2. SIPRI (Stockholm International Peace Research Institute), *The Problem of Chemical and Biological Warfare*, Vol. 1: *The Rise of CB Weapons* (New York: Humanities Press, 1971).

3. "Terrorist Gangs Reaching for Nerve Gas, Gruesome New Weapons," *Boston Globe*, November 7, 1976; and "Terrorist Use of Gas Feared," *Washington Post*, May 13, 1975.

4. For an excellent unclassified discussion of precision-guided munitions, see James Digby, "Precision-Guided Weapons," Adelphi Paper No. 118 (London: International Institute for Strategic Studies, Summer 1975).

5. Brian Jenkins, *Terrorism: Trends and Potentialities* (Santa Monica, Calif.: Rand Corp., 1977), p. 80.

6. Eric C. Ludvigsen, "The Weapons Directory," *Army*, October 1977, p. 154.

7. Advanced Concepts Research (ADCON Corp.: B. J. Berkowitz et al.), *Superviolence: The Civil Threat of Mass Destruction Weapons* (Santa Barbara, Calif.: ADCON Corp., September 1972); Robert K. Mullen, *The International Clandestine Nuclear Threat* (Gaithersburg, Md.: International Association of Chiefs of Police, 1975); and Robert K. Mullen, *The Clandestine Use of Chemical or Biological Weapons* (Gaithersburg, Md.: International Association of Chiefs of Police, 1978).

8. Advanced Concepts Research, *Superviolence*.

9. Mason Willrich and Theodore Taylor, *Nuclear Theft: Risks and Safeguards* (Cambridge, Mass.: Ballinger Publishing Co., 1974).

10. Ibid.

11. Far more extensive discussions of the effects of nuclear weapons appear in Samuel Glasstone, *The Effects of Nuclear Weapons* (Washington, D.C.: U.S. Energy Research and Development Administration, 1977).

12. Ibid.

13. Robert H. Kupperman, *Facing Tomorrow's Terrorist Incident Today*, Report prepared for the Department of Justice (Washington, D.C.: Government Printing Office, October 1977), p. 4.

14. Robert Morrison and Robert Boyd, *Organic Chemistry* (Boston: Allyn and Bacon, 1959); Advanced Concepts Research, *Superviolence*.

15. Frederick Pattison, *Toxic Aliphatic Fluorine Compounds* (New York: Elsevier Publishing Co., 1959).

16. E. Chadwick, "Actions on Insects and Other Invertebrates," in G. E. Koelle, ed., *Cholinesterases and Anticholinesterase Agents*, Handbuch der experimentallen Pharmakologie (Berlin: Springer-Verlag, 1963), pp. 741–798.

17. Advanced Concepts Research, *Superviolence*; Robert K. Mullen, "Mass Destruction and Terrorism," *Journal of International Affairs*, Spring/Summer 1978, pp. 68–69.

18. Advanced Concepts Research, *Superviolence*.

19. Brian Beckett, "Nerve Gas Secrets Leak Out," *The Observer* (London), November 19, 1978, p. 1.

20. SIPRI, *Problem of Chemical and Biological Warfare*, pp. 86–87.

21. Hans Riemann, "Botulinum Types A, B and F," in Hans Riemann, ed., *Food-Borne Infections and Intoxications* (New York: Academic Press, 1969), pp. 291–327; and G. Hobbs, Kathleen Williams, and A. T. Willis, "Basic Methods for the Isolation of Clostridia," in D. A. Shapta and R. G. Board, eds., *Isolation of Anerobes* (New York: Academic Press, 1969), pp. 1–23.

22. H. D. Hatt and E. F. Lessel, *The American Type Culture Collection (Bacteria)* (New York: American Type Culture Collection, 1974); and U.S. Army, *Military Biology and Biological Agents*, Training Manual TM 3-216 (Washington, D.C., 1964).

23. J. H. Rothschild, *Tomorrow's Weapons: Chemical and Biological* (New York: McGraw-Hill Book Co., 1964).

24. I. W. Dawes and J. Mandelstam, "Biochemistry of Sporulation of *Bacillus subtilis* 168: Continuous Culture Studies," in I. Malek et al., eds., *Continuous Cultivation of Microorganisms* (New York: Academic Press, 1969), pp. 157–162; and J. Ricica, "Sporulation of *Bacillus cereus* in Multistage Continuous Cultivation," in ibid., pp. 163–172.

25. Advanced Concepts Research, *Superviolence*.

26. National Academy of Sciences/National Research Council, *Health Effects of Alpha-Emitting Particles in the Respiratory Tract*, EPA 520/4-76-013 (Washington, D.C.: Environmental Protection Agency, 1976), Appendix A.

27. Henry Tanner, "Terrorist Bombs Severely Damage Rome Power Plant," *New York Times*, June 18, 1978, p. A8.

28. Merrill Sheils, "Can Oil Be Guarded?" *Newsweek*, June 12, 1978, pp. 79–80.

29. Ibid.

30. Maynard M. Stephens, "Vulnerability of Natural Gas Systems" (Washington, D.C.: Defense Civil Preparedness Agency, June 1974); Maynard M. Stephens, "Vulnerability of Total Petroleum Systems," Report prepared for the Defense Civil Preparedness Agency, DAHC 20-70-C-0316 (Washington, D.C.: Department of the Interior, May 1973); and Maynard M. Stephens, "Minimizing Damage to Refineries from Nuclear Attack, Natural and Other Disasters"

(Washington, D.C.: Department of the Interior, Office of Oil and Gas, February 1970).

31. Michael Arbib, *The Metaphorical Brain: An Introduction to Cybernetics as Artificial Intelligence and Brain Theory* (New York: Wiley-Interscience, 1972).

CHAPTER 3

1. United States Sinai Support Mission, Report to the Congress, April 13, 1977.

2. Gerard I. Nierenberg, *The Art of Negotiating* (New York: Simon and Schuster, 1971); J. Godey, *The Taking of Pelham 123* (New York: Dell Publishing Co., 1974); H. Schlossberg and Lucy Freeman, *Psychologist with a Gun* (New York: Coward, McCann and Geoghehan 1974); David Hubbard, *The Skyjacker: His Flights of Fantasy* (New York: Macmillan Co., 1971); Julius Fast, *Body Language* (Philadelphia: J. P. Lippincott, 1970); Royce A Coffin, *The Negotiator: A Manual for Winners* (New York: American Management Association, 1973); and Stanley Cohen, *Three Thirty Park* (New York: G. P. Putnam's Sons, 1977).

3. Herman Kahn, *Thinking about the Unthinkable* (New York: Horizon Press, 1962); and Herman Kahn, *On Thermonuclear War* (Princeton: Princeton University Press, 1960).

4. R. A. Howard, J. E. Matheson, and D. W. North, "The Decision to Seed Hurricanes," *Science*, June 16, 1972, pp. 1191–1202.

5. B. Fischhoff, P. Slovic, and S. Lichtenstein, "Fault Trees: Sensitivity of Estimated Failure Probabilities to Problem Representation," *Journal of Experimental Psychology: Human Perception and Performance*, May, 1978, pp. 330–344. R. M. Hogarth, "Methods for Aggregating Options," Paper presented at Fifth Research Conference on Subjective Probability, Utility and Decision-Making, Darmstadt, West Germany, September 1975; Ryukichi Imai, "Safeguards against Diversion of Nuclear Material: An Overview," *Annals of the American Association of Political and Social Science*, March 1977, pp. 58–69; D. Kahneman and A. Tversky, "Judgment under Uncertainty: Heuristics and Biases," *Science*, September 27, 1974; pp. 1124–1131; and William W. Lawrence, *Of Acceptable Risk* (Los Altos: William Kaufman, 1976).

CHAPTER 4

1. See David Hubbard, *The Skyjacker: His Flights of Fantasy* (New York: Macmillan Co., 1971); Frederick Hacker, *Crusaders, Criminals, and Crazies: Terror and Terrorism in Our Time* (New York: W. W. Norton, 1977); and Frank Ochberg, "The Victim of Terrorism: Psychiatric Considerations," *Terrorism: An International Journal* 1, no. 2 (1978): 147–168.

CHAPTER 5

1. Stanley Hoffman, "Choices," in Robert J. Pranger, ed., *Detente and Defense: A Reader*, American Enterprise Institute Foreign Affairs Study No. 40

(Washington, D.C.: American Enterprise Institute, October 1976), p. 84; also in *Foreign Policy*, Fall 1973.

2. Quoted in Leo Gross, "International Terrorism and International Criminal Jurisdiction," *American Journal of International Law*, January 1973, p. 509.

3. John Dugard, "Towards the Definition of International Terrorism," *American Journal of International Law*, July 1973, pp. 94–100.

4. Quoted in Steven J. Rosen and Robert Frank, "Measures against International Terrorism," in David Carlton and Carlo Schaerf, eds., *International Terrorism and World Security* (New York: John Wiley and Sons, Halsted Press, 1975), p. 67.

5. Dugard, "Towards the Definition of International Terrorism," p. 94.

6. See ibid.; John Norton Moore, "Toward Legal Restraints on International Terrorism," *American Journal of International Law*, July 1973, pp. 88–94; and Jordan J. Paust, "A Survey of Possible Legal Responses to International Terrorism: Prevention, Punishment, and Cooperative Action," *Georgia Journal of Comparative Law* 5, issue 2 (1975): 431–465.

7. Dugard, "Towards the Definition of International Terrorism," p. 98.

8. Ibid.

9. Moore, "Toward Legal Restraints," p. 88.

10. Ibid.

11. Paust, "Survey of Possible Legal Responses," p. 433.

12. Ibid., p. 461.

13. Ibid., p. 437.

14. Paust, quoting 1972 U.N. Document A/C 6/418, p. 436.

15. Testimony of David E. McGiffert, in U.S. Congress, Senate, Committee on Governmental Affairs, *An Act to Combat International Terrorism, Hearings on S. 2236*, 95th Cong., 2nd sess., February 22, 1978, pp. 195–198.

16. "Head of the German Raid Is Linked to Entebbe," *New York Times*, October 22, 1977, p. 7; "Getting Tough," *Newsweek*, October 31, 1977, p. 51; and Gregory F. Rose, "The Terrorists Are Coming," *Politics Today*, July/August 1978, p. 52.

17. "13 Nations Training Commandos to Save Air Hijacking Hostages," *New York Times*, October 22, 1977, p. 7.

18. Ibid.

19. Ibid.

20. Ibid.

21. Ibid.

22. Erwin Lanc, quoted in Claire Sterling, "The Terrorist Network," *The Atlantic*, November 1978, p. 47.

23. For a highly detailed discussion of the material that follows, see statement of A. Atley Peterson (May 8, 1978), in U.S. Congress, Senate, Committee on Governmental Affairs, *An Act to Combat International Terrorism*, pp. 1071–1098.

24. See testimony of James H. Scheuer, in ibid., February 22, 1978, p. 235.

CHAPTER 6

1. Peter Kihss, "Notes on Kennedy in Suspect's Home," *New York Times*, June 6, 1968, p. 1.

2. Quoted in Gregory F. Rose, "The Terrorists Are Coming," *Politics Today*, July/August 1978, p. 22.

3. U.S. Congress, Senate, Committee on Governmental Affairs, *Reorganization Plan No. 3 of 1978, Establishing a New Independent Agency, The Federal Emergency Management Agency*, Report No. 95-1141, 95th Cong., 2nd sess., August 23, 1978, p. 27.

4. Statement of Ambassador Anthony Quainton, in U.S. Congress, House, Committee on International Relations, Subcommittee on International Security and Scientific Affairs, "International Terrorism: Legislative Initiatives," Hearing on H.R. 13387, September 12, 1978 (mimeographed), pp. 2–3.

5. U.S. Congress, Senate, Committee on Governmental Affairs, *Reorganization Plan No. 3 of 1978*, p. 2.

6. White House Fact Sheet on Reorganization Plan No. 3, Office of the White House Press Secretary, June 19, 1978.

7. Anthony Quainton, "Doing Something about Terrorism—Abroad and at Home," *Christian Science Monitor*, September 7, 1978, p. 23.

8. U.S. Congress, Senate, Committee on Governmental Affairs, *Reorganization Plan No. 3*, p. 27.

9. U.S. Congress, House, Committee on Government Operations, *Reorganization Plan No. 3 of 1978 (Emergency Preparedness)*, Report No. 95-1523, 95th Cong., 2nd sess., August 21, 1978, p. 2.

10. U.S. Congress, Senate, Committee on Governmental Affairs, *Reorganization Plan No. 3*, p. 27.

11. Ibid.

12. Testimony of James T. McIntyre, in U.S. Congress, Senate, Committee on Governmental Affairs, Subcommittee on Intergovernmental Relations, "The Disaster/Preparedness Reorganization Plan," Transcript of Proceedings, June 20, 1978, p. 8.

13. Harry S. Truman, "Letter to the Director, Office of Defense Mobilization, on Federal Activities in the Flood Disaster Areas," July 19, 1951, in *Public Papers of the Presidents of the United States* (Washington, D.C.: Office of the *Federal Register*, National Archives and Records Service, 1948–), 1951.

14. Jonathan Daniels, *Frontier on the Potomac* (New York: Macmillan Co., 1946), pp. 31–32.

15. White House Fact Sheet, June 19, 1978, p. 2.

16. Graham T. Allison, *Essence of Decision* (Boston: Little, Brown and Co., 1971), p. 85.

Bibliography

Advanced Concepts Research (ADCON Corp.: B. J. Berkowitz et al.). *Superviolence: The Civil Threat of Mass Destruction Weapons*. Santa Barbara: Calif.: Adcon Corp., September 1972.

Allison, Graham T. *Essence of Decision*. Boston: Little, Brown and Co., 1971.

Anable, David. "Terrorism: How a Handful of Radical States Keeps It in Business." *Christian Science Monitor*, March 15, 1977, pp. 14–15.

———. "Terrorism: Loose Net Links Diverse Groups; No Central Plot," *Christian Science Monitor*, March 14, 1977, pp. 16–17.

Alexander, Yonah. "Terrorism and the Mass Media in the Middle East." Paper presented at the Conference on International Terrorism, Ralph Bunche Institute, New York City, June 9–11, 1976.

———. ed. *International Terrorism: National, Regional and Global Perspectives*. New York: Frederick Praegar, 1976.

Apple, R. W. "A Loose Alliance of Terrorists Does Seem to Exist." *New York Times*, October 23, 1977, sec. 4, p. 1.

Arbib, Michael. *The Metaphorical Brain: An Introduction to Cybernetics as Artificial Intelligence and Brain Theory*. New York: Wiley-Interscience, 1972.

Bakunin, Michael. *Writings*. Edited by Guy Aldred. New York: Kraus Reprints, 1972.

Barringer, Richard E., and Whaley, Barton. "The MIT Political-Military Gaming Experience." *Orbis*, Summer 1965, pp. 437–458.

Bassiouni, M. Cherif, ed. *International Terrorism and Political Crimes*. Springfield, Ill.: Charles C. Thomas, 1975.

Beckett, Brian. "Nerve Gas Secrets Leak Out," *The Observer* (London), November 19, 1978, p. 1.

Beecher, William. "Terrorist Gangs Reaching for Nerve Gas, Gruesome New Weapons." *Boston Globe*, November 7, 1976.

Begin, Menachem. *The Revolt: Story of the Irgun*. Translated by Samuel Katz. Los Angeles: Nash, 1972.

Bell, J. Bowyer. *Transnational Terror*. Stanford and Washington, D.C.: Hoover Institution and American Enterprise Institute, 1975.

———. "Transnational Terror and World Order." *South Atlantic Quarterly*, Autumn 1975, pp. 404–417.

Bloomfield, Lincoln P., and Gearin, Cornelius T. "Games Foreign Policy Experts Play: The Political Exercise Comes of Age." *Orbis*, Winter 1973, pp. 1012–1013.

Bouthoul, Baston. "On International Terrorism: Historical and Contemporary Aspects 1968–1975." Paper presented at the State Department Conference on International Terrorism in Retrospect and Prospect, March 25–26, 1975.

Bradshaw, Jon. "A Dream of Terror." *Esquire*, July 18, 1978, pp. 24–50.

Brewer, Gary D. "Existing in a World of Institutionalized Danger." Technical Report No. 102. New Haven: Yale University School of Organization and Management, 1976.

Burton, Anthony. *Urban Terrorism: Theory, Practice and Response*. New York: Free Press, 1975.

Carlton, David, and Schaerf, Carlo, eds. *International Terrorism and World Security*, New York: John Wiley and Sons, Halsted Press, 1975.

Central Intelligence Agency. *Annotated Bibliography on Transnational and International Terrorism*. PR 76 10073U. Washington, D.C., December 1976.

Chadwick, E. "Actions on Insects and Other Invertebrates." In G. E. Koelle, ed., *Cholinesterases and Anticholinesterase Agents*. Handbuch der experimentallen Pharmakologie. Berlin: Springer-Verlag, 1963.

Cherio P. "Security Requirements and Standards for Nuclear Power Plants." *Security Management*, January 1975, pp. 22–24.

Clutterbuck, Richard. *Living with Terrorism*. New Rochelle: Arlington House, 1975.

———. *Protest and the Urban Guerilla*. London: Abelard-Schuman, 1973.

———. "Terrorist International." *Army Quarterly and Defense Journal* (London), January, 1974, pp. 154–159.

Coffin, Royce A. *The Negotiator: A Manual for Winners*. New York: American Management Association, 1973.

Cohen, Stanley. *Three Thirty Park*. New York: G. P. Putnam's Sons, 1977.

Crozier, Brian. "Terrorism: The Problem in Perspective." Paper presented at the State Department Conference on Terrorism in Retrospect and Prospect, March 25–26, 1976.

———, ed. *Annual of Power and Conflict* [for years 1972–1973 to 1975–1976]. London: Institute for the Study of Conflict, 1973–1976.

Daniels, Jonathan. *Frontier on the Potomac*. New York: Macmillan Co., 1946.

Dawes, I. W., and Mandelstam, J. "Biochemistry of Sporulation of *Bacillus subtilis* 168: Continuous Culture Studies." In I. Malek et al., eds., *Continuous Cultivation of Microorganisms*. New York: Academic Press, 1969.

DeLeon, Peter. "Scenario Designs: An Overview." R-1215-ARPA. Santa Monica, Calif.: Rand Corp., June 1973.

Demaris, Ovid. *Brothers in Blood*. New York: Charles Scribner's Sons, 1977.

Digby, James. "Precision-Guided Weapons." Adelphi Paper No. 118. London: International Institute for Strategic Studies, Summer 1975.

Dobson, Christopher. *Black September: Its Short, Violent History*. New York: Macmillan Co., 1974.

———, and Payne, Ronald. *The Carlos Complex: A Study in Terror*. New York: G. P. Putnam's Sons, 1977.

Doub, William O., and Duker, Joseph M. "Making Nuclear Energy Safe and Secure." *Foreign Affairs*, July 1975, pp. 756–772.

Dugard, John. "International Terrorism: Problems of Definition." *International Affairs*, January 1974, pp. 67–81.

———. "Towards the Definition of International Terrorism." *American Journal of International Law*, July 1973, pp. 94–100.

Falk, Richard A. "Terror Liberation Movements and the Processes of Social Change." *American Journal of International Law*, July 1969, pp. 423–427.

Fallaci, Oriana. "A Leader of Fedayeen: 'We Want a War Like the Vietnam War': Interview with George Habash." *Life*, June 12, 1970, pp. 32–34.

Fanon, Frantz. *The Wretched of the Earth*. New York: Grove Press, 1967.

Fast, Julius. *Body Language*. Philadelphia: J. P. Lippincott, 1970.

Finger, Seymour Maxwell, and Alexander, Yonah, eds. *Terrorism: Interdisciplinary Perspectives*. New York, John Jay, 1977.

Fischhoff, B., Slovic, P., and Lichtenstein, S. "Fault Trees: Sensitivity of

Estimated Failure Probabilities to Problem Representation," *Journal of Experimental Psychology: Human Perception and Performance*, May 1978, pp. 330–344.

Friedlander, Robert A. "Terrorism: What's Behind Our Passive Acceptance of Transnational Mugging?" *Barrister*, Summer 1975, pp. 10–71.

Fromkin, David. "The Strategy of Terrorism." *Foreign Affairs*, July 1975, pp. 683–698.

Gann, Lewis. *Guerrillas in History*. Stanford: Hoover Institution Press, 1975.

Girard, Edward W. "History of Gaming." In Murray Greyson, ed., *Second War Gaming Symposium Proceedings*. Washington, D.C.: WORC, 1962.

Glasstone, Samuel. *The Effects of Nuclear Weapons*. Washington, D.C.: U.S. Energy Research and Development Administration, 1977.

Godey, J. *The Taking of Pelham 123*. New York: Dell Publishing Co., 1974.

Goldhamer, Herbert, and Speier, Hans. "Some Observations on Political Gaming." *World Politics* October 1959, pp. 71–83.

Gross, Leo. "International Terrorism and International Criminal Jurisdiction." *American Journal of International Law*, January 1973, pp. 508–511.

Guevara Ernesto Che. *Guerrilla Warfare*. New York: Random House, 1969.

Hacker, Frederick J. *Crusaders, Criminals, and Crazies: Terror and Terrorism in Our Time*. New York: W. W. Norton, 1976.

Hatt, H. D., and Lessel, E. F. *The American Type Culture Collection (Bacteria)*. New York: American Type Culture Collection, 1974.

Hermann, Charles F. *Crisis in Foreign Policy: A Simulation Analysis*. Indianapolis: Bobbs-Merrill, 1969.

———. "Time, Threat and Surprise: A Simulation of International Crisis." In Charles F. Hermann, ed., *International Crisis: Insights from Behavioral Research*. New York: Free Press, 1972.

Hobbs, G., Williams, Kathleen, and Willis, A. T. "Basic Methods for the Isolation of Clostridia." In D. A. Shapta and R. G. Board, eds., *Isolation of Anerobes*. New York: Academic Press, 1971, pp. 1–23.

Hoffman, Stanley. "Choices." In Robert J. Pranger, ed., *Detente and Defense: A Reader*. American Enterprise Institute Foreign Affairs Study No. 40. Washington, D.C.: American Enterprise Institute,

October 1976, pp. 75–99. Also in *Foreign Policy*, Fall 1973.

Hogarth, R. M. "Methods for Aggregating Options." Fifth Research Conference on Subjective Probability, Utility and Decision-Making, Darmstadt, West Germany, September 1975.

Holsti, Ole R., et al. "Perceptions and Action in the 1914 Crisis." In T. David Singer, ed., *Quantitative International Politics*. New York: Free Press, 1968.

Holton, Gerald. "Reflections on Modern Terrorism." *Jerusalem Journal of International Relations*, Fall 1977, pp. 96–104.

Hoveyda, Fereydoun. "The Problem of International Terrorism at the United Nations." *Terrorism: An International Journal* 1, no. 1 (1977): 71–84.

Howard, R. A., Matheson, J. E., and North, D. W. "The Decision to Seed Hurricanes." *Science*, June 16, 1973, pp. 1191–1202.

Hubbard, David. *The Skyjacker: His Flights of Fantasy*. New York: Macmillan Co., 1971.

Hyams, Edward. *Terrorists and Terrorism*. London: J. M. Dent, 1975.

Imai, Ryukichi. "Safeguards against Diversion of Nuclear Material: An Overview." *Annals of the American Association of Political and Social Science*, March 1977, pp. 58–69.

Jack, H. A. "Terrorism: Another U.N. Failure." *America*, October 20, 1973, pp. 283–285.

Jackson, Geoffrey. *Surviving the Long Night: An Authobiographical Account of a Political Kidnapping*. New York: Vanguard, 1974.

Jenkins, Brian M. "High Technology Terrorism and Surrogate War: The Impact of New Technology on Low-Level Violence." P-5339. Santa Monica, Calif.: Rand Corp., January 1975.

———. "Hostage Survival: Some Preliminary Observations." P-5627. Santa Monica, Calif.: Rand Corp., April 1976.

———. "International Terrorism: A Balance Sheet." *Survival*, July-August 1975, pp. 158–164.

———. "International Terrorism: A New Mode of Conflict." In David Carlton and Carlo Schaerf, eds., *International Terrorism and World Security*. New York: John Wiley and Sons, Halsted Press, 1975, pp. 13–49.

———. *International Terrorism: Trends and Potentialities*. Santa Monica, Calif.: Rand Corp., 1977.

———. "Should Corporations Be Prevented from Paying Ransom?"

P-5291. Santa Monica, Calif.: Rand Corp., September 1974.

———. "Terrorism and Kidnapping." P-5255. Santa Monica, Calif.: Rand Corp., June 1974.

———. "Terrorism Works—Sometimes." P-5217. Santa Monica, Calif.: Rand Corp., April 1974.

———. "Will Terrorists Go Nuclear?" California Seminar on Foreign Policy and Arms Control, January 1976.

———, and Johnson, Janera. "International Terrorism: A Chronology, 1968–1974." R-1597-DOS/ARPA. Santa Monica, Calif.: Rand Corp., March 1975.

Kahn, Herman. *On Thermonuclear War*. Princeton: Princeton University Press, 1960.

———. *Thinking about the Unthinkable*. New York: Horizon Press, 1962.

Kahneman, D., and Tversky, A. "Judgment under Uncertainty: Heuristics and Biases." *Science*, September 27, 1974, pp. 1124–1131.

Kihss, Peter. "Notes on Kennedy in Suspect's Home." *New York Times*, June 6, 1968.

Kupperman, Robert H. *Facing Tomorrow's Terrorist Incident Today*. Report prepared for the Department of Justice. Washington, D.C.: Government Printing Office, October 1977.

———. "Treating the Symptoms of Terrorism: Some Principles of Good Hygiene." *Terrorism: An International Journal* 1, no. 1 (1977):35–40.

Laqueur, Walter. "The Futility of Terrorism." *Harper's*, March 1976, pp. 99–105.

———. "Guerrillas and Terrorists." *Commentary*, October 1974, pp. 40–48.

———. *Terrorism*. Boston: Little, Brown and Co., 1977.

Lasky, Melvin J. "Ulrike and Andreas: The Bonnie and Clyde of West Germany's Radical Subculture May Have Failed to Make a Revolution, but They Have Bruised the Body Politic." *New York Times Magazine*, May 11, 1975, pp. 14 ff.

Lawrence, William W. *Of Acceptable Risk*. Los Altos: William Kaufman, 1976.

Leachman, Robert B., and Althoff, Phillip, eds. *Preventing Nuclear Theft: Guidelines for Industry and Government: Security Measures Conferences*. New York: Frederick Praeger, 1972.

Lewis, Flora. "The New Terrorism." *New York Times*, October 23, 1977, sec. 4, p. 1.

——— "Western Europe's Militant Minorities Find Common Cause in Secret Meeting." *New York Times*, July 8, 1975, p. 4.

Livingston, Marius, ed. *Proceedings of the Conference on Terrorism in the Contemporary World*. Westport, Conn.: Greenwood Press, 1976.

Mallin, Jay, ed. *Terror and Urban Guerrillas: A Study of Tactics and Documents*. Coral Gables: University of Miami Press, 1971.

Mandel, Robert. "Political Gaming and Foreign Policy Making during Crises." *World Politics*, July 1977, pp. 610–625.

———. "Political Gaming and Crisis Foreign Policy Making." Ph.D. dissertation, Yale University, 1976.

Mao Tse-tung. *Basic Tactics*. New York: Frederick Praeger, 1966.

———. *On Guerrilla Warfare*. New York: Frederick Praeger, 1961.

Marighella, Carlos. "Minimanual of the Urban Guerilla." *Tricontinental* (Havana), January–February 1970, pp. 15–56; (Also in Jay Mallin, ed., *Terror and Urban Guerrillas*. Coral Gables: University of Miami Press, 1971.)

May, W. F. "Terrorism as Strategy and Ecstasy." *Social Research*, Summer 1974, pp. 277–298.

McKnight, Gerald. *The Mind of the Terrorist*. London: Michael Joseph, 1974.

McPhee, John. *The Curve of Binding Energy*. New York: Farrar, Straus and Giroux, 1974.

Means, John. "Political Kidnappings and Terrorism." *North American Review*, Winter 1970, pp. 16–19.

Mickolus, Edward. *Codebook: ITERATE (International Terrorism: Attributes of Terrorist Events)*. Ann Arbor: Inter-University Consortium for Political and Social Research, University of Michigan, 1976.

Milbank, David L. "International Terrorism: Diagnosis and Prognosis." Research Study PR 76 10030. Washington, D.C.: Office of Political Research, Central Intelligence Agency, April, 1976.

Miller, Judith. "Bargain with Terrorists?" *New York Times Magazine*, July 18, 1976, pp. 7, 38–42.

Moore, John Norton. "Toward Legal Restraints on International Terrorism." *American Journal of International Law*, July 1973, pp. 88–94.

Morrison, Robert, and Boyd, Robert. *Organic Chemistry*. Boston: Allyn and Bacon, 1959.

Moss, Robert. *Counter-Terrorism*. Economist Brief Books, no. 29. London, 1972.

――――. "International Terrorism and Western Societies." *International Journal*, Summer 1973, pp. 418–430.

――――. *Urban Guerrillas: The New Face of Political Violence*. London: Maurice Temple Smith, 1977.

Mullen, Robert K. *The Clandestine Use of Chemical or Biological Weapons*. Gaithersburg, Md.: International Association of Chiefs of Police, 1978.

――――. *The International Clandestine Nuclear Threat*. Gaithersburg, Md.: International Association of Chiefs of Police, 1975.

――――. "Mass Destruction and Terrorism." *Journal of International Affairs*, Spring/Summer 1978, pp. 63–89.

National Academy of Sciences/National Research Council. *Health Effects of Alpha-Emitting Particles in the Respiratory Tract*. EPA 520/4-76-013. Washington, D.C.: U.S. Environmental Protection Agency, 1976.

Nierenberg, Gerard I. *The Art of Negotiating*. New York: Simon and Schuster, 1971.

Niezing, Johan, ed. *Urban Guerilla: Studies on the Theory, Strategy and Practice of Political Violence in Modern Societies*. Rotterdam: University of Rotterdam Press, 1974.

Ochberg, Frank. "The Victim of Terrorism: Psychiatric Considerations." *Terrorism: An International Journal* 1, no. 2 (1978):147–168.

Paine, Lauran. *The Terrorists*. London: Robert Hale and Co., 1975.

Parry, Albert. *Terrorism: From Robespierre to Arafat*. New York: Vanguard, 1976.

Pattison, Frederick. *Toxic Aliphatic Fluorine Compounds*. New York: Elsevier Publishing Co., 1959.

Paust, Jordan J. "A Survey of Possible Legal Responses to Terrorism: Prevention, Punishment and Cooperative Action." *Georgia Journal of Comparative Law* 5, issue 2 (1975):431–469.

Possony, Stefan T. "Coping with Terrorism." *Defense/Foreign Affairs Digest*, February 1973, pp. 6–7.

――――. "Terrorism: A Global Concern." *Defense/Foreign Affairs Digest*, January 1973, pp. 4–5.

――――, and Bouchey, L. Francis. *International Terrorism—The Communist Connection*. Washington, D.C.: American Council for World Freedom, 1978.

Pryee-Jones, David. *The Face of Defeat: Palestine Refugees and Guerrillas*. New York: Holt, Rinehart and Winston, 1972.

Quainton, Anthony. "Doing Something about Terrorism—Abroad and at Home." *Christian Science Monitor*, September 7, 1978.

————. Statement, in U.S. Congress, House, Committee on International Relations, Subcommittee on International Security and Scientific Affairs, "International Terrorism: Legislative Initiatives." Hearing on H. R. 13387, September 12, 1978.

Raditsa, Leo. "Letter from Rome." *Midstream*, December 1976. pp. 24–31.

Ricia, J. "Sporulation of *Bacillus cereus* in Multistage Continuous Cultivation." In I. Malek et al., eds., *Continuous Cultivation of Microorganisms*. New York: Academic Press, 1969, pp. 163–172.

Riemann, Hans, ed. *Infections and Intoxications*. New York: Academic Press, 1969.

Rose, Gregory F. "The Terrorists Are Coming." *Politics Today*, July/August 1978, pp. 22 ff.

Rosen, Steven J., and Frank, Robert. "Measures against International Terrorism." In David Carlton and Carlo Schaerf, eds., *International Terrorism and World Security*. New York: John Wiley and Sons, Halsted Press, 1975.

Rothschild, J. H. *Tomorrow's Weapons: Chemical and Biological*. New York: McGraw-Hill Book Co., 1964.

Schlossberg, H., and Freeman, Lucy. *Psychologist with a Gun*. New York: Coward, McCann and Geoghehan, 1974.

Shaw, Eric D., et al. "Analyzing Threats from Terrorism." Washington, D.C.: CACI, April 29, 1976.

Shiels, Merrill. "Can Oil Be Guarded?" *Newsweek*, June 12, 1978, pp. 79–81.

SIPRI (Stockholm International Peace Research Institute). *The Problem of Chemical and Biological Warfare*, Vol. 1: *The Rise of CB Weapons*. New York: Humanities Press, 1971.

Sobel, Lester A., ed. *Political Terrorism*. New York: Facts on File, 1975.

Stephens, Maynard M. "Minimizing Damage to Refineries from Nuclear Attack, Natural and Other Disasters." Washington, D.C.: Department of the Interior, Office of Civil Defense, February 1970.

————. "Vulnerability of Natural Gas Systems." Washington, D.C.: Defense Civil Preparedness Agency, June 1974.

————. "Vulnerability of Total Petroleum Systems." Report prepared for the Defense Civil Preparedness Agency, DAHC 20-70-C-0316. Washington, D.C.: Department of the Interior, May 1973.

Stohl, Michael, ed. *The Politics of Terror: A Reader in Theory and Practice*. New York: Marcel Dekker, 1977.

Tanner, Henry. "Terrorist Bombs Severely Damage Rome Power Plant." *New York Times*, June 15, 1978, p. A8.

Taylor, Theodore B., and Colligan, Douglas. "Nuclear Terrorism: A Threat of the Future." *Science Digest*, August 1974, pp. 12–17.

——, Van Cleave, W. R., and Kinderman, E. M. "Preliminary Survey of Non-National Nuclear Threats." Stanford Research Institute Technical Note SSC-TN-5205-83. Menlo Park, Calif.: Stanford Research Institute, September 1968.

"Terror International." Transcript of *60 Minutes* as broadcast over CBS Television Network, Sunday, April 9, 1978.

Truman, Harry S., "Letter to the Director, Office of Defense Mobilization, on Federal Activities in the Flood Disaster Areas," July 19, 1951. *Public Papers of the Presidents of the United States*. Washington, D.C.: Office of the *Federal Register*, National Archives and Records Service, 1948–, 1951.

"USSR: 'Greatest Subversive Center in the World.' " *Human Events*, May 31, 1975, p. 5.

U.S. Army. *Military Biology and Biological Agents*. Training Manual 3-216. Washington, D.C., 1964.

U.S. Congress. House. Committee on Government Operations. *Reorganization Plan No. 3 of 1978 (Emergency Preparedness)*. Report No. 95-1523. 95th Congress, 2nd session, August 21, 1978.

U.S. Congress. House. Committee on Internal Security. *Terrorism, Hearings*. 93rd Congress, 2nd session, February-August 1974, Parts 1–4.

U.S. Congress. House. Committee on Internal Security. *Terrorism: A Staff Study*. 93rd Congress, 2nd session, August 1, 1974.

U.S. Congress. Senate. Committee on Governmental Affairs. *An Act to Combat Terrorism, Hearings on S. 2236*. 95th Congress, 2nd session, 1978.

U.S. Congress. Senate. Committee on Governmental Affairs. *Reorganization Plan No. 3 of 1978, Establishing a New Independent Agency, The Federal Emergency Management Agency*. Report No. 95-1141. 95th Congress, 2nd session, August 23, 1978.

U.S. Congress. Senate. Committee on Governmental Affairs, Subcommittee on Intergovernmental Relations. "The Disaster/Preparedness Reorganization Plan." Transcript of Proceedings, June 20, 1978.

U.S. Congress. Senate. Committee on the Judiciary. Subcommittee to Investigate the Administration of the Internal Security Act and Other Internal Security Laws. *Terrorist Activity: International Terrorism, Hearings*. 94th Congress, 1st session, May 14, 1975.

United States Sinai Support Mission. Report to the Congress, April 13, 1977.

Walter, Eugene Victor. "Violence and the Process of Terror." *American Sociological Review*, April 1964, pp. 248–257.

Walzer Michael. "The New Terrorist: Random Murder." *New Republic*, August 30, 1975, pp. 12–14.

———, Bell, J. Bowyer, and Morris, Roger. "Terrorism: A Debate." *New Republic*, December 27, 1975, pp. 12–15.

Watson, Francis M. *Political Terrorism: The Threat and the Response*. Washington, D.C.: Robert B. Luce, 1976.

Watson, John W. "An Operation Model of Crisis Decision-Making." In Joann Langston, ed., *6th Symposium in Gaming*. Washington, D.C.: Technical Operations, Inc., 1967.

Weinraub, Bernard. "Libyans Arm and Train World Terrorists." *New York Times*, July 16, 1976.

Weis, Paul. "Asylum and Terrorism." *Review of the International Commission of Jurists*, December 1977, pp. 37–43.

Wilkinson, Paul. "A Fatality of Illusions: Dominant Images of International Terrorism." Paper presented at the State Department Conference on International Terrorism in Retrospect and Prospect, March 25–26, 1976.

———. *Political Terrorism*. London: Macmillan, 1974.

———. "Three Questions on Terrorism." *Government and Opposition*, Summer 1973, pp. 290–312.

Willrich, Mason, ed. *International Safeguards and Nuclear Industry*. Baltimore: Johns Hopkins University Press, 1973.

———, and Taylor, Theodore B. *Nuclear Theft: Risks and Safeguards*. New York: Ballinger Publishing Co., 1974.

Wohlstetter, Roberta. "Terror on a Grand Scale." *Survival*, May-June 1976, pp. 98–104.

Zivic, J. "The Nonaligned and the Problem of International Terrorism." *Review of International Affairs* (Belgrade), January 20, 1973, pp. 6–8.

Index

Luebbe, Hermann, xvi
Lufthansa jet hijacking, 23, 34, 41, 155, 339, 342
Lumumba (Patrice) University, 30
Luxemburg, Rosa, xi

Machine guns, 52, 54, 81
McIntyre, James T., quoted, 171
McKinley, William, 16
Mafia, 39, 191
Magnetometers, 80, 81, 82, 83, 95
Mahasabha, 17, 18
Mahler, Horst, 25; quoted, 25–26
Malta, cave bombing on, 350, 376, 377
Manhattan, 60, 68
Maoism, 25n, 39
Mao Tse-tung, 20, 185, 189
Marcuse, Herbert, quoted, xv
Marighella, Carlos, 20, 25n, 187, 188, 189, 192, 334; quoted, 195n, 333
Marseilles, 142
Martinez, Carlos. See Carlos
Marx, Karl, 15
Marxism, Marxists, xii, 5, 16, 17, 19, 24, 26, 36, 39, 40, 186
Marxist-Leninists, 36
Maryland Chapter Society of Professional Journalists, 344
Mass casualties. See Medical care, mass-casualty
Mass-destruction technology, 46, 47; national use of, 50, 51; terrorists' use of (see Mass-destruction terrorism). See also Biological agents, Chemical agents; Nerve agents; Nuclear weapons; Radiological agents
Mass-destruction terrorism, 118, 128, 161, 193, 237; counter-measures in, 100–102, 110, 121; and national disruption, 6, 17, 45–52; plausibility of, 49–52, 58, 63–69 passim, 83–84, 100, 103, 112, 113n, 125, 141, 179
Mass transit facilities, as targets, 5, 97, 99, 118, 156. See also Aircraft; Hijackings
Matheson, J. E., 103
Mauritania, 146
Media, 58; as contributor to disorder and terrorism, 11, 20–21, 70, 114, 121, 334, 336–339, 340–343, 345; as helpful in terrorist incidents, 339–340, 345, 373; public and police opinion on coverage of terrorism by, 340–341; responsibilities of, 10, 184, 340, 343–346; and terrorist incidents, 38, 92–93, 131–132, 184, 282, 334–340 passim; as terrorist

target, 196, 197, 334; terrorist use of, 7, 21, 39, 41–42, 43, 92–93, 132, 332–335, 340, 345. See also Press; Television
Medical care, for terrorists, 188
Medical care, mass-casualty, 75, 98, 136, 349–392, 403; inadequacy of existing systems of, 375–378; model for national system of, 379–388; as national counterterrorist measure, 138, 349; philosophy of rescue in, 374–375; and secondary psychological effects, 372–374; and target site, 352–353; and types of casualties, 350–352; and types of injuries, 353–374; unified resuscitative model of, 378–379
Meinhof, Ulrike, 23, 32
Meir, Golda, 247
Mercedes-Benz company, 334
Mercury, liquid, terrorist use, 45
"Metalanguages," 230
Metal detectors, 87–88
Meuniers case, 149
Mexican guerrillas, 34
Mexico, 205, 334
Mexico, Gulf of, 159, 209, 217
Michigan, 221
Middle East, 5, 56, 81, 89, 141; terrorism in, 3, 163, 186, 187; U.S. and conflict in, 162–163. See also Arab-Israeli conflict
Middle Eastern terrorists, 42, 187. See also Arab terrorists; Palestinian terrorists
Midland, Texas, 217
Milan, 24
Military force, 202; in incident management, 75, 94, 95, 115, 116, 139, 167, 178; international paramilitary, need for, 139, 153, 156, 178; members of, as victims, 196, 197; for prevention of terrorism, 107, 115, 116, 153–156. See also Commando teams
Miller, Bowman, H., 183
Minimanual of the Urban Guerrilla (Marighella), 25n, 195n, 333
Missile crash, Soviet, 154
Missile injuries, treatment of, 353–355
Missile launchers. See Antiaircraft missiles; Antitank weapons
MIT (Massachusetts Institute of Technology), 58
Mitla Pass, 87
Mogadishu incident, 3, 23, 38–39, 41, 92, 93, 139, 140, 141, 155, 156, 178, 190
"Mohammed Boudia Commando," 29
Moluccan (South) terrorists, 3, 156, 252, 281, 339

About the Authors

ROBERT KUPPERMAN is Chief Scientist of the U.S. Arms Control and Disarmament Agency. He is the scientific adviser to the director as well as the principal representative of the agency on scientific matters. Dr. Kupperman's responsibilities cover the spectrum of agency activities, including SALT, nuclear proliferation, physical safeguards, technology transfer, and the control of conventional arms sales. Additionally, he has directed a series of interagency studies of terrorism. Dr. Kupperman has served as Deputy Assistant Director for Military and Economic Affairs of the Arms Control and Disarmament Agency and as Assistant Director for Government Preparedness in the President's Office of Emergency Preparedness. While serving in the White House, he held the position of Deputy Executive Director of the Property Review Board. He has been a member of the faculties of the University of Maryland, the California Institute of Technology, and the Courant Institute of Mathematical Science of New York University, from which he holds a Ph.D. in applied mathematics. He is a member of the American Association for the Advancement of Science, and a fellow of the New York Academy of Sciences and the Operations Research Society of America. Dr. Kupperman has published numerous research articles, reports, and books on operations research and crisis management.

DARRELL M. TRENT is Associate Director and Senior Research Fellow at the Hoover Institution of Stanford University. He served the federal government from 1969 to 1974 in a series of Presidential appointments in the Executive Branch. From 1970 through 1973 he assumed management responsibility for the civil emergency apparatus of the federal government, first as Deputy Director and then as head of the President's Office of Emergency Preparedness, serving concurrently as a statutory member of the National Security Council. In 1971, when President Nixon assigned the Office of Emergency Preparedness to organize and manage the wage-price-rent freeze, Mr. Trent had the primary operational responsibility for this task. The agency was also in charge of coordinating plans for emergency mobilization of the nation's resources, formulating policy for management of the national stockpile of strategic materials, and directing the federal government's disaster relief and recovery efforts. Mr. Trent's experience in federal crisis management is extensive: he helped establish White House coordination as Deputy Assistant to the President and as Executive Director of the Property Review Board, served as chairman both of the Joint Board of Fuel Supply and Fuel Transport and of the President's Advisory Council on Civil Defense, and was a member of the Cost of Living Council, the Oil Policy Committee, and the NATO Senior Civil Emergency Planning Committee. Before his government service, Mr. Trent was the developer, major stockholder, and chief executive of several corporations in the Midwest. He received a B.A. degree from Stanford University (1961) and an M.B.A. from the Graduate School of Business of Columbia University (1964).